BENEATH THE SURFACE

THEORY IN FORMS *A series edited by* Nancy Rose Hunt and Achille Mbembe

`

BENEATH THE SURFACE

A Transnational History of Skin Lighteners

LYNN M. THOMAS

Duke University Press   *Durham and London*   2020

Library of Congress Cataloging-in-Publication Data

Names: Thomas, Lynn M., [date] author.
Title: Beneath the surface : a transnational history of skin lighteners /
    Lynn M. Thomas.
Other titles: Theory in forms.
Description: Durham : Duke University Press, 2019. | Series: Theory
    in forms | Includes bibliographical references and index.
Identifiers: LCCN 2019013462 (print)
LCCN 2019980443 (ebook)
ISBN 9781478005384 (hardcover)
ISBN 9781478006428 (paperback)
ISBN 9781478007050 (ebook)
Subjects: LCSH: Colorism—South Africa. | Human skin color—
    Social aspects—South Africa. | Human skin color—Economic
    aspects—South Africa. | Racism—South Africa. | Race relations.
    Classification: LCC GN197 .S524 2019 (print) | LCC GN197 (ebook) |
    DDC 612.7/927—dc23
LC record available at https://lccn.loc.gov/2019013462
LC ebook record available at https://lccn.loc.gov/2019980443

COVER ART: Stills from the short film
Yellow Fever, 2012. © Ng'endo Mukii.

Duke University Press gratefully acknowledges the Department of
History and the College of Arts and Sciences at the University of
Washington, which provided funds toward
the publication of this book.

FOR MICHAEL AND IN MEMORY OF STEPHANIE

Contents

Acknowledgments

Like the history of skin lighteners, the history of this book is a layered one. The research and writing unfolded over many—likely, too many—years. In the process, I benefited from the support of many people and I accumulated many debts. Some of the deepest layers and greatest debts date back over fifteen years. Soon after joining the Department of History at the University of Washington in 1997, I began working with Tani E. Barlow, Madeleine Y. Dong, Uta G. Poiger, Priti Ramamurthy, and Alys Eve Weinbaum in the Modern Girl Around the World Research Group. That collaboration introduced me to new research themes, and it helped me to see how the history of skin lighteners might merit a full-length study. Concepts and insights that we developed together—from the modern-girl heuristic to the method of connective comparison—form much of the backbone of this book.

A Charles Ryskamp Fellowship from the American Council of Learned Societies and a National Endowment for the Humanities Fellowship enabled early phases of my individual research in South Africa and the United States. In both countries, I benefited from the help of skilled archivists and librarians, and speaking with a range of people knowledgeable about the history of skin lighteners. I am grateful to all those who kindly agreed to talk with me. Some of those people are cited in footnotes as interviewees while others provided more general background. I am also grateful to Patricia Njuki in Kenya, and Moss Lulama and Sarah Espi-Sanchis in South Africa for providing invaluable assistance in arranging and undertaking some of the interviews with me. Pauline Njuki generously hosted me in Nairobi, and Peter Cherutich and Carol Weloba helped guide my research there. In the final stage of writing, Susan Ziki tracked down helpful sources in Zimbabwe.

A number of people voiced enthusiastic support for this project early and often. They include Julie Livingston, Luise White, Stephanie M. H. Camp, Uta G. Poiger, Priti Ramamurthy, Janelle Taylor, Sarah Abreveya Stein, Jordanna Bailkin, Timothy Burke, and James Campbell. Some of them also shared their encouragement and insights through writing groups. Three such groups were essential: the body-antibody group, with core members Julie Livingston, Steven Feierman, Nancy Rose Hunt, Sinfree Makoni, and David Schoenbrun; the African history group with Laura Fair, Lisa A. Lindsay, and Stephan Miescher; and my "lady chairs" group with Uta G. Poiger, Priti Ramamurthy, and Janelle Taylor. I am especially thankful to Uta, Priti, and Janelle for guiding me through multiple versions of each chapter, steadying me when my confidence wavered, and coming up with a title.

Conducting my research in South Africa enabled me to deepen old friendships and to forge new ones. Catherine Burns and Keith Breckenridge have taught me a tremendous amount about South African history. Through welcoming me into their intellectual worlds at the University of KwaZulu-Natal and the University of the Witwatersrand, they ensured the rigorous discussion of my work and introduced me to other colleagues from whom I learned a great deal. These colleagues include Prinisha Badassy, Belinda Bozzoli, Sarah Duff, Natasha Erlank, Bill Freund, Clive Glaser, Jeff Guy, Shireen Hassim, Isabel Hofmeyr, Mark Hunter, Vashna Jagarnath, Vukile Khumalo, Robert Morrell, Vanessa Noble, Julie Paarl, Nafisa Essop Sheik, Stephan Sparks, and Jonny Steinberg. A workshop on the history of technology in Ithala organized by Keith and Gabrielle Hecht first encouraged me to think more deeply about the materiality of skin lighteners. I am grateful to Keith, Gabrielle, Kelly Askew, Derek Peterson, Pamila Gupta, and others who spearheaded the University of Michigan/WISER Mellon Collaboration for allowing me to participate in a number of their workshops. In Johannesburg and, a few years before in Seattle, Sarah Nuttall and Achille Mbembe offered invaluable encouragement for this project. In Cape Town and its environs, Andrew Bank, Wayne Dooling, Patricia Hayes, Anne Mager, and Ciraj Rasool offered intellectual guidance.

I have also learned much from others studying skin lighteners in South Africa. Hilary Carman opened my eyes to doctors' campaigns against them in the 1980s by sharing her personal archive. In more recent years, Ncoza Dlova has shared her ongoing research and been a model of intellectual generosity and collegiality. I especially appreciated Ncoza's invitation for me and fellow historian Zinhle Thwala to present our work to medical students at the University of KwaZulu-Natal. A few years earlier, an interdisciplinary workshop on skin lightening at the University of Cape Town organized by Lester Davids and Susan Levine allowed me to learn from them and others, including June Bam-Hutchinson, Meagan Jacobs, Yutende Mercy Olumide, and old friend Divine Fuh.

Many people and programs at the University of Washington have generously supported this project. Current colleagues in the Department of History, especially Jordanna Bailkin, Purnima Dhavan, Susan Glenn, Laurie Marhoefer, and Joel Walker have answered research questions and offered moral support. Financial support from the department's Hanauer and Keller faculty development funds and the Giovanni and Amne Costigan Endowed Professorship, and from the College of Arts and Sciences helped with research and book-production expenses. History chairs John Findlay and Anand Yang, and Social Sciences Divisional Dean Judy Howard ensured that I had time for research and writing before and after my own tenure as department chair. History staff members Josh Apfel, Matt Erickson, Wanjiku Gitahi, and Jeri Park helped me to squeeze in research bits (and fun bits) during that tenure. I am also grateful for the excellent research assistance provided by a number of University of Washington undergraduate and graduate students, including Ali Bilow, Holly Boyce, Jessie Kindig, Kristy Leissle, Teresa Mares, Azmera Melashu, Jesse Meredith, Kathryn Moffat, Bonnie Mosley, Amy Scott-Zerr, Taylor Soja, Kelly Ward, and Sharae Wheeler. History librarian Theresa Mudrock graciously answered countless research queries.

The University of Washington's Walter Chapin Simpson Center for the Humanities and its director, Kathleen Woodward, generously supported the Modern Girl Around the World research project and my own writing through a Society of Scholars Fellowship. This book would not exist without writing retreats at the Helen Riaboff Whiteley Center, a place of breathtaking beauty now imprinted on my soul. I am grateful to Kathy Cowell and other Whiteley Center staff for facilitating those visits. My African Studies colleagues have also been a great support, especially Johanna Crane, Danny Hoffmann, Nora Kenworthy, Ron Krabill, and Amanda Swarr. And, finally, at the University of Washington, I thank my own dermatologist, Dr. Jay Vary, for discussing hydroquinone and inviting me to a grand rounds.

I have had the good fortune to present this research in many venues where I received feedback that sharpened my thinking. Those venues, not already named, include UCLA, Harvard University, the University of Chicago, Rutgers University, Yale University, Washington University, University of Virginia, Northwestern University, University of Florida, University of Birmingham, University of the Western Cape, University of Johannesburg, University of Wisconsin, Oxford University, Whitman College, Central Washington University, Rice University, the University of Michigan, Columbia University, and a Max Planck workshop in Moshi, Tanzania. I thank all who organized those events. People who offered especially useful commentary at those events or in other venues include Emily Callaci, Jean Comaroff, Robert Edgar, James Ferguson, Karen Flint, Bodil Frederickson, Jonathon Glassman, Matthew Guertl, Rebecca Herzig, Preben Kaarsholm, Paul Landau, Nina Lerman, Helen Lunn, Daniel Magaziner, Greg Mann, Simphiwe Ngwane, Ope Ofodile, Shanti Parikh, Richard Rottenberg, Keith Shear, Rhiannon Stephens, Krista Thompson, Helen Tilley, Robert Vinson, Keith Wailoo, and Eric Worby. What David William Cohen and

Fred Cooper taught me in graduate school about embracing history's complexity while remaining attentive to its political stakes has remained a target throughout.

I am also thankful to those who ensured that the book got to press. Elizabeth Ault at Duke University Press has been an ideal editor, a perfect combination of champion and intelligent taskmaster. In the final stretch, I received invaluable comments on specific chapters from Andrew Bank, Catherine Burns, Catherine Cole, Jennifer Cole, Laura Fair, Gabrielle Hecht, Rebecca Herzig, Nancy Rose Hunt, Stephan Miescher, Kenda Mutongi, and Alys Eve Weinbaum. Lisa A. Lindsay and Robert Ross, along with three anonymous reviewers for the press, performed the heroic feat of commenting on the entire manuscript. Collectively, they encouraged me to be a bit bolder and told me it was time to let go.

I am grateful to Ng'endo Mukii for allowing stills from her excellent short film, *Yellow Fever* (2012), to serve as cover art. Thanks, too, to the entire production staff at Duke University Press for getting the manuscript and design in good shape and to Fred Brown for creating the index.

Through all the layers of research and writing, family members have warmed my heart. My mother, my four siblings and their families, and my in-laws have been steady sources of love. Best buddies from Ryther Child Center enriched my life by sharing Seattle outings and their uncanny and empathetic views of the world.

Two people provided close support from the start. Michael A. Sanderson, my husband, never doubted that I could figure out the conundrum of this book and finish it. Yet, with humor and affection, he often provided persuasive arguments for why I should be away from my desk. This book's completion marks the beginning of new adventures together. Stephanie M. H. Camp, my dear departed friend, kept this project afloat as she wrote her own history of black beauty. With wit and grace, she taught me much about history and about life. This book is dedicated to Michael and to the memory of Stephanie, in love and gratitude.

Introduction

A LAYERED
HISTORY

From corseting and hair coloring to tanning and plastic surgery, the history of beauty is the history of bending the material body to meet social desires. It is a history of struggle. And few beauty practices have been the site of more struggle than skin lightening. For centuries, elites in some parts of the world used paints and powders to create smoother, paler appearances, unblemished by illness and the sun's darkening and roughening effects. By the twentieth century, legions of working- and middle-class consumers had joined them, making skin lightening creams some of the most commonly sold cosmetics worldwide. This book examines the long and layered history of skin lightening from the vantage point of South Africa, a place where people have invested the body's surface with often deeply divisive meanings.

Today, despite the controversies surrounding them, skin lighteners are a booming global business. Sales extend across Asia and the Americas and through Europe, the Middle East, and Africa, and they are expected by industry insiders to reach US$31.2 billion by 2024. Whereas for decades Japan has been the most lucrative national market for skin lighteners, it is now being supplanted by India and China.[1] Within many African countries, skin lightening is a commonplace practice. Skin lighteners are used by the world's richest— including Hollywood and Bollywood celebrities—and by the world's poorest, those living in slums on just a couple dollars per day. International and local journalists routinely run stories profiling the women and sometimes men who use skin lighteners as well as the uphill efforts of others trying to end the practice.[2] The sizable and growing demand for skin lighteners is striking given the known toxicities of many of these products and repeated condemnation of them by antiracist activists. Like other potentially dangerous beauty practices, skin lightening pits the promise of bodily enhancement against the threat of bodily harm. It is a practice that seemingly defies the logic of progressive political ideologies, and that raises challenging historical questions.

What do the long history and contemporary ubiquity of skin lightening tell us about the politics of beauty? What do these controversial cosmetics reveal about the historical relationship between bodily practices and personal desires, on the one hand, and large-scale social and economic transformations, on the other? What do they reveal about the relevance of skin color and colorism— prejudice based on preference for lighter skin tones—to conceptions of race and racism? *Beneath the Surface* answers these questions by reconstructing a history of skin lighteners that is centered in South Africa, and looks outwards, most notably to the United States and East Africa. It traces the changing meanings of skin color and examines how those changes have informed racial hierarchies and antiracist resistance. At the same time, it insists that racism alone cannot explain skin lightening practices. To understand them, we must also attend to intersecting political and affective formations of class, gender, and sexuality, and to a variety of transregional and multisited processes. Peoples' everyday experiences of skin color have been produced through institutions of slavery, colonialism, and segregation as well as the collateral development of consumer capitalism, visual media, techno-medical innovations, and protest politics.

South Africa is an instructive site for considering the history of skin lightening. Compared with other parts of the African continent and even the world, it is a region that has long encompassed people with a wide range of skin tones and with varied ways of conceptualizing and caring for the body's surface. Over more than two centuries of European colonial rule, those ways became increasingly entangled. Colonialism, segregation, and apartheid heightened scrutiny to bodily surfaces by casting skin color as one of the most visible markers of racial distinctions. White supremacist rule in twentieth-century South Africa depended on identifying and dividing the population into four categories: Native or Bantu, European, Asian, and Mixed or Coloured. This racial order did not rely on a binary distinction between black and white or, as in the United States, the legal principle of the "one-drop rule." Rather, it relied on racialized geographic and linguistic affiliations while admitting—through the category of Coloured—the failure of simple affiliations to capture complex social realities. For those living within this four-tiered racial hierarchy, even slight differences in skin tone could carry significant social and political weight. That weight helped to make skin lighteners into prominent commodities in apartheid South Africa, the country with the most developed capitalist economy on the sub-continent. Advertisements for skin lighteners became a fixture in apartheid-era popular media, with market researchers declaring them among the most common personal products used in urban African households. Activists, in turn, saw their popularity as overdetermined evidence of racial capitalism's pathological effects and made opposition to skin lighteners into a corollary of the anti-apartheid movement. Their activism ensured that today South Africa possesses—on the books, at least—the world's most extensive prohibitions on skin lighteners.

The topic of skin lighteners in South Africa and elsewhere can elicit strong, even visceral, reactions that are often racialized. People who first learn about skin lighteners from news reports and other secondhand sources—generally, white people—are frequently surprised, asking, "Why do people use them?" Behind this question lies others. Why would people want to alter the color of their skin? Why would some black and brown people want to "look white"? Why would they do so at the risk of harming their health? And, in the case of the many poor consumers of skin lighteners, why do they devote any of their scarce resources to frivolous cosmetics? These questions alternately cast skin lightening as irrational, dangerous, or trivial. For those more familiar with the practice—often people of color—public discussion of skin lightening can generate unease. In racially mixed settings, especially in the United States, skin color itself is a rarely broached topic. For scholars of race and gender, skin lightening raises knotty political and conceptual issues: issues of self-expression versus social control, informed choice versus false consciousness, and politics versus aesthetics.

This book historicizes such reactions and challenges such distinctions. Answering the question of why people have used skin lighteners requires attention to overlapping and, at times, contradictory dynamics. Rather than separating matters of self-fashioning, beauty, and affect from political and economic structures, such dynamics bind them together. Understanding this history requires a layered approach, an approach that reconstructs sedimented meanings and compounded politics. Attending to such meanings and politics adds nuance and new fields of inquiry to the study of gender history and African history. Like

FIGURES I.1–I.7. These seven ads—four of them full-page—appeared in a single issue of *Drum* magazine. Skin lightener ads were a ubiquitous part of apartheid-era popular culture. Modeled after U.S. pictorials like *Life* and *Ebony*, *Drum* was founded in Johannesburg in 1951 and grew to be one of the most influential publications in Africa, with regional issues published in Lagos, Accra, and Nairobi. *Drum* (Central and East African Edition), June 1962.

Catherine Burns's call to compose history "in chords," this approach seeks to understand a "world of complexity and multiple layers of causation."[3] People's words and actions provide vital starting points for understanding why skin lighteners are used. Yet, similar to all historical artifacts, these words and actions exist both as sources of information and as expressions of a particular time and place. Interpreting them requires situating them in relation to other evidence and finding insight in their form as well as their content. It also requires an openness to the multiplicity, ambiguity, and opacity of meaning. The history of skin lighteners reveals the importance of both surface appearances and the layers that lie beneath them.[4]

Modern Girls and Slippery Things

Take a rich, if brief, reference to skin lighteners from a letter written in 1941 by a young African woman. The letter is part of correspondence, now archived at the University of Witwatersrand, between Zilpah Skota and Mweli, her beloved husband. Mweli was a prominent member of the African National Congress, and the editor of the *African Yearly Register*, an extraordinary "Who's Who" published in 1930 that chronicled the achievements of black people in Africa, aiming to inspire those "tempted to feel ashamed of their race." Zilpah, the daughter of an African Methodist Episcopal church minister, was younger than Mweli when they met in Soweto and married in 1938. Resembling other members of South Africa's mission-educated black elite, the couple struggled to make ends meet under segregation's many barriers. Soon after marrying, financial difficulties compelled the Skotas to sublet part of their house in Johannesburg and forced Zilpah to return to her family home in the provincial town of Klerksdorp. Zilpah's letters convey a passionate longing for Mweli and a modern-girl sensibility. Around the world in this period, modern girls distinguished themselves by their schooling, their passion for romance, and their sense of style.[5] Zilpah paid keen attention to appearances, expressing some insecurity about her own. In one letter she decided not to send a photo of herself, writing, "It's not nice I'll try to take a better one." In others she noted whether she had grown "fat" or "thin" and requested new clothes and other commodities. In her April 1941 letter, sandwiched between news of loved ones, Zilpah asked, "Can you send me one jar of Karoo [sic] I am already dark through the sun."[6] At the time, Karroo was one of South Africa's most popular brands of skin lighteners.

This correspondence provides clues to the use of commercial skin lighteners in segregationist South Africa. By the early 1940s, skin lighteners—like love letters and photos—had become routine items for some African modern girls. Zilpah's request is noteworthy given the financial difficulties that she and Mweli faced, and because of his standing as a prominent African nationalist dedicated to promoting racial pride. Widespread condemnation of skin lighteners by black nationalists was still a couple of decades away. For Zilpah, skin lighteners were neither an unthinkable luxury nor a testament to racial shame. A jar of cosmetics would have expressed her husband's care and affection, easing the emotional and material effects of her provincial stay. By the interwar period, many modern girls recognized as white in South Africa, the United States, and elsewhere had embraced tanning as evidence of a healthy and leisure-filled lifestyle that imparted an alluring, seasonal glow. Such consumers had begun to replace skin lighteners with tanning products. By contrast, for Zilpah and some other black modern girls, tanned skin was a sign of hardship endured, not privilege gained. They viewed skin made "dark through the sun" as evidence of outdoor, menial toil that dimmed and dulled their appearances. This perspective challenged the rigidity of racial thinking. It posited gradations of darkness and lightness as existing within—not just between—racial categories and as features that might be added or removed. Some of the roots of this perspective lay in the region's earlier history.

Even prior to the arrival of European colonizers, southern Africa was a place of marked diversity in skin tones. Melanin, the biochemical compound that makes skin colorful, serves as a natural sunscreen. Variations in melanin evolved to ensure that human bodies absorb the appropriate levels of ultraviolet radiation vital for good health and successful reproduction. Too much ultraviolet radiation produces the short-term effect of sunburn and the long-term effect of molecular damage that can both result in skin cancer and impair egg health, sperm production, and fetal growth. Too little radiation hinders the production of vitamin D, weakening bones and hampering the ability of female bodies to support fetal development and provide nutritious breastmilk. Humans who lived, for tens of thousands of years, in equatorial Africa or at high altitudes, places where sun exposure is the greatest, evolved to have higher levels of melanin and, hence, more darkly pigmented skin. People living farther from the equator in places with strong but seasonal sun, such as along the Mediterranean coast or the southern tip of Africa, evolved to have more lightly pigmented skin that could still become deeply tanned.[7] When European travelers and traders first set foot in southern Africa around 1500, they encountered people who spoke Khoesan and Bantu languages, and whose skin color spanned from light tan to the richest brown. These people sought, in various ways, to protect their bodies from the elements and to render their surfaces attractive and spiritually potent.

When the Dutch established a colonial outpost at the Cape in 1652, they further expanded southern Africa's sepia spectrum of skin tones and introduced new bodily practices and politics. Older concerns of gender, beauty, and status confronted newer ones rooted in race, class, and respectability. Colonialism brought people from other parts of Africa, Southeast Asia, South Asia, and East Asia as slaves, political prisoners, and indentured servants, whereas people from Western and Eastern Europe and North America arrived as soldiers, merchants, farmers, wage laborers, and, later, missionaries and miners. These people interacted with one another and those already living in southern Africa through often violent political and sexual relations. The children born of those relations contributed to the region's already diverse palette of skin tones. Through imperial conquest, slavery, and settler colonialism, a political order structured by white supremacy took root. South Africa's racial order emerged alongside the development of the transatlantic slave trade and as part of the elaboration of European colonial rule across much of the globe.[8] European colonizers invested skin color and associated physical differences with fierce political meanings, using them to distinguish the enslaved and vanquished from the free, and to justify the former's subjugation. They paired pale skin color with beauty, intelligence, and power while casting melanin-rich hues as the embodiment of ugliness, inferiority, and abjection.[9] By the time Zilpah was a young woman, South Africa's segregationist government attached differential rights and privileges to the four official racial categories.

Within this political order, where minute racialized differences in physical appearances could carry great import, some people sought to whiten and lighten the body's surface. It is useful here to distinguish between two types of preparations. *Skin whiteners* are powders and paints that contain light-colored materials, including clay, chalk, flour, rice powder, and white lead. People in many parts of Africa had long used kaolin or white clay as part of ritual and spiritual transformations while elite women from Europe and Asia used white-colored cosmetics to create refined and privileged appearances. *Skin lighteners*, in turn, are compounds, creams, and lotions—often also called "freckle removers" or "skin bleaches"—that generated a less painted effect by removing rather than concealing blemished or darker skin. Skin lighteners containing acidic compounds or ingredients like lemon juice or milk can produce real, if subtle and temporary, lightening effects by acting as irritants and exfoliants that remove the top, tanned layers of the epidermis, revealing the lighter layers beneath. Skin lighteners have also often contained harsher chemicals like sulfur, arsenic, and, most notably, mercury.

Whether made at home or purchased in shops, skin lighteners defy easy distinctions between cosmetics and medicines. Pharmacists and doctors have prepared and prescribed skin lighteners for people who desire overall lightening. They have also prescribed them to treat dermatological disorders and hyperpigmentation, darkened patches left by sun exposure, infection, inflammation, and melasma. Hyperpigmentation tends to be more visible and long-lasting on complexions rich in melanin, providing additional reasons why some black and brown consumers and patients have turned to skin lighteners. By the early twentieth century, many biomedical experts and cosmetic manufacturers recognized the toxicity of ammoniated mercury and mercuric chloride but regarded them as the most effective lightening agents available. In addition to exfoliating the skin, mercurial compounds, through their antibacterial properties, can clear infections like acne and syphilis. Moreover, at a biomolecular level, they inhibit the body's production of melanin by interfering with the enzyme tyrosinase.[10] Skin lighteners' multiple names and uses, and varied active ingredients and effects, render them fluid substances and slippery things to analyze. They continually slide between being beauty preparations and being therapeutic treatments, between being common cosmetics and caustic poisons.

Tracking the slipperiness of skin lighteners introduces a fresh set of thematic concerns to African historiography. Over thirty years ago, Arjun Appadurai's edited volume *The Social Life of Things* demonstrated how salient, and often surprising, political and historical connections could be elucidated by following and analyzing things from production to consumption. That volume explored how people invest value in things and how, in turn, things give value to human relations.[11] Subsequent scholars ran with these insights, producing social biographies of singular objects and commodity-chain analyses of goods like cotton, coffee, and salt.[12] The more recent flourishing of science and technology studies (STS) has similarly directed scrutiny to the social lives of things and, more specifically, to their material properties and how those properties act in the world.[13] Tracing how things like skin lighteners move and are remade pushes African history beyond the social history of specific communities and the political history of colonies and metropoles. It opens the field to multiple geographic locales, a wider cast of characters, and a new attention to materiality.

Beneath the Surface proceeds chronologically and thematically. Chapter 1 examines how precolonial ways of caring for the body's surface encountered and eventually became entangled with ideas and practices brought by European colonizers and immigrants from elsewhere. Chapter 2 focuses on the 1930s, when South Africa's mission-educated black elite began debating the propriety of using skin whiteners and lighteners as part of a new consumer culture. Their debates pivoted on how to define feminine beauty and racial respectability amid the influx of cultural forms and commercial products from the United States. Chapter 3 examines the growth of cosmetics manufacturing in South Africa, exploring why such companies increasingly catered to black and brown consumers. The local pharmacist who developed Karroo, for instance, did so with a white clientele in mind. By the 1940s, however, young women like Zilpah Skota were more likely to purchase his product.

The second half of the book considers what happened in the decades after Zilpah's correspondence, when South Africa became one of the world's most robust markets for skin lighteners. This vitality coincided with the unfolding of apartheid rule, introduced in 1948. Chapter 4 examines how the expansion of black consumer markets and black media—especially photo magazines like *Zonk!* and *Drum*—during the 1950s and 1960s fueled this commercial boom, helping to situate skin lighteners as tools that women and some men could use to achieve greater social visibility amid shrinking political possibilities. Chapter 5 explores how this boom fed off the accidental discovery of a new active ingredient, hydroquinone, and entailed the marketing of South African–made products elsewhere in Africa. Concerns about skin lighteners intensified in the 1970s as political and regulatory debates ricocheted between the United States, postcolonial East Africa, and apartheid South Africa. Chapter 6 examines how those debates came to a head when Black Consciousness activists and biomedical professionals in South Africa compelled the apartheid government, in its waning months, to ban skin lighteners. The conclusion considers the uneven afterlives of that achievement and today's growing global market for skin lighteners.

To reconstruct this layered history, I draw on a variety of sources. The first chapter delves into archaeological and linguistic evidence as well as travelers' and missionaries' writing and early anthropological accounts. Subsequent chapters weave together analysis of advertisements, beauty competitions and advice columns, business and marketing reports, regulatory investigations and legislative debates, medical and social scientific studies, and protest literature with attention to popular fiction, memoirs, personal correspondence, and oral history interviews. The breadth of these sources reveals how struggles surrounding skin lighteners have extended from their manufacturing and marketing to their consumption and condemnation.

Connective Comparison and Affective Consumption

I first came to this historical topic through my own astonishment: I was surprised by the ubiquity of skin lighteners in Kenyan popular and political culture in the early 1990s. Later, I realized that their postcolonial presence raised important and largely unanswered questions for the fields of gender studies and African history: questions about race, consumer capitalism, and transnational connections; and questions about visual media, beauty, and affect. Growing up white on U.S. Air Force bases and in an even more racially segregated suburb north of Pittsburgh, I do not recall ever seeing or hearing about skin lighteners. As an undergraduate, at the height of the anti-apartheid movement on U.S. college campuses, I began studying African history and reading the work of African political theorists and novelists, nearly all of them men. What I took from those texts left me unprepared to make sense of the skin lightening products that I saw for sale in Nairobi's shops and informal markets. Discussions by Jomo Kenyatta, Chinua Achebe, Frantz Fanon, and Ngũgĩ wa Thiong'o about the integrity of African cultural practices and the power of anticolonial nationalism seemed a world apart from the advertisements in Kenyan magazines that promised glamour and success to those who lightened their skin. I soon learned that skin lighteners were not just common but highly contested commodities, and that men, as well as women, sometimes used them. Male politicians, nonetheless, condemned the use of skin lighteners as evidence of young women's embrace of debased Western values and rejection of African traditions and looks. Newspapers frequently carried editorials decrying the ill health effects of various products while letter-to-the-editor writers urged their compatriots to embrace the motto "Black Is Beautiful."

Few academics took note of these debates in Kenya or elsewhere. One exception was Audrey Wipper, a Canadian sociologist working in postcolonial East Africa in the early 1970s. Wipper, while acknowledging the physical and psychological dangers of skin lighteners, argued that male politicians' denunciations of them were a piece of broader, worrisome efforts to use urban women as scapegoats for national problems and to safeguard politicians' puritanical and patriarchal authority.[14] Two decades later, Timothy Burke returned to the topic in *Lifebuoy Men, Lux Women*, the first history of commodity culture in Africa. Burke examined how skin lightener advertisements in Zimbabwe during the 1960s and 1970s conflated lightness and whiteness with sexual attraction and social mobility. He described how black users hailed from the country's highest or lowest income group, those "successful or desperate for success." Moreover, he demonstrated that African nationalists' criticism of skin lightening as a betrayal of African culture overshadowed alternative perspectives.[15] These accounts left me wondering what the history of skin lighteners might look like from South Africa, the country where white-minority rule lasted the longest and where, not coincidentally, consumer capitalism was the most advanced, extending its tendrils north to places that included Kenya and Zimbabwe.

These questions partly inspired my participation in a collaborative project, the Modern Girl Around the World Research Group. Comprising six University of Washington faculty members, our group developed the modern girl as a heuristic device to examine the global emergence during the 1920s and 1930s of female figures who embraced an explicit eroticism, appeared to disavow domestic duties, and used commodities like cigarettes and cosmetics.[16] That collaboration altered my perspective on gender in Africa by foregrounding how transnational and transregional histories had shaped twentieth-century developments. Whereas my earlier work examined the *historical entanglement* of indigenous and colonial concerns in one African locale, the collaboration pushed me to see a more varied set of forces at play, and to find analytical value in connecting similar processes across different locales.[17] To produce such histories, our research group developed the method of *connective comparison*. This method draws attention to how "things previously understood to be local come into being through complex global dynamics" that are neither derivative nor linear.[18] Connective comparison entails attending to developments in multiple places, and then determining when those developments are linked and when they diverge. Identification of linkages and divergences, in turn, throws into sharp relief the causal ties and grounded peculiarities that merit further investigation. Like Anna Tsing's *friction*, connective comparison questions the simplicity of globalization narratives that presume unimpeded and undifferentiated flows between various parts of the world. Both concepts focus on when, where, and why things, people, and ideas that move gain traction, and how, in the grip of those encounters, novel formations are born.[19]

The method of connective comparison helped me to identify the importance of U.S. developments to the history of commercial skin lighteners in Africa, and the importance of transnational conversations to American political and regulatory debates. When I first began this project, I imagined that South Asia would be an important touchstone, given the pervasive presence of skin lighteners in India today and South Africa's many ties to South Asia. For the period prior to the 1980s, however, I found little evidence of South Asian involvement in the trade. By contrast, American connections loomed large.

Beginning in the late nineteenth century, South Africa's racial order and capitalist economy evolved in close conversation with the United States.[20] Government officials and businesspeople alike looked across the Atlantic for political and economic inspiration while U.S. investors and entrepreneurs turned to South Africa in search of new opportunities. U.S. companies, some of them black-owned, shaped South Africa's skin lighteners market by recognizing resonances between the two racial and commercial orders, and by exporting their products and formulas. American-made skin lighteners encountered friction and gained traction in South Africa. At the same time, local cosmetic manufacturers used cultural forms first developed in the United States to promote their own skin lighteners in South Africa and elsewhere on the continent. These forms ranged from beauty contests and photo magazines to Hollywood starlets and testimonial advertisements. South Africa, in turn, exported these forms north of the Limpopo River. To elucidate the influence of the South African trade elsewhere on the subcontinent and to compare the politics of skin lightening under apartheid and postcolonial regimes, I turn to East Africa and especially to Kenya as a case study in chapter 5. Kenya is a place where some South African companies had business connections and where I had previous research experience. The manufacturing and marketing of skin lighteners in South Africa and Kenya often followed developments in the United States, including guidelines developed by the Food and Drug Administration (FDA). When it came to opposition to skin lighteners, however, influences were more multidirectional.

In addition to directing my attention toward transnational and diasporic connections, the Modern Girl collaboration helped me to see beauty and commerce as topics neglected by historians of women and gender in Africa. Previous studies, including my own, presented mission Christianity, colonial law, and labor migrancy as the main forces that fueled twentieth-century gender transformations. Focus on those forces, in part, mirrored the priorities of the missionaries and state officials who produced the written archives on which we have often relied. Focus on those forces also reflected social historians' and second-wave feminists' desire to challenge racist and sexist representations of African women, to document women's productive and reproductive labors, and to demonstrate African agency. Less easily captured by our archives and research agendas were new forms of commerce and media that circulated internationally and that worked to alter appearances and aspirations. Apart from dress, historians of Africa have largely ignored matters of bodily aesthetics and beauty.[21] Yet, some time ago, Sylvia Ardyn Boone, the pioneering art historian of Sierra Leone, argued for the centrality of beauty and especially the beauty of pubescent girls and young women to African social worlds. Forms of female initiation across the continent have consistently equated the cultivation of beauty with fertility and sexual desirability.[22]

Over the past twenty years, scholars from a range of disciplines have argued for taking beauty seriously as a subject of study. One of the central insights of that scholarship is that the development of a global beauty industry has depended upon consumer capitalism's insistence on the body's malleability. Much feminist scholarship on beauty has debated whether practices like wearing makeup and high heels, hair straightening, and cosmetic surgery simply uphold patriarchal and racist structures, or whether some women find agency and empowerment through those very same practices.[23] A few South African cultural studies scholars have contributed to these debates by exploring beauty as a "peculiarly dense transfer point for relations of power," one used to include some and exclude others.[24] Regarding the politics of hair in South Africa, Zimitri Erasmus has importantly argued that while "'race' is always present," efforts to reduce hair straightening to aspirations for "whiteness" miss the complexity of black cultural politics and how such practices have also enabled black women to *feel* "proud," "confident," and "beautiful."[25]

Recent anthropological research on beauty similarly combines an attention to politics with an attention to emotions. In his ethnography of plastic surgery in Brazil, Alvaro Jarrín, for one, theorizes that "beauty's value" stems from the intertwining of biopolitics and affect. Michel Foucault's conception of biopower helps explain how "the discursive contrast between beauty and ugliness" permeates the social landscape, working to produce and reproduce inequalities, while attention to affect helps explain peoples' "visceral attachment to beauty as a form of hope." Perceptions of beauty, Jarrín insightfully argues, operate as "gut reactions that are entirely social, but which are not subject to modification, at least not with ease, because they have become habitual at a preconscious level."[26] Theorization of the interplay between the politics of beauty and its affective dimensions is especially useful for understanding the appeal of skin lightening in the past and present.

Such theorization also opens new perspectives on the history of consumer capitalism in Africa. Archaeologists and historians long ago identified consumption and commerce as key agents of change in Africa. Consumption of mundane and luxury goods was vital to the development of centralized polities like the West African kingdoms and Swahili city-states, and long-distance trade within the continent and across the Atlantic and Indian oceans. African demand for consumer goods figured prominently in Walter Rodney's analysis of how Europe "underdeveloped" Africa through slavery and colonialism while the fashioning of new consumer practices was central to John L. Comaroff and Jean Comaroff's account of the seismic transformations engendered by nineteenth-century mission Christianity.[27] Efforts to explain why capitalist relations of production developed relatively late on the continent have also singled out consumption. John Iliffe, for example, argued that pragmatic considerations prompted people, living in Africa's "often harsh and insecure" environments, to invest in social relations by consuming and enjoying material wealth rather than stockpiling it.[28] Over the past two decades, anthropologists and sociologists have posited consumption, together with the debt and disappointment that often accompanies it, as a driving force in postcolonial and post-apartheid political life. Consumer goods are essential to sustaining social ties while their conspicuous display provides sharp reminders of rising inequality.[29] Yet we have few accounts of how this form of capitalism that coupled consumption with new modes of manufacturing, merchandising, and marketing emerged in different parts of Africa over the twentieth century. The few historical accounts we do have focus almost exclusively on alcohol, foregrounding the consumer practices of men.[30]

Skin lighteners center the practices of women and foreground affective consumption. Zilpah Skota requested a jar of Karroo for lightening her tanned skin while writing about whether she had grown fat or thin, needed new clothes, and looked nice in photos. Despite or perhaps because of her family's trying circumstances, Zilpah drew Mweli's attention to *her* personal needs and *her* individual appearance, affirming her own self-worth. Poor people have repeatedly stunned researchers by using their meager resources to purchase cosmetics, commodities that the researchers themselves have often deemed frivolous, unnecessary, or ineffectual.[31] Compared with other capitalist enterprises, cosmetics companies are unusually dependent on cultivating desire and selling hope. Over the past century, they have devoted a larger portion of their revenues to advertising than almost any other type of manufacturing.[32] Success in the cosmetics industry hinges on convincing consumers that seemingly small and intimate products can alter how they look and feel within wider publics. Across the globe, cosmetics marketing has championed the body's malleability and the possibility of self-fashioning, helping to deepen the entanglement of consumption and affect.[33] Skin lighteners are an especially revealing category of cosmetics through which to track that entanglement in Africa. From the middle of the twentieth century, in South Africa at least, skin lightener manufacturers invested considerable resources in elaborate marketing campaigns that sparked wide-ranging debates over beauty, respectability, and authenticity.

Antiracist Retorts and Technologies of Visibility

Barack Obama, in his autobiography *Dreams from My Father: A Story of Race and Inheritance*, recounts learning about skin lighteners as a formative childhood experience. He tells a story of browsing through issues of *Life* magazine at the U.S. embassy library in Jakarta, when he and his American mother, Ann Dunham, lived there. Amid the glossy advertisements and photo spreads, the nine-year-old Obama came across a story of a black man who had paid for a "chemical treatment" to lighten his complexion. The accompanying photos showed the man's "strange, unnatural pallor" along with his "crinkly hair" and "heavy lips and broad, fleshy nose." Obama recalls experiencing the story and photos as an "ambush attack," a "frightening discovery." Raised by a liberal white mother who had swaddled her biracial son in the achievements of civil rights heroes and repeatedly pronounced Harry Belafonte as the world's best-looking man, Obama was unprepared for the revelation that some black people might seek to pass for white and use "bleaching creams" to do so. He wondered, "Did my mother know about this?" The young Obama kept that question to himself, continuing to trust his "mother's love," but knew, from that point forward, that "her account of the world, and my father's place in it, was somehow incomplete."[34]

This story is apocryphal. No article that fits the description ever appeared in *Life*. Obama may have read instead "A Whiter Shade of Black," an article published in *Esquire* in 1968. That article sensationalized the work of a white dermatologist in Washington, D.C., who treated black patients suffering from the depigmenting disorder vitiligo with a cream containing monobenzyl ether of hydroquinone.[35] Vitiligo became more well known in the 1990s when the entertainer Michael Jackson explained that his increasingly pale skin color was a side effect of the condition. Jackson's doctors, in fact, treated his vitiligo by prescribing creams like those discussed in the *Esquire* article.[36] The crucial point here is not the accuracy of Obama's recollection but how learning about skin lighteners operated in his memory and autobiographical narrative as a decisive moment in his journey toward color consciousness and racial awareness: "my vision had been permanently altered."[37]

Obama's story reveals how, by the late 1960s, encounters with skin lightening could stir visceral reactions and alter everyday perceptions. Over the past thirty years, scholars have explored race as a fundamental social and historical construction that is continually being remade and always in formation. Race importantly intersects with other social categories such as class and gender but is not reducible to them.[38] Thomas C. Holt, drawing on the earlier work of W. E. B. Du Bois and Frantz Fanon, pointed historians to its everyday salience: "race is reproduced via the marking of the racial Other.... It is at this level that race is reproduced long after its original historical stimulus—the slave trade and slavery—have faded."[39] Similarly, scholars of South Africa also called for more nuanced understandings of "how race works" by exploring intimate realms of action.[40] Following such calls, historians of Africa have begun to examine the centrality of racial thinking and processes of racialization to the continent's past and present. Significantly, they have demonstrated that European colonizers were not the only purveyors of racial discourses and that white settler colonies were not the only African locations where race mattered.[41] Skin lighteners provide another way to track the history of racialization, a way that foregrounds commonplace conceptions of skin color and beauty, and influences that crisscrossed the Atlantic.

Across the twentieth century, black women writers in the United States pointed to the body and contested beauty ideals as fundamental to everyday experiences of blackness, especially for girls and women. Writers from Zora Neale Hurston to Toni Morrison have explored how dominant American ideals that equate beauty with whiteness powerfully and painfully shaped social possibilities and internal longings. Describing the anguish and self-contempt felt by a young black girl who longed for blue eyes, Morrison's narrator in *The Bluest Eye* (1970) conjectures that "physical beauty," along with romantic love, are "probably the most destructive ideas in the history of human thought."[42] The roots of racialized ideals of beauty go back, at least, to the eighteenth century, the height of the transatlantic slave trade, when Enlightenment science bolstered white supremacy by associating bodily features, including skin color, with intelligence and beauty and denying those virtues to Africans. As Stephanie M. H. Camp put it, "Blackness and beauty have an ugly history."[43] Partly a product of this deeply racialized history and partly an antiracist retort to it, a vibrant African American beauty culture emerged. In the early twentieth century, black beauty entrepreneurs became emblems of pride and progress. They also, though, faced criticism for promoting a "white look" that valorized straight hair and light complexions.[44]

Despite stirring sharp debates, skin lighteners have garnered little in-depth historical analysis. Analysts of U.S. black beauty culture have paid more attention to hair practices and politics.[45] Otherwise astute scholars have mistakenly dismissed skin lightening as entirely ineffective and, hence, inconsequential.[46] In her social history of cosmetics, Kathy Peiss countered this neglect by documenting how a variety of consumers in the early twentieth-century United States, including recent immigrants from Southern and Eastern Europe as well as African American women, used skin lighteners. Notably, she argued that they did so for diverse reasons, ranging from a desire to fade blemishes and even out skin tone to the racialized pursuit of overall bleaching.[47] Some subsequent scholars have questioned Peiss's account for casting black beauty practices, including skin lightening, as acts of political agency and resistance, while downplaying how they more often accommodated, rather than contested, racial hierarchies.[48]

Although historical analysis has been scarce, interest in contemporary practices of skin lightening has grown in recent years. This growth has coincided with renewed attention to the relationship between racism and colorism, a term put into prominent usage by the writer and activist Alice Walker in the early 1980s.[49] Sociologists and legal scholars, focused mainly on the United States and Latin America, have demonstrated that discrimination based on skin tone continues to have a profound effect on income, health, and other social indicators. Color hierarchies suffuse inter- and intraracial relations. Whites discriminate most against black people with dark skin tones while blacks discriminate more against people with very dark or very light complexions than those with medium skin tones.[50] The volume *Shades of Difference*, edited by Evelyn Nakano Glenn, paired stark findings of color discrimination in the Americas, Asia, and Africa with analysis of the complexity of that discrimination. Skin color is always read in relation to other factors, including bodily comportment, dress, hair, age, gender, and even season. Skin-color hierarchies can both confirm and disrupt racial logics. Glenn's chapter and my own explored how the commercial trade in skin lighteners has shored up colorism by yoking the privileging of paler skin tones to corporate profits.[51]

Anthropologists have offered incisive, if divergent, answers to the question of why people use skin lighteners. Yaba Amgborale Blay and Jemima Pierre, in separate studies of skin lightening in Ghana, counter popular narratives that pathologize users. Instead of dismissing the practice as irrational or the result of "racial self-hatred," Blay and Pierre argue that people, living in economically precarious circumstances, lighten their skin for very practical and very political reasons. Many Ghanaians believe, according to Blay's trenchant analysis, that light-colored skin enables both women and men to be "noticeably beautiful," to "stand[] out in a crowd," and to look modern. Users seek to make themselves more visible to bolster their social networks, attract sexual and romantic attention, and secure and maintain marital partners. The conflation of beauty and success with light-colored skin in present-day West Africa, argue Blay and Pierre, results from the power of global white supremacy dating back to the era of the transatlantic slave trade and European colonialism.[52]

By contrast, other ethnographic analyses foreground historical influences that extend beyond Western racism and highlight localized conceptions of dignity and personhood. To explain Indonesian preferences for lightness, L. Ayu Saraswati points to the impact of European colonialism and American popular culture but also to the effect of Indian beauty ideals, dating back to the ninth century, and the Japanese occupation during World War II. In the very country where Obama recalled first learning of skin lightening from an American magazine, the practice was already well established.[53] Saraswati finds that Indonesian women today use skin lighteners more to avoid shame and embarrassment than to look good.[54] Her account that emphasizes affect and a variety of cultural influences resonates with Jonathan Friedman's interpretation of Congolese *sapeurs*, poor men who famously dedicate themselves to haute couture and often practice skin lightening. Friedman attributes *sapeurs'* actions and aspirations to long-standing central African aesthetic sensibilities that equate elegant and luminescent appearances with the accumulation of "life force."[55]

Similarly, cultural studies scholars have insisted that in Jamaica skin bleaching should not be interpreted as a quest for whiteness but rather in relation to the privileged Jamaican identity of "browning" or mixed race. While acknowledging the health dangers, these scholars argue that poor Jamaicans' use of skin bleaches partly disrupts essentialized notions of blackness by pointing to the unstable relationship between bodily appearances and racial identities.[56] Building on that work, Krista Thompson, an art historian, has insightfully linked skin lightening in Jamaican dancehalls during the 1990s and 2000s to the aesthetics of film and photography. Thompson examines how people use lighteners as visual technologies to make their faces and bodies more "representable" to the video camera. Skin lightening, she argues, operates as both a response to videography and a tool that enables marginalized and disenfranchised people to gain recognition in Jamaica and the United States, where the videos often circulate.[57] Together, these studies situate skin lightening as a site of disruptive politics and aesthetic expression.

Beneath the Surface places the political, economic, affective, and aesthetic dimensions of skin lightening in historical perspective. Eva Illouz calls such an approach to studying consumer capitalism a "post-normative critique." It aims to produce a "critical effect" by historically elucidating—instead of morally evaluating—the interconnectedness of things and human beings, and emotions and consumption: understanding emerges from identifying and describing the "chain of causes" that creates consuming subjects.[58] The early chapters of this book delve back in time to demonstrate how practices of skin lightening have moved between geographic locations and across cultural frontiers, appealing to diverse and shifting groups of people. I then turn to the commercial manufacture and marketing of skin lighteners, reconstructing the history of particular companies and advertising campaigns. This examination reveals how skin lighteners often operated as technologies of visibility. People used them to attract favorable attention and enhance their appearances and, as the twentieth century unfolded, to render themselves legible in new visual media and cultural forms ranging from photos and film to magazine spreads and beauty contests. They also deployed them as technologies of visibility to negotiate deeply racialized and sharply gendered social worlds. Whereas little evidence suggests that black consumers in South Africa used skin lighteners specifically to obtain official reclassification within apartheid's four-tiered racial hierarchy, they did use them to enhance prospects in social and work settings that privileged light skin. In the mid-1980s, an activist campaigning against skin lighteners explained their appeal: "I don't know if many blacks have tried to get reclassified by lightening their skin color, but psychologically they believe that they will have more opportunities and be more successful in whatever they do if their skin is whiter."[59]

In addition, *Beneath the Surface* chronicles the history of opposition to skin lighteners, and it is the first study to do so. I examine efforts to curtail their sale and use by medical professionals and consumer health advocates, on the one hand, and by antiracist thinkers and activists, on the other. Attention to these two forms of critique highlights the unique and distinct positions that South Africa and the United States occupy in the global history of skin lighteners. It also helps to explain episodes like Obama's apocryphal encounter with an American magazine article in Jakarta. By the late 1960s, antiracist activists had framed skin lighteners as overdetermined evidence of the psychical effects of structural racism. Raising her son at the height of the Black Power movement and at a distance from the United States, Dunham sought to instill in him what bell hooks would later term "loving blackness," an ethic that rejected white beauty standards and named Harry Belafonte the world's most attractive man.[60] The ethic stuck but left the young Obama unprepared for a world where people who looked like him and his Kenyan father might want to lighten their skin.

UNDERSTANDING WHY SOME PEOPLE have used skin lighteners in the past and continue to do so in the present requires a layered history, a history that attends to lighteners' slippery status as both cosmetics and medicines and to connections between seemingly disparate domains. The political and affective dimensions of skin lightening have been forged through social and material processes that have spanned centuries and crossed oceans. Racism is utterly integral but alone insufficient for making sense of this history. Skin lighteners have proliferated through the spread of mass manufacturing, marketing, and media, and the linked rise of the modern girl, one of consumer capitalism's chief protagonists. By purchasing and using skin lighteners, some young women, like Zilpah Skota, and, later, men participated in new forms of consumption and self-fashioning. They engaged skin lighteners as technologies of visibility that simultaneously worked to challenge and entrench existing racial and gender hierarchies. Over time and as part of broader social movements, antiracist activists took aim at these forms and invested bodily appearances and affective consumption with new, liberatory meanings. It was the presence of skin lighteners *despite* the power of those movements that so confounded Obama.

To understand these twentieth-century developments, we must start earlier. How did people in precolonial and colonial southern Africa conceptualize and care for bodily surfaces? What part did whitening or lightening play as different ideas and practices intersected and became entangled on the decidedly uneven terrain of colonialism? Answering these questions requires paying attention to the significance of the body's surface as well as to what lies beneath.

One

COSMETIC PRACTICES
AND COLONIAL CRUCIBLES

In 1931, Monica Hunter (later, Wilson) with the indispensable assistance of Mary Soga undertook ethnographic research in Pondoland, an isiXhosa-speaking area of the Eastern Cape. Hunter had grown up in the area as the daughter of European missionaries. In her early twenties, she was pursuing a doctorate in social anthropology that would result in the richly detailed publication *Reaction to Conquest*. Twenty years Hunter's senior, Soga ran a local trading store. She was the daughter of a Scottish woman and a Xhosa medical doctor, William Anderson Soga, and was the granddaughter of Tiyo Soga, the first black ordained minister in South Africa.[1] During their research together, Hunter and Soga encountered young women using two different homemade preparations to lighten their complexions.

The first was a "strong bleaching agent" derived from the green roots of sweet-smelling Tambookie grass (*umgqungu*). Hunter explained that during the period of seclusion that followed the onset of puberty and, ideally, preceded marriage, female initiates chewed the root and then smeared their faces and bodies, "usually at least twice" per day, with "saliva and the juice of the chewed root." The root's effect, combined with the darkness of the seclusion hut and lack of exercise, made the women "lighter in complexion and fatter than normal," features that they considered beautiful. The acids and citronella oil contained within this plant species (*Cymbopogon*) likely worked as irritants, stripping away the top, tanned layers of the epidermis.[2] Such physical effects signaled ritual transformation and depended on proper social and spiritual relations. Some informants told Hunter and Soga that lightening, in fact, was the "most essential" part of the ceremonies and that if the initiate's mother violated the prohibition on family members entering the seclusion hut, the initiate would "not bleach properly."

The second lightening preparation was egg whites used by young Christian women about to marry. Hunter described how in the weeks after a wedding was announced but before the ceremony actually occurred, Christian brides would confine themselves in huts, near their parents' homes. During confinement, they would rub egg whites onto their faces and bodies to give themselves "a light complexion." Hunter noted that whereas this appeared to be an obvious reworking of non-Christian practices, Christians were "indignant at any suggestion that this seclusion is really an adaptation of the initiation ceremonies." Hunter's account reveals how, in this rural locale, both "pagan" and Christian young women practiced skin lightening. Hunter was one of the earliest anthropologists to carefully record girls' and women's activities. After presenting informants' commentary on their skin lightening practices, however, she offered no further assessment of the practices' meanings or longevity.[3] Were such lightening practices a traditional part of female initiation ceremonies and wedding preparations in the area? Or were they a more recent development, a response to the racial ideologies and inequities of colonial and segregationist rule?

Answering these questions entails reconstructing a long and layered history of peoples' efforts to care for and embellish their bodies. Attention to surface appearances and skin tones, as we shall see, predated European colonialism but occurred in different social and cultural registers. In precolonial times, southern African bodily practices centered on smearing and brightening the skin, and they were tied to gendered and generational beauty ideals rather than to racial designations. Under colonial rule, these ways of cultivating the body's surface became entangled with practices, ideas, and institutions introduced by settlers and migrants from elsewhere.

Smearing, Brightening, and Lightening

As with many other aspects of precolonial African history, the task of reconstructing bodily practices and meanings before the arrival of literate travelers and colonizers is challenging. Early southern African societies did not possess systems of writing, so no documents exist for this period. To imagine everyday life, we must piece together clues garnered from archaeological and linguistic sources as well as latter-day written accounts, most often penned by European travelers, traders, officials, ethnographers, and missionaries. Though partial, these sources suggest that the region's inhabitants invested considerable energy and resources in protecting and brightening their skin in ways that combined pragmatic concerns with aesthetic preferences.

Smearing the body's surface with red ochre and other bright minerals are among the most ancient of human practices. Recent archaeological excavations of the Blombos Cave, located on the Western Cape coast, have unearthed engraved ochre pieces and ochre processing toolkits dating back 100,000 years. Remarkably, the engraved pieces appear to be the very earliest evidence of humans anywhere in the world engaging in symbolic behavior. Archaeologists believe that early *Homo sapiens* used the toolkits to combine ochre powder with animal fat and then smeared the mixture on their bodies for decorative and practical purposes, including protection from the sun, wind, and insect bites. Recovered bits of powder demonstrate a clear preference for the reddest, most saturated, and brightest forms of ochre.[4] Research at another site, Tsodilo Hills in present-day Botswana, has revealed that tens of thousands of years later, somewhere between 800 and 1000 AD, another mineral used for bodily protection and decoration—specularite—helped to fuel long-distance trade networks that stretched across much of southern Africa. Specularite is a silvery, bluish variety of hematite that, when combined with animal fat and smeared, creates glittery and glistening appearances. In the early nineteenth century, European travelers observed men and especially women in the Northern Cape whose "hair was copiously adorned with *sibilo* (specularite in Setswana)" so that their heads sparkled "like diamonds" when they moved.[5] Specularite was a precious trade good whose use conveyed status and wealth. Southern Africans used specularite, like the reddest ochres, as technologies of visibility, tools for distinguishing themselves and rendering their bodily surfaces brilliant.

When Europeans first came ashore, around 1500, they encountered people who embraced this aesthetic preference, who spoke languages belonging to one of two broad linguistic families, and whose skin color varied greatly. Speakers of Khoesan languages, distinctive for their click sounds, had the deepest historical ties to the region. Their ancestors began arriving there, likely emigrating from eastern Africa, somewhere between forty thousand and ten thousand years ago. Living between the Kalahari Desert and the Cape of Good Hope, relatively high latitudes by sub-Saharan African standards, Khoesan ancestors evolved to have complexions with less melanin.[6] Khoesan communities, in this relatively arid terrain, sustained themselves through gathering, hunting, and sometimes keeping cattle and mining. Their moderately pigmented skin contrasted with the darker skin tones of Bantu speakers from equatorial Africa and the Great Lakes area, who began moving into the region about 2,500 years ago. As farmers and cattle keepers, these Africans eventually gravitated toward the

FIGURE 1.1. An illustration of a young woman wearing specularite in her hair to create a shiny and bright appearance. For centuries, specularite, a variety of hematite, had been mined at Tsodilo Hills and traded across southern Africa for use in bodily adornment. William J. Burchell, *Travels in the Interior of Southern Africa, Volume II* (London: Longman, Hurst, Rees, Orme, Brown, and Green, 1824).

eastern portions of southern Africa where rainfall was greater and more reliable. Despite and, in part, because of these differences in livelihood and location, these two broadly defined groups interacted through raiding, trading, and marrying. Over the course of generations, the more sedentary, larger, and often wealthier and more powerful Bantu societies incorporated significant numbers of Khoesan, especially women, and, as a result, southern Africa's skin-color palette developed further gradations.[7]

For early European colonists and travelers, the most striking feature of southern Africans' appearances was not their skin color but the substances with which they covered it. One visitor after another to the Cape described, in disparaging terms, the sight and smell of Khoekhoe bodies and cloaks "smeared with grease and filthy" and covered in fat mixed with black powder so that "they stink and shine horribly."[8] The oil and fat derived from plants, cattle, and even whales that washed ashore; the black powder came from crushed charcoal or black stones, or soot scraped from cooking utensils.[9] Observers agreed that the application of this oil and powder mixture made Khoekhoe skin appear much darker than it actually was. Their natural skin color, Europeans testified, ranged from being as "white as our women in Holland" to being moderate brown.[10] Bantu speakers also practiced smearing. Over the eighteenth and nineteenth centuries as Europeans moved farther to the east and north of the Cape colony, they documented Africans rubbing oil or fat, often mixed with red ochre, on their bodies and clothes. A missionary evangelizing among the Tswana disapprovingly noted that they left "the colour of their greasy red attire" on everything they touched. Increasingly, over time, colonizers cast smearing not just as evidence of African "barbarity" and pagan backwardness but also as a trait of racial inferiority.[11]

From the perspective of many others in southern Africa, there was much to recommend the practice. Smearing, as Timothy Burke has argued, created a protective layer that shielded skin from dirt and other menaces, prevented the skin from drying and cracking under strong winds and intense sunlight, and imparted a sensual and glossy sheen that was pleasing to the eye and touch.[12] Smearing was also a sign of affluence; by covering their bodies in animal fat, people demonstrated their wealth in cattle.[13] In his 1931 study of Xhosa life and customs, John Henderson Soga, Mary's uncle, argued that the application of fat and ochre was an ancient practice used to adorn the body and protect it from the sun and insects. The red shale known as *itchitywa* was especially renowned for its ability to create a "bronze appearance" and leave the skin feeling smooth and silky.[14] Some people created patterns on their skin by removing smeared charcoal and ochre with their fingernails while others painted decorative designs on their faces in a variety of colors, including red, yellow, white, and black, by using a fine stick or quill.[15] A smeared and painted body was a body well cared for.

The colors in which people enveloped their bodies conveyed metaphysical qualities and ritual states. Across broad swathes of Africa, redness, especially as achieved through ochre, has signified protection from dangers, and a normal, undisturbed, state of being.[16] Among isiXhosa speakers, over the nineteenth century, redness came to embody the distinction between those who believed in conserving traditions, including offering sacrifices to their ancestors, and those who embraced colonial ways, most notably mission Christianity and schools. The latter group self-identified as the school people or "dressed people" (*abantu basesikolweni*), while the former described themselves as the "red people" (*abantu ababomvu*). Less politely, those with schooling often referred to red people as the "smeared or ochred ones" (*amaqaba* or *oonombola*), suggesting just how powerfully bodily appearances and practices expressed social and spiritual divides.[17] The medical anthropologist Harriet Ngubane, writing in the 1970s, argued that, among isiZulu speakers, red ochre carried a somewhat different ritual significance, signaling transition and transformation, especially between the mundane and otherworldly.[18]

People in many parts of Africa have also associated white clay or kaolin with liminal states. Initiates, nursing mothers, apprentice diviners, and healers have all painted their bodies and especially their faces with white clay. This covering has signified their positive and potent connections to the spiritual world and ancestors, and it warned others to approach them with caution. The wearing of white clay has been one of the most marked features of seclusion for both male and female initiates, ensuring and expressing their state of ritual transformation.[19] The wide geographic distribution of this practice from west and central to eastern and southern Africa belies deep historical roots.

Linguistic evidence extending back to the nineteenth century suggests that the aesthetic ideals of shininess, brightness, lightness, and ritual—not racial—whiteness have overlapped in dense and complex ways, and these ideals have often been associated with feminine beauty, sexual availability, and marriage. In his early isiZulu-English dictionary, J. W. Colenso used the well-known phrase "The bride goes off having anointed herself" (*umlobokazi uhamba esagcobile*) to illustrate the verb for to anoint, grease, or smear over.[20] Two Zulu linguists working in the mid-twentieth century translated the same phrase, more pointedly, as "The new bride goes while still well greased."[21] The descriptive verb in isiZulu and isiXhosa (both Nguni languages within the larger Bantu-language family) for "to shine" and "to be bright," *kanya* or *khanya*, denotes the quality of being clear and light. It also carries connotations of purity and ritual whiteness. Ngubane, in her discussion of color symbolism in Zulu medicine, explained the complex relationship between *khanya* and *mhlophe*, the adjective generally used for the color white. Whereas the adjective for black, *mnyama*, also encompasses dark, the distinction between lightness and whiteness has long been divided between *khanya* and *mhlophe*. Yet, at times and especially in their more metaphorical uses, these terms have been used interchangeably, as both can carry positive associations of goodness and ritual success. Ngubane provides the example of words spoken at a nubility rite in which the ancestors were called upon to make a young woman's future white and light: "Pathways hers be white / Let there be light, let her [be able to] see" (*Izindlela zakhe zibe mhlophe / Kukhanye, abone*).[22] Speakers of Sesotho and Setswana have also associated feminine beauty with shininess, brightness, lightness, and ritual whiteness. In early dictionaries, the verb for "to shine and glitter," *galalèla*, is also translated as "to be glorious." To smear one's face with fat, *iphôtlha*, signaled shininess and beauty and, more recently, to "smarten oneself." Moreover, as in isiZulu and isiXhosa, both the verb for "to become light" or "to be clear or bright," *phèpahala*, and the color white, *chweu*, especially in ritual contexts, carried positive connotations of clarity, purity, innocence, and rebirth.[23]

These dense and overlapping associations between shininess, brightness, lightness, and ritual whiteness almost always reference substances applied to skin rather than the skin itself. These associations seem, however, to have extended to the color and texture of skin through the historically deep and geographically diffuse practice of initiates wearing white clay. Such preparations not only covered the skin in ritual whiteness; they also produced some of the same effects sought by the initiates whom Hunter and Soga encountered in the 1930s and by others, in later decades, who purchased commercially made skin lighteners. Kaolinite, the main mineral in white clay, has been used, in many different parts of the world, to help smoothen skin, clear blemishes and rashes, and shield complexions from the sun. By applying and then washing away kaolin preparations, people have sought to clarify and soften their skin, often in the hopes of looking more youthful.[24] Today, in South Africa, white clay persists as a cosmetic treatment and skin protector. It is not uncommon to see African women, who work outdoors and cannot afford commercial sunscreens, using a mixture of white clay (*umcaku* in isiZulu/isiXhosa) or red clay (*ibomvu* in isiZulu/isiXhosa), water, and glycerin to protect their faces from the sun and other elements.[25]

When initiates have used white clay, they usually remove it at the end of seclusion and then apply oils and fats to make their clarified and lightened skin shiny and bright. The ideal for girls and young women, in particular, has entailed emerging from seclusion—whether following initiation and childbirth, or prior to marriage—rested and fattened, and with skin that is glistening, smooth, and lightened. According to an anthropologist working in northern Tanzania in the 1990s, for instance, initiates sought to return their skin to the pristine condition of a "newborn child." Men associated such appearances with women who were sexually pliable.[26] The initiates and brides whom Hunter and Soga encountered sought this same effect but by different means. Rather than using an opaque mixture of white clay, they applied chewed Tambookie grass roots and translucent egg whites. Why they used these substances rather than kaolin is unclear; Hunter wrote that white clay was sometimes used during the initiation of diviners, though it was difficult to find.[27] Roots and eggs were likely easier to find, less expensive, and, perhaps by this time, considered more efficacious. Another researcher, studying cosmetic practices in the Eastern Cape in the early 1960s, noted that young people liked to "try new products . . . even where ritual is involved."[28] Egg whites, as we shall see, often appeared as an ingredient in cosmetic recipes that circulated across the British Empire. AmaPondo may have regarded egg whites as more "Western" and, hence, a more appropriate substance for preparing for Christian weddings. Eggs also carried gendered and sexualized meanings. Elsewhere in her ethnography, Hunter explained that women were forbidden from eating eggs for fear they would "make them lascivious."[29] Whatever the reasons for the specific ingredients, the use of such preparations during initiation and premarital seclusion suggests that the appeal of skin lightening in Pondoland stemmed, at least in part, from long-standing notions of ritual transformation and feminine beauty.

Extant sources offer few insights into how Africans living in precolonial times understood variations in skin color. Oral traditions collected from isiZulu speakers and recorded during the mid-nineteenth century frequently describe Africans as having particular and varied skin colors, including "light brown," "like brass," "dark but not black," and "black." These sources, though, attach no aesthetic preferences to these skin-color distinctions.[30] Two well-known and stylized travelers' accounts represent southern African leaders as voicing contradictory preferences when confronted with the novelty of Europeans' pale or reddish, sunburned skin.[31] According to Henry Francis Fynn, an English trader, Shaka Zulu found white skin to be ugly and "not pleasant to the eye."[32] By contrast, a Tswana rain doctor described by David Livingstone affirmed Victorian derision of black African appearances. In Livingstone's scripted account of a conversation between himself and a rain doctor, the latter states that God made "white men . . . beautiful" in comparison with "black men." Elsewhere, in the same volume, Livingstone explained that a preference for lighter skin tones was common in the highveld where he traveled and that some women, most notably "Mokololo ladies," turned to botanical substances to promote such appearances: "The whole of the colored tribes consider that beauty and fairness are associated, and women long for children of light color so much, that they sometimes chew the bark of a certain tree in hopes of producing that effect."[33]

What Mokololo women chewed sounds like *ummemezi,* a bark derived from various indigenous trees and still sold today by South African herbalists for skin lightening. Rather than chewing the bark, contemporary users crush it, mix it with water, and then apply the mixture to their faces. The term *ummemezi* derives from the isiXhosa verb *ukumemeza,* meaning "to call aloud," "to be attractive," or, even more specifically, "to be conspicuous as a result of a glowing shine or bright coloration." *Ummemezi* helps users stand out and attract favorable attention by making their complexions shiny and bright.[34] Recently, researchers have identified chemical compounds in *ummemezi* that inhibit melanin production in ways similar to commercially made skin lighteners, namely by interfering with the enzyme tyrosinase.[35] Today, when South Africans refer to skin lightening with commercial products, they often use the isiZulu term *ukucreamer*, "applying creams," or the isiXhosa term *ukutsheyisa,* "chasing" or "chasing beauty." Both terms are examples of linguistic borrowing from English, suggesting how black South Africans have associated such products with English-speaking settings and cultural influences.[36] *Ukucreamer* also suggests how isiZulu speakers have conflated commercial skin lighteners, perhaps because of their ubiquity, with the broader category of facial creams. *Ukutsheyisa*, in turn, evokes meanings closer to the root of *ummemezi*, aligning skin lightening with a desire to look attractive and beautiful. In parts of nineteenth-century southern Africa, at least, the ideal of well-oiled and shiny bodily surfaces coexisted with an aesthetic preference for young women with lightened skin tones. Though operating in distinct visual and tactile registers, both ideals extolled eye-catching brightness. Like ochre and specularite, *ummemezi* has operated as a technology of visibility.

The "colored tribes" that Livingstone encountered as he traveled across the southern African interior encompassed a great deal of skin-color diversity. Livingstone described people whose complexions spanned from a "light brownish-yellow color" to "very dark, with a slight tinge of olive." Revealing his own racialized preference for purity, Livingstone wrote that he found the "dark color... much more agreeable" than the "sickly" and "tawny hues" that resemble those of "the half-caste."[37] As Paul Landau has argued, long before the arrival of Europeans, the highveld was a place of *métissage*. It was a place where people accrued wealth and power by embracing "the potential value of foreigners" and traversing differences of language, culture, and color. For centuries, the rulers and aspirant rulers of Bantu-speaking chiefdoms married out, forging trade relations and political alliances with foreigners, often Khoesan speakers. Bodily appearances that combined or mixed different peoples' physical traits, including light and dark skin hues, became a sign of aristocratic or elite status.[38] What Livingstone described as an aesthetic preference for "fairness" among Mokololo women may have been part of this historical privileging of connection, incorporation, and admixture among highveld peoples. Beginning in the eighteenth century, new groups of people, fleeing the Cape Colony and its immediate borderlands, became part of this social world. These relative newcomers often arrived with their own *métis*, or "coloured," pedigrees that included speaking European and African languages, and ancestry that extended to Europe and across the Indian Ocean. By moving into the highveld, they sought to build lives beyond the Cape's evolving racial order. At the same time, they spread that order's political and cultural influences into new territories.

Whitening and Lightening

The cosmetics that European colonists brought with them to southern Africa included skin whitening and lightening preparations developed in the Mediterranean world and far beyond. Elites in ancient times used these cosmetics to craft appearances considered refined, feminine, and youthful. During the early modern period, as trade increased and Europeans colonized much of the globe, these cosmetics experienced a revival. Eventually, they became more commonplace goods, accessible to increasing numbers of middle- and working-class consumers.

In the Mediterranean and Near Eastern worlds, skin whiteners had been part of elite women's toiletries for centuries and even millennia. Cosmetics users in ancient Mesopotamia, Egypt, Greece, and Rome created dramatic appearances by pairing face paints containing white lead or chalk with eye makeup of black kohl, and rouge and lip colorants derived from red ochre, mercury, and lead. On occasion, crushed mica was added to eye preparations for a glistening effect. The pale, smooth skin that resulted from white face paint provided a striking contrast to dark, colorful, and shiny features. In these highly stratified societies, it also evidenced one's entitled avoidance of agricultural and other outdoor labor. For women especially, pale skin color embodied elite status and a refined lifestyle.[39]

The most prized skin whitener in classical Greece and the Roman Empire was white lead, also known as ceruse. It was the same substance used to paint buildings and works of art white. When used in cosmetics, ceruse was ground finely to avoid a gritty look or feel. Compared with other whitening preparations made from chalk, flour, or rice, white lead was valued for its smooth texture, its ability to adhere to the skin without an oil base, and the capacity for even a thin layer to provide an opaque covering that could conceal blemishes, marks, and freckles. When users ventured outside, white lead also blocked the sun and prevented tanning. These effects came at a price. Several classical writers recognized the health hazards of lead-based cosmetics, including the loss of the skin's youthful tone, severe abdominal pain, paralysis, and, in some cases, death. Such writers ridiculed users who continued to apply white lead despite these dangers.[40] The collapse of the Roman Empire around the fifth century CE reduced the trade in many luxury goods, including cosmetics. The beauty ideal of a white face with pink or reddened cheeks, however, persisted in many parts of Europe.[41]

White lead regained prominence in the seventeenth century, when trade within and beyond Europe increased once again. The most prized preparations were imported from Venice, then a center of European high fashion. Elizabeth I of England may have used Venetian ceruse. Elites frequently turned to white lead to conceal scars left by diseases such as smallpox.[42] By covering white face paint with a thin glaze of egg white, they created masklike appearances. Over time, users often required more ceruse to cover up the grayish pallor and premature aging of the skin caused by the lead itself. Some offset white facial paint by applying black patches, pieces of taffeta, velvet, or leather cut into various shapes, to cover more prominent blemishes or simply to look fashionable.[43]

The seventeenth century also witnessed the publication of whitening and lightening recipes, formerly handed down within families, and an increase in itinerant traders selling cosmetic ingredients and preparations. Aimed at the more middling classes, recipes to "blanch" skin and remove freckles rarely called for costly white lead but instead included ingredients ranging from egg whites, lemon juice, white wine, flour, plantain juice, almonds, rose water, and rosemary to borax, tartar, sulfur, and mercury. White ingredients reduced to powder and blended with water, oil, or fat would have, like lead, provided a white-colored covering. By contrast, lighteners containing acidic ingredients or mercury contributed to more natural, less "painted," appearances by removing the top layers of the epidermis or by impeding the production of melanin.[44]

The heightened use of skin whiteners and lighteners, and other cosmetics in early modern Europe stemmed from various motivations and provoked mixed reactions. Cosmetics signaled wealth and glamour, a life free of outdoor toil. They also helped to create dramatic and youthful appearances. Renewed interest in whiteners and lighteners may also have been fueled by greater contact with Asian cultural practices and trade goods. In China and Japan, elite women and some men used white lead preparations and rice powder to achieve flawless complexions and a color that classical writers likened to translucent white jade or fresh lychee. As in Europe, smooth, untanned skin conveyed one's entitled avoidance of outdoor labor.[45]

The privileging of pale skin in early modern England also coincided with the rise of the Atlantic slave trade and contributed to emerging notions of national and racial difference rooted in the distinction between "fairness" and "blackness." In Elizabethan England, references to Aesop's fable about the

FIGURE 1.2. In this portrait, the Flemish artist Anthony van Dyck underscored his subject's regal whiteness by positioning behind her a dark-toned servant boy holding a parasol that shielded her from the sun's rays. *Marchesa Elena Grimaldi Cattaneo*, 1623. Oil on canvas, 95.625 × 54.5 in. Courtesy National Gallery of Art, Washington.

impossibility of "washing an Ethiopian white" commonly featured in engravings, poetry, and collections of proverbs. This fable drew attention to the darkness of Africans' skin color and taught the moral that a person's true nature could not be changed.[46] Fairness was a highly gendered attribute; femininity was closely associated with whiteness and its aligned virtues of virginity and innocence. Painters of this period frequently placed black servants in the background of their portraits of aristocratic women to highlight their pale skin and superior status and to convey their purity and refinement. To attain the fairness idealized in such portraits, some women used cosmetic whiteners and lighteners.[47]

Yet the use of such cosmetics was frequently condemned. Critics argued that the opacity of whiteners concealed women's true nature and sentiments, especially as expressed through blushing. Cosmetics use stirred long-standing concerns about the relationship between surface appearance and inner substance. Popular discourse associated excessive use with licentious behavior and prostitution. During the eighteenth century, as sumptuary codes loosened across much of Europe, some observers voiced increasing concern about women using cosmetics to pass for statuses that exceeded their actual stations. Women's greater access to formerly rare beauty preparations meant that carefully painted visages no longer correlated to noble rank. At the same time, cosmetics could be evoked to impugn national identities as when English writers compared their womenfolk's moderate use of makeup to French women's garish and deceitful use.[48]

Within the Netherlands, a center of early modern trade and the home of many of South Africa's first European colonists, cosmetic practices and debates raised similar issues. Few foreign visitors failed to be impressed by the Dutch obsession for cleaning their streets, houses, and, usually, themselves. An Englishman, Joseph Shaw, who traveled there in 1709 admired ordinary Dutch women for their beautiful yet plain faces. When he visited the house of correction for "fallen women" in Amsterdam, however, he saw dozens of women "patched and painted" and "clothed in the gay habiliments of love." Calvinist preachers' frequent condemnation of facial cosmetics and dyed wigs suggests that some in their congregations were tempted to wear them. Portrait paintings indicate that, as in England, the Dutch ideal of feminine beauty included smooth, white visages with pinkish cheeks.[49]

Debates over the morality and health effects of cosmetics intensified in eighteenth-century France where elites, most famously Louis XV's court, took paint and powder to new extremes and expanding consumer markets placed cosmetics within the reach of more people. Around midcentury, doctors joined the chorus of those warning of the dangers of cosmetics containing lead, mercury, arsenic, and other toxic compounds. In so doing, they extended male medical expertise into the largely female domain of the *toilette*. Rather than adopting the position of the Enlightened *philosophes* that condemned all cosmetics for sustaining aristocratic debauchery and encouraging social deceit, doctors wrote beauty manuals and columns that distinguished cosmetics containing "natural" vegetable and animal ingredients from those with mineral ingredients. They promoted the former, sometimes their own products, as beneficial while denouncing the latter as harmful. Such advice fit well with an emerging consumer ethos that shunned practices, including the use of white lead paint, which smacked of aristocratic excess but embraced the availability of small and affordable luxury goods for the urban bourgeoisie and working classes.[50] Advertisements for whiteners and lighteners that appeared in the *Times* of London in the late eighteenth and early nineteenth centuries similarly stressed both the natural look they produced and their safety.[51] As cosmetics extended beyond the preserve of elites, their application often became more subtle.

Overseas colonial empires contributed to the increased use of cosmetics by stoking early modern Europe's economic revolutions and by drawing greater attention to skin-color distinctions. The extraction of resources and trade in products from colonies in the Americas, Asia, and Africa enabled European economies to transition from mercantile capitalism to industrial and, later, consumer capitalism. As Sidney Mintz demonstrated in his pioneering history of sugar in the Caribbean and Britain, colonialism and slavery not only entailed new forms of production on various sides of the Atlantic, but also spurred new patterns of consumption across the class spectrum.[52] Cosmetics use in Europe was part of the broader consumer revolution engendered by imperial economic growth.

Increased consumption of cosmetics also coincided with the strengthening of anti-black ideologies to justify racial slavery and European colonial rule. During the sixteenth and seventeenth centuries, Spanish, Portuguese, French, and British explorers and traders frequently distinguished themselves from the inhabitants of the Americas and Africa by religion and morality: they were Christians and righteous while those they conquered and enslaved were pagan and sinful. Early European colonizers, like those at the Cape, also distinguished themselves by pointing to features like smell or clothing. Beginning in the late eighteenth century, Europeans developed systems of racial classification that increasingly focused on the somatic feature of skin color to differentiate races and especially to distinguish themselves from Africans and people of African descent.[53] The rooting of colonial power in white supremacy ensured that whitening and lightening—beauty practices primarily associated in earlier times with creating a refined, feminine, and youthful appearance—became more pointedly linked to claiming racial privilege.

Colonial Crucibles and Commercial Cosmetics

When Europeans colonized new places and peoples, they took with them cosmetic practices of whitening and lightening. The cookbooks and medical manuals that British colonists brought with them to the Americas, for example, routinely contained recipes for "Italian" whiteners and for removing freckles and sunburn. Such preparations were also among the most common skin-care products advertised in early southern U.S. newspapers.[54] They were especially popular in colonial locales where the sun was strong and social distinctions were finely graded. A number of observers in the West Indies, in the 1760s and 1770s, described how both black and white women (and, on occasion, men) used cashew oil, an irritant, to remove freckles and sunburn, and bonneted their heads and "masked" their faces to avoid being tanned. White creole women reportedly adopted the practice of masking from "free mulatto women" while some even sent their daughters to England, away from the tropical sun, to obtain "red and white roses" complexions. In colonial societies, long-standing practices of whitening, lightening, and sun avoidance acquired sharper, racialized meanings, particularly among those trying to ascend the social ladder or fearful of sliding down it.[55]

At the early Cape Colony, well-to-do women who used white paints and powders were part of a small and highly stratified society. Most Dutch East India Company (Vereenigde Oost-Indische Compagnie; VOC) employees were of Dutch or German origin. Before the end of the seventeenth century, they were joined by Huguenots seeking escape from religious persecution in France and other VOC employees, who, on return voyages from Batavia and other colonies farther east, decided to settle at the Cape. While some immigrants were reasonably affluent, many others came from the lowest rungs of European society. By 1717, the free population of the Cape amounted only to two thousand. Throughout the eighteenth century, free men outnumbered free women by about three to two, while the entire free population was slightly outnumbered by enslaved peoples brought mainly from Madagascar and Indonesia and, later, from India, Ceylon, and Mozambique. Colonial conquest devastated the Cape's Khoesan communities. European colonizers, having ruthlessly decimated their communities through warfare, theft, and the spread of disease, pushed the remaining Khoesan into the colony's underclass or toward its outskirts. By 1795, the year the British first took over the Cape Colony (only to lose it to the Dutch in 1803 and regain it in 1806), the total population stood at approximately thirty thousand, divided nearly equally between free people and slaves.[56]

We know little about the cosmetics practices that people from South and Southeast Asia and Madagascar brought to the Cape. In much of the Indian Ocean region, turmeric was rubbed over the bodies of brides and grooms to create an auspicious yellow or golden hue that promised success and fertility. Applied together with a rice paste, turmeric was said to "cool" and "comfort" the couple. People used sandalwood powder alone or with turmeric to clear blemishes, as well as soften and smoothen the skin. Oils also were applied to moisturize, and some may have used botanical preparations to lighten complexions. In Madagascar, women often used white clay, sometimes mixed with saffron, to create designs of white and yellow dots and lines on their foreheads and cheeks. Such designs aimed to beautify, to protect the wearer from malicious spirits and female rivals, and to reignite the passions of former lovers and unfaithful husbands. People also used clay and botanical preparations to soften and smoothen their skin. When possible, enslaved peoples and indentured servants likely continued these practices.[57] Another practice that traveled westward to the Cape was the use of parasols and umbrellas. Mimicking Asian elites, well-heeled Dutch colonizers wielded parasols to both convey social rank and prevent tanning.[58]

Over the course of the eighteenth century, skin color increasingly became a defining feature of status and respectability at the Cape. Although at the start of the century, it was possible, if not common, for a freeborn person of mixed parentage and with the support of a well-connected European father to be assimilated into the respectable ranks of Cape society, by the end, it had become much more difficult.[59] The racialization of respectability directly shaped the politics of personal appearance. Revealing an increasing color-consciousness in Cape law, in 1765, the government responded to white unease with free black women who placed themselves on par or above "respectable burghers' wives" by prohibiting black women from wearing colored silk clothing, hooped skirts, fine lace, fancy hats, curled hair, and jeweled earrings.[60] Whites identified free black women's crafting of stylized European appearances as a direct threat to the colony's evolving racial order.

The cultivation of fashionable appearances continued to be part of black efforts to garner resources and respect into the nineteenth century. In an account of Cape Town's social life from 1822, William Wilberforce Bird, a British official stationed there, described the "rainbow balls," whose name referenced the people of "different hue[s]" who attended in "this many coloured town." Following the British takeover of the Cape Colony, officials began using "coloured" (*kleurling* in Dutch) to describe people of visibly mixed ancestry along with all enslaved people. They also included in this category the small group of free blacks and the remaining Khoekhoen. The category of Coloured became a distinguishing feature of southern Africa's racial order as officials used it to designate those deemed of slave, Khoesan, and mixed ancestry, and more elite members of this group used it as a form of self-identification.[61] The dances that Bird observed brought together wealthy, mainly white, men and black women, both enslaved and free. Bird described how, at these gatherings, black women imitated the manners of wealthy white women and "nearly equal[ed] them in dress."[62]

Following the abolition of slavery in 1834, colonial elites relied more heavily on racial thinking to sustain their power, and skin color became a more salient marker of status distinctions. Such Manichean thinking left whites with little ability to see beauty and refinement in black behavior. In the 1850s, Lady Duff Gordon, an English visitor, wrote a letter home expressing her incredulity at the expense and attention that black women from Cape Town and its environs devoted to their dressing tables: "The first few shillings that a coloured woman has to spend on her cottage go in[to]—what do you think—a grand toilet table of worked muslin over pink, all set with little '*objets*.'" During the Victorian era, dressing tables covered with combs, brushes, mirrors, jewelry boxes, and jars of powders, creams, and perfumes became standard features in many middle- and working-class homes. Yet, for Gordon, poor black women's possession of such items devoted to beautifying and pampering themselves was nothing less than absurd: "Now, what is the use or comfort of a *duchesse* [a dressing table with a mirror] to a Hottentot family? I shall never see those toilets again without thinking of Hottentots—what a baroque association of ideas!"[63]

Although we have no way of knowing what filled those dressing-table jars, we do know that commercial skin whiteners and lighteners were available by this time. In 1840, James Divine, a merchant in Cape Town, advertised a range of cosmetics, including white face powders and rouges imported from France. Other ads appeared in local newspapers for Rowland's "Kalydor," a lightening preparation made in London that promised to render "the most sallow complexion delicately fair, clear, and delightfully soft" and to eradicate "freckles, tan, pimples, spots, [and] discoloration." Reflecting both the appeal of exotic beauty preparations to European consumers and growing concerns about the harmful effects of some ingredients, Rowland's touted its product as "an eastern botanical discovery" that was free of "all mineral admixture." Chemical analyses undertaken by U.S. physicians in the 1870s and 1880s found, in fact, that Kalydor contained mercury.[64]

Such cosmetics advertisements reflected wider shifts in fashion and manufacturing. By the mid-nineteenth century, in much of Europe and the United States, powders and lotions that promised pale yet "natural" appearances had replaced white lead paint. This change in cosmetic fashion was spurred by rejection of the ostentatious displays associated with the ancien régime, the ascension of the youthful and modest Victoria to the British throne in 1837, and growing health concerns over lead. The nineteenth century also saw the growth of commercially manufactured cosmetics. Rather than going to a local perfumer or chemist to order a powder or cream or mixing it up at home, many women now purchased prepackaged cosmetics from the shelves of trading, drug, and department stores.[65]

Some of these products posed health problems. British and American physicians joined their French predecessors to warn that commercial cosmetics often contained dangerous ingredients—arsenic, lead, and mercury—that were rarely disclosed on labels. Patients, they reported, presented in various stages of poisoning, some too late to be saved.[66] Whereas physicians and pharmacists consistently denounced cosmetics containing arsenic and lead, many continued to recommend mercury, in limited amounts, as an effective treatment for skin infections, particularly acne and syphilis, and for fading freckles, scars, and other areas of darker pigmentation.[67] Mercury-based skin lighteners slipped between being marketed as cosmetics and being prescribed as medicines. Publications conveyed mixed messages. In the United States, *Scientific American* and trade journals like *Druggists' Circular and Chemical Gazette* carried articles warning of the dangers of mercury in cosmetics as well as recipes for freckle creams that contained it.[68] Some beauty advice columns in South African and U.S. periodicals, including African American newspapers, recommended milder bleaches containing lemon juice, buttermilk, and peroxide rather than mercury.[69]

The South African market for cosmetics grew in the early twentieth century as diamond and gold mining fueled economic expansion. The formation of the Union of South Africa in 1910, following Britain's defeat of the South African Republic and the Orange Free State in the South African War, combined the two Boer republics and the two British colonies of the Cape and Natal into a single dominion of the British Empire. A far cry from the single, sparsely populated colony that Britain seized in the early nineteenth century, the new Union encompassed nearly six million people, classified by the 1911 census into one of three racial groups: "Native" or "Bantu" (67 percent of the total population), "European or White" (21 percent), and "Mixed and Coloured" (11 percent). Cosmetic manufacturers targeted the wealthier white population through advertisements

Protect Your Skin

against sunburn, windburn and chap with

NYAL
FACE CREAM
with Peroxide

A bleaching cream excellent for the complexion. It is non-irritating, greaseless, and vanishing. Leaves no shine or sticky after-feeling. Helps to make the skin clear and soft. Will not cause or promote the growth of hair. Pleasingly perfumed.

Two Sizes

FOR SALE AT ALL NYAL CHEMISTS SHOPS

FIGURE 1.3. Ad marketing a skin-bleaching cream to white South African women. *Rand Daily Mail* (Johannesburg), August 1927.

Bring Out the Hidden Beauty

Beneath the soiled, discolored, faded or aged complexion is one fair to look upon. Mercolized Wax gradually, gently absorbs the devitalized surface skin, revealing the young, fresh, beautiful skin underneath. Used by refined women who prefer complexions of true naturalness. Have *you* tried it?

Mercolized Wax in one ounce package, with directions for use, sold by all druggists.

FIGURES 1.4 AND 1.5. These ads for an American-made skin lightener containing mercury targeted consumers in Washington, D.C., and South Africa. Such products ranked among the most common cosmetics used by white women in the early twentieth century. *Washington Post*, October 1916; *South African Pictorial*, October 1920.

Complexion Soft and Clear as Baby's

EVERY woman has it, you know, UNDERNEATH. But how to remove the soiled, weather-worn outer skin with all its blemishes, is a secret at present little known. In America the women submit themselves to

THE HEROIC PROCESS OF SKINNING

i.e., having the outer cuticle removed by a carbolic acid solution. The process is not only extremely painful, but necessitates the patient keeping to the house for several weeks. In this country

SCIENCE HAS PROGRESSED

so far that any woman, or man, may confidently remove their skin without pain or inconvenience of any kind. All that they need do is to get a little mercolized wax from the Chemist, and smear it over the face and neck.

IT TAKES ABOUT TEN DAYS

to complete the transformation. and nobody will be any the wiser, except of course for the great improvement in your appearance. Don't simply ask for wax: it must be

MERCOLIZED.

in newspapers as well as in the country's early pictorial magazines like the *South African Lady's Pictorial and Home Journal* and *South African Pictorial: Stage and Cinema.* The latter magazine, in particular, promoted American and European film stars as beauty icons. It featured close-ups of actresses and beauty queens with pale, flawless complexions and carried cosmetic ads and advice columns about achieving the same photogenic look.

Promises of smoother, whiter, and lighter skin were ubiquitous in South African magazines. Salons touted their ability to remove blemishes, moles, and superfluous hairs through "electrolysis" and "electric face bleaching massage."[70] Purveyors of blood and liver purifiers claimed that their pills and tonics clarified complexions and eliminated sallowness.[71] A number of products marketed as "soaps" and "skin food" promised to whiten the skin and remove all "sunburn, freckles, and wrinkles."[72] Still others were marketed as "freckle waxes" or "freckle creams." An ad for one claimed to work overnight and offered a money-back promise: "Here's a chance, Miss Freckle-face, to try a new remedy for freckles with the guarantee of a reliable dealer."[73] While advertisements rarely mentioned ingredients, most products marketed as freckle waxes and creams contained mercury.[74]

"Mercolized Wax," a product manufactured in the U.S. Midwest and sold in South Africa beginning in the 1910s, definitely contained mercury. The Dearborn Company specifically targeted sunny imperial outposts like Australia, India, and South Africa. Soon after the company trademarked the product, the American Medical Association denounced Mercolized Wax as a "caustic poison." Tests revealed that it contained 10 percent ammoniated mercury, a high amount even by the period's standard.[75] The formula could produce dramatic short-term results. One user, a white American woman who had traveled with her father, a naval officer, to Samoa in 1912, testified in a letter home to her aunt: "I can't say enough in praise of mercolized wax—have used it [for two months] ... and now have a complexion like 'baby's.'"[76]

Government efforts to regulate cosmetics containing mercury and other harmful ingredients were limited. Some health authorities in the United States required manufacturers of skin lighteners to label their products as poisons with skull and crossbones warnings.[77] During the 1920s, the American Medical Association included such cosmetics in its compendium of "nostrums and quackery" afflicting public health and called for federal regulation.[78] Whereas local authorities in the United States and Germany, on occasion, ordered manufacturers to identify certain cosmetics as poisons, no comprehensive national law on cosmetics safety existed anywhere in the world prior to the passage of the U.S. Food, Drug and Cosmetics Act in 1938.[79] In Britain, statutes governing food and drug safety, inaugurated during the mid-nineteenth century, did not include cosmetics.[80] The South African government also paid little attention to cosmetics safety until the 1970s.

Domestic Work and Mission Schools

Black southern Africans first encountered the world of European cosmetics through domestic work in white households. Such work exposed them to new ways of caring for the body's surface and conceiving of its color. Domestic work, in fact, was the earliest and most effective means by which colonists incorporated indigenous and enslaved peoples into their households and colonial society, more generally. Krotoa (Eva), a Khoi woman who married the VOC's Danish surgeon and became the company's most adept local mediator, gained her fluency in Dutch language, dress, and manners through serving as a nursemaid in the household of Jan Van Riebeeck, the founding commander of the colony. Indicating just how important bodily appearances were in demarcating the colonial world from the Khoi, the young Krotoa swapped her Dutch clothes for smeared skins when visiting her relatives.[81] Many enslaved people, especially women owned by either VOC officials or other townspeople, also worked as household cleaners, cooks, and child minders, often sleeping in their owners' kitchens.[82] Working and living in such close quarters, they and other domestic laborers gained firsthand knowledge of how European colonists as well as fellow subalterns cared for and cultivated their bodies.

As European settlers moved into the Northern and Eastern Cape, Natal, the Orange Free State, and the Transvaal during the nineteenth century, domestic work remained a core colonial institution. From the start, black women dominated this labor force in Cape and Orange Free State. By contrast, black men initially made up the bulk of domestic workers in Johannesburg, Pretoria, and Durban. The "black peril" scares of the 1890s and early 1900s, which stirred racist anxieties over black men raping white women, erased these regional differences. By the 1940s, black women outnumbered men as domestic workers in all parts of the country. Remarkably, three out of every four employed women, classified as either African or Coloured, were domestic workers. And, as the anthropologist Philip Mayer observed in East London during the 1950s, such employment provided African girls and women with unparalleled knowledge of white domestic habits and their associated consumer goods.[83]

Mission schools also helped to impart such knowledge. From the establishment of the first continuous stations at the Cape in the 1790s, missionaries taught black students the importance of cleanliness and clothing to Christianity. In keeping with Victorian ideologies, they positioned women as the custodians of the home, and linked domesticity and hygiene to salvation, "civilization," and racial progress. Alongside reading, writing, and arithmetic, mission schools taught African girls and young women domestic science, laundry work, needlework, cookery, and home nursing. The intent of this curriculum was twofold: to prepare African girls and women to be Christian wives and mothers, and to work as domestic servants. While a few female mission graduates became teachers and, later, nurses, the vast majority found employment in white households.[84]

Cosmetics were never a part of mission-school curricula. Whereas soap was a key component of Christian domesticity, cosmetics embodied the immodest and self-indulgent elements of Western culture that most nineteenth-century missionaries rejected. By the twentieth century, mission-school regulations often specifically forbade the wearing of cosmetics.[85] Nonetheless, in a couple of vital ways, mission schools helped to lay the foundations for southern Africa's black consumer culture that grew to include skin lighteners and other cosmetics. First, through teaching literacy, schooling exposed students and graduates to newspapers and magazines that featured advertisements and advice columns on matters ranging from cleanliness to beauty. Second, mission schools taught that new bodily and consumer routines were essential to becoming Christian, "civilized," and, later, "modern." Whereas at the start of the nineteenth century, many missionaries and their converts made their own soap, by the turn of the century, they bought bar soap manufactured by British companies like Lever Brothers and Pears, or by local competitors such as the Transvaal Soap Company. Similarly, with little marketing from the U.S. manufacturer Chesebrough, southern Africans adopted Vaseline as the preferred substance for smearing. One researcher reported in the 1960s that Vaseline had so completely replaced animal fat that many amaXhosa no longer knew that the latter had ever been used.[86] Mission schools laid the groundwork for such commodity adoptions and adaptations by denigrating African bodily practices as "barbaric" and "backward" and yoking Christianity to domestic regimes that relied on commodities.[87]

As the most intimate and sustained sites of colonial interaction, domestic work and mission schools contributed to a racialized commodity fetishism that imbued toiletries with the power to domesticate unruly bodies and subjects. Some of the most disturbing visual evidence of this fetishism are soap and detergent advertisements that evoked and updated Aesop's fable of "washing the Ethiopian white." Appearing at the height of the "scramble for Africa" and the elaboration of "scientific" racism, advertisements for Pears soap mockingly played on the impossibility of turning black people's skin white despite their adoption of European dress and hygiene routines.[88] For imperial sensibilities, the jest that some commodities might whiten black skin was both a source of humor and an anxious assertion of white superiority.

African American missionaries and performers, who began arriving in South Africa in the 1890s, offered, in part, an antiracist retort to this commodity fetishism. Their presence conjoined Christianity and cleanliness with "racial uplift" rather than with whiteness. The most popular were the Virginia Jubilee Singers from the Hampton Institute, who toured between 1890 and 1898, performing hundreds of concerts of American Negro spirituals and dramatic and comedic skits. With their stage talent and "smart and tidy" appearances, they moved white audiences to tears and became, for black viewers, powerful role models of what might be achieved through advanced schooling, Christian devotion, and commercial enterprise. In the decades that followed, as more people, publications, and products moved between South Africa and the United States, a transatlantic dialogue developed over what it meant to be "modern" and black.[89] As we shall see in the next chapter, African American influences importantly shaped South African debates over consumption and cosmetics.

THE SKIN LIGHTENING practices that Hunter and Soga observed in early 1930s Pondoland were likely the entanglement of indigenous and colonial ways of cultivating bodily surfaces. By enlisting Tambookie grass roots and egg whites to lighten complexions, women and girls drew together disparate aesthetic and ritual traditions. Hunter chose Pondoland as her research site, in large part, because the area was colonized in the late nineteenth century and, hence, by South African standards, European influences were relatively shallow. Nonetheless, Christian missionaries and European traders had been active in the area for nearly a century. Many of the Christian brides whom Hunter and Soga encountered would have attended mission schools for a few years while some of the older women who helped to organize their weddings would have worked in white households.[90] The egg whites that the Christian brides used suggest the mark of colonial institutions. Egg whites were part of cosmetic traditions of whitening and lightening that extended back centuries in Europe and elsewhere. Colonists brought those traditions to southern Africa. By the early twentieth century, lightening recipes that called for egg whites and other ingredients existed alongside the marketing of commercially made soaps and creams that promised to bleach skin. These new technologies of visibility proliferated in colonial and segregationist contexts where racialized beauty ideals held sway and minute distinctions in physical appearance could open or foreclose social opportunities.

Pondo young women's desire for lightened and smoothened complexions also resonated with the long-standing regional aesthetic of brightness. But rather than applying ochre or specularite, or limiting themselves to fats and oils, they cultivated bright and auspicious appearances by avoiding the sun and lightening their skin tones. Livingstone's account of the Mokololo women of the highveld suggests that, in some areas, a preference for light brown tones might have predated European colonial rule. Yet the explanations that initiates and brides offered Hunter and Soja reveal just how challenging it is to reconstruct histories of aesthetic and political thought from bodily and ritual practices. For the Pondo initiates, proper "bleaching" depended on smearing chewed Tambookie grass roots on their bodies *and* keeping their own mothers at a safe distance. Moreover, whereas for Hunter, brides' seclusion and lightening practices looked like an obvious adaptation of older initiation ceremonies, Christians insisted that they were unconnected and incommensurate.

Such perspectives remind us that, by attending to the body's surface, people have sought not only to alter or enhance their appearances. They have also sought to forge fresh relations between the social and the spiritual, their inner selves and their outer worlds. The next chapter examines discussions in the South African newspaper *Bantu World* about female beauty and black women's use of skin whiteners and lighteners. Many of the mission-educated Africans who wrote and read this newspaper understood women's looks and cosmetic practices as linked to morality and racial respectability, though not always in the same ways.

Two

MODERN GIRLS
AND RACIAL RESPECTABILITY

Just about the same year that Monica Hunter observed initiates and brides in the Eastern Cape lightening their complexions, one of the earliest skin lightener advertisements to target African consumers appeared. In 1933, *Bantu World*, a black South African newspaper founded by a white businessman, carried an advertisement for Apex beauty products that included a skin bleach. Whereas many of the ads that ran in such newspapers crossed over from the white South African press, this one originated in the black U.S. press. The Apex Company was founded by an African American woman who mainly sold beauty products to her compatriots. The ad in *Bantu World* marketed modern black glamour with a U.S. provenance.

The Apex campaign reveals the early arrival of commercial whiteners and lighteners among school-educated Africans. This chapter examines that campaign and other discussions of beauty in *Bantu World* to demonstrate how black women engaged commercial cosmetics as technologies of visibility to craft eye-catching and photogenic appearances. By this period, nineteenth-century ideologies of Christian domesticity and modesty had run headlong into a new consumer culture wedded to the mass production of commodities and their aggressive marketing through print and visual media. *Bantu World* helped to spread this new consumer culture by being the first black South African newspaper to advertise cosmetics, offer women's pages, and hold a beauty contest.

Not coincidentally, *Bantu World* was also the first black paper to feature extensive discussion of the "modern girl," a figure who emerged in cities around the world in the 1910s and 1920s and appeared to reject the roles of dutiful

FIGURE 2.1. A *Bantu World* ad for cosmetics manufactured by the African American company Apex, featuring a modern girl reflecting on herself. This was one of the first ads for a skin bleach or skin lightener to target black consumers anywhere in Africa. *Bantu World*, July 1933.

daughter, wife, and mother by engaging in the new consumer culture. "Girl" was first stretched beyond its reference to female children in 1880s England where it popularly denoted unmarried working-class and middle-class young women who seemingly occupied "a provisional free space."[1] It was this contingent independence from conventional female roles that people in Africa and elsewhere evoked during the 1920s and 1930s when they deployed "girl" or variants of it to reference young women. Whites' uses of "girl" and "boy" to refer to African adults in segregationist South Africa, as in the Jim Crow United States, were racial insults. But when black writers prefaced "girl" with "modern," they signaled something humorous and unsettlingly progressive rather than decidedly pejorative.[2]

The black modern girl emerged through and posed challenges to categories of race and respectability. Writers in South Africa's dominant press imagined the modern girl—a privileged, if troubling, figure—as undoubtedly white.[3] *Bantu World* writers, on the other hand, debated whether school-educated black young women, often referred to as "modern girls," contributed to "racial uplift" through their professional careers and cosmopolitan looks, or instead "prostituted" their sex and race by imitating the ways of white, Coloured, and Indian women. During the 1930s, the use of whitening and lightening cosmetics, especially face powder, ranked among the most contentious of these young women's practices as it drew attention to the visual dimensions of racial distinctions.

Bantu World's Beauty Contest

Bantu World viewed women readers as crucial to increasing its early circulation figure of six thousand copies per week. Bertram Paver, a white advertising salesman, founded *Bantu World* in 1932. In the midst of the Great Depression, Paver sought to expand the market for white companies by establishing the only black commercial newspaper with a nationwide circulation. In interwar South Africa, newspapers easily surpassed magazines and radio as the preferred medium for advertisers.[4] Like other black newspapers, *Bantu World* struggled financially, and white mining interests soon held the majority of shares in the paper's parent company, Bantu Press.[5] About half of the paper appeared in English, with the rest appearing in isiZulu, isiXhosa, Sesotho, and Setswana, and, to a lesser extent, Tshivenda, Xitsonga, and Afrikaans. The women's pages—like the front page—appeared in English to ensure an audience that better cut across ethnolinguistic divides.

Bantu World distinguished itself from *Umteteli wa Bantu* (Mouthpiece of the people), an older multilingual paper funded by the mine managers' association, by having a looser editorial policy. Liberal African nationalists edited and staffed *Bantu World*, and they held considerable sway in determining its content. R. V. Selope Thema, the editor from 1932 to 1952, was a leader of the South African Native National Congress (a precursor to the African National Congress). He used his position at the paper to criticize discriminatory government policies and to highlight African achievements. *Bantu World*, according to a historian of South Africa's alternative press, quickly became "the arbiter of taste in urban African politics and culture and by far the most important medium of mass communication for the literate African community." Although this community (literate in any language) amounted to only about 12 percent of the total African population of 6.6 million in 1936, it was a vocal and visible group.[6]

Bantu World embodied the concerns and aspirations of Africans who worked as clerks, teachers, domestic servants, nurses, and clergy, and who struggled, under increasingly difficult circumstances, to achieve elite status. Amid the diverse ideologies that shaped interwar black politics, *Bantu World* advocated a "progressive but moderate" agenda. This agenda insisted, in the face of white racism and intensifying segregation, on the importance of school-educated blacks to South Africa's future. At times, others referred, somewhat derisively, to such Africans as the *AmaRespectables* (respectable people) for their fervent embrace of Christianity and their elite ambitions. The English root of this Xhosa term suggests the importance of respectability to this group's self-presentation and their political goal of gaining access to the same educational, social, and economic opportunities available to white South Africans.[7] The respectability that the *AmaRespectables* sought was deeply racialized. In segregationist South Africa, racial categories informed what behavior merited positive public recognition and who might obtain it. Visual markers of race made bodily and sartorial appearances into matters of grave importance. Yet what counted as a respectable practice or look was often contested.[8] *Bantu World*'s women's pages reveal the gendered dimensions of these political struggles and highlight how shifting conceptions of feminine beauty and changing cosmetic practices fueled debate over how to define and achieve racial respectability.

Bantu World announced a beauty competition in its inaugural women's pages, inviting "All African Ladies" to submit their "best photos" and promising cash prizes. "The Son of Africa," likely the editor Thema, justified the paper's new attention to women by stating that "no nation can rise above its women-folk," an axiom common to contemporary nationalist discourse. He then explained the multiple motivations behind the beauty competition: to prove that "there are beautiful women and girls in Africa," to promote "diligent perusal of enterprising Bantu newspapers," and to encourage "careless or lazy [ladies] to give a little more attention to their toilet."[9] According to this logic, the competition would foster race pride, a female readership, and conscientious consumption. Through its very format—the submission of portrait photos to a commercial newspaper—the contest encouraged young black women to engage with new visual media and to cultivate a conception of beauty focused on the face and upper torso. The entries published as part of *Bantu World*'s competition constitute a unique archive of interwar photographs of young African women. Although many photographs of African women taken during the late nineteenth and early twentieth centuries sought to cast them as ethnographic or erotic subjects, *Bantu World*'s beauty competition highlights another tradition dating back to at least the 1870s: African women commissioning and sharing their own photographs.[10]

Feminine beauty, as we have seen, was a long-valued attribute in southern Africa. When it came to assessing beauty, people considered a range of bodily features and surface appearances. Nineteenth-century white travelers and traders reported that Africans considered "stout" young women to be the most beautiful. Groups of such women attended the compounds of senior chiefs, demonstrating the chief's wealth and sexual prowess.[11] When they became "old and flabby in the cheeks," according to one turn-of-the-twentieth-century isiZulu-speaking man, they were married off.[12] In their accounts of conceptions of beauty in rural Setswana- and isiXhosa-speaking areas from the early 1930s, the anthropologists Isaac Schapera and Monica Hunter also emphasized the importance of bodily attributes. They noted the appeal of young women with "somewhat heavy build[s]," and prominent and firm breasts, buttocks, hips, and calves.[13] They also observed that people preferred "light-skinned girl[s]" and young women with "thin lips, an aquiline nose, and light brown skin."[14] By contrast, their colleague Eileen Krige observed that while "a large number of Zulus have relatively light skin, dark complexions are held in the highest esteem."[15] This difference mirrors the evidence for the precolonial period presented in chapter 1: whereas young women were widely associated with the aesthetic ideals of brightness, lightness, and ritual whiteness, some Setswana and isiXhosa speakers—but not isiZulu speakers—also expressed preferences for skin tones that were lightened through either seclusion or the use of white clay and botanical agents.

The fifty or so entries to *Bantu World*'s contest provide striking evidence of shifting ideas of beauty and proper bodily comportment. Most submissions feature young women wearing conservative clothing and somber countenances. Like the photos of well-groomed African converts that often appeared in mission fundraising literature as proof of "success," these portraits situated their subjects as "civilized."[16] When hung on the walls in black homes, collected in family albums, and enclosed in love letters, such portrait photos also became a medium for expressing and claiming a black Christian respectability.[17]

Photo beauty contests, in fact, first emerged in the United States to make displays of female beauty into reputable spectacles. American showman P. T. Barnum inaugurated such contests in the 1850s after realizing that respectable

BANTU WORLD BEAUTY COMPETITION

BEACONSFIELD

KRUGERSDORP

GRAHAMSTOWN

WORCESTER

FIGURE 2.2. Some of the entries that *Bantu World* received for its "Miss Africa" competition. Most entrants wore dignifies, if modest, dress and struck unassuming poses. *Bantu World*, November 1932.

women would not parade before judges but would submit daguerreotypes. By the end of the century, newspapers throughout the United States had picked up his idea.[18] Beauty photo contests soon spread to other parts of the world through illustrated magazines. According to the German sociologist Siegfried Kracauer, such magazines ranked among the most disorienting media of the interwar period. As part of their effort to reproduce "the world accessible to the photographic apparatus," Kracauer wrote, illustrated magazines filled their pages with film divas and "beautiful girls."[19]

By the early 1920s, South African magazines reported on British and U.S. competitions to find film stars and sponsored their own beauty photo contests.[20] Although these magazines targeted white audiences and only published photos of contestants who looked white, the intimacy of the country's racial

Page Of Interest To Women Of The Race

What Love Is
(By Maud J. Gacula)

Love: What It Is

Helpful Pages

Mr. Rakgomo's Futile Effusion

Miss J. G. Phahlane's Merry Makers' Troupe of Bloemfontein who will tour the O.F.S beginning with Kimberley on Apri. 20.

When Girls Leave School

geographies meant that they were perused and sometimes purchased by blacks.[21] Because South Africa had no pictorial magazine that catered to black readers during the 1930s, *Bantu World*'s editors saw both a duty and an opportunity in providing elements like beauty contests and love advice columns that, in the white press, were normally found in magazines.[22] Its women's pages, in effect, operated as a women's magazine within the bounds of a newspaper.

From its defense of black womanhood to its crowning title of "Miss Africa," *Bantu World*'s beauty competition also bears the marks of African American inspiration. Black journalists in interwar South Africa were influenced by the works of Booker T. Washington, Marcus Garvey, W. E. B. Du Bois, and by discussions of the "New Negro."[23] They were also familiar with the African American press as copies of Garvey's *Negro World* and Du Bois's *Crisis* circulated in South Africa.[24] *Bantu World* sometimes reprinted articles from those two periodicals and might have modeled its title and women's pages after those from Garvey's paper.[25] When these African American publications sponsored beauty contests, they, like other U.S. periodicals, sought to boost circulation. In addition, they aimed to combat racist disparagement of black women's appearances; showcasing beautiful black women was an antiracist retort.[26] The very title of the contest, "Miss Africa" as opposed to "Miss Bantu," evoked a Garveyite notion of "Africa" that emphasized the continent's heroic past and asserted a singular racial identity.[27] Through this title, the men behind *Bantu World* situated attractive and carefully groomed women as contributing to racial uplift.

Bantu World relied on readers to select the competition winner. Beneath each photo entry, the paper printed the name of the town or mission station from which the entrant hailed. Readers were instructed to cut out the three photos they thought were "best," to number them 1 to 3, and then to post them back to the paper.[28] At a time when *Bantu World* was protesting an ultimately successful political campaign to abolish black men's limited voting rights in the Cape Province, the paper invited all readers to elect "Miss Africa." This beauty competition, like others the world over, drew disparate entrants and readers into new circuits of citizenship by granting voting rights to all consumers and by insisting that what one looked like defined who one was, and that appearance mattered more than one's family, clan, or class.[29]

What most readily distinguishes the beauty competition's top two finishers is their rejection of the somber countenance, an early convention of portraiture photography. Mrs. Flora Ndobe of Cape Town, the first-place finisher, and Miss Elizabeth Hlabakoe of Johannesburg, the second-place finisher, sport teeth-revealing smiles. Publicity photos of film stars and advertisements for toothpaste and other toiletries had made this full-smile look a feature of the

Hail, Miss Africa, Queen of Beauty!

Miss AFRICA.

3. Mrs. Nellie L. Duna, (100 votes)
Grahamstown.

1. Mrs. Flora Ndobe, (230 votes)
Cape Town.

2. Miss Elizabeth Hlabakoe, (110 votes)
Johannesburg.

6. Miss E. Dhlamini,
Bethlehem.

5. Miss Hilda Landela,
Kimberly.

4. Miss E. R. Lulu Radebe
Krugersdorp.

FIGURE 2.4. The top six finishers in the beauty competition as selected by reader-voters. *Bantu World*, March 1933.

international modern-girl style during the 1920s.[30] In announcing the *Bantu World* competition, "The Son of Africa" had, in fact, encouraged entrants to smile: "Smile sweetly while the camera clicks and post the result to the Editor of this paper.... The trouble with some of our ladies is that they do not know how to smile. Yet what a glorious transformation a smile can give to your features! Practise it in front of your mirror every morning before or after meals it does not matter when."[31] This editorial dismissed any notion that smiling was an immodest gesture, and linked it to another common element in modern-girl representations: mirror-gazing.[32] By encouraging entrants to smile before a mirror, "The Son of Africa," like so many contemporary advertisements (see figure 2.1), claimed that young women could transform themselves through careful attention to their appearance.

The fact that Ndobe garnered more than twice as many votes as her closest competitor suggests that *Bantu World* reader-voters embraced a conception of

Modern Girls and Racial Respectability   55

FIGURE 2.5.
Mrs. Flora Ndobe,
winner of the "Miss
Africa" competition,
in cosmopolitan
flapper attire and
with a teeth-revealing
smile. *Bantu World*,
December 1932.

CAPE TOWN.

beauty rooted more in the twentieth century's modern glamour than the nineteenth's Victorian propriety. Her cloche hat, string of pearls, drop neckline, and ostrich-feather tippet were in keeping with the apparel worn by the film stars and socialites who featured in white South African and foreign magazines, and by the fashionable African American women who appeared in *Negro World* and *The Crisis*.[33] Ndobe's cosmopolitan dress may be attributable to her eclectic social circle in Cape Town. Flora was the wife of Bransby Ndobe, the prominent Independent African Native Congress (IANC) organizer in the Western Cape. Born Flora Motinya in the Orange Free State, she married Bransby by the age of nineteen. Bransby's left-wing activism in Cape Town brought him and possibly Flora into contact with diverse political figures, including the black Garveyite James Thaele, fellow IANC organizers Eliot Tonjeni and Amoth Plaatjes, and white communists Eddie Roux, Jack Simons, and Ray Simons.[34] Such connections would have exposed Flora to an internationalist set of ideas and styles. *Bantu World* reader-voters likely delighted in Ndobe's audacious and successful expression of a cosmopolitan glamour not readily associated with black South Africans.

Ndobe's facial features and skin tone were also more reminiscent of the white and light-skinned women who appeared in illustrated publications, including African American ones, than most of the other contest entrants. Her slender nose and lips, and light-colored skin combined to create an appearance that, in terms of South Africa's racial classifications, was more "Coloured" than "Bantu." By the 1930s and especially in the urban areas and mission stations where many *Bantu World* readers lived, colonialism's and segregation's insidious privileging of racial whiteness had become entangled with aesthetic preferences for brightness and lightness. Given the many elements that distinguished Ndobe's photo from those of her competitors, it is difficult to know if or to what extent her relatively pale color appealed to reader-voters. As we shall see below, *Bantu World* editors spent considerable ink discussing and decrying African women whose faces appeared too white. Whereas Ndobe's light visage may have appealed to some reader-voters, it might have also contributed to the ambivalent attitude that the editors expressed at the contest's close.

In the editorial that accompanied the competition results, Thema claimed that the competition's purpose had been to promote reading and, by extension, schooling for girls and women. He did not mention the earlier stated motivations of proving that there are "beautiful girls and women in Africa" and encouraging women to pay "more attention to their toilet." Instead, Thema insisted that deeds were more important than looks: "[While the] Bantu race is certainly proud of its beautiful women ... it will be more proud of women who take interest in the welfare of the people."[35] This reformulation of the contest's purpose suggests that something about its conduct or conclusion caused the men behind *Bantu World* to worry that excessive attention to appearances might undermine racial respectability. These worries perhaps also ensured that this was *Bantu World*'s first and last beauty competition.

Interwar Debates about Whitening and Lightening

In February 1933, a few weeks before the beauty competition winner was announced, a *Bantu World* headline playfully announced "Daughters of Ham Take to Powdering Their Faces." The article's author, "Tommy," described how face powder caused him to mistake a young black woman in Cape Town for an Italian. It was not until she asked in "faultless vernacular" about who had won the competition that he recognized her as nonwhite. Tommy responded coyly that she had probably won, and was promptly invited to her birthday party in the "Malay Camp's 'aristocratic' tenements," likely somewhere in District Six.[36] What is so striking about this account is how the woman's use of face powder, in combination with her language and the party venue, cast her as a racially ambiguous figure. Her powdered face and pink cheeks caused Tommy to mistake her for an olive-skinned European while her interest in *Bantu World*'s beauty competition, expressed most likely in isiXhosa, marked her as African. Finally, the location of her upcoming birthday party signaled Coloured affinities. Tommy's partner in this flirtatious exchange may well have been Flora Ndobe. The woman's curiosity about the competition suggested to Tommy that she was an entrant, and Ndobe was one of only two from Cape Town. Moreover, Ndobe's competition photo conveys racial ambiguity and her light-colored face appears powdered.

By the 1930s, it was commonplace for women, in many parts of the world, to use face powders and other cosmetics as technologies of visibility to enhance their appearances for portrait photographs. Even women who did not normally apply paints, powders, rouges, and eye makeup would use them before sittings in the hope of creating a photogenic look that could conceal blemishes and highlight their most alluring features. Richard Dyer, in his now-classic study of whiteness and racial representation, demonstrated how photography, a technology of light that developed with pale faces as the presumed norms, bolstered the use of white paints and powders.[37] Powders, in particular, helped produce an even complexion and remove shininess. Stage and film actresses who generously used cosmetics to achieve dramatic and flawless appearances set the standard for portrait photographs. Cosmetics became so closely associated with portraiture that some photography handbooks included recipes for them. American photographers also, at times, used cosmetics to retouch negatives and prints, enlivening women's faces with traces of rouge. Some customers with dark complexions requested photographs that would make them look lighter.[38] A skin lightener advertisement that appeared in an African American newspaper in 1935 referenced this practice by promising that its product could achieve the same look produced by photographers: a lighter complexion free of blemishes.[39] By drawing attention to the face and encouraging cosmetics use, portrait photography heightened the aesthetic valuation of smooth and often light-colored skin.

In interwar South Africa, black women who wanted to apply powder had little choice but to use a pale shade. Up through the mid-1930s, South African stores sold face powders in a very limited range of colors extending from light beige to pink. This range reflected a narrow commercial vision of what skin tones mattered, and ensured that on black women, face powder functioned as a skin whitener.[40] When criticizing black women's use of light-colored powders, as we shall see, observers never mentioned the unavailability of darker shades. Nor did they consider that the look achieved with such powders was similar to that produced by a thin application of white clay and yellow ochre, as was sometimes done locally. Instead, critics interpreted black women's use of light-colored powder as beyond the bounds of middle-class feminine propriety and as a vain attempt to look white.

Whereas Tommy was charmed by the powdered "daughter of Ham" he encountered, most *Bantu World* writers disapproved of black women wearing cosmetics. A month after Tommy's article, R. R. R. Dhlomo, the "editress" of the women's pages, launched a campaign against white powder and, to a lesser extent, red lipstick. Dhlomo was one of the period's most important black writers in English and isiZulu, and he was the first to publish a novel. His early life provides insight into the social background of those who criticized cosmetics. Born in Pietermaritzburg in 1901, he attended mission schools. In 1912, the Dhlomo family moved to Johannesburg where his father worked as a medical assistant for a mining company and his mother washed laundry for white customers. After further schooling, R. R. R. worked as a mine clerk and, in the late 1920s, turned his full attention to writing. He and his younger brother Herbert, also an accomplished writer, were very close to their mother, Sardinia Mbune Caluza Dhlomo, who dominated the Dhlomo household with her storytelling, her Victorian and Christian values, and her keen attention to appearances.[41] In many regards, Dhlomo was a strong advocate for women. He celebrated black women's educational and professional achievements, and endorsed companionate marriages.[42] Yet when it came to black women wearing makeup, Dhlomo saw nothing redeemable.

Many letter writers, particularly men, supported Dhlomo in his anticosmetics campaign. Their condemnation was part of widespread class concerns about natural versus artificial beauty. Many contemporaries wrote elsewhere in *Bantu World* in 1933 that "the original meaning of the word 'Beauty'...[is] 'Natural Beauty'" and not the "modern meaning of 'artificial beauty'" achieved through "powders and paints."[43] As we saw in the previous chapter, moral concerns had long animated discussions of cosmetics. By the nineteenth century, "painted woman" was a common English-language euphemism for a prostitute or sex worker as some used powder, rouge, and eye makeup to advertise their trade. Critics associated cosmetics' use with women's ability to deceive men and take their money. Over the twentieth century, cosmetics in the United States and many other places underwent a remarkable transformation, moving, in the words of U.S. beauty historian Kathy Peiss, from being "a sign of disrepute" to becoming "the daily routine of millions."[44]

Most South Africans approved of only modest cosmetics use. One marketing report from 1931 found that white and Coloured women tended to use face powder, rouge, and lipstick sparingly: "its free use usually draws forth unfavourable comment."[45] Such remarks likely impugned the woman's sexual morality and class standing. By the mid-1930s, such concerns had reached Fort Hare Native College, South Africa's premier institution of black higher learning, in the rural Eastern Cape. In her autobiography, Phyllis Ntantala describes how her boyfriend persuaded her to stop wearing makeup with a line from Shakespeare's *As You Like It*: "good wine needs no bush."[46] Such condemnation of black women's use of cosmetics coincided with broader notions of middle-class respectability in South Africa, the United States, and elsewhere.

In 1930s Johannesburg where most Africans lived close to poverty, appearances were especially important in defining class differences and claiming respectability. Dhlomo castigated face powder and lipstick for giving "the impression of cheapness."[47] He did not tolerate divergent viewpoints. When S. H. D. Lee Mnyandu wrote that powder and paint made Johannesburg's ladies beautiful and "suitable for marriage," Dhlomo dismissed his letter as naïve by appending the following note: "This writer has just arrived in the city from Natal."[48] Dhlomo's concern about urban femininity is evident as early as 1928 when he published *An African Tragedy*, the first English-language novel by a black South African. Dhlomo's novel chronicles the moral destruction of a male labor migrant in Johannesburg at the hands of a prostitute, contrasting this domineering urban female figure with the migrant's obedient and Christian wife in rural Zululand.[49]

In the years following the publication of *An African Tragedy*, urban populations continued to grow with the number of Africans residing in Johannesburg reaching a quarter million by the mid-1930s. Many female migrants found employment as domestic workers while a few worked as teachers and nurses. Faced with such limited employment opportunities, others washed laundry and sold beer from their homes, or earned money by providing domestic and sexual services to male migrants.[50] Poor women ranked among black South Africa's urban innovators. Social anthropologist Ellen Hellmann documented that young women living in Johannesburg's slums during the early 1930s regularly wore lipstick, rouge, and powder.[51] Similarly, a couple of decades later, a black columnist explained, "The fashion of hair straightening had moved upward from loose women to the middle class."[52] It is possible that poor and working-class women were the first black women to wear makeup, thereby contributing to Dhlomo's unease about *AmaRespectable* cosmetics use.

Alongside expressing class anxieties, Dhlomo's anticosmetics campaign resonated with interwar efforts by black male leaders to reassert patriarchal control. Confronted with women's increasing social and economic independence, these men promoted gender relations and conduct that bolstered their authority as fathers and husbands.[53] In *Bantu World*, men charged women who wore makeup with other offenses: smoking cigarettes, drinking alcohol, speaking "township languages," wearing trousers, and fixating on romance.[54] Like complaints about the modern girl elsewhere in the world, they criticized young women for simultaneously embracing masculine habits and neglecting feminine duties through self-indulgence.[55] One letter writer argued that African women would not achieve a "modern and up-to-date" look by wearing powder and lipstick but only by "behav[ing] in a lady like way."[56] Such writers admitted that modern conditions demanded new forms of black femininity. But they insisted that these forms revise rather than topple the gender norms prevalent in black Christian homes.

Critics of cosmetics interspersed these complaints about class and gender transgressions with charges of racial betrayal. As scholars of U.S. beauty culture have argued, concerns about natural versus artificial beauty took on a unique salience when directed at black women living under segregation. More so than white women, black women's cosmetics use made them vulnerable to accusations of racial shame. Critics charged black women who used makeup and hair-straightening products of acquiescing to white beauty standards.[57] Countering such charges, some scholars have argued that young black women wore powder, rouge, and lipstick not to "look white" but to "draw[] attention to their faces" and distinguish themselves from "the 'natural' look of their mothers and grandmothers," or to cover and clear blemishes, scars, and "complexion problems that had little to do with color per se."[58] Nonetheless, in segregationist South Africa, too, where light-skinned people held privileges denied those who were darker, some interpreted black women's use of light-colored powder in racial terms.

Dhlomo's condemnation of cosmetics, in fact, centered on racial unsightliness. He argued that powders and lipsticks did "not suit dark skins." Black women, Dhlomo wrote, should abandon their desire "to turn themselves white," recognize "the beauty of their natural coloring," and limit their use of cosmetics to moisturizing creams and hair lotions.[59] Letter writers similarly accused black women who wore makeup of foolishly copying white women. M. F. Phala singled out powder use as evidence of how "Bantu people" were not "proud" of their skin color.[60] Another writer noted that black women's "imitative" habits were not reciprocated by "European ladies" who never wore *imbola*, the ochre used to redden skin, hair, and blankets.[61] At other times, *Bantu World* with its moderate political agenda situated white women as appropriate role models. In announcing the beauty competition, for example, "The Son of Africa" had encouraged women "to emulate your white sisters in all that is noble, true and good."[62] For Dhlomo and his allies, rather than being noble, wearing makeup sullied racial respectability.

Although men authored most of *Bantu World*'s commentary, a few women, or perhaps Dhlomo masquerading behind female pseudonyms and hoping to stir controversy, voiced their opinions. One mother agreed that makeup was among the more disagreeable practices that young women had recently adopted.[63] Another letter writer, under the pseudonym "Swanee," joined the racialized condemnation of cosmetics. Testifying as a repentant cosmetics user, she explained how a male friend had recently convinced her that wearing face powder and lipstick made her look like a "guinea baboon." By comparing herself to a monkey, "Swanee" drew on racist insults that disparaged Africans as apelike. She warned: "Use a hundred powders and lip-sticks, you'll never change from black to white."[64]

A few women took the opposite stance, dismissing those who criticized cosmetics and ignoring their racialized charges. They offered few specifics, however, on why they or other women might choose to use face powder. Sarah Ngcobo of Durban, for one, rejected criticism of cosmetics as part of a smear campaign against young women, writing that she was "fed up" with reading articles that blamed "women, particularly young girls, for everything . . . [including] for powdering their faces, for going out at night, for snaring other women's husbands, for dressing expensively."[65] Similarly, "Powdered Face" expressed frustration with the critics of cosmetics as part of a longer litany. She noted that while previously African women wore *imbola*, smoked pipes, and were only "clothed from the waist downwards," today young women are admonished for using powder, smoking cigarettes, and wearing short sleeves.[66] By identifying African antecedents for a number of modern-girl practices, "Powdered Face" challenged the sentiments of racial nationalism that underlay most *Bantu World* criticism of cosmetics.

On a couple of occasions, Dhlomo mentioned receiving letters from women who claimed that powder had made their faces "look nicer." Confronted with charges that cosmetics use was ill-conceived racial mimicry, these black women insisted that they simply sought to improve their appearances.[67] But as Dhlomo did not publish these letters, it is unclear how exactly these women felt their appearances were improved: Did powder leave their complexions smoother and more even? Did it make their skin look lighter or brighter? Did it render them more fashionable or photogenic? As with cosmetics users in other time periods and places, a combination of pragmatic reasons and affective desires likely stirred black women to apply powder. Yet their critics ignored this multiplicity of motivations and reduced black women's use of face powder to a matter of race. Middle-class notions of female modesty prevented all but a couple of women from challenging this simplification. *Bantu World*'s lopsided debate over face powder highlights how in twentieth-century South Africa black women's efforts to cultivate what they deemed fashionable or modern appearances could readily be interpreted by others as unsightly imitations of white ways. For help in negotiating this tricky cultural terrain, some turned to black people living on the other side of the Atlantic.

African American Influences

Apex, the first skin lightener advertised in *Bantu World*, was the product of African American enterprise. U.S. influences were integral to the spread of such products in Africa. One of the earliest references to commercial skin lighteners in the black African press was a speech delivered and published in Lagos in 1909. In that speech, S. M. Harden, a minister and teacher who was raised locally as the son of an Americo-Liberian father and Sierra Leonean mother but had attended a Baptist College in Virginia, criticized "Negro[s] in America" and their newspapers for advertising hair straighteners and face bleaches, presenting those advertisements as evidence that they were "devoid of all race pride."[68] Two decades later, an African newspaper a couple of thousand miles south of Lagos carried the same types of advertisements. The Apex ads in *Bantu World* promoted a skin bleach that promised to "instantly lighten" complexions and to remove "tan, freckles, liver spots, blackheads, pimples, collar marks, sunburns, acne, etc." (see figure 2.1).

In the early twentieth-century United States, cosmetics companies were some of the largest and most profitable African American businesses. Black entrepreneur Anthony Overton pioneered the field by developing and successfully selling "High-Brown" face powder as an alternative to inappropriate light-colored powders. With the product's name, Overton evoked the skin tone commonly expressed as a beauty ideal in black popular culture.[69] By the 1920s, several of the most successful African American cosmetic companies—like Madam C. J. Walker, Poro, and Apex—were women-owned, and sold their products through door-to-door agents. These companies provided black women with some of their few employment opportunities outside of field, laundry, or domestic work. As scholars of African American beauty culture have argued, the success of these companies was, in part, an antiracist retort, a form of race-conscious economic nationalism that made beauty the right of every woman. The beauty salons they spawned became coveted sites of black female sociality and affirmation. Even more than the white beauty industry, historians Shane White and Graham White write, "Black cosmetics were associated with modernity and, most importantly, with progress."[70]

At the same time, some African Americans criticized the companies and their advertising campaigns for promoting a "white look" that valorized straight hair and light complexions. They argued that rather than fostering race pride, the black beauty industry traded on racial shame. The advent of powder in "all shades" did not resolve black debates over cosmetics but simply shifted them to other products. Although black publications like *The Afro-American* and *Negro World* received 30 to 50 percent of their revenue from advertising such products, their editors, most notably Marcus Garvey and his wife, Amy Jacques Garvey, frequently condemned them. African American women reformers such as Anna Julia Cooper and Nanny Burroughs also denounced these products for contributing to superficial notions of beauty and supporting some black men's misguided preference for light-colored women. As a matter of race pride, Madam C. J. Walker refused to sell hair straighteners and skin lighteners. Following her death in 1918, however, the C. J. Walker Company began to manufacture the skin lightener "Tan-Off" and, by the late 1920s, it had become one of its best-sellers.[71]

The appeal of skin lighteners and hair straighteners highlighted color hierarchies within the Jim Crow United States that extended into African American communities. During slavery, paler African Americans and those with less curly hair frequently received preferred work tasks and, sometimes, skilled training. They were also more likely to be manumitted as many of their fathers were white slave owners. Following the end of slavery, straighter hair and lighter skin continued to correspond to higher social status and real material benefits such as greater income, job security, and more affluent marriage partners. Some exclusive churches and clubs, and certain fraternities and sororities at black colleges, deployed the "paper-bag test," only admitting members whose complexion was lighter than that of the bag's brown color. According to critics, many users of skin lighteners and hair straighteners were not so much trying to pass for white as to join the ranks of this light-colored black elite. Marketing appeals provided additional fodder for such criticism. With promises that products would deliver "that refined light tone so valuable in business and social life," manufacturers promoted a form of racial uplift that privileged pale skin tones.[72]

Such contradictions captured the imagination of fiction writers. In 1931, the African American author George S. Schuyler published a satiric novel, *Black No More* (the name of an actual brand of skin bleach), about a roguish black businessman who cashes in on a scientific invention that turns black people white. Schuyler's novel parodied white supremacy and lampooned "race leaders" for condoning skin lightening.[73] H. I. E. Dhlomo—the younger brother of R. R. R. Dhlomo—picked up on some of these same themes in a science fiction short story published four years later in the liberal South African magazine *The African Observer*. "An Experiment in Color" bears several striking similarities to Schuyler's novel. Like *Black No More*, Dhlomo's story about the absurdity of racial logics pivots on the scientific discovery of a process for turning black people white and back again. The protagonist, a black scientist named Frank Mabaso, deploys his discovery to experience life beyond the color bar and to develop a romantic relationship with a white woman. But whereas Schuyler ridicules cosmetics companies, black leaders, and the racism of white America, Dhlomo's tone is consistently somber. Mabaso's experiment ends in tragedy when he reveals his discovery and is then assassinated by an Afrikaans-speaking white man who declares, "*Goed! Ons wil nie wit kafers in ons land bie nie. Waar sou ons vrow-mense wees?*" (Good! We do not want white kaffirs in our country. Where would our women be?). Written a few years after the passage of the 1928 Immorality Act that prohibited sexual relations between whites and Africans, Dhlomo's Afrofuturist story points to the intimacy of racial transgressions and sexual threats under segregationist rule. It also casts surface appearances as simultaneously superficial and a matter of life and death.[74]

Such debates accompanied African American cosmetics as they crossed the Atlantic. By the 1930s, the United States was only second to the United Kingdom as a source of imports for South Africa.[75] Nonetheless, African American–manufactured goods were a novelty. One *Bantu World* advertisement proudly declared Apex the first "all Negro Company" in South Africa. Apex's agent in Johannesburg was an American man, apparently white, named "Jolly" Jack Bernard.[76] As such, he was a significant departure from Apex's U.S. marketing strategy of working through black female sales agents. Barnard introduced Apex products as part of his trade in "American Negro Books and Photographs." Since the mid-1920s, at least, Barnard operated a bookstore in Johannesburg that sold African American newspapers, including the *Negro World* and the *Messenger* alongside photos of Marcus Garvey, boxers, and other black celebrities, and an eclectic set of booklets on how to interpret dreams, give toasts, and write love letters. A staunch supporter of South Africa's Industrial and Commercial Workers Union, a radical black organization with a membership that spanned urban and rural areas, he sold their newspaper, *The Worker's Herald*, and advertised his shop in it and in the *Sun*, a Coloured newspaper published out of Cape Town.[77]

From reading black U.S. newspapers, Barnard and his customers would have learned about African American cosmetic enterprises. Images for the first Apex advertisements in *Bantu World* were borrowed wholesale from the African American press.[78] Later advertisements sought to assure readers of the products' local resonance by featuring the photo and Johannesburg address of Mrs. E. Garson, described as a "regular user of and firm believer in Apex products." In contrast to the drawings, the photo, with its greater pretensions to realism, aimed to provide testimonial evidence. By using stories and photos of actual women, advertisers capitalized on what Roland Barthes termed photography's "myth of 'naturalness.'"[79] Garson's profile portrait highlighted her relaxed hair and light-colored skin, perhaps suggesting to *Bantu World* readers someone classified as Coloured. In a further attempt to localize Apex's message, some ads provided product descriptions in Sesotho. Whereas the opening sentence of the earlier English-language description—"It not only bleaches but is a skin purifier"(see figure 2.1)—assumed a reader familiar with the basic claims of commercial skin lighteners, the Sesotho one undertook the pedagogical work of explaining the product's purpose: "It is an oil/lotion that lightens/whitens a person's skin. It removes sores/pimples and dirt from the skin. It makes a person beautiful and makes their skin and face very soft and smooth."[80]

Several months into the Apex campaign, *Bantu World* ran an article about the company's founder and president, Sara Washington. Such features were a common publicity tool used by black beauty companies in the United States.[81] This article positioned Washington as an African American success story, discussing how Apex had created "legitimate business" opportunities for many in the United States. It explained that the company's arrival in South Africa meant that the "Bantu race" could now benefit from products "manufactured for them by their brothers and sisters in America."[82] According to the article's logic, cosmetics consumption enabled racial solidarity and progress. Such logic ignored criticism of certain beauty products as embodying racial self-loathing and overlooked how black diasporic connections might include a white middleman.

Bantu World's founder ensured that the Apex advertisements and others reached an audience larger than the newspaper's readers by including them in a "Bantu World Trade Exhibition" in May 1934. True to *Bantu World*'s founding vision, Paver promoted the exhibition as facilitating the expansion of white capital and improving race relations: "The European business man who participates in it will discover the fact that the Africans are a potential market

FIGURE 2.6. This Apex ad from an African American newspaper served as the basis for the Apex ad that appeared one year later in *Bantu World* (see figure 2.1). *New York Amsterdam News*, June 1932.

APEX GLOSSATINA

Ke poo ea mafura a otlollang moriri. A etsa moriri gore obe boleta go feta mafura a mefuta e meng. Gape a sebedisoa ke banna, basadi le bana.

APEX SPECIAL GROWER
(Double Strength)

Ana ke mafura a godisang le go tisa moriri o hlobegaeg. A nea matla medu ea moriri, gomme a etse gore o gole,

APEX SKIN BLFACH

Ke Mafura a sueufatsang letlalo la motho. A tlosa diso le ditshila tse ding letlalong. A etsa gore motho a be motle, a dira letlalo la gagoe boleta gamogo le sefahlogo sa gagoe.

THE APEX HAIR Co. Inc.
1725 Arctic Avenue
Atlantic City, N. J.

Mrs E. GARSON,
66a. Gold St.,   Johannesburg.
Who is a regular user of and firm beleiver in APEX products.

Join the APEX SCHOOL
OF BEAUTY CULTURE
& HAIRDRESSING

It will make you **independent** by giving you a valuable profession.

Write for particulars :—

APEX HAIR Co., (S.A.)
P.O. Box 5731,   JOHANNESBURG.

FIGURE 2.7. An Apex ad that localized its message for black South African consumers by providing product descriptions in Sesotho and featuring the photo of a Johannesburg user. *Bantu World*, September 1933.

for his commodities, and, therefore a useful citizen [*sic*] of South Africa.... [H]ere the two races will meet not as masters and servants but as producers and consumers."[83] Paver provided all advertisers with a stall and an African translator to help them communicate with those who perused their displays. He also gave each of them five thousand leaflet-reprints of their ads. These same ads were compiled into a slide show that toured four thousand miles across the country, disseminating commercial images, including those for Apex, far and wide.[84]

Mme. Sara Spencer Washington. Founder and President of the Apex Hair Company.

Remarkable Business Acumen of Negro Woman Shown in Her Work

FIGURE 2.8. A photo of African American beauty entrepreneur Sara Washington. The accompanying article lauded Apex's opening of a Johannesburg office as allowing the "Bantu race" to follow in the footsteps of "their brothers and sisters in America." *Bantu World*, November 1933.

It is difficult to know what Dhlomo and other critics of black women's use of cosmetics made of the Apex campaign. Dhlomo's condemnation of face powder often appeared on the same page as the ads. Yet he never commented on them. While he and others may have welcomed the arrival of powders in more diverse shades, they probably disapproved of Apex's skin bleach. As was the case with the African American press, the revenue to be gained from cosmetics advertising likely placed these products beyond reproach. As editress, Dhlomo urged women readers to attend the 1934 exhibition and purchase products from *Bantu World*'s advertisers.[85] Afterward, Dhlomo noted that the cosmetics stall proved especially popular with women visitors. Recounting his own visit with his wife and child, Dhlomo described how "sweet smelling fats and oils . . . drew cries and cries of enthusiasm from our fair companions." Cosmetics provoked olfactory and affective reactions. When writing about the exhibition, Dhlomo did not criticize cosmetics per se but rather explained that they were beyond the means of people like himself who were "not paid a living wage."[86]

Despite their cost, Apex products gained traction in South Africa. In 1936, *Apex News*, the company's bimonthly magazine published out of Atlantic City, listed the Bantu World Building in Johannesburg as its first international office. A few years later, the magazine published an article by a South African male correspondent dispelling stereotypes of Africans as "primitive" and "uncivilized," and encouraging beauticians to move to South Africa where they could become "pioneers in the field of scientific beauty culture." Accompanying the article were photos of an Apex Beauty Parlour near a modern Johannesburg apartment building, as well as the adjoining offices of the Apex Hair Co. and *Bantu World*. The magazine's "News from Abroad" column also included messages from agents based in the Cape Province. Their last names—Coleman, Sissing, Gow, and Benjamin—suggest that they, like Garson, the company's local spokesmodel, may have been classified as Coloured and that Apex products may have been especially attractive and accessible to that segment of South Africa's population.[87]

During the 1930s, *Bantu World* ran an advertisement for another African American cosmetics company, Valmor Products, recruiting local agents. The ad featured drawings of a man with a white face and a woman whose face was half light and half dark, a crude representation of the results purportedly achieved through their products.[88] During his 1938 trip to South Africa, Ralph Bunche, the African American scholar and activist, visited a dressmaking and hair shop in Sophiatown run by a Sotho woman who used Valmor's products. Revealing that Bunche preferred the older black cosmetics companies that appealed to race pride, he "put her on to Poro."[89] Advertisements for other skin lighteners and hair straighteners imported from the United States also appeared in the *Sun*.[90] Their appearance and the Apex and Valmor campaigns demonstrate how, in interwar South Africa, skin lighteners and other cosmetics became linked to concerns about racial respectability through the transatlantic circulation of products, people, and new print and visual media.

As part of that traffic, at least one black South African woman traveled across the Atlantic and gained in-depth knowledge of African American beauty culture. In 1935, Rilda Marta, a Xhosa woman from the Eastern Cape, published a series of articles in *Bantu World*, describing her adventures in the United States. Marta explained that while she had planned to study medicine or law, she ended up attending a beauty college. When she arrived in New

AGENTS WANTED

To Sell Sweet Georgia Brown Beauty Products

Here is a big chance for you to be our Agent and make a lot of money. Men and Women wanted to be agents for our big line of **SWEET GEORGIA BROWN** Beauty Products made especially for dark-skinned people. We have everything—Hair Dressing Pomade, Skin Brightener, Bleach Cream, Hair Strength, Face Powder, Vanishing Cream, Perfumes—300 different products. Everywhere you go, you make a sale because you have the things people want. Don't wait! **HAVE MONEY;** work in spare time or full time; work when you please; be independent when you are our agent. Write today for Agents Offer and **FREE** Samples. Do it today before you forget.

VALMOR PRODUCTS CO. Dept. F66 2241 Indiana Avenue Chicago, Ill., U.S.A.

FIGURE 2.9. An ad recruiting sales agents for another African American cosmetics company, Valmor, that purported to sell three hundred different products, including a face powder, a bleach cream, and a "skin brightener." *Bantu World*, February 1936.

York, she noticed to her surprise that the skin of "the American Negro" was like that of the African—"some are very light, and others are very dark in complexion." Marta's misconception may have stemmed from the predominance of photos of light-colored African American notables in the U.S. black press. Where Africans and African Americans actually differed, Marta explained, was in their hair: "I was always proud to call myself as African . . . [but] What really made me feel strange [was that] nearly every girl and woman has long hair and I among them looked like a boy dressed in girl's clothes."[91] Marta soon learned that their "long and beautiful" hair was the work of a beautician and, within a year, she "looked just like them[]." "Before" and "after" photos that accompanied the article demonstrated her own transformation from a plain schoolgirl to a sophisticated lady, and suggested what she might do for customers at her newly opened East London beauty salon.[92]

Marta added her voice to *Bantu World's* ongoing cosmetics discussion. She urged "African ladies" to take the advice of African American beauty culturist Madam C. J. Walker: "The key to Happiness and Success is a good appearance. You are often judged by how you look." Walker's dictum insisted that looking good was crucial to being satisfied with oneself and achieving respectability in a racialized world. Appearances were both an affective and political matter.

Miss Rilda Marta, before her visit to America.

Miss Rilda Marta, after her return from America. Note the remarkable change in her appearance. Her interesting article will be continued next week.

FIGURE 2.10. Photos of Miss Rilda Marta before and after she traveled from South Africa to the United States, where she attended an African American beauty college and transformed her appearance. *Bantu World*, June 1935.

Marta agreed that beauty products helped black women feel good, win the respect of their menfolk, and contribute to building "a clean, educated nation." Noting that even white women used "powder to make themselves lighter," Marta cautiously endorsed black women's use of makeup: "I do not mean that you should go and use lipstick and rouge because our colour is different to theirs; but if you do want to use some, remember there is a way of doing everything."[93] According to Walker and Marta, cosmetics enabled rather than undermined racial respectability.

For all of the connections that the Apex campaign and Marta's articles articulated between South Africa and the United States, profound differences existed in the relationship between cosmetics and racial respectability in the two countries. Whereas in the United States black women shaped discussions of beauty culture and owned some of the largest cosmetics companies, in South Africa, black men dominated the cosmetics discussion in *Bantu World* and white men owned the companies that imported and, later, manufactured cosmetics for black women. Black beauty culture in the United States, in part, gained positive recognition from making individuals like Sara Washington and Madam C. J. Walker into millionaires, and removing thousands of women from backbreaking field, laundry, and domestic work and turning them into sales agents. Such highly successful black businesswomen did not exist in interwar South Africa. Washington and Walker must have appeared as unusual figures to *Bantu World*'s readers. While black South African writers routinely referenced African American male intellectuals and leaders, they rarely evoked African American women. As others have argued, within these political circles, strong African American women provoked more ambivalence than admiration.[94] That ambivalence stemmed from a continuing faith in the propriety of patriarchy. For Dhlomo and his allies, independent women were not *AmaRespectable* women.

DISCUSSIONS OF BEAUTY in *Bantu World* demonstrate how, during the 1930s, concerns over cosmetics became tied to political struggles over racial respectability that spanned the Atlantic. Through its beauty competition, the newspaper sought to foster race pride and black consumption. The submitted photos drew aesthetic attention away from bodily shapes and toward bodily surfaces. This focus likely encouraged some black women to enlist powders as technologies of visibility to look more photogenic. The wide margin by which Flora Ndobe won the competition suggests that some combination of her glamorous style, alluring smile, and pale appearance appealed to *Bantu World*'s reader-voters, if not necessarily its editor and other staff. Aesthetic attention to the upper body and head supported *AmaRespectable* aspirations by providing a counter to photos of Africans that focused on sparsely clothed lower halves and cast women, especially, as primitive and erotic. But attention to the face and facial cosmetics could confound racial respectability when it seemed to endorse segregationist South Africa's skin-color hierarchy by valorizing light skin tones.

More than other contentious modern-girl practices like smoking cigarettes, wearing provocative fashions, and courting romance, the use of cosmetics emphasized the corporeal dimensions of racial distinctions. Black women may have worn white face powder to even out their skin tone, conceal blemishes, or draw attention to their faces. Until the mid-1930s, most only had access to powders in pale shades. Yet, for Dhlomo and his fellow critics of cosmetics, such multiple desires and consumer constraints mattered less than the impression that black women were trying to look white. This impression called into question women's pride in being African and their commitment to racial uplift. Cosmetics use provoked such strong reactions from some *Bantu World* writers because it combined a challenge to middle-class notions of gender propriety with intimations of racial shame. Although all participants in this debate agreed that appearances mattered, they disagreed as to what consumptive practices enabled both a modern and respectable look. *AmaRespectable* women had to walk the very thin line between paying too little and too much attention to their appearances.

To navigate that line, some turned to the products and advice of African American cosmetics manufacturers. "Jolly" Jack Bernard, Rilda Marta, and the women who admired Apex products at *Bantu World*'s trade exhibition all saw a resonance between African American women's efforts to look good and those of black South African women. But different histories and politics of race and gender in the two countries ensured that their circumstances and concerns were never identical. In 1939, James R. Korombi wrote a letter to *Bantu World* chiding "African youth" who "attempted to change their colour with expensive cosmetics." This letter is striking both for its seemingly early condemnation of skin lighteners and in its account of racial mimicry. Whereas previous authors had criticized black women's use of face powder as a vain attempt to mimic whites, Korombi pointed elsewhere: "African youth could be taught to be proud of their race and colour and should not be encouraged to pretend to be Indians or Coloureds."[95] According to Korombi, the use of skin lighteners was not about looking white but passing for brown. Once exported, U.S. skin lighteners quickly encountered the particularities of local racial hierarchies. In South Africa, the group that often appeared most analogous to African Americans were those classified as Coloured.

Yet as Tommy's flirtatious exchange attested, passing for another racial designation was never simply a matter of skin color. To ascertain a person's racial status, officials and laypeople alike considered language and accent, dress and bodily comportment, place of residence and employment, and the status of family members and friends as well as skin color, facial features, and hair. Skin whiteners and lighteners played into a subtle calculus of color, beauty, and status that nonetheless had significant material consequences. As small and intimate commodities that promised to transform one's appearance before and beyond the camera, cosmetics generated commercial revenues and social controversies. The next chapter examines how South African pharmacists entered this fray by marketing their own products to black consumers.

Three

LOCAL MANUFACTURING
AND COLOR CONSCIOUSNESS

The same year that the first Apex ad appeared in *Bantu World,* a South African cosmetics manufacturer named Karroo began marketing skin lighteners to local black consumers. But whereas Apex would disappear from the market within a decade, Karroo would grow to be the largest manufacturer of skin lighteners in South Africa with, by the 1970s, its products advertised as far afield as Ghana.[1] An early ad for Karroo Freckle and Complexion Cream appeared in the *Sun,* a Cape Town newspaper with a largely Coloured readership. It featured a blonde-haired woman and promised to remove freckles and blemishes, leaving a "clear, white complexion."[2] At four shillings per pot—about one week's wages for the average domestic worker countrywide and about one-third of a week's wages for a newly appointed female factory worker in Cape Town—Karroo was a considerable but conceivable expense.[3]

By the 1930s, some South African pharmacists recognized a market for their locally made cosmetics among Coloured and African consumers. Karroo began in Middelburg, a small sheep and cattle farming town located midway between Cape Town and Johannesburg. The Karroo name referenced Middelburg's location in the semidesert area known as the Karoo, with an additional "r" included for trademark purposes. Sometime in the 1910s or 1920s, W. C. Turpin, a pharmacist in Middelburg, began manufacturing a skin lightener containing mercury.[4] His pharmacy catered to an in-store clientele that was predominantly white. Yet, similar to pharmacists in other parts of South Africa, Turpin saw the financial advantages of offering services and products, perhaps through the pharmacy's back door or through hawkers, to the area's black residents.[5] The temptation to tap that market was considerable: Middelburg's black population (4,000 classified

She looks a different girl . . .

now that she's lost those ugly freckles

So easily done, too. Just a few applications and those ugly freckles and skin blemishes vanished as though they were mud spots wiped off with a clean towel.

Every woman, whether she has freckles or not, loves the soft beauty of a clear, white complexion. Hundreds of South African women have tried and proved KARROO Freckle and Complexion Cream. In three strengths — Mild, Medium and Strong. Medium suits most Complexions. Price 4/- at chemists, or 4/4 post free from W. C. Turpin & Son, Chemists, Middelburg, C.P.

KARROO FRECKLE AND COMPLEXION CREAM

FIGURE 3.1. By the early 1930s, some South African manufacturers of skin lighteners began marketing their products to black consumers. Karroo, developed by a pharmacist in Middelburg, grew to be one of the best-selling brands in the country. *Sun*, January 1934.

FIGURE 3.2. Turpin's Karroo Pharmacy (Apteek, in Afrikaans) with its ornate store-front and location on a central corner in Middelburg's business district. Although Turpin's initially catered to a white clientele, its skin lightener grew to be popular among Coloured and African consumers. Courtesy of Frannie Roux, General Manager, Rolfe Laboratories, Middelburg.

as Coloured; 5,500 as African) was more than double its white.[6] Turpin's involvement with black consumers soon extended beyond Middelburg. As we already know, by 1941, a woman living more than six hundred kilometers to the northeast requested a jar of Karroo from her beloved husband.

This chapter examines the early history of Karroo and other South African cosmetic manufacturers to demonstrate how, during the 1930s and 1940s, the main demand for skin lighteners shifted from white to brown and black consumers. It also reveals how and why pharmacists played a key role in the layered history of skin lighteners, ensuring that their manufacture existed on the cusp between medicines and cosmetics. When it came to cosmetics, pharmacists struggled to sell their products to those classified as European. Cosmetics' status as luxury commodities and the racialized history of manufacturing in southern Africa prompted white consumers to prefer imported cosmetics. In the specific case of skin lighteners, other influences also worked to ensure that those classified as Coloured and African became their main consumers. For some black consumers, the everyday salience of even slight distinctions in skin color—a refined "color consciousness"—made skin lighteners desirable commodities. By contrast, the emergence of tanning as a healthy and privileged pastime encouraged many white consumers to abandon skin lighteners for other kinds of cosmetics.

Pharmacists and Cosmetics

To turn a profit, pharmacists, also referred to as chemists and druggists, sold a range of nonmedicinal products, including cosmetics, perfumes, soda water, candies, and photographic equipment.[7] The sale of such products helped protect pharmacists' bottom line. Illustrating the significance of such enterprises, the inaugural issue of the *South African Pharmaceutical Journal* in 1934 carried a full front-page ad for an imported skin lightener, "Ysabel" Lemon Cold Cream, that promised "an excellent margin of profit."[8] Such enterprises could, in fact, dwarf sales of medicines. A pharmacist in Atlanta, for one, developed "Coca-Cola" while some of the twentieth century's largest cosmetics and toiletry companies also began in drug stores.[9]

With few exceptions, pharmacy was an all-white profession in segregationist South Africa. Pharmacies either were independently owned businesses or belonged to one of three chains.[10] Pharmacists and their professional associations ensured racial exclusion by controlling who apprenticed.[11] Yet such tight controls did not eliminate all competition. In the sale of patented medicines, poisons, and cosmetics, pharmacists competed with shopkeepers and general traders. In dispensing other medicinal preparations, they vied with black healers and white biomedical doctors.

Playing, in part, on racist fears, white pharmacists lobbied for and achieved significant protections under the Medical, Dental, and Pharmacy Act of 1928. The Act banned African healers (outside of Natal Province) from practicing their craft and selling medicines, and it required registered doctors who mixed and dispensed medicines to purchase a special license while barring them from operating full-blown pharmacies. The Act also restricted the keeping, sale, and supply of "poisons"—including mercuric chloride, one of the forms of mercury used in skin lighteners—to medical doctors, dentists, and pharmacists. This provision sought to safeguard the public by curtailing the sale of toxic substances by lay traders, frequently depicted in inflammatory terms as Indians, Chinese, and recently immigrated Jews.[12] In distinction from regulations in the

United Kingdom and the United States, a 1937 amendment to the Act required that the managing directors of all companies that produced preparations containing poisons be locally registered pharmacists.[13] This stipulation ensured that pharmacists played a more dominant role in cosmetics manufacturing in South Africa, and that the manufacture of skin lighteners remained closely tied to the manufacture of medicines.

The most profitable products for pharmacists to sell were those that they manufactured themselves. Trade journals carried articles on how to manufacture these products, and pharmacists routinely and successfully steered customers toward their own preparations.[14] Gerald Schap—a pharmacist who first learned to manufacture medicines when he apprenticed at a retail chemist in East London during the late 1940s and 1950s and later went on to make and sell diet pills ("Slimming Dradgings"), laxatives ("Movies"), and de-worming medication ("Early Bird") in Cape Town—explained this business logic. Schap recalled that selling his own products generated two to three times more income than those he purchased wholesale and then resold.[15] South African pharmacists developed a number of medicinal preparations, such as Lennon's "Dutch medicines," a line of supplements drawing on colonial and indigenous pharmacological knowledge, which grew to have wide national distribution and have remained popular brands today.

Pharmacists had more difficulty convincing white consumers to buy locally manufactured cosmetics. In 1931, the Port Elizabeth office of the U.S. advertising and marketing firm J. Walter Thompson undertook a survey of the South African cosmetics market for Lehn & Fink Products Co., a U.S. manufacturer. Imagining the cosmetics market as almost exclusively white, that report ranked chemists along with hairdressers, beauty parlors, department stores, and general dealers as the main purveyors of cosmetics.[16] Conveniently in accordance with the interests of Thompson's U.S. client, the survey found that white South African women preferred imported face creams and cosmetics. The United States reportedly held the reputation for the best creams and nail preparations, France for makeup items, and England for hair lotions. In a brief reference to black women, the report noted that Coloured women too preferred imported face powder. Over the next decade, imports continued to dominate the South African cosmetics market. A 1944 government survey of the industry found that cosmetic and toiletry importers outnumbered local manufacturers by more than three to one. In addition, a number of in-country manufacturers were simply subsidiaries of international cosmetic and pharmaceutical companies including Bristol Meyers, Colgate-Palmolive, Johnson & Johnson, and Richard Hudnut & Co.[17]

The dominance of imported cosmetics and luxury toiletries persisted despite the South African government's effort to spark local manufacturing. Beginning in the mid-1920s, politicians sought to diversify the economy and create more jobs for white workers by promoting secondary industry through the introduction of extensive protections. The government imposed taxes on hundreds of imported semidurable consumer goods.[18] Cosmetics, perfumery, and toilet preparations garnered the highest level of customs duty: 40 percent on the value of the imported product.[19] Such protections gave rise to sixteen registered firms dedicated to pharmaceutical and cosmetics manufacturing.[20] In 1940, the duty on cosmetics increased to 50 percent.[21] Policy makers figured that, as nonessential goods that could be manufactured in South Africa, cosmetics and toiletries merited elevated protection. Officials soon counted more than forty local manufacturers of perfumes, cosmetics, and toiletries, and, by 1950, it was a total of fifty-seven.[22]

These developments had limited impact on the more affluent segments of the market. In 1937, the South African subsidiary of Unilever concluded that local manufacturing of luxury toiletries did not make financial sense as "the tariff on toilet preparations was too low" and "the consumer preference for imported goods remained too strong."[23] When it came to cosmetics, luxury commodities imbued with the power to transform appearances, white women were willing to pay more for foreign brands deemed superior. Similarly, in the United States, early consumers preferred cosmetics manufactured by French companies that were often of higher quality than U.S. products and evoked Paris's reputation as the international capital for fashion and cosmopolitan elegance.[24] In South Africa, white women's strong and enduring preference for imported cosmetics was also shaped by the country's racialized history of manufacturing. In the early twentieth century, white consumers frequently disparaged South Africa–made goods as "Kaffir products."[25] Derived from the Arabic word for "unbeliever," "Kaffir" was used in southern Africa since the sixteenth century to refer to black Africans. Over time, the term became a racial insult. The epithet "Kaffir product" simultaneously posited locally made goods as inferior and likely to be purchased by black consumers.[26]

World War II only heightened these negative associations. Interruptions in the importation of many products, including cosmetics and toiletries, prompted a boom in local manufacturing, much of which was of poor quality.[27] Following the war, a local lipstick manufacturer complained to government officials that "the buying public" was now "prejudiced against local products irrespective of their quality."[28] Pointing to the same problem, a local toiletries company requested government assistance in contacting a foreign company that might

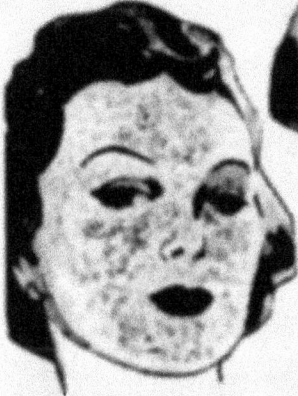

FIGURE 3.3. This Karroo ad encouraged readers of a popular Afrikaans-language photo magazine to reveal their "hidden beauty" and boost their "self-confidence" by creating a smooth, white complexion. *Die Huisgenoot,* October 1946.

BRIGHTEN UP YOUR SKIN

Nothing looks worse than a person with pimples all over chin, cheeks, and neck. Young men are worried about it, young ladies know it ruins their happiness, married men feel that people look at them with suspicion and disgust. Keppels have a treatment for you—an excellent ointment that clears away pimples and gives you a new skin altogether. It is called Keppels Acne Cream and costs 3/6 per pot. Get one to-day at your chemists!

Keppels
ACNE CREAM

FIGURE 3.4. Keppels was one of the earliest South African cosmetics companies to target black consumers. This ad promoted an acne cream for men and women, an olive tint face powder for "dark ladies," and a freckle wax that "makes the face lighter in colour and brings out its true beauty." *Bantu World*, April 1939. Cropped image reproduced courtesy of Bantu World Newspaper Digitized Collection, Historical Papers Research Archive, the Library, University of Witwatersrand, Johannesburg.

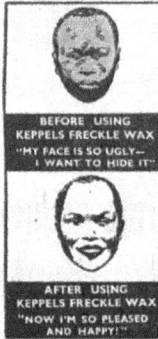

BEFORE USING
KEPPELS FRECKLE WAX
"MY FACE IS SO UGLY—
I WANT TO HIDE IT"

AFTER USING
KEPPELS FRECKLE WAX
"NOW I'M SO PLEASED
AND HAPPY!"

KEPPELS FRECKLE WAX
MAKES THE SKIN LIGHTER
AND BRINGS OUT
YOUR BEAUTY

It is very unpleasant for a lady to have blotches, patches, or marks in her face. Remove them with Keppels Freckle Wax! This lovely cream makes the face lighter in colour and brings out its true beauty. Keppels Freckle Wax costs 4/- per pot.

SHE'S THE SMARTEST WOMAN IN THE HALL—

thanks to Keppels Face Powder, Olive Tint

Keppels Face Powder (Olive tint) is especially recommended for dark ladies. Don't use pink or naturelle—insist on Olive colour! This wonderful powder stays on all night at dances and costs only 3/6 per large box.

YOUNG MEN!
BUY YOUR LADY FRIEND A BOX OF KEPPELS FACE POWDER (OLIVE TINT)

THE FOLLOWING HIGH-CLASS CHEMISTS STOCK KEPPELS BEAUTY PRODUCTS:

Lennon Ltd., Garrard (Pty.) Ltd., Newlyn Pharmacy and all high-class Johannesburg chemists. | *Geo. Pirie, Germiston, E. J. Adcock Ltd., Krugersdorp, B. Owen Jones Ltd., Boksburg, Koedoe Pharmacy, Pretoria.*

YOUR OWN FAVOURITE CHEMIST WILL SUPPLY YOU

serve as its "foster parent": "with an English firm's name and address upon the label there would exist no field for prejudice to operate."[29] The Board of Trade and Industries itself recognized the substandard reputation of locally manufactured products when, in 1945, it advised *against* requiring companies to mark their goods as "Made in the Union of South Africa."[30] Cosmetics' status as luxury goods combined with white consumers' strong preference for imports to ensure that some of the largest South African cosmetics manufacturers catered to black consumers. And for those manufacturers, skin lighteners grew to rank among their biggest sellers.

Karroo, Keppels, Bu-Tone, and Be-A-Beauty

Pharmacists had easy access to formulas for skin lighteners. Handbooks and trade journals had long carried recipes for cosmetics alongside those for medicines. Such publications from the late nineteenth and early twentieth centuries listed a range of active ingredients for "face bleaches," including citric, lactic, and acetic acid; hydrogen, zinc, and magnesium peroxides; the perborates of sodium, zinc, and magnesium; as well as ammoniated mercury and mercuric chloride. While, at times, pharmacy handbooks and journals warned of the ill-health consequences of mercury, they also described it as effective in treating skin infections and hyperpigmentation, and provided formulas for producing mercurial creams and ointments.[31] Turpin, the pharmacist who developed Karroo, likely obtained his recipe from such a source and used mercury imported from either Italy or Spain.[32]

During the 1940s, demand for Karroo grew, prompting its manufacturing operations to move from the modest facilities of Turpin's pharmacy to a newly built factory across town. The factory produced a range of cosmetic and medicinal products, including a foundation cream, foot powder, and an analgesic. The best-selling product was the skin lightener. People who worked in the factory or grew up in Middelburg recall that each week truckloads of it left the factory for distribution across the country.[33] Ads in *Die Huisgenoot* (The house companion), the most popular Afrikaans-language photo magazine, suggest that throughout the 1940s, Karroo still envisioned a significant market among white consumers. Ads promised to remove freckles and "colourization" (*verkleuring*) caused by the sun, leaving a complexion that was "satin smooth" (*satyngladde*) and "snow white" (*sneeuwitte*). By using cognates of racial terms—*kleuring* and *witte*—to describe the products' before and after effects, Karroo ads tied cosmetic use to the broader social order. The company also claimed their creams could boost women's "self-confidence" and make them more "attractive to men."[34] By the early 1950s, Karroo was renowned both for the full-page ads it ran in the black photo magazines *Zonk!* and *Drum* and for the black beauty competitions that it sponsored. It also became one of Middelburg's largest employers while its owners, by then a group of seven Afrikaans men known locally as the *Skewe Sewe* (the crooked seven), ranked among the town's wealthiest residents. One long-term resident remembered that they were the first people in Middelburg to own expensive cars with air conditioners.[35] Manufacturing cosmetics for black consumers turned out to be a profitable endeavor.

Other local skin lightener manufacturers also targeted black consumers. Keppels Cosmetic Laboratories originally plied its face powders and creams in the *Rand Daily Mail*, an English-language paper published in Johannesburg for a predominantly white readership.[36] Established in Ladybrand, a small town located near South Africa's border with today's Lesotho, Keppels struggled in the late 1930s to turn a profit. It unsuccessfully lobbied the government's board of trade and industries to reduce the import duties on the raw materials and fancy bottles necessary for cosmetics manufacturing.[37] Failing in its efforts to reduce import costs and perhaps with some preliminary success among black consumers around Ladybrand, Keppels began advertising in *Bantu World*. A 1939 Keppels ad instructed readers to "brighten up" their skin, an exhortation that, intentionally or not, evoked long-standing aesthetic ideals. The freckle wax or skin lightener was the most expensive of the products promoted, costing the same as Karroo: four shillings per container. The ad promised black readers happiness and glamour through before-and-after illustrations and an image of a stylish dancing couple.[38]

Keppels's ads, like those of other manufacturers, paired images of beauty and refinement with descriptive and relatively spare text. South African advertisers partly followed marketing methods pioneered in the United States. Trade publications such as *South African Business Efficiency* recognized U.S. advertisers as the world's leaders and encouraged readers to learn from their cutting-edge techniques. Yet, overall, ads in the English-language South African press were more subdued. In 1936, a U.S. Commerce Department report on advertising in South Africa referred to the dominant type of copy as "reason why." Whereas "testimonial" and "scare" copy were common in the United States, the report explained that South African advertisers preferred "simple, straightforward, conservative copy devoid of extravagant claims and complex expressions." Many South African consumers regarded ads as providing a "guarantee of quality."[39]

In addition to suggesting a product's trustworthiness, ads served as shopping aids. At most retail stores, sales agents stood behind counters and handed requested items to consumers. Through ads, consumers learned of specific brands. They then sometimes presented clippings to ensure their proper procurement.[40] When it came to cosmetics, clipped ads were an especially noteworthy practice because pharmacists and their counter help preferred to direct customers to their own products. Ads, as bearers of product names and logos, assisted consumers, particularly those with limited literacy or familiarity with the English, in securing specific brands and fending off the pressures of sales agents. In a 1953 article for *South African Retail Chemist*, Mr. Braude, who operated a pharmacy in Athlone, a Coloured township in Cape Town, described how African and Coloured shoppers often arrived with ads in hand: "they come with the cuttings . . . and will not take an alternative." The article's author further explained that "the Native provides an outstanding example of the success of large-scale advertising. He is ultra-conservative and tends to distrust any medicine or cosmetic that is not familiar to him through lavish radio programmes or great splashes in the newspapers."[41]

During the 1940s, another major brand of skin lighteners emerged: Bu-Tone Freckle and Complexion Cream. A Johannesburg-based pharmacist, Mr. L. Arenband, developed Bu-Tone under the auspices of Crowden Products Ltd.[42] Like other pharmacists, Arenband seems to have initially marketed his product to white and Coloured consumers. Ads that appeared in *Die Huisgenoot* and the *Cape Times* promised that Bu-Tone could keep skin "forever young" (*jeugdig die uwe*) and "soft, pliant and smooth in the face of harsh winds and searing sun."[43] Within a few years, Bu-Tone ads began appearing in the *Sun*, the same Coloured newspaper where Karroo first marketed its products to black consumers. These early Bu-Tone ads featured white-looking figures and emphasized the cream's ability to remove freckles and blemishes.[44] By the 1950s, Bu-Tone filled the pages of black photo magazines and vied with Karroo as the most heavily marketed brand in South Africa.

Ads for another, less widely distributed product, Be-A-Beauty Complexion Cream, reveal how at least one African entrepreneur also marketed skin lighteners. Israel Alexander was a fascinating, if not unique, figure within segregationist South Africa's landscape of medicinal and cosmetic producers: a wealthy black healer who operated several herbal shops and a very successful mail-order business.[45] Originally from Lesotho, Alexander became familiar with the trade when working as a typist in the mail-order department of a Durban chemist. Alexander soon developed his own business in Natal where the Medical, Dental and Pharmacy Act of 1928 afforded licensed African healers or *inyanga* greater allowances. According to local white pharmacists, Alexander sometimes exceeded those allowances. They accused him, together with some other African healers, of advertising themselves as "qualified doctors" and owning

FIGURE 3.5. An early Bu-Tone ad in a newspaper that targeted a primarily Coloured readership. *Sun*, March 1949.

establishments "with all the outward appearance of European chemist shops." In 1932, much to their dismay, Alexander even managed to be listed in the Durban city directory under "European Chemists."[46]

Around 1940, Alexander advertised a skin lightener in one of his mail-order catalogs. In translation from the original Sesotho, the ad copy read:

"BE-A-BEAUTY" COMPLEXION CREAM

The ointment that BEAUTIFIES. If your face is black and your color is not lovable, use "BE-A-BEAUTY" Complexion Cream. This ointment will remove your dark complexion, you will glow/shine and as a result your complexion will be lighter/whiter and more lovable. It also removes dark patches and wrinkles that come with old age.

Buy yourself this amazing ointment to beautify yourself. Boys and girls who value beauty use this ointment daily.

The price for "BE-A-BEAUTY" COMPLEXION CREAM is 5/6 postage included.[47]

> **"BE-A-BEAUTY" COMPLEXION CREAM**
> Setlolo se etsang BOTLE. Ha u le mots'o sefahlehong 'mala oa hau o sa ratehe, sebelisa setlolo sena se bitsoang "BE-A-BEAUTY" Complexion Cream. Setlolo sena se tla tlosa bots'o bona, u khanye u be mosueu hantle, u ratehe. Hape e bile ke setlolo se tlosang lihloba hang mahlong esita le masoebe a etsoang ke boqheku.
> Iphumanele Setlolo sena se makatsang u be motle. Bahlankana le Baroetsana ba ithatang ba sebelisa setlolo sena.
> Theko ea "BE-A-BEAUTY" COMPLEXION CREAM ke 5/6 feela ka poso.

FIGURE 3.6. This skin lightener ad appeared in the mail-order catalog of a successful African healer, Israel Alexander. The graphic features a glamorous black woman while the Sesotho text promises a light and glowing complexion. South African National Archive Repository, Pretoria, GES, 1788, 25/30M, Israel Alexander pamphlet, c. 1940.

The ad promised that Be-A-Beauty would provide a "glow/shine" (*u khanya*), a quality that southern Africans had long associated with beauty, especially that of young women. Speaking directly to the affective appeal of cosmetics, the ad proclaimed the ability to make one's skin color "lovable" (*ratehe*). By casting his cream as a kind of charm with the power to attract others, Alexander made explicit a faith that was generally implicit in English-language cosmetic ads. In another one of his mail-order catalogs, Alexander conveyed the power of Be-A-Beauty through a modern-girl parable about two young women—Lena and Anna—who went to a dance. Anna, who used Be-A-Beauty along with Alexander's "Keep Skeet" deodorant and "Love Drops" perfume, was the belle of the ball. One boy even told her, in English, that she was "the prettiest girl in the room." In contrast, no one even noticed Lena.[48] More directly than some other skin lightener ads, Alexander's expressed an aversion to "black" complexions, a sentiment that was seemingly more common in the Sesotho- and Setswana-speaking areas from which he hailed than in the largely Zulu-speaking province where he lived. Alexander further pushed the boundaries of skin lightener marketing by hailing men and women, both young and old. In comparison with contemporary white manufacturers, Alexander imagined a broader market for his skin lighteners.

Color Consciousness

Whereas ads provide insight into the contours of the trade, other kinds of sources reveal what motivated specific consumers. In the correspondence discussed in the introduction, Zilpah Skota explained that she used Karroo to fade skin tanned through outdoor work.[49] Similarly, in Belinda Bozzoli's history of labor migrancy, *Women of Phokeng*, one interviewee, Mrs. Mokale, recalled that being out of the sun was one of the positive aspects of working in white households during the 1920s and 1930s: "what we liked about being indoors was . . . our complexion lightened and turned very beautiful."[50] These remarks suggest how some women grew to associate urban life and its related forms of indoor labor with lighter skin. Whereas, in rural areas, the only extended periods that most girls and women spent free from outdoor labor were during initiation, premarital or postpartum seclusion, in cities, working inside buildings protected their skin from the sun's darkening and roughening effects.

Such sun-induced differences in skin color could be rendered in racial terms. In her book on beauty culture, Nakedi Ribane, a former South African model and fashion journalist, recounts the practice of brides-to-be in Sepedi-, Setswana-, and Sesotho-speaking areas remaining indoors for several days to avoid "the harsh rays of the sun" and develop a "radiant look." On their wedding day, well-wishers would then sing, "Come out and behold, the bride is so pretty she looks Coloured!" Ribane notes that in post-apartheid South Africa, where people became more self-conscious of employing the old regime's racial schema, singers sometimes stumbled on the last word and replaced "Coloured" with "*naledi*," meaning star.[51] By comparing the lightened and clarified skin of a bride to that of a Coloured person, earlier well-wishers yoked beauty ideals of brightness and lightness to a racial classification. In doing so, they evoked not only the lighter skin tones associated with this classification but also its more privileged social, economic, and political status.

By 1941, when Zilpah Skota requested a jar of Karroo, those classified as Coloured, especially in urban areas, possessed significant material advantages over those recognized as African. They were not subject to pass laws and curfews that restricted mobility. The 1923 Native Urban Areas Act, which gave municipal authorities enhanced power to restrict African migration and deport those deemed "idle and undesirable," did not apply to Coloureds. Moreover, they generally garnered higher salaries, had access to superior housing and social services, and exerted more influence in national politics. Whereas the South African parliament eviscerated Africans' limited voting rights in 1936, Coloureds possessed a qualified franchise that allowed for direct representation for twenty more years. In the Western Cape, where the Coloured population was the largest and carried the most political clout, employers and unions frequently barred Africans from semiskilled positions, reserving them for Coloureds.[52] During the 1930s and 1940s, such advantages encouraged some classified as African to pass, whether officially or unofficially, for Coloured. The 1936 Native Representation Act, the very law that whittled away African voting rights, stipulated that well-educated "natives" could obtain the franchise by petitioning for "promotion" to "Coloured."[53] Although very few Africans pursued such legal channels, they could pursue some of the advantages of looking Coloured by cultivating a paler appearance.

Segregation's hierarchy of racial privilege also encouraged some classified as Coloured to pass for white and many others to valorize white attributes. Up until at least the early twentieth century, the racial boundary between Coloured and white in the Cape was somewhat permeable; those with wealth, skills, and more European-looking features were generally accepted as white. Liberal observers estimated, in the 1930s, that given the country's long history of European colonization and sexual relations across color lines, more than one-quarter of those classified as white were, in fact, of "mixed blood."[54] Those classified as white enjoyed access to better jobs, housing, and schools. With such marked advantages in mind, one South African writer pointedly defined "Coloured" as any person who "failed to pass as a White."[55]

Within Coloured communities, people with the highest status frequently possessed lighter skin and less curly hair, spoke English over Dutch or Afrikaans, and embraced practices deemed Western and bourgeois. In 1920, one commentator described such intra-Coloured social distinctions as "white-mindedness."[56] An article published around the same time in the A.P.O., the newspaper of the main Coloured political body, the African People's Organization, contested this mind-set. The author implored Coloured women to foster "race pride" by first combating prejudice in their own homes: "Do not let us be loud in our condemnation of the European policy of prejudice and insolent pride and at the same time teach our children that lightness of colour, regularity of features, texture of hair, have special values of their own, and allow these physical accidents to influence our affections for our children."[57] Such pleas suggest the intimate and heart-wrenching effects of color consciousness.

During the 1930s, the Coloured press included debates over beauty and racial respectability that were similar to those in *Bantu World*. One reader, Henry C. A. Cloete, wrote a letter to the *Sun* in 1934 complaining of young women who wore scanty clothing. He blamed this and other unsuitable trends in "modern fashion" on racial mimicry facilitated by domestic service: "Our girls, especially those in domestic employment, are apt to copy their mistresses, and it is from their mistresses that they have copied the art of powdering, painting and smoking."[58] Readers rebuked Cloete by insisting that such practices were simply part of being "modern" and not the preserve of any particular race or class. Two domestic servants pointed out that "factory girls" also frequently wore makeup and smoked cigarettes while a male reader observed that women's magazines regularly featured such commodities.[59] Responding to these rebukes, Cloete argued that such "modern" practices looked strikingly "primitive." He joked that dancers of the Charleston looked like "first class Zulu warrior[s]" and that some white mistresses copied their makeup practices from "the Native races who smeared their faces with red stone."[60] Cloete insisted on the absurdity of white and Coloured women flirting with African practices.

Concerns over respectability also surfaced in relation to an early Coloured beauty pageant. The *Cape Standard*, another weekly newspaper published in Cape Town, reported in late 1936 on difficulties that organizers faced in recruiting beauty contestants for the "Western Province Pageant Sports Meeting" to be held over the New Year's holiday. In contrast to the *Bantu World* competition that simply required entrants to submit portrait photographs, this one entailed a public appearance, something that caused concern among parents who sought to safeguard their daughters' reputations. Eventually, the event organizers succeeded in securing entrants, including a young woman from Kimberley, Miss Hazel Kensley, described as possessing "good looks and figure" as well as a "pleasing singing voice and a flair for classic dancing."[61] By considering competitors' talents, these organizers, like those who sponsored similar contests in the United States and elsewhere, sought to allay criticisms that they promoted a superficial conception of beauty. Mention of Kensley's figure, however, likely only confirmed some readers' suspicions about the titillating intent of such events.

Discussion of beauty and racial respectability in the Coloured press frequently entailed talk of skin color and hair texture. A 1940 article, which enumerated and criticized the "economic and moral" reasons why some Coloureds chose to pass for white, opined: "In the eyes of very many Coloured people the fairness of the skin conferred on the bearer both beauty and the right to be respected." The author further argued that this valorization of light colored skin was so deep-seated that, for most people, it operated on a "subconscious" level.[62] Expressing similar sentiments, editorials and letters to the editor called for a positive "race consciousness" among Coloureds. They derided those with "lily-white" complexions who passed for European or discriminated against those with darker skin and hair that was not straight like a "horsetail" (*perdestert* in Afrikaans).[63] Turning the language of respectability on its head, one letter writer explained that such prejudice caused young men to lose respect for their elders. He gave the example of parents of "long-haired daughters" who refused to allow "young men of woolly hair" to befriend them, explaining that when such men politely asked for permission, they faced "blunt refusal[s]" and often "insulting remarks."[64] Within the relatively progressive political sphere of Coloured newspapers, intra-Coloured prejudice was indefensible. Yet the presence, on some of the very same pages, of ads for skin lighteners and hair straighteners demonstrates that sellers remained confident of their products' appeal.

Tanning's Allure

At the same time that manufacturers and sellers increasingly targeted black South African consumers, skin lighteners were becoming less popular with white consumers. This decline stemmed, in large part, from the newfound appeal of tanning. In 1903, a Danish physician won the Nobel Prize in Medicine for demonstrating that ultraviolet light was beneficial for tuberculosis patients. This recognition spurred the establishment of sanatoria in warm, dry climates and contributed to medical experts' growing enthusiasm for heliotherapy— sun treatment—as a cure for other ailments including rickets and lupus, and an overall boon for mental and physical well-being.[65] By the mid-1920s, for example, a school in Natal required "daily sun-baths" for all students recovering from malaria, pneumonia, and other ailments.[66] In the name of health, people in a wide range of locales took up sunbathing as well as outdoor activities such as swimming, golf, and tennis. This embrace of sunshine and sports dovetailed with eugenicist efforts to improve the "fitness" of racially defined populations as well as the emergence of new forms of femininity, personified by the "New Woman" and, later, the modern girl, that promoted athleticism and a passion for the outdoors.

These trends began to reverse the enduring association in Europe and the United States of pale, white skin with elite status. For many urban white women and men, tanned skin became a badge of health and fitness. It also became a beauty attribute, and an expression of class and racial privilege. By the 1930s, pale skin, especially during the summer months, signaled someone who was sickly or confined to long hours of factory or office work whereas tanned skin signaled someone who was fit, attractive, and had the luxury of spending holidays at the beach or afternoons on the tennis court. From socialites like Coco Chanel sunning herself in the South of France to working-class young men and women flocking to Coney Island and Cape Town's beaches on summer weekends, temporarily darkened skin became a prized achievement.[67]

White South Africans' embrace of tanning and outdoor leisure is chronicled in the pages of *South African Pictorial: Stage and Cinema*, a weekly illustrated magazine. Whereas the U.S. press often reported tanning as a fad that Americans copied from upper-class Europeans, *South African Pictorial* placed the United States and specifically California at the trend's epicenter. A 1917 issue featured a photograph of sunbathers with the caption "wealthy and fashionable Americans at Palm Beach."[68] A few years later, the magazine launched a "bathing beauty contest," sponsored by the U.S. film and camera company Kodak. Through this competition, Kodak promoted its "Brownie" snapshot cameras as the best way to capture active and tanned bodies. To show what a Brownie could do, the magazine published photos of sunbathing Hollywood stars.[69] Subsequent issues featured dozens of snapshots, submitted by readers from across southern Africa, of people sunbathing and swimming. Few of those photographed wore hats or carried parasols; most posed in full view of the sun.[70]

Contemporary beauty advice columns and toiletry marketing also reflect the rise of tanning among white South African women. A 1925 column in the *South African Lady's Pictorial and Home Journal* offered advice on how to avoid the reddening and damaging effects of sunburn while acknowledging, "it looks very nice to be burnt to a deep tan."[71] In a marketing survey conducted a few years later for the U.S. manufacturer of a skin ointment, the South African office of J. Walter Thompson explained that climatically the country was "comparable to Arizona, California, and Texas" and that sunburn was common, especially among city dwellers who enjoyed coastal resorts during summer months.[72] Amid tanned skin's newfound popularity, skin lightener manufacturers sought to remain relevant by touting their products' ability to reduce the roughening results of sunburn and windburn (see figure 1.3). Karroo explained that its cream could vanquish the freckles caused by "excessive sunburns" (see figure 3.3) while Keppels promoted its products as a defense against South Africa's climate that "ravages complexion."[73] The appeal of skin lighteners for white consumers no longer stemmed from preserving a refined, pale complexion but removing the marring effects of outdoor leisure.

Discussion in the U.S. press about tanning occasionally pointed to the racial politics of this increasingly international practice. By the late 1920s, articles in trade journals declared that the "tan fad" was here to stay. A piece that appeared in *Advertising and Selling* likened young women's embrace of tanned skin and colorful makeup to members of "savage tribes" who painted and distorted their faces to "indicate relative position."[74] Similarly, another in *Printers' Ink Monthly* mockingly suggested how the trend unsettled racial distinctions: "[Flappers] flocked to the beaches day after day in bathing suits as close to the ultimate zero as was permitted...and return[ed] to their Northern and Eastern haunts to display an expanse of deeply tanned skin that would arouse the envy of an Indian."[75] According to these authors, modern girls challenged the boundaries of "civilized" and respectable femininity. Yet racial privilege ensured that they remained white even when they darkened their skin.[76] Contemporary developments in filmmaking further encouraged young women to cultivate darker, "exotic" skin tones. With the rise of Technicolor films, Hollywood combined forces with cosmetics companies, most notably Max Factor, to highlight the new technology's advantages through using a fuller palette of face makeup. "Colorful" ethnic beauties, including Rita Hayworth, Dolores Del Rio, and Anna May Wong, became film stars while fair actresses like Joan Crawford, Joan Bennett, and Marlene Dietrich were made more exotic and alluring through dark-hued cosmetics and tans.[77]

Beauty advice columns and skin lightener ads that cast tanning as a seasonal fashion also situated white women's skin color as a matter of consumer choice. Throughout the interwar period, beauty columnists in major U.S. publications like the *Washington Post* and *Vogue* advised women to cultivate moderate tans over the summer or while on holiday but to remove them soon after.[78] Seeking to maintain their products' relevance, skin lightener manufacturers seconded this advice with slogans such as "vacation is over—off with the tan" or "bleach your way to autumn beauty."[79] Letters written to *Hygeia*, the consumer health magazine of the American Medical Association, and to the U.S. Food and Drug Administration (FDA) reveal that not all women were as sanguine about either removing tans or the stability of their racial identities. In the mid-1920s, two women wrote to *Hygeia* explaining that they had lived for a number of years in "tropical" countries where they had become "very tanned" and "unusually dark." They requested advice on how to regain their "natural complexion[s]" before returning to the United States. Although one knew of "patent preparations" used by "Negroes," she was reluctant to try them as she was unsure of their ingredients.[80] About fifteen years later, a desperate woman holed up in Chicago sent the following plea to the FDA: "Will you please tell me how I can take the skin off my neck, hands and arms? I have a tan that is terrible that I got in Phoenix and Los Angeles. I have used Drug Store bleaches for six months and now want to take the skin off as that is the only way to get this tan off. My home is Washington, D.C. and I can't come back black. Do let me hear from you."[81] The FDA officials joked among themselves about the woman's "true" color before advising her to see a physician. What was deemed an acceptable shade of tan varied not just seasonally but between countries and across regions of the United States. For some, like this woman, the palpable fear of being taken for "Negro" under Jim Crow spurred her search for an effective skin lightener.

Commentators in the African American press also took note of the fad for tanning, frequently comparing it in jest with skin lightening. Articles published in a number of black papers in 1929 identified Europe as the source of the trend. Observing that much money had already been spent on trying to change "colored skins to white," a short piece in the Baltimore *Afro-American* hailed tanning as "another kind of assault on the color line."[82] A satirical piece in the *New York Amsterdam News*, commenting on a German scientist's recent claim to have developed a pill that could turn black people white, chided the trend of American men and women bathing on beaches and taking "great pride in seeing just how near to colored people they can become."[83] Also with a bemused tone, a *Chicago Defender* columnist pointed to the absurd appearances created by a white girl darkening her face with a "sun-tan" colored powder but leaving her ears and neck untouched, and a "colored girl" lightening her face and ignoring the same.[84]

The tanning fad did not diminish the prevalence of skin lightener ads in the African American press but it did influence their messages. In the mid-1920s, the Madam C. J. Walker company launched its first skin lightener, Tan-Off. With this name, the company alluded to the increasingly popular pastime and cast black women's use of these products in a less racialized idiom. Through exhortations to "enjoy this summer's sunshine" and figures of young women swimming, boating, and playing tennis and golf, Tan-Off ads situated African American young women as modern girls and acknowledged that outdoor activities could darken brown as well as ivory skin. Fan Tan, one of the most heavily marketed skin lighteners in the 1930s, also related skin color to sun exposure rather than racial categories, promising that one's tone could be easily adjusted. With resulting shades described as "Sun-Brown," "Spanish," and "Ivory White," Fan Tan ads situated black women's desire for lighter skin outside of the racial binary of white and black by evoking the contemporary craze for tanning and a more cosmopolitan color palette.[85]

FIGURE 3.7. Marketed to African Americans, this skin lightener—Fan Tan—played off the new fad for tanning. Its pitch emphasized the diversity and malleability of skin tones. *Baltimore Afro-American*, October 1929.

The sparse discussion of tanning in South Africa's black press makes it more difficult to discern the practice's racial politics there. A 1938 beauty advice column for "holiday-makers" that appeared in *Cape Standard* offered the same counsel found in contemporary white newspapers: tans should be cultivated gradually to avoid damaging sunburn.[86] Some of the paper's Coloured readership likely embraced seasonal tanning as part of outdoor leisure. Yet skin lightener ads continued to encourage consumers to remove tans, and some consumers, like Zilpah Skota, clearly agreed with that advice.[87]

As tanning took root during the 1930s, the marketing of skin lighteners to white consumers in both South Africa and the United States declined while the promotion of sunning products took off. In 1931, the New York office of J. Walter Thompson compiled a list, focused mainly on the white cosmetics market, of over two hundred "skin bleaches" manufactured in the United States. Although the length of this list attests to skin lighteners' status as commonplace cosmetics, the accompanying report chronicled their plummeting popularity. According to trade sources, sales of Mercolized Wax were "small and declining."[88] Similarly, a 1934 handbook for cosmetic manufacturers explained that "bleaching creams are not as popular as they once were when people favored lily white complexions instead of the outdoor tan which has won current favor."[89] For the remainder of the decade, cosmetic companies and their marketers spent considerable energy responding to the trend for "color" by developing sunburn preparations, suntan lotions, and tinted powders and foundations.[90] Sunbathing had become a favorite pastime for many white people, a development whose commercial consequences were quickly felt. Sunbathing's most serious health consequence—increased risk for skin cancer—did not garner significant popular attention until the 1970s.[91]

SKIN LIGHTENERS BECAME a lucrative product for South African manufacturers like Karroo and Bu-Tone during the 1930s and 1940s. After earlier efforts to target white consumers floundered, pharmacists realized that locally made cosmetics and especially skin lighteners held considerable appeal among some Coloured and African consumers, a clientele less able to afford costly imports. The roots of apartheid South Africa's skin lighteners boom—the subject of the next chapter—lay in that realization and the ongoing racialization of aesthetic ideals.

Segregation's social and political inequities produced visual sensibilities attuned to even slight differences in skin color. Yet peoples' use of skin lighteners focused less on movement across official racial boundaries than on nuanced gradations within them. Skota's letter, Alexander's ads, and discussions in the Coloured press all reveal subtle yet deeply felt distinctions in skin color and tone. Through avoiding sun exposure and using skin lighteners, people sought to cultivate "bright," "lovable," and smooth complexions that would signal their escape from outdoor labor and their attainment of modern femininity and, possibly, urbane masculinity. Such distinctions cast the body's surface as a site for attracting favorable attention and expressing gendered forms of racial respectability. Not all accepted this logic. Progressive contributors to the Coloured press, from the 1920s through the 1940s, denounced the insidious favoring of lighter skin and straighter hair within families and communities, and instead called for a positive "race consciousness." Other expressions of this sentiment never made it into print. In 1947, a South Africa literary journal rejected a poem submitted by Marie Kathleen Jeffreys, a Cape Town archivist and writer, entitled "Though I Am Black, I Am Comely."[92]

The tanning fad inspired jokes and also raised questions about the stability of racial categories. Initially prescribed as a health aid, sunbathing grew into a leisure activity and another sign of white privilege. Writers in both the mainstream U.S. and African American press greeted the tanning craze with gibes about formerly pale-skinned flappers being mistaken for members of "savage tribes." Humor also pervaded writing that equated tanning with skin lightening. African American columnists first penned such equations in the late 1920s, pointing to the absurdity of white people trying to look "colored" while "colored" people tried to look white. In subsequent decades, as we shall see, others in the United States and South Africa teasingly cast tanning and skin lightening as racially inverted but equivalent practices. The crux of all these jokes lay in the visceral recognition that while surface appearances might be malleable, the politics of race were much more durable.

Four

BEAUTY QUEENS
AND CONSUMER CAPITALISM

Between the late 1940s and mid-1970s, commercial skin lighteners became a ubiquitous part of South African popular culture. Bu-Tone advertisements framed the masthead of *Bantu World.* Newly established photo magazines like *Zonk!, Drum,* and *Bona* carried five or more such ads per issue, making skin lightening synonymous with cover-girl glamour and the magazines' beauty contests. Glitzy commercials for skin lighteners played in cinemas and in promotional spots on radio. Pharmacists ranked them among their best-selling personal care products.[1] A marketing survey reported that over 60 percent of urban African women used bleaching/lightening creams, making them one of the most commonly purchased household goods.[2] Miriam Makeba, the South African singer who rose to international fame in the 1960s, recalled growing up inundated by messages that equated beauty and success with lightness and whiteness.[3]

South Africa's skin lightener boom coincided with the elaboration of apartheid rule. With greater political will and institutional muscle than prior governments, the National Party sought to ensure that racial designations structured all aspects of everyday life. This included determining where one could reside, attend school, and work, and with whom one could socialize, marry, and share a family. One of a battery of apartheid laws, the Separate Amenities Act of 1953 introduced "petty apartheid," strengthening the state's ability to segregate public facilities ranging from parks, graveyards, and beaches to restaurants, hospitals, and drive-in cinema parking spaces.[4] Skin color, as one highly visible marker of race, loomed large in this world where whiteness was synonymous with power and privilege, and small differences in appearance could carry significant consequences. Skin lightener ads reinforced this racialized reality by

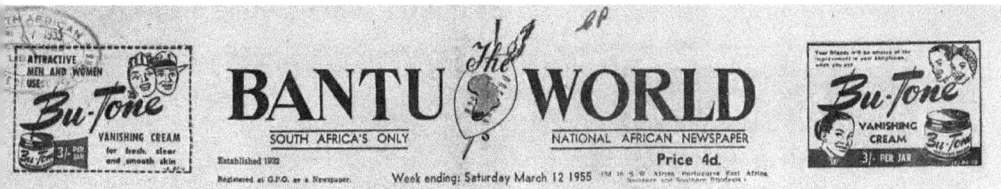

FIGURE 4.1. By the 1950s, skin lightener ads featured prominently in the black South African press. *Bantu World* sometimes carried three on its front page alone with two, like this, framing the masthead. *Bantu World*, March 1955. Cropped image reproduced with permission courtesy of Bantu World Newspaper Digitized Collection, Historical Papers Research Archive, the Library, University of Witwatersrand, Johannesburg.

FIGURE 4.2. Skin lightener manufacturers sponsored the photo magazines' beauty contests with the winners then becoming spokesmodels and cover girls. *Zonk!*, January 1955. Courtesy of the Library of Congress, LC-DDSO-9859.

drawing heightened attention to bodily surfaces. In hindsight, the ads' promises of happiness, glamour, and fame seem at odds with apartheid's tightening of political control.[5] Their affective tone, however, was very much in keeping with consumer capitalism's aspirational essence.

The popularity of skin lighteners in early apartheid South Africa is a revealing episode in the history of consumer capitalism. In *Advertising the American Dream* (1985), one of the first cultural histories of advertising, Roland Marchand used the concept "social fantasy" to denote what historians can learn from the idealized images of class privilege featured in mid-twentieth-century U.S. advertisements. Marchand argued that ads reveal a great deal about "social fantasies" if not "social realities."[6] This chapter expands Marchand's conception by exploring social fantasies of race and gender as well as class, and by considering how such fantasies circulated, within and beyond advertisements, in a context of emerging consumer capitalism. The mass production and purchase of consumer goods was vital to South Africa's postwar economic growth. Numerous businesspeople staked their financial future to extending consumer markets across the country's racial divides and geopolitical borders. Such economic ambitions often ran headlong into the state's political vision of racial separation. It was amid these varied and, at times, conflicting social fantasies that apartheid's skin lightener trade flourished.

Black Markets

World War II spurred profound social and economic changes in southern Africa as elsewhere. Wartime production demands and the enlistment of many white workers in the armed forces prompted the government to relax pass laws. This encouraged greater numbers of Africans to move to urban areas where many filled manufacturing positions that demanded a better trained and more stable labor force. Between 1921 and 1959, the country's black urban population grew dramatically from 750,000 to 3.1 million. Living in areas that ranged from makeshift slumyards to middle-class townships, Africans became a more visible and vocal presence in South Africa's cities. During the 1948 election campaign, the right-wing National Party pointed to an increasingly urbanized black population as justification for its policies of racial separation or apartheid. Although opposition to black urbanization helped ensure the National Party's narrow electoral victory, it placed party ideology at odds with the labor needs and market ambitions of a key sector of the economy. By the end of World War II, manufacturing had surpassed mining and agriculture as the single greatest contributor to South Africa's gross domestic product. Continued growth of the country's capitalist economy, many liberal observers argued, depended on expanding African markets for locally produced goods.[7]

White advertising men and owners of the black commercial press ranked among the most outspoken proponents of African markets. In 1945, South Africa's oldest advertising and marketing journal, *Selling*, began highlighting the economic potential of black consumers.[8] Pushing the argument further, its competitor *Selling Age*, under the editorship of outspoken liberal Ralph Horwitz, insisted that the future of South African capitalism depended on increasing black consumption.[9] Bantu Press, with a pamphlet entitled *Black Gold!*, similarly urged white companies to tap the buying power of black southern Africans—estimated in 1945 at £57,000,000 per year—by advertising in their newspapers and magazines. They emphasized the scale of African purchases ranging from groceries, clothing, and farm tools to cigarettes, used cars, and beauty preparations.[10] Assuring potential advertisers of the proximity of this market, Bantu Press noted a prominent feature of South Africa's racialized consumer culture: many Africans possessed intimate knowledge about commercial products from working as domestic servants in white households.[11]

Domestic work was especially vital in gaining knowledge of toiletries and cosmetics. By 1960, one out of every two Coloured women and three out of five African women in a "gainful occupation" were domestic workers.[12] Such work provided African girls and women with unparalleled knowledge of and, in some cases, access to diverse consumer products.[13] Describing domestic workers' backyard living quarters, one social scientist observed that cosmetics, together with radios, took "pride of place." For workers from rural areas, their "cosmetic universes expanded greatly upon their arrival in the city" where they encountered more ads and "took cues from their madams' dressing tables."[14] More so than other consumer products, cosmetics provided domestic workers the rare opportunity to indulge their own needs and appearances rather than those of their employers or their own families.

Postwar optimism about the potential of African markets surged in 1959, the year before the Sharpeville massacre prompted international condemnation of the apartheid government and the banning of internal opposition groups including the African National Congress and Pan-Africanist Congress. In June of that year, *Selling Age* teamed up with reporters from *Drum* to profile the consumer habits of the African middle class. Noting that the African population now possessed a 30 percent literacy rate and an annual purchasing power of £400 million, the article described how well-off Africans enjoyed consumer lives that looked a lot like those of whites. It listed the expenditures of a married couple who had recently acquired a five-room house through a government scheme, documenting how their purchases included costly furniture, psychology books and jazz albums, and burglar proofing for their windows.[15]

A national advertising conference held the same year also devoted substantial attention to African consumers. The conference heard a paper from Dr. Werner W. M. Eiselen, who was unable to attend. As the secretary of Bantu administration and development, Eiselen was one of the chief architects of apartheid policy. His paper emphasized the increasing purchasing power of Africans, especially future homeland residents, and Africans' preference for advertising in vernacular languages.[16] The head of the African market division of J. Walter Thompson, Nimrod Mkele, spoke immediately after Eiselen's presentation and challenged some of his key points. Mkele was the most senior black marketing agent in South Africa at the time. He had a master's degree in psychology and was familiar with anthropology. As an undergraduate at Fort Hare, Mkele had coauthored and published a study of an African separatist church.[17] At the conference in 1959, he evocatively referred to the contemporary moment as the "advertisers' scramble for Africa." Mkele shared Eiselen's optimism about the African consumer market, singling out women as "the vanguard of progressive ideas." Yet he contradicted Eiselen by noting that the African market was growing "in spite of low wages" and that urban rather than rural residents possessed greater purchasing power. Moreover, explaining that no African-language equivalents existed for English words such as "face powder" and "face cream," Mkele insisted that Africans preferred English ads as the copy read as "less artificial and stilted." He concluded his presentation by declaring, "The African first and foremost wants to be Westernised."[18] This integrationist sentiment, while exaggerating the unanimity of black opinion for his nearly all-white audience, directly challenged apartheid's social fantasy of entrenched cultural differences.

Mkele insisted that African women with even modest incomes were avid consumers of cosmetics. To illustrate, he listed the twenty-three cosmetic and toiletry products—including one skin lightener, Bu-Tone—found on the dressing table of a domestic worker in Johannesburg.[19] Eighty percent of urban African women, Mkele reported, used face creams while 30 percent used face powder. According to both Mkele and Eiselen, Africans were discerning consumers and concerned with more than just price.[20] Although African women purchased locally produced cosmetics, they, like their white counterparts, avoided products regarded as cheap due to concerns about poor quality and "prestige-value." Mkele explained that in the case of one inexpensive face cream deemed of good quality, women would buy it and then place it in "more prestige-bearing containers."[21] Low salaries prevented most African women from owning and furnishing middle-class homes. That did not, however, prevent them from pampering themselves by purchasing a local face cream and repackaging it into a fancier form.

During the 1950s, many black consumers continued to purchase skin lighteners and other cosmetics directly from pharmacists. *South African Retail Chemist* ran articles and ads announcing the release of new skin lighteners and encouraged chemists to anticipate demand by stocking up.[22] In this period too, pharmacists began to face new competition from large retail chains like Checkers and Pick n Pay that offered cosmetics at discounted prices.[23] Black consumers frequently purchased cosmetics at shops also patronized by white consumers. At pharmacies in and around Johannesburg, white shoppers encountered prominent displays of skin lighteners targeting black consumers.[24] In his 1959 address, Mkele emphasized that although some shops located in rural towns might still serve blacks at "separate counters and through holes-in-the-wall," in larger towns and cities most shops accepted the African "as a customer against whom it is not good business to discriminate."[25] Black urban consumers preferred white stores because their prices were generally lower than those charged at smaller township shops that experienced slow turnover and little competition.[26] Moreover, white stores assured black consumers access to the same quality of goods. A survey from the late 1960s found that Africans purchased more than 40 percent of their cosmetics in the central business districts of cities and towns.[27]

The remainder were purchased in township shops or trading stores. Don Vaphi recalled that in the 1960s his aunt's trading store in Langa, the oldest African township in Cape Town, sold skin lighteners alongside a very wide range of products, including groceries, medicines, clothes, blankets, hardware, and toiletries. In line with older forms of retail organization, customers requested products from a clerk standing behind a counter. Vaphi and his wife, Leticia, explained that customers would often hear about new brands of skin lighteners on the radio and then would come to the shop to buy and "test themselves." According to Mrs. Vaphi, people wanted to make themselves "look more beautiful" in preparation for weekend parties they attended in the township. Her husband noted that skin lighteners and other cosmetics were good sellers, especially just before the December holidays. People would buy large quantities to take home to the Eastern Cape where they would give them as presents or resell them in small towns or rural communities at still higher prices.[28] Through such trading networks, skin lightener sales extended from cities to the country's far corners.

As in earlier decades, multiple desires prompted consumers to purchase skin lighteners. In apartheid South Africa where even small distinctions in skin color could open or foreclose a range of opportunities, cosmetics could help those with racially ambiguous appearances pass for a paler and more privileged racial designation. Apartheid laws like the Population Registration Act of 1950, aimed at clarifying and hardening the country's racial distinctions, drew renewed attention to passing. The progressive Coloured press highlighted the absurdity of these laws by noting that many with Coloured origins successfully "masqueraded" as Europeans.[29] In a witty article entitled "Playing White," journalists George Manuel and Gerard Van de Haer pointed to the "heavy disguise of cream and powder" as a common element of the masquerade. They also noted that it was easier to be a "Pass-for-White" in Johannesburg than in the Cape Province, where Coloureds were "very numerous and easily recognized" by all.[30] Another Coloured leader described how many with "fair skin" had become "'play-white' ... [and then] permanently 'White'" to improve prospects in "jobs, admission to places of entertainment, membership of sports clubs, residence and even marriage."[31] Others adjusted their appearances to secure jobs at stores and offices that advertised for "'slightly Coloured' girls."[32] In turn, some classified as Africans, notably in the Western Cape, sought to claim the privileges of being Coloured that, by the 1950s, included official hiring preferences. Africans "passing for Coloured," according to one historian, took place on a "wide scale."[33]

Some people with racially ambiguous appearances sought official reclassification. Among the nearly four thousand cases filed with South Africa's Race Classification Appeal Boards by 1964, one-third involved "Coloureds" requesting reclassification as "white" while the remaining two-thirds entailed "Bantu" seeking the status of "Coloured." In her analysis of these cases, Deborah Posel highlights two remarkable facts: over 70 percent of the appeals were successful, and the few thousand appeal cases represented a tiny fraction of the country's total population of nearly twenty million, suggesting that the state's racial classifications resonated closely with people's "common sense."[34] Although skin color was perhaps the most discussed marker of race in apartheid South Africa, it was never read in isolation from other bodily features and social facts. When seeking to determine "race," both officials and laypeople also considered a person's facial physiognomy, hair texture, language fluency and accent, bodily comportment, residence, and known associates. To pass, one had to ensure that a composite of these features and facts—not just skin color—accorded with the claimed classification.[35] Beginning in the late 1960s, Posel explains, apartheid officials began to place greater emphasis on social facts than physical appearances by requiring that a person's racial classification follow that of his or her parents; when parents were classified differently, the "lower" racial ranking prevailed.[36] For most people, the slight, if noticeable, changes in tone that skin lighteners provided would have been insufficient to catapult them from one official racial designation to another.

When explaining why skin lighteners were so popular under apartheid, instrumental reasons of passing or racial reclassification are outweighed by the pervasive sentiment that skin lighteners improved people's appearances. This, of course, was the social fantasy promoted in ads: lighteners would make one beautiful, glamorous, and modern.[37] Beauty-advice columnists also recommended lighteners for treating acne, fading dark spots, and making "deep tribal marks" less conspicuous.[38] As before, skin lighteners easily slid between use as cosmetics and medicines. Columnists linked pimply and "dull" skin to various health problems, including inadequate diet, constipation, and "impure blood."[39] South Africans, like people in so many other times and places, viewed the skin's appearance as evidence of one's overall health and vitality, providing people with more reasons to purchase products that promised to clarify as well as lighten.

Apartheid's carefully graded social order further heightened attention to surface appearances. Writing in the early 1960s, the anthropologist Leo Kuper noted that the modest incomes of even the "African bourgeoisie" left them with few opportunities for "conspicuous consumption." This situation, combined with the omnipresent "wealth of the White man," Kuper argued, encouraged some black people to imbue even "minor differences" with social significance.[40] Such attention could quickly turn to scrutiny and shame. A fictional account—based on real events—of growing up Coloured during the 1960s features skin lightening as a Sunday ritual, and a formative and painful episode in coming to racial awareness: an aunt lathered the brand Ambi on her nieces each week in the failed hope of making them light enough to receive parts in school plays.[41] Progressive Coloured leaders criticized such skin-color "snobbery" within families and neighborhoods. Richard Van Der Ross, a leading educationalist and activist, provided heart-wrenching examples of parents who left darker children at home while taking lighter ones on public outings or sequestered them in back rooms when suitors came calling for their light brown siblings. He denounced such "colour conscious tendencies" as undermining the community's broader struggle against apartheid.[42]

Many associated skin lighteners with schoolgirls. A 1966 *South African Medical Journal* article on skin conditions in rural areas noted that "sophisticates, such as girl students," used Bu-Tone and Karroo.[43] Attending high school and college often gave girls and young women, among other privileges, access to "pocket money" from relatives and boyfriends. With that cash, schoolgirls purchased small commodities including cosmetics.[44] Joyce Molefe and her friend Notumato Tyeku, who were nursing students in the 1960s, recalled in an interview how they used skin lighteners then, even though they were "light already," because they wanted "to be yellow": "when . . . [you] come back from college, people must admire you and see that you are beautiful."[45] With their references to "light already" and "yellow," Molefe and Tyeku offered descriptions of skin color that strayed from the binary of black or white, and bore the mark of African American cultural influences. They also pointed to how skin lighteners continued to act as technologies of visibility, satisfying the desire to be seen and noticed. A woman who was a schoolgirl in the 1950s told another historian that her parents purchased lighteners for her, regarding them as an "investment in their daughter's future"; if she looked more attractive to men, they might receive a higher *lobola*, or bridewealth, when she married.[46] For some, lighter skin was a readily recognizable manifestation of the transformation and transcendence afforded by advanced schooling, a rare and coveted achievement for young black women in apartheid South Africa. Moreover, schooling, like older practices of premarital seclusion, allowed them to spend more time indoors and away from the tanning and roughening effects of outdoor labor.

The association of beauty with schooling, consumption, and lightness affirmed apartheid's class and color hierarchies. In his presentation at the 1959 advertising conference, Mkele sought to make the complex argument that although blacks had largely accepted "European standards" for measuring success and status, their use of skin lighteners did not mean they wanted to be white. He explained to his nearly all-white audience: "I know that in some of the surveys carried out on face creams, Africans have said they prefer certain creams because they made them 'light,' which might be interpreted as meaning that they want to be white. Personally, however, I do not think that would be correct, but by the word 'light' I hold they mean the improvement of the 'glow' of their skin."

With "glow," Mkele evoked the older, regional aesthetic ideal that paired lightness with brightness, and he suggested a nonracialized interpretation of skin lightening: young black women used skin lighteners to attract favorable attention rather than to appear white or Coloured. Moreover, Mkele explained, the look they desired was different from the oiled, moisturized, and shiny faces that their mothers and grandmothers sought by using petroleum jelly: "For the younger women are more interested in titivating themselves, as they put it, and in looking attractive." Both "glow" and the neologism "titivate," an apparent melding of titillate and cultivate, signaled a desire to rouse interest and convey refinement.[47] Leticia Vaphi, who worked at a trading store in Langa, explained the appeal of skin lighteners in terms very similar to those used by Mkele: "You know, if you want to be beautiful even if you just have . . . [little money], you go to buy [skin lighteners]. . . . You go outside and then people could see that you were a lady."[48]

As the size of the black consumer market grew, manufacturers and advertisers sought to gain greater knowledge of it. Between 1960 and 1970, the black share of the country's income increased from around 20 percent to between 25 and 30 percent. This increase, as Robert Ross has argued, was the result of the incremental expansion of an urban African middle class, spurred by the "welfare paternalism" of early apartheid and a rise in skilled employment positions for black workers. It was also the result of African population growth. By 1970, Africans made up 65 percent of South Africa's 19.2 million population total, rising to 67 percent of nearly 24 million by 1980. Beginning in the mid-1960s, manufacturers and advertisers funded the Bureau of Market Research (BMR), attached to the University of South Africa, and, later, the South African Advertising Research Foundation to conduct extensive surveys of black household expenditure.[49]

The BMR first introduced "lightening/face bleaching cream" as a separate cosmetic category in 1970. Although shifts in the geographic areas surveyed by the BMR make it difficult to use their studies to chart skin lightener expenditures over time, they provide useful snapshots of the market and reveal what researchers found most notable about it. For 1970, the BMR estimated total spending on skin lighteners by "non-white" households in the five major metropolitan areas—the Cape Peninsula, the Port Elizabeth/Uitenhage area, the East London area, the Durban complex, and the Pretoria/Witwatersrand/Vaal Triangle—to be 3.1 million in South African rand (R). Three-fifths of these households were classified as "Bantu." Despite having lower overall income, these households reportedly accounted for 88 percent of skin lightener expenditure while "Coloured" and "Asian" households accounted for 9 percent and 3 percent, respectively. Africans living in Johannesburg represented the largest group of skin lightener consumers, responsible for over one-quarter of all skin lighteners purchased.[50] Based on different survey data, J. Walter Thompson estimated in 1973 that 27 percent of the adult urban population—including both men and women—used skin lighteners.[51] What was more noteworthy to the researchers than the total expenditure figure was the fact that a "large number of Africans spend relatively small amounts" on skin lighteners and other personal care items, and that the amount spent per household was increasing. These trends made them "important target markets."[52] The skin lighteners market was also notable for the high level of brand consciousness. One researcher concluded, in 1966, that beauty preparations, together with patent medicines and other "pharmaceuticals," were the only products where "advertising directly to the Bantu can be presumed to have reaped rewards."[53]

Skin lighteners' commercial success largely lay in their status as relatively inexpensive luxuries that promised visible results. In 1965, the average African female domestic worker in the Witwatersrand area earned R14 in cash per month. At 50 to 86 cents per jar or tube (100 cents equal one rand), skin lighteners

And she just couldn't pass the Modern Cosmetics Swanlake room without trying them all out . . .

FIGURE 4.3. The cosmetics room at an "Ideal Homes Exhibition" in Johannesburg. Displaying its founding mission to promote local, mainly white, businesses to black consumers, *Drum* ran a sixteen-page spread on the exhibition. *Drum* (Central and East Africa edition), June 1962.

were a significant but imaginable expense. Between 1958 and 1965, wages for domestic workers nationwide rose by approximately 35 percent while the price of skin lighteners remained relatively constant, making them an increasingly affordable commodity.[54] Whereas during the 1930s, a jar cost about one week of a domestic worker's earnings, by the 1960s, it cost one day. Although *Selling Age*'s articles on the African market touted household possessions like sewing machines and radios, less expensive products were within the reach of many more consumers.[55] Acknowledging this reality, a 1962 "Ideal Homes Exhibition" for Africans featured a cosmetics display alongside rooms filled with appliances and furniture.[56] Unlike big-ticket items that remained in one's home, cosmetics affirmed consumers' self-worth while attracting favorable attention in public spaces where modest gradations in skin color carried social and political significance. By purchasing and applying skin lighteners, black women participated in the social fantasy of modern consumer citizenship and sought recognition within the bounds of apartheid's racial order.[57] New forms of media played a vital role in visualizing that recognition.

Black Media

Reaching new markets required new media. The birth of black photo magazines, tabloid newspapers, cinema, and FM radio in the post–World War II period enabled skin lighteners to become commonplace commodities. These media offered manufacturers places to promote their products. In turn, manufacturers provided publishers and broadcasters with significant advertising revenues. By the late 1960s, beauty preparations ranked as the fifth largest source of advertising revenue for black print and radio media in South Africa, and skin lighteners ranked among the most heavily promoted of those preparations.[58] Through new media, skin lighteners and pale models became a key element of black visual culture.

Businessmen and journalists active in the black press had frequently argued for the establishment of magazines for Africans. Such publications, they insisted since at least the 1930s, could serve as attractive advertising venues.[59] Against the postwar backdrop of rising black literacy rates and purchasing power, white entrepreneurs launched *Zonk!* and *Drum* in 1949 and 1951, respectively. Embodying optimism and glamour in both their form and content, these magazines used spot color on front and back covers, dramatic type, and plenty of photos. They filled their pages with contests, advice columns, and stories about cover girls, entertainers, criminals, and middle-class professionals.[60] Eiselen and Mkele agreed, at the 1959 advertising conference, that they marked a new era. Black magazines, Mkele explained, "imposed upon the advertiser an obligation to accept the African on his own definition of himself."[61] Advertisers sought to ensure that that definition included using their products.

White impresario Ike Brooks founded *Zonk!*—"The African People's Pictorial"—as an English-language monthly, modeled after successful African American photo magazines. Brooks served in World War II as a lieutenant who organized entertainment for the troops. Following the war and facing unemployment, some of the black soldiers-entertainers with whom he worked asked Brooks to organize a civilian performance group. The result was the enormously successful *Zonk!* stage show that played to an estimated countrywide

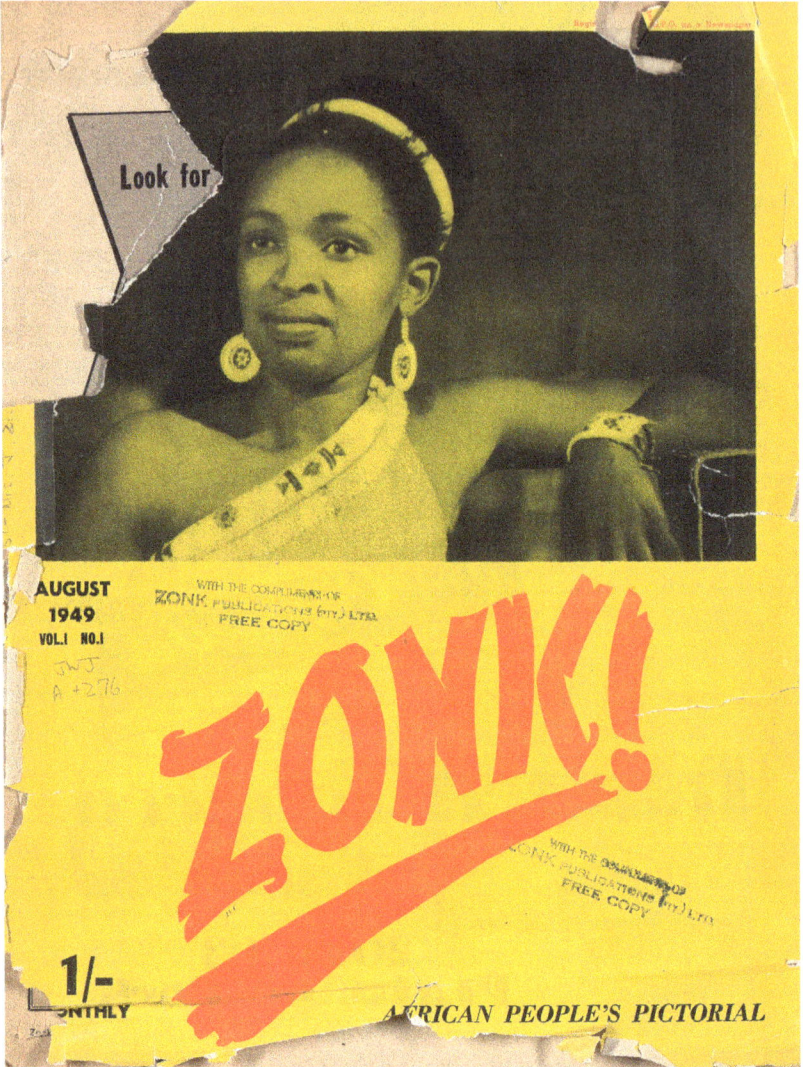

FIGURE 4.4. The inaugural cover of *Zonk!* featured Dolly Rathebe, the female star of *African Jim*, the first black South African feature film. This cover showcased a filmic aesthetic that privileged faces made pale through cosmetics, intense lighting, and other photographic techniques. *Zonk!*, August 1949. Courtesy of the Beinecke Rare Book and Manuscript Library, Yale University.

audience of 500,000, and was eventually filmed and ran for years in black cinemas. While touring, Simon Sekaphane, one of the lead *Zonk!* cast members, shared with Brooks copies of the African American magazines *Our World* and *Ebony*, suggesting that he start a local version.[62] *Zonk!* echoed *Ebony's* self-proclaimed mission of showcasing "the zesty side" of black American life.[63] *Ebony*, according to U.S historian Adam Green, gave birth to the very "concept of the black celebrity."[64] *Zonk!* followed suit, filling its pages with stories about African American achievements and images of "Negro" stars. Its 1949 inaugural issue featured a full-page photo of a light-skinned Lena Horne with a message from black America: "I extend my heartfelt greetings to the African people. I and fifteen million other American people share the same aims for a happy, prosperous and peaceful life."[65] Horne was a three-time *Ebony* cover girl and familiar to South African audiences through her leading roles in films like *Cabin in the Sky* (1943) and *Stormy Weather* (1943).[66] Earlier in her career, she had also served as the spokesmodel for a skin lightening cream.[67] Horne's presence in the first issue of *Zonk!* placed the visual imprimatur of African American success and pale black beauty on the start of black South African photo magazines. A few years later, Horne also appeared on the cover of *Drum*.

 Zonk! began in Johannesburg with capital from fifteen shareholders, all white. Brooks trained black performers from the stage show to staff the magazine as writers and photographers while whites held all the senior editorial positions. In contrast to *Bantu World*, which still targeted a small, educated elite, *Zonk!* aimed for the masses or, in the words of the historian Irwin Manoim, "the poorly educated—even illiterate—township workers [who] would appreciate pictures more than words."[68] Early issues encouraged active involvement in the magazine by holding contests and publishing readers' letters and photos. *Zonk!* declared itself as a "non-political" magazine that fostered "pride of race through pride in his own national magazine."[69] It rarely reported on anti-apartheid demonstrations and strikes organized by the African National Congress, Pan-Africanist Congress, and other opposition groups during the 1950s. As Manoim has argued, *Zonk!* represented the most politically conservative element of the black press, pretending, "during times of peace, that apartheid did not exist" and propagating, "during times of strife, that apartheid *must* exist." The magazine's political acquiescence was institutionalized in 1958 when the National Party's printing house, Afrikaanse Pers, purchased nearly all shares of the magazine.[70]

 Although *Zonk!* quickly sold out of its first twenty thousand copies, Brooks struggled to attract advertisers. Mass circulation newspapers and magazines in South Africa, as in the United States, regularly sold for below production costs and depended on advertising revenue to generate profits.[71] The editors of *Zonk!*

AMERICAN LETTER

To the African People,
With all my good wishes
Lena Horne

To the Editor of Zonk,
        It is with great pleasure that I extend my heartfelt greetings to the African people.
        I and fifteen million other American people share the same aims for a happy, prosperous and peaceful life.
                Sincerely,
                Lena Horne.

For the story of Miss Lena Horne's rise to stardom, turn to page 40.

Zonk, August, 1949

FIGURE 4.5. A letter and photo from African American film star Lena Horne congratulating *Zonk!* on its inaugural issue. Horne's pale complexion was in keeping with the vision of black beauty promoted by the magazine. *Zonk!*, August 1949. Courtesy of the Beinecke Rare Book and Manuscript Library, Yale University.

FIGURE 4.6. Lena Horne appeared on *Drum*'s cover holding an earlier issue of the magazine that featured a cover girl doubling as a spokesmodel for Karroo skin lightener on the back cover. *Drum* (West Africa edition), October 1954.

encouraged readers to patronize the magazine's advertisers.[72] The magazine lost £5,853 during its first year but, by 1955, had earned £11,523, making it the first black publication in South Africa to generate profits over an extended period. Its margins, however, were not great. As one former senior editor recalled, "*Zonk!* never made any *real* money—just enough to keep our heads above water."[73]

Skin lightener manufacturers ranked among the magazine's most prominent advertisers. Lightener ads appeared early and, by the mid-1950s, issues regularly included four or more. A study done a decade later found that only laxatives and men's clothing were advertised more frequently in photo magazines than face creams. Lightener ads, though, were generally more prominent than ads for those other products. By the mid-1960s, 70 percent of the time, they occupied the highly visible inside front cover and the back cover.[74] A sister magazine, *Hi Note*, published between 1954 and 1957 and targeted to Indian and Coloured readers, included the same ads.[75] Brands commonly advertised included Karroo and Bu-Tone, and the later upstarts Super Rose, Ambi, and Artra (see chapter 5). Ads for shorter-lived brands with wildly diverse names also littered the pages of *Zonk!*: Superskin, Sweet Sue, Sweet Dream, Glyco-Lemon, Metamorphosa, Sunco Skin-Wite, Ebony, Black Crow, Jive, Vaseline Honey-Gold, Italienne, Kamak, Tru-Glam, Desire, Parasol, and Aloma. Some names evoked glamour and transformation while others, science or nature. Skin lightener ads went hand-in-hand with the beauty contests. Manufacturers sponsored the contests while winners then became cover girls and the subject of feature stories as well as company spokesmodels (see figures 4.2, 4.10, 4.11, 4.13, and 4.14).[76]

Drum, launched two years after *Zonk!*, promoted a similar vision of black beauty. Its cover girls and beauty queens were light-colored and, by 1953, skin lightener manufacturers ranked among its most prominent advertisers. Jim Bailey (the son of a South African mining magnet) and a group of Cape Town businessmen started *Drum* with the express aim of advertising to local black consumers as well as to buyers across Africa.[77] South African interest in tapping broader African markets grew after World War II as the country's manufacturing capacity began to exceed domestic demand. Newspapers ran articles proclaiming the "danger of losing the African market" while a trade journal exclusively devoted to the topic was established.[78] *Drum* was a piece of this "pan-African" strategy. In its first year, *Drum* shipped issues to Nigeria and Ghana. Soon after, it opened offices in Lagos. By the early 1960s, these offices published West African editions while an office in Nairobi published an East African edition.[79] *Drum* became an enormous cultural influence across the

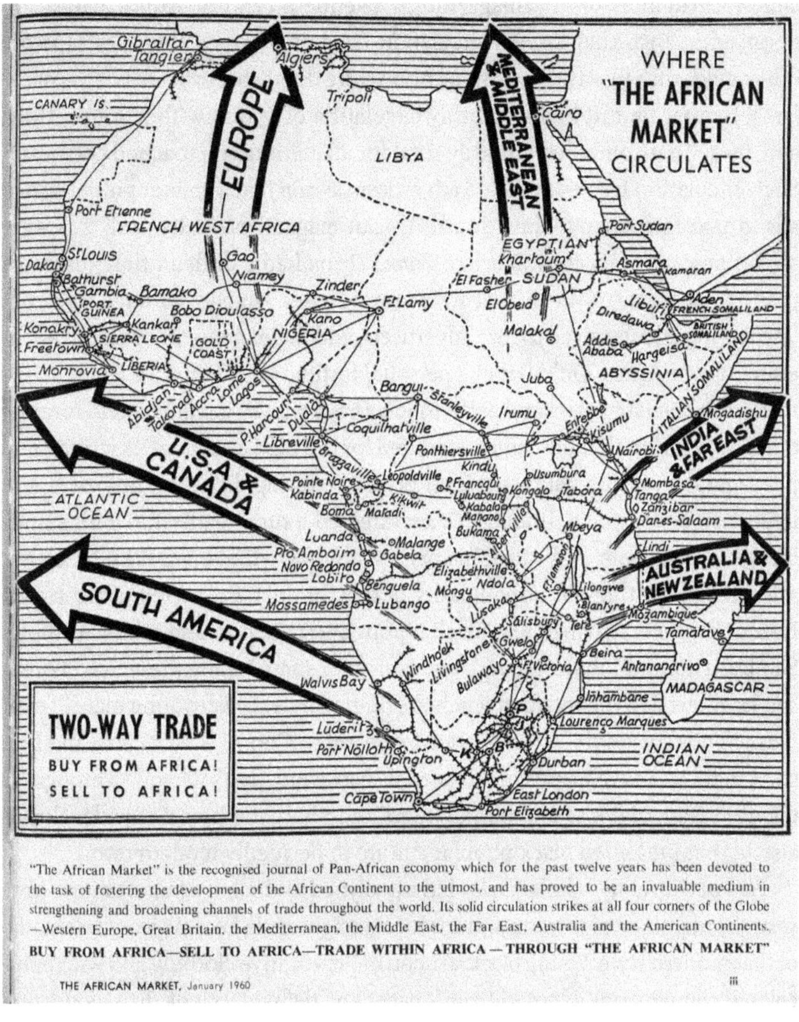

FIGURE 4.7. *The African Market*, a trade journal established in 1947, heralded the advent of a "pan-African economy" in which South African companies could sell anything from "a safety pin to a bulldozer" across the continent. This map visualizes the promise of those commercial relations. *African Market*, January 1960. Courtesy of the Library of Congress, LC-DDSO-9859.

continent. According to Nigerian writer Wole Soyinka, African readers of the era were "weaned on" *Drum*.[80]

Although *Zonk!* initially outsold *Drum*, the latter soon grew to have the largest circulation of any magazine in twentieth-century Africa. Bailey announced in 1956 that *Drum*'s circulation "had outstripped the sales of every other magazine in Africa, white or non-white, English, Afrikaans or vernacular."[81] By that time, it had a monthly circulation of 75,000 within South Africa and, by 1969, a combined monthly total for all editions approached 500,000.[82] Such circulation figures attracted advertisers. *Drum* had a greater proportion of ads to text than many white South African magazines. At its peak, ads were 50–60 percent of its copy. But like *Zonk!*, *Drum* had a difficult time turning a profit, losing £71,568 in its first four years. Losses largely stemmed from the uneconomical rates used to lure advertisers, and the expense of opening offices elsewhere in Africa. Only Bailey's personal fortune kept *Drum* afloat.[83]

During the late 1950s and early 1960s, *Drum* gained a regional and international reputation that has largely endured for the high quality of its writing and photography and its willingness, on occasion, to highlight the injustices and hypocrisy of apartheid. Initially, *Drum* targeted a rural readership with stories on elders, ancestors, and "tribal history," written by white men. With lackluster sales demonstrating the unpopularity of this formula, Bailey requested Henry Nxumalo, the magazine's first black reporter, to take him and editor Anthony Sampson around Johannesburg's townships for some "market research." Sampson later recalled the instructive rebuke offered by a stylish young man: "Tribal music! Tribal history! Chiefs! We don't care about Chiefs! Give us jazz and film stars, man! . . . You're just trying to keep us backward, that's what!"[84] Through its talented team of white and black writers and photographers, *Drum* developed a style that presented black popular culture in decidedly modern terms.

Few of the many scholars who have analyzed *Drum* have failed to note how sexualized photos of women and ads for skin lighteners became iconic elements of that modern style. Young black women in provocative clothing and with light-colored complexions adorned *Drum*'s pages and defined its look. In a pioneering critique of *Drum*'s gender politics, literary scholar Dorothy Driver interpreted the prevalence of such imagery as part of the magazine's construction of an urban patriarchy modeled after "Western" gender norms that "through a set of gestures ranging from domestication to eroticization" belittled "intelligent, active and energetic women" and reduced them to objects of male desire.[85] Building on Driver's critique, Rob Nixon described *Drum*'s Sophiatown literary milieu as "airlessly male and sometimes misogynistic": "thus the 'new' woman found herself increasingly bombarded with the trappings and standards of Western beauty, while being projected as a threat to the urban man's virility and a drain on his pocket."[86] Similarly, Christopher Ballantine has identified *Drum*'s representations of women as a response to a "crisis of masculinity" generated by apartheid policies. In the face of South Africa's migrant labor system that ravaged families, Ballantine argues, "women responded creatively, taking over the position of household heads, embarking upon a[n] era of unprecedented women's activism, and developing a fierce anger towards men for what they perceived to be their selfishness and impotence." But rather than reflecting these new gender realities, *Drum* sought to counter them by promoting a masculinity that situated men as "supremely dominant at the same moment that it handicapped and infantilized women, making them bearers of sexual allure."[87] Such analyses rightly highlight the sexist and racist politics that informed *Drum*, and they convincingly locate some of the roots of those politics in apartheid's brutality.

These analyses, however, do not fully acknowledge how the sexualized and glamorous images of women that populated *Drum*'s pages were also the product of transnational—not just local—influences and, like all prominent symbols, were open to multiple interpretations. As Joanne Meyerowitz in her study of American pin-ups has argued, "The proliferation in the mass media of sexual representations of women is, arguably, among the most significant developments in twentieth-century U.S. women's history, the history of sexuality, and the history of popular culture." And, as Meyerowitz documents, white and black American women at the time debated whether such representations were degrading or affirming: did they belittle women, or celebrate their beauty and sexuality? From its inception in 1945, *Ebony* featured scantily clad, light-colored cover girls. Some of its readers argued that cover girls and pin-ups were an anathema to black progress and respectability as they reinforced pernicious stereotypes of black women as oversexed and immoral. Others applauded them as both proof of black women's "equality in beauty" and appealing symbols of racial pride. Even those who criticized the magazine for favoring light-colored models did not necessarily reject these sexualized figures wholesale; instead, they demanded cover girls and pin-ups with darker skin tones.[88]

In Africa, too, readers frequently found such images inspiring rather than demeaning. Some readers copied the look, and magazines published photos submitted by readers of themselves posing in bathing suits.[89] A man from Tanganyika wrote a letter to *Zonk!* offering high praise for one of its 1962 cover girls: "Thank you for the April cover of the wonderful Madondo.... She ought to be in Hollywood and give stiff competition to Marilyn Monroe, Liz Taylor, and Zsa Zsa Gabor, or compete in the 'Miss World' competition."[90] In contexts where photos of black women of any kind were rarely published, full-page shots of

SHY GIRL WITH A WINNING SMILE

The search for the prettiest girl in the country, to take the Calendar Girl Contest prize, finally led the organisers — DRUM and the South African Bottlers of Coca-Cola — to Natal. In a Durban hospital they found the winner — working as a nurse — and probably the shyest beauty contest winner they had ever come across. She is 20-year-old Monhlanhla Mabaso.

"I'M sure you've got the wrong name, Nomsa would never enter a beauty contest," said the staff nurse at Durban's King Edward VIII hospital when DRUM asked for 20-year-old Nonhlanhla Mabaso to tell her she had won the Calendar Girl contest.

Nomsa, a student nurse from Northern Natal, was almost as difficult to convince that she had won the contest which was organised by DRUM and the bottlers of Coca-Cola.

Quiet and shy, she said she entered the contest just for fun and had not told her friends about it.

She must rate as one of the prettiest and yet shyest girls to win a beauty contest. She would not model in a bathing suit. "Never wore one; even if I did, I won't be photographed in one. It is not in keeping with my profession," was her frank comment.

A SHY SMILE FROM THE WINNER

But though Nomsa does not love tight-fitting jeans and natty bathing suits, she certainly loves nursing. "I derive great satisfaction from nursing and it is a profession I won't exchange for any other. I love doing something as exciting and human as nursing," she says.

Nomsa does not know what she will do with the money she won in the contest. "This has been so sudden that I can't even think. But you can be sure that whatever use I put the money to, it will not be spent foolishly," she laughed. ●

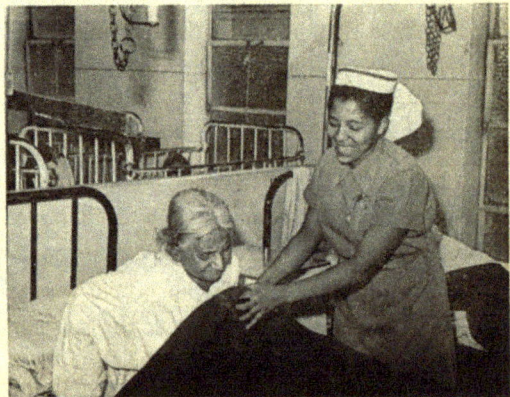

SECOND, PRETTY LILLY TSOTETSI

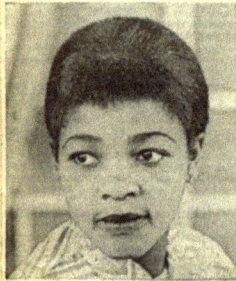

THIRD, MARIA SEUDE

"NOMSA" TENDS AN AGED PATIENT — A HAPPY SMILE ON HER FACE.

FIGURE 4.8. The second-place finisher in this "Calendar Girl Contest" struck a pin-up pose in her swimsuit while the face of the third-place finisher seems to have been lightened with cosmetics or during the photo's development process. Contest photo entries like these demonstrate how readers mimicked and engaged the photo magazines' visual aesthetics. *Drum,* September 1961.

black South African women in the same poses and clothing as American and white South African celebrities attracted attention and could inspire pride.

Whereas *Zonk!* featured local film and musical stars as its early cover girls, *Drum* most often presented as-yet-unknown young women. A style sheet reveals the magazine's logic for selecting eye-catching cover girls. Manoim, who obtained the guide from an ex-editor, rightly described it as "invaluable" to understanding Bailey's "thoughts on journalism and his magazine's readers."[91] Bailey sought images with a youthful and dynamic aesthetic, finely tuned to apartheid's racial distinctions and public decorum.

> The cover girl must be happy and good looking—preferably aged 15 to 18 so that she appeals to young readers. Every second or third cover girl should be Coloured, preferably Africanish. The cover must be bright and striking and this depends on the use of a model who is not static—movement is an important part of the cover's appeal. The girl must be doing something—cheerfully. Be careful not to use girls exhibiting too much flesh. Our public and the censor are squeamish. Make sure the girl is not too light-skinned. The model must be beautiful. However excellent the photography, a mediocre model makes a mediocre cover.[92]

By insisting that some cover girls be "Coloured, preferably Africanish" and "not too light-skinned," Bailey sought to craft a vision of beauty and glamour with which many black South Africans might identify. That vision was weighted toward lighter skin shades while remaining recognizably black. Fear of government censors influenced choices regarding models' dress and may have also influenced choices regarding their skin tone. The magazine's success and survival depended on getting the cover girl just right.

Just as the popularity of cover-girl and pin-up photos suggests the need for latter-day analysis rather than mere condemnation, so too does the ubiquitous presence of skin lightener ads. Scholars of *Drum* have generally interpreted their overbearing presence as evidence of the cultural and racial mimicry promoted by the magazine and its ultimately accommodationist political position.[93] For these progressive scholars whose political sensibilities were forged in the wake of the Black Power and Black Consciousness movements and second-wave feminism, skin lightener ads with their beauty-queen spokesmodels offer irrefutable evidence of *Drum*'s less than radical politics and serve as painful reminders of apartheid's insidious privileging of whiteness and degradation of black women. The acuity and elegance of this critique has left little room to consider the material and affective dynamics that made these ads so pervasive and enduring.

FIGURE 4.9. This cover girl, Maureen Koorbanally, satisfied *Drum*'s goal to showcase attractive and cheerful models with often racially ambiguous appearances. The magazine often sought models whose looks fell between apartheid's categories of African and Coloured. *Drum*, September 1961.

Like in *Zonk!*, skin lightener ads dominated *Drum*'s inside front cover and back covers, the only advertising pages with color graphics. These ads generated a significant portion of *Drum*'s advertising revenue as they ranked among the few full-page ads consistently commissioned.[94] Manufacturers also supported *Drum* by underwriting its beauty contests. Bu-Tone sponsored *Drum*'s first competitions, providing cash awards for the top three finishers and skin lightening creams as consolation prizes for the next one hundred runners-up. Illustrating the overlapping importance of the contests to the magazine and the manufacturers, the same layout and photo of a beauty queen appeared on *Drum*'s March 1954 cover and in subsequent Bu-Tone ads. Whereas *Zonk!* readers occasionally criticized skin lighteners, such breaches never occurred in *Drum*'s more polished pages. As was the case in much of the interwar African American press, the revenue to be gained from advertising skin lighteners appears to have placed them beyond reproach in all of the magazine's regional editions. One Bu-Tone ad—part of a two-page promotional spread—proclaimed in 1958–59 that its products were available in thirteen African countries or colonies, including as far north as Nigeria and Kenya.[95] *Drum* did more than any other single publication to generate a pan-African market for skin lighteners.

As publishers sought to reach deeper into the black market, skin lightener ads went with them. In addition to bracketing *Bantu World*'s masthead, skin lightener ads featured prominently in the paper's weekly supplement, *Mayibuye*. Although its title—"Let it (better times) return"—evoked the slogan of the 1952 Defiance Campaign and resistance to apartheid, *Mayibuye* did not provide political coverage but rather mimicked the photo magazines by focusing on entertainment and crime stories.[96] Other publications owned by Bantu Press, including *Ilanga Lase Natal* (The Natal sun), *Imvo Zabantsundu* (Bantu opinion), and *Izwi Lama Swazi* (The voice of the Swazis), also carried skin lightener ads.[97] In 1955, *Drum* owner Jim Bailey launched a weekly *Golden City Post*, modeled after British tabloids. The *Post*'s lowbrow journalism proved enormously popular among black readers, providing a formula that other papers, including *Bantu World* (renamed *The World* in 1956), soon copied. Alongside countless articles on violent crime, love potions, witchcraft, and interracial sex, the *Post* ran up to five skin lightener ads per issue, most identical to those that appeared in *Drum*.[98] In 1956, Dagbreekpers, a publishing house closely aligned with the apartheid government, launched *Bona*, a photo magazine published in isiZulu, isiXhosa, Sesotho, and, later, English. *Bona*'s circulation figures soon surpassed *Zonk!* and *Drum*, as Henrik Verwoerd, then minister of native affairs, made it a compulsory part of Bantu education.[99] Intended as a government-approved alternative, *Bona* imitated the look, if not all the content, of the other magazines. Suggesting that

FIGURE 4.10. Bu-Tone sponsored *Drum's* 1954 "Miss Africa" contest. The magazine featured Ruth Bosman, the winner, as the cover girl. Like the winner of *Bantu World's* 1933 contest, Bosman was selected by reader-voters. *Drum* (International edition), May 1954.

BY *Bu-Tone* SHE'S BEAUTIFUL

RUTH BOSMAN
"Miss Africa" and
DRUM Cover Girl says:

I could never have gained the "Miss Africa" crown without the help of BU-TONE. Bu-tone, Number 3, Cream has given me a "cover girl" complexion, and I would ask you to start the Bu-tone Beauty Treatment NOW. Here's what I do . . . I apply Bu-tone, Number 3, Cream to my face each evening and leave the cream on all night. In the morning after washing with lovely Bu-tone Complexion Soap, I apply Bu-tone, Number 3, Cream again and after a few minutes remove it with a dry towel. The result is a fresh and lighter skin which is free from all blemishes. Yes, take my advice, use only BU-TONE.

Buy *Bu-Tone* and be Beautiful!

Bu-Tone **NUMBER 3 STRONG**

FRECKLE AND COMPLEXION CREAM

BU-TONE, Number 3, Cream is obtainable from your chemist, or price 4/5 from Crowden Products (Pty.) Ltd., P.O. Box 4043, Johannesburg, South Africa.

NUMBER 3 STRONG

FIGURE 4.11. A few months after Ruth Bosman appeared on *Drum*'s cover, the same photo featured in a Bu-Tone ad, revealing the close relationship between the magazine's beauty contests and cover girls, and the marketing of skin lighteners. *Drum,* October 1954.

apartheid officials did not see the promotion of skin lightening as incompatible with the racial order they sought to build, lightener ads appeared in *Bona's* pages. Karroo in fact sponsored the first "Miss Bona" competition.[100]

Some *Bona* ads appeared in African languages, but others remained in English. Skin lightener manufacturers who kept their ads in English seem to have agreed with Mkele that translations of words like "face cream" sounded stilted, and that the glamour of modern cosmetics was best conveyed in English.[101] The fact that the two most common expressions used today in South Africa for lightening with commercial products—*ukucreamer* and *ukutsheyisa*—are both linguistic borrowings from English ("applying creams" and "chasing beauty") reveals how English associations remained even after African languages domesticated the products.

The promotion of skin lighteners stretched beyond print media to include commercials played in cinemas. Karroo's 1956 short featured Hazel Futa, a *Zonk!* cover girl and "Miss South Africa." Situating Futa as a cosmopolitan and affluent star, it included scenes of her disembarking from an airplane with a copy of *Zonk!* in hand and applying Karroo cream while seated at a luxurious vanity.[102] Two years later, Bu-Tone debuted a film ad starring nineteen-year-old singer (and later "Miss Bu-Tone") Ruth Nkonyeni and the Bu-Tone Boys performing a theme song: "Hey, beautiful, so bright and gay what makes your skin look thata-way? Why, Bu-Tone! .... To make my skin look lovely as a dream I always use this wonder cream." A print ad claimed that the song had proven so popular with cinema audiences that Bu-Tone planned to release it as a single.[103]

In subsequent years, radio would become another vital nonprint media for advertising skin lighteners. In the mid-1950s, a Cape Town pharmacist described the effectiveness of radio ads: "To them [African and Coloured consumers] the radio slogan is often synonymous with the name of the product and they recite it in asking."[104] To support its policy of "separate development," the apartheid government introduced Bantu Radio in 1962. Its programming quickly grew to include full-day broadcasts in seven African languages that, by the late 1960s, boasted an audience of 2.3 million daily listeners.[105] Its urban reach of 36 percent exceeded black weekly newspapers' and monthly magazines' coverage of 28 and 24 percent, respectively.[106] Radio played an important role in promoting specific brands of skin lighteners.[107]

These various forms of black media made skin lightener ads a fixture of apartheid popular culture. Jeremy Taylor, a white English-born teacher-cum-entertainer, pointed to this fact in his song "Black-White Calypso." Taylor first performed it in 1961 in Johannesburg as part of a musical revue that later

FIGURE 4.12. Skin lighteners headlined *Bantu World*'s weekly supplement, *Mayibuye*. Covers paired an ad for Bu-Tone products with photos of models with light skin tones. *Bantu World*, September 1955. Reproduced with permission courtesy of Bantu World Newspaper Digitized Collection, Historical Papers Research Archive, the Library, University of Witwatersrand, Johannesburg.

FIGURE 4.13. Another Karroo ad featuring beauty queens that appeared in the isiXhosa edition of *Bona*, a government-funded alternative to *Zonk!* and *Drum. Bona* (Xhosa edition), October 1958.

toured regionally and abroad. Taylor's lyrics echoed the humor that an earlier generation of African American journalists found in tanning and lightening:

The other day reading *Drum* magazine
I'll tell you some of the things I seen (repeat)
Advertisements for a special cream in every section
Give you a soft and pale complexion
Making your black skin lighter creamier and whiter
But when I look in the *Star* [a large daily newspaper] what do I find
But advertisements of a different kind
Because it seems that the white people have a notion
To make themselves black with suntan lotion

Other verses described black South Africans purchasing products to straighten their hair and fatten their bodies while white South Africans permed their hair to make it curly and dieted to make their bodies slim. Taylor's refrain asked, "Tell me, tell me, tell me why I want to know the fact why all the black people want to go white and the white people want to go black." The song's final verse proposed interracial marriage and sex—practices that violated apartheid law—as the solution:

Don't waste your time buying creams and jellies
Trying to change the color of your bellies
But follow the example of my brother
He married a black girl, they love each other
And she gives him a little bit of black in the night
And he gives her a little bit of white

Taylor's South African recording company excised this final verse from his best-selling album *Ag Pleez Deddy*, in the hopes of avoiding government censors. Even without the verse, the South African Broadcast Corporation refused to play "Black-White Calypso" on radio.[108] Drawing attention to apartheid's political absurdities generated official consternation in a way that the promotion and actual use of skin lighteners did not.

Photo Magazines and Technologies of Visibility

Photo magazines heightened the status of skin lighteners as technologies of visibility in two important ways. First, by allowing skin lightener manufacturers to sponsor their beauty contests, the magazines explicitly positioned skin lighteners as tools for claiming broader recognition and achieving modern success. Beauty contests were a hallmark of apartheid popular culture. Such contests, in the words of cultural critic Rita Barnard, enlisted young women to signify the nation's "tenuously imagined" communities.[109] Near the end of the apartheid era in 1993, the *New York Times* reported, "Few countries take beauty pageants quite as seriously as South Africa."[110] An ethnographer described their prevalence and importance: "an average Soweto girl will have competed in dozens of beauty pageants at the crèche, primary school, high school, in the streets after school.... [The pageants assign] a sense of value to each girl's understanding of her looks and that has a strong impact upon her reckoning of future life prospects."[111] Beauty contests were sites for both public recognition and personal scrutiny. This combination was particularly potent in a country where quick, racialized assessments of peoples' appearances mattered so much in the ordering of everyday life.

South Africa's beauty-contest craze took off in the 1950s. The white "Miss South Africa" competition garnered much attention, boosting sales of the newspapers that sponsored it.[112] That attention soared in 1958 when white South African Penny Coelen won the "Miss World" competition. The press hailed Coelen's victory as a national achievement.[113] During the 1960s, growing international condemnation of apartheid threatened South Africa's continued participation in the global pageant. In response, the organizers, in 1970, adopted the ungainly strategy of sending two contestants to Miss World: a white "Miss South Africa" and a black "Miss Africa South."[114] The country's black media, delighted when, in the initial match-up, the country's black representative, Pearl Jansen, won first runner-up, outperforming her white compatriot.[115] Black media similarly delighted in reports of black beauty queens caught with white lovers and charged under the Immorality Act that prohibited interracial sexual relations.[116] Such incidents affirmed black women's irresistibility and white men's weakness.

Photo magazines and their readers began with a more expansive definition of who might compete. For its inaugural contest, *Zonk!* invited submissions from both women and men.[117] When *Drum* and Bu-Tone launched their first contest a few months later, they solicited photos for "Miss Africa" only, but the response from men was so great that they were compelled to crown a "Mr. Africa." As historian Lindsay Clowes has insightfully argued, submissions by men demonstrate the presence of an alternative conception of masculinity that celebrated male beauty.[118] By restricting submissions in subsequent contests to women, the magazines asserted the primacy of Western standards and promoted the principle that only women should be judged solely by their appearances.

When contests were live, female entrants frequently faced physical intimidation and sexual harassment. Marion Welsh, one of *Drum*'s few woman writers, offered a harrowing portrait of the auctionlike atmosphere at a Cape Town pageant. Contestants endured male spectators' "wolf-whistles," pawing, and shouts of "Can I put down payment on the Winner Princess?"[119] For black parents, especially those struggling to maintain or achieve middle-class status, such untoward attention spelled danger. Joyce Molefe, who grew up in Langa during the 1960s, recalled that when her father learned that she had done a photo shoot for a magazine, he said, "Listen here, you are not going there any longer. I do not want you to become a beauty queen."[120] Her father feared that such activities would jeopardize her training to become a nurse, leaving her without a respectable profession or spouse.

Photo magazines' beauty queens were more sexually provocative than those that appeared in *Bantu World* in 1933. Bu-Tone frequently featured each beauty queen in little more than a crown, swimsuit, and high heels. One especially bawdy promotion featured eight photos of women in bathing suits, providing readers with two of three measurements (bust, waist, hips) and inviting them to guess the third after "tak[ing] a tape-measure ... [to] your girl friends, or your wife."[121] An earlier *Drum* cover had visualized how this might be done. These black modern girls were a far cry from the *AmaRespectables* who submitted their portraits to *Bantu World* but were instead close cousins to American postwar pin-ups and the gender politics that produced them.

In his 1959 presentation, Mkele explained the rise of black South African beauty queens. He noted that "the cult of the American Negro" had begun to decline as Africans had found inspiration among "their own political leaders, educated and wealthy men, their Miriam Makebas and fashionable women." "Advertisers," Mkele continued, "have discovered that African models make as good symbols for identification as the Negro and perhaps even better since the local model represents a[n] attainable ideal. The proliferation of 'Misses'— Miss Africa, Miss South Africa, Miss Butone, Miss Palmolive ... —shows that the glamour of the American Negro has been superseded by the glamour of the African beauty queen."[122] The look of the "attainable ideal" had been forged through transatlantic conversations yet the prime exemplars were now firmly South African. As elsewhere, local spokesmodels proved effective and cost-efficient in promoting personal commodities.[123] Skin lightener manufacturers and the photo magazines fueled the shift from American to African celebrities by sponsoring the biggest beauty contests and turning the winners into cover girls.

Beauty contests were ideal vehicles for marketing skin lighteners. First, they generated tremendous publicity and produced low-paid spokesmodels. Former beauty queens recalled earning little, if anything, to appear in skin lightener ads.[124] Moreover, beauty queens made compelling spokesmodels because

FIGURE 4.14. Bu-Tone quickly turned Selina Kolae, "Miss Africa 1957," into a spokesmodel for their skin lightener. Photos like this one drew as much attention to curvaceous figures as to light-colored skin. *Zonk!*, January 1957. Courtesy of the Library of Congress, LC-DDS0-9859.

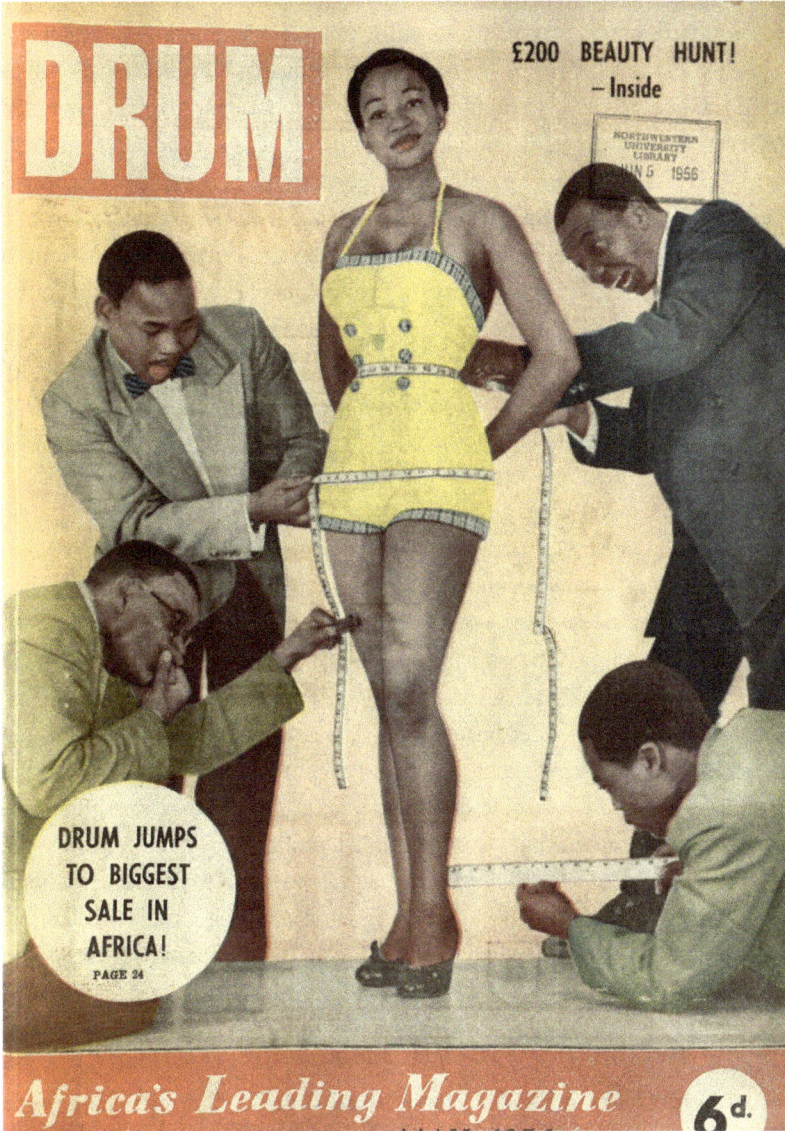

FIGURE 4.15. In this infamous cover, *Drum*'s male staff pushed the objectification of female beauty to new heights by wielding tape measures against a mannequinlike model. *Drum*, May 1956.

they embodied one of consumer capitalism's core social fantasies: through consumption and self-cultivation, one could move from obscurity to visibility and thereby achieve happiness.[125] Beauty queens made this trajectory appear within reach, providing advertisers with valuable testimonials. As Marchand argued in his cultural history of American advertising, "Testimonial ads tell us which public figures a well-informed and highly motivated advertising elite believed the consumers would identify with and accept as adequate authorities."[126] For skin lightener manufacturers, beauty queens were those authorities. In one advertisement after another, they credited their happiness to skin lighteners. Such testimonials tied skin lighteners and success to self-worth. A *Zonk!* article entitled "What Makes a Beauty Queen?" articulated this affective value as "poise": "It's the way people behave who believe in themselves, who know they are important and worthwhile. It's the true sign of a happy, self-confident person."[127] Other businesses also sought to capitalize on beauty queens' appeal, including, astoundingly, fish wholesalers.[128] Through light-colored beauty queens, advertisers sought to associate their products with good looks and the good life.

The fervor for beauty contests did not go unchallenged. Some *Drum* readers criticized the magazine for showing "greater interest in physical beauty than in cultural matters" and not providing competitions for those "who are not so beautiful."[129] Prompted by similar complaints, *Zonk!* invited readers to explain the value of beauty contests and offered a prize for the best reply. Responses "poured in." Some defended beauty contests for offering contestants prizes and the chance to be discovered as film stars. Rather than making people "feel inferior and miserable," as some detractors argued, defenders claimed that contests offered the opportunity to overcome "inferiority complexes" and provided readers with "ideas for self-improvement." These same psychological idioms would soon be wielded by those opposing skin lightening. Others insisted that beauty contests fostered race pride by bringing "to the fore our own African beauties."[130] When Mary Kel Masuabi, the first *Zonk!* beauty queen, visited a local hospital, the children's ward reportedly erupted into the pan-African anthem, "Nkosi Sikelela Afrika!"[131] Defenders of the contests reveled in the recognition of black women as beautiful. Critics complained, increasingly so by the mid-1960s, that beauty contests imposed "Western" standards on African women and impugned their morality.[132]

Even among those who enjoyed beauty contests, some questioned their privileging of light-colored skin. *Zonk!* published a letter insisting that competitions should not be restricted to light-colored girls: "I should like to advise those who think that they are dark and can't win, that they are mistaken.

MEET THE WINNERS of the

EAT MORE FISH

BEAUTY COMPETITION

Miss Caroline Motsamai
c/o P.O. Box 235, Witbank, TRANSVAAL

1ST PRIZE OF **£75**

Wouldn't you like to be as attractive as Miss Caroline Motsamai?
A smooth skin, bright eyes and a lovely figure
come from eating the right food.
Eat plenty of fish and be beautiful.
Fish tastes so good and costs so little.

Mr. Richard M. Dludla,
258, Church Street, Vryheid, Natal,
Wins £75
His was the first correct entry opened, naming
the 3 beauties in the correct order.

Mrs. Sophie Skosana,
990, Lebelebele Avenue, Bopwelvug Location,
Van der Byl Park, Transvaal,
Wins £20
Her entry was the 2nd correct one opened

Miss Francina Moeletjie
1050, Leflow Street, Lady Selborne, Pretoria
2ND PRIZE £25

Miss Nancy Mugadi
52, Mary Road, Mayville, Durban, Natal
3RD PRIZE £15

Prizes of £5 each will be sent to the other nine finalists.

FOR HEALTH AND STRENGTH

EAT MORE FISH

THE CHEAPEST, TASTIEST FOOD YOU CAN BUY

FIGURE 4.16. The use of beauty contests as a marketing tool extended beyond cosmetics manufacturers. Here, fish wholesalers feature the winners of their contest, all young women with strikingly pale faces. The copy promises that eating fish makes "skin smooth." *Bona,* December 1956.

There may be a marvelous face hidden behind that mask!" Taking no issue with this description of dark skin as a "mask," the editor noted that the letter writer was "quite right."[133] Selina Khumalo, who described herself as "very dark," evoked a similar response when she wrote to "Aunt Thandi," explaining that she had used "face creams since 1949 without success." The columnist for *Zonk!* responded with frank advice and proposed a dark-skinned African American role model: "Look my dear, if you were born dark, no cream in the world can make you light. All you can do is try to develop a smooth and clear skin. Hazel Scott the American pianist is dark, and is regarded as one of the most beautiful women in America."[134] Despite such assurances, the women who won *Zonk!* contests usually had light brown skin. And, subsequently, when they appeared as cover girls or in close-up shots, their faces looked whitish, seemingly altered by a combination of skin lighteners, face powders, and strong lighting.

When images of South African beauty queens made their way across the Atlantic, they garnered mixed reactions. *Zonk!* proudly reported in 1954 that the African American weekly *Jet* had profiled their recent "Miss Golden Girl," Mercia Marshall.[135] *Jet's* reporting emphasized how definitions of beauty in Africa were changing:

> Because U.S. standards of beauty run to light skin, straight nose, thin lips and straight hair, American Negroes have often looked down upon their African cousins whose preferences in pulchritude often run to the opposite extreme. But today even African Zulus and Swazis are beginning to accept beauty standards of the white world.... Chosen as their African beauty queen was a pert, oval-faced, tea-colored Swazi-Xhosa girl who well might have run off with honors in beauty contests in any U.S. Negro community.

The choice of Marshall, the article insisted, marked a departure from beauty standards in "many African tribes": "for them light skin is not an asset any more than straight hair."[136] This interpretation underscored how the "white world" had altered African conceptions of beauty while occluding the possibility that some Africans may have long preferred lighter or "brighter" complexions. It also missed how dominant beauty standards, in part, reached Africa after being refracted through African American cultural forms. Voicing a different perspective, a regular reader of *Drum* living in Harlem lauded the magazine for its alternative representations of black beauty. Contrasting its darker-skinned "pinups" to those in American magazines, John Banks wrote, "[I] like the girls you pick for your pin-ups. You pick girls who are pure African.... When it comes to

AFRICAN BEAUTY QUEEN

Among the many different races and nationalities around the earth, the criterion of what makes a woman beautiful is as different as their diets, their clothes and their homes. "Miss America" may be considered ugly in far-off Tibet or Timbuctoo, where beauty standards are entirely different than in Atlantic City. And conversely the sex appeal of Greenland's "Miss Eskimo" or a lovely lass in Liberia may be entirely lost on the most cosmopolitan New Yorker who thinks only in terms of white beauty.

Throughout the w o r l d standards of beauty are set by the mores and customs

of a particular country and despite color and race those standards are usually adhered to.

Because U. S. standards of beauty run to light skin, straight nose, thin lips and straight hair, American Negroes have often looked down upon their African cousins whose preferences in pulchritude often run to the opposite extreme. But today even African Zulus and Swazis are beginning to accept beauty standards of the white world. The new trend was demonstrated in the first national beauty contest held by South A f r i c a n natives. Chosen as their African beauty queen was a pert, oval-faced, tea-c o l o r e d Swazi-Xhosa girl who well might have run off with honors in beauty contests in any U S Negro community.

The winner, Mercia Marshall, is pretty of face by any standards, but would be considered short and even a trifle dumpy by such an arbiter of beauty as E.

African beauty "queen" Mercia Marshall likes to read, play piano at home.

In bathing suit, shapely Mercia belies her 17 years.

FIGURE 4.17. A spread about *Zonk!* beauty queen Mercia Marshall in an African American monthly. The article emphasized how black beauty preferences in the United States and South Africa had begun to converge, pointing to Marshall's "pert" face and "tea-colored" complexion as features that could have swayed American judges. *Jet,* April 1952.

beauty, no woman in the world can match a black woman."[137] While Banks was impressed by the genuinely African appearance of *Drum*'s models, black South African readers would have recognized Bailey's cover girls as including a mix of young women classified as African and Coloured. Local readers were likely more struck by their modern appearances than concerned with their purity or authenticity.

Beauty contests both challenged and breathed new life into racial orders that sought to deny black beauty. When contest winners appeared in skin lightener ads, they personified the fantasy that ordinary young women could attain stardom, and they situated skin lighteners as indispensable technologies for achieving such visibility. Those messages fit well with consumer capitalism's broader promises that the body's surface was malleable and that, through consumption, one could find happiness and attract adulation.

Beauty Queens and Consumer Capitalism   135

The second important way that magazines heightened skin lighteners' status as technologies of visibility was through photography's technical dependence on lighting and its aesthetic affinity for lightness. As Bailey explained in *Drum*'s style sheet, "Photographs are more important than text."[138] What many black urban South Africans considered beautiful or "titivating" by the 1950s had been deeply influenced by the techniques and representational limitations of black and white photography. To present-day eyes, such faces often look whitish, overlit, and unnatural (see figures 4.2, 4.8 (lower left corner), 4.13, and 4.16). Film stars pioneered this pale look. Dolly Rathebe (figure 4.4) graced the cover of the *Zonk!* inaugural issue, the same one where Lena Horne appeared on page four (figure 4.5). Rathebe was the female lead from *African Jim* (1949), the first black South African feature film. Anticipating its popularity, *Zonk!* made Rathebe its first cover girl, two months before the film's release. In the process, *Zonk!* introduced filmic aesthetics to South Africa's photo magazines.[139] Rathebe's face appeared strikingly light and bright—even white—on screen, on the magazine's cover, and in subsequent skin lightener ads. Many cover girls who followed shared the same look.

To achieve this look, a combination of cosmetics and strong lighting was used. Abigail Khubeka, a renowned black South African singer who began her career in the late 1950s and was featured in magazine articles and skin lightener ads, explained, in an interview, that both skin lighteners and face powders were applied.[140] Filmmakers in the United States and Europe pioneered the use of heavy white makeup together with strong lighting during the 1910s and 1920s. The techniques aimed to focus audience attention on lead actors, most especially white women. Richard Dyer, in his study of whiteness and representation, details how photographers and filmmakers created a visual aesthetic that emphasized lightness and radiance, which reinforced dominant beauty ideals rooted in white supremacy. A technology of light, photography evolved with pale faces as the presumed norm. Manufacturers calibrated film and equipment based on this presumption, making it difficult for photographers to capture the detail and skin tones of darker faces. "Movie figure lighting," which was standard in Hollywood by the 1920s, sought to separate actors from their surroundings and highlight facial expressions through a "three-point" overhead system of keylight, softer fill-light, and backlight. For faces to appear as luminescent as possible without producing glare, makeup artists applied copious amounts of white foundation and powder to actors' faces.[141] Beginning in the 1930s, cakelike applications of white cosmetics waned as seasonally tanned skin became a beauty ideal for many white women and Technicolor processing encouraged filmmakers to showcase more "colorful" stars such as Steffi Duna, Dolores Del

FAMOUS AFRICAN FILM STAR *says* . . . .

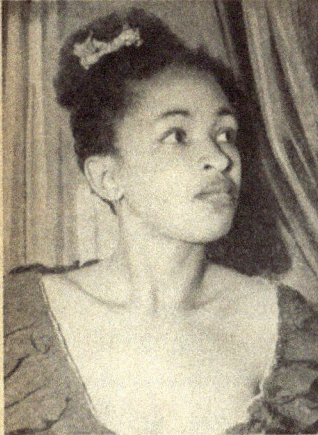

"Use Two KARROO CREAMS to look attractive!"

Beautiful Dolly Rathebe is one of the best known of our African Lovelies. And one of the attractions that has helped to make Dolly famous is her clear, light skin. But let Dolly tell you her secret; it's so simple!

KARROO MATT CREAM in the daytime

Dolly says "Night cream is only part of this beauty treatment. You must have a good day cream, too. Now there's a wonderful new KARROO MATT CREAM. It gives you a smooth, non-shiny make-up. You will look really beautiful if you use KARROO MATT CREAM. Just try it!" Take Dolly's advice, try KARROO MATT CREAM. When you open the jar, you'll see what a really good cream it is. You can use powder if you like.

KARROO FRECKLE CREAM at night

"Just rub KARROO FRECKLE CREAM into your face and shoulders every night. Next morning, wash it off. Even if you haven't used KARROO FRECKLE CREAM before, you'll soon begin to notice an improvement. Your skin gets lighter quickly. You begin to look much more attractive." Yes, Dolly is right! She's told you something that most of our beautiful African women know well. Don't forget — she says "It must be KARROO FRECKLE CREAM".

You all know beautiful Dolly Rathebe. We don't have to tell you about her great film successes, her broadcasting and her stage tours. She has a wonderful, bright personality whether she's acting or not. She always looks attractive — and on this page she tells you two of her beauty secrets. Listen to her — you can look very attractive, too!

KARROO *MATT Cream for Daytime use* at *Night use* **KARROO** *FRECKLE Cream*

IN THE MORNING, USE THIS

KARROO MATT Cream TARNISHING

2/- PER JAR

AT NIGHT, USE THIS

KARROO CREAM

5/- PER JAR

FIGURE 4.18. Dolly Rathebe as a spokesmodel for Karroo. The copy attributes her "clear, light skin" to her use of a matte cream during the day and a skin lightener at night. Yet Rathebe's whitish appearance in the photograph was likely also the result of strong lighting and other photographic techniques. *Zonk!*, August 1953. Courtesy of the Beinecke Rare Book and Manuscript Library, Yale University.

Rio, and Dorothy Lamour.[142] Yet all of these actors as well as African American film stars like Lena Horne and Dorothy Dandridge remained on the decidedly light end of the skin-color spectrum.[143]

The filmic association of light skin tones with glamour crossed the Atlantic. Writing in the early 1960s, anthropologist Absolom Vilakazi, for one, blamed South Africa's skin lightener boom on Hollywood. Describing beauty preferences in a rural isiZulu-speaking community, he wrote, "The skin colour of the woman is of little importance. A fair-skinned Zulu (i.e. light brown) has as much chance of winning a beauty competition as a dark-skinned one—what they call *itshe lamazi* i.e. a river stone or *omnyama njengendoni*, i.e. like a black berry. The new craze for light skins which leads to the use of face creams and other beauty preparations is a result of the Hollywood films and is typically an urban phenomena."[144] Vilakazi's point that the feminine beauty preference for light-colored skin was a recent innovation accords with Eileen Krige's observation from the 1930s that among isiZulu speakers "dark complexions" were highly regarded.[145] Vilakazi contended that by the early 1960s, urban beauty ideals, even in Natal, had become entangled with filmic aesthetics. Dolly Rathebe's reappearance on the *Zonk!* cover in August 1953 illustrates how the photo magazine represented varying aesthetic sensibilities through attention to facial surfaces as well as to dress and hair. The cover contrasts Rathebe as a respectable new mother with a photo of her as a glamorous celebrity. The brightly lit or lightened face—along with the off-one-shoulder evening gown and carefully coiffed hair—mark the right-hand image as that of a movie star.

Readers of photo magazines—not just their staff and advertisers—embraced this look. A market survey done in Soweto found that respondents most often selected a model with a whitish and overlit complexion as the most beautiful and modern (see figure 4.20).[146] Moreover, a good number of the black and white portraits submitted for the magazines' beauty competitions (see figures 4.8 and 4.21) and for publication in their "photo album" sections feature faces that appear unnaturally light as the result of heavy cosmetics, strong lighting, or some combination of the two. Local studio photographers, whose work in black communities took off in the 1950s, played decisive roles in crafting these images.[147] In the United States, photographers with black clienteles had long used special makeup and lighting techniques to counter film's calibrated bias toward peach-colored skin. For example, photography scholar Brian Winston explains that some photographers would "augment lighting, by bouncing reflected light back into the face from a low angle . . . so as not to lose details."[148] The photos submitted to *Zonk!, Drum,* and *Bona* suggest that studio photographers in South Africa developed similar techniques.

FIGURE 4.19. Dolly Rathebe returned as a mother to a *Zonk!* cover for its fourth anniversary issue. Apart from dress and hair, the distinguishing element of Rathebe's prior appearance is her lightened face, demonstrating just how synonymous that look was with film star glamour. *Zonk!*, August 1953. Courtesy of the Beinecke Rare Book and Manuscript Library, Yale University.

FIGURE 4.20. Survey respondents in Soweto considered this model, with her fashionable dress, straightened hair, and pale and made-up face, to be the most beautiful. Interestingly, she was the model whom female respondents most wanted to be like and also the one they thought would be least likable! Her flashy appearance inspired desire and distrust. Van der Reis, *Some Aspects of the Acceptability of Particular Photographic Models to the Bantu* (1972).

Photographers also lightened portraits after shots were taken. Political activist Emma Mashinini, in her autobiography, explains that it was commonplace during the 1960s for photographic "negatives" to be "lightened" to make black people "look as much like white people as possible."[149] Sometimes black and white negatives were retouched and other times adjustments were made during the development process.[150] Developers could lighten faces through techniques of overexposure and "masking and dodging." The former technique entailed lightening the entire print while the latter lightened only designated areas, like faces, allowing them to look lighter relative to the rest of the print and lighter than they would have appeared in real life. A *Zonk!* cover image from June 1951 (figure 4.23), a composite of three different head shots of the same model, Onicca Morake, bears the mark of these techniques. The overly bright pearls and lack of detail in her hair suggest overexposure of the entire print. The marked transition to darker skin tones on the upper forehead and chin together with the lack of facial shadows on the middle image suggest

Choose Miss Bona
— And Win A Grand Prize

What You Must Do

On this page and on pages 17 we
publish the photos of 14 of the
best entries received for the Miss
Bona competition. These 14 photos
were chosen out of several hundreds
received by a panel of six judges.
Every photo has a number. All
you have to do is to arrange on the
enclosed form the four most beauti-

ful photos in order of your choice. If
photo No. 10 is your first choice you
only fill in 10 behind First, etc.
Post your forms back to The Edit-
or, Bona, P.O. Box 3788, Johanne-
burg, and mark your envelope Miss
Bona Competition.
The closing date of your entries is
the 14th of July.

- - - - - ENTRY FORM - - - - -

The Editor, BONA, P.O. Box 3788, JOHANNESBURG.

MISS BONA COMPETITION

First: Photo No. _____
Second: Photo No. _____
Third: Photo No. _____
Fourth: Photo No. _____

I am:
Name _____
Address _____

1 — MISS MAALE, George.

2 — CORAL SWELAKOMO, Alexandra Township.

3 — Jemimah Makgatsha, Seokmekaar.

4 CYNTHIA NEMBILA, Maraka.

5 — SPERO CALUZA, Orlando.

6 — AGNES NKOAHE, Krugersdorp.

7 — SOPHIE M. SENOSI, Krugersdorp.

9 — MAGSIE NZIMA, Pretoria.

10 — IRIS HONGO, Johannesburg.

11 — GLADYS MKHOMBE, Uschlodi.

8 ROSEMARY NDABA, Durban.

12 — JOYCE BROWN, Bloemfontein.

13 — ALICE IYAZI, Middledrift.

14 — CAROLINE SOGI, East London.

FIGURE 4.21. Some of these entries to *Bona's* beauty contest (note 4, 6, 11, and 12) feature faces that appear to have been lightened through the use of heavy cosmetics and bright lights, or through retouching negatives and other development techniques. *Bona*, June 1956.

masking and dodging. *Zonk!* was particularly proud of this cover's "modern style."[151] Photographers at the magazines and in local studios used a range of techniques in pursuit of a visual aesthetic that equated light-colored complexions with attractive and up-to-date appearances.

The introduction of color photographs to the magazines' front and back covers, beginning in the early 1960s, partly altered this aesthetic, underscoring the previous limits of black and white photography in representing the rich diversity of human skin tones. Cover girls' complexions now appeared in various shades of brown rather than looking whitish, and the color contrast between their faces, necks, and limbs became less stark. *Drum's* practice of frequently using "Coloured" models with "Africanish" appearances abetted this shift (see figure 4.9). By featuring young black women with tan complexions, *Drum* contributed to a more natural-looking but still light-colored aesthetic. The skin lightener ads that now appeared on the magazines' colored inside and back covers similarly presented light- to medium-brown skin tones.[152] But between

FIGURE 4.22. Of these photos submitted to *Zonk!*, images in the upper center and bottom left feature faces that have seemingly been lightened by photographers, perhaps at the request of their clients or as part of their standard studio practice. *Zonk!*, December 1953. Courtesy of the Library of Congress, LC-DDSO-9859.

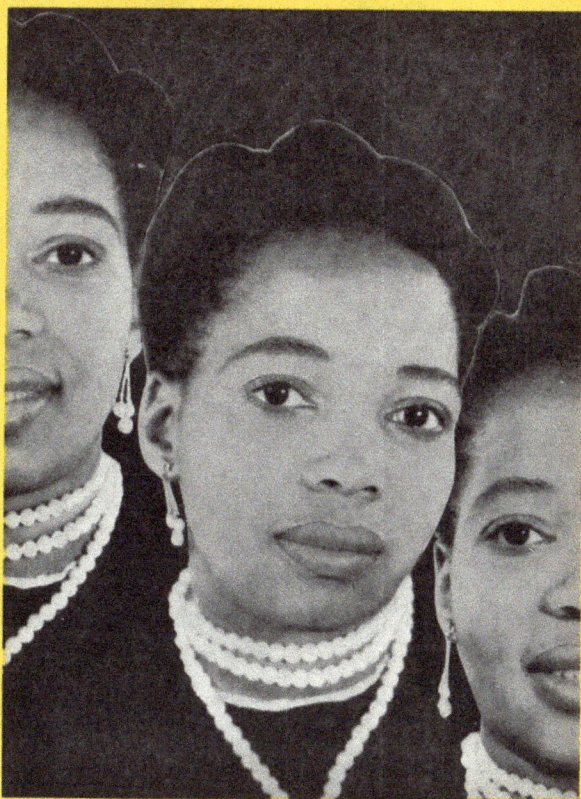

FIGURE 4.23. The *Zonk!* production team likely used techniques of overexposure and masking and dodging to render these faces whitish. In an article, the magazine explained that this was created through an arduous process of "posing, lighting and photography" and by "experimenting" with different prints. *Zonk!*, June 1951. Courtesy of the Beinecke Rare Book and Manuscript Library, Yale University.

the covers, photographs remained black and white, and the visual aesthetic of whitish and overlit surfaces most often prevailed.[153]

Real-life embrace of that aesthetic could result in "two-tone" appearances in which pale faces appeared atop darker necks and limbs. When viewed in person, it struck some as artificial and unappealing. In 1955, Johnny Seboni, a sharp-witted advice columnist, penned an attack. He warned teenage girls that skin lighteners would only create unsightly appearances with dark arms and torsos contrasting with much lighter faces, and they would damage their complexions. Skin lighteners, Seboni declared, were "for the birds."[154] Similarly, in her autobiography, Miriam Makeba recalled how cosmetics made women's faces a "different shade" than their necks, giving them the appearance of "wearing a mask."[155] Beginning in the 1970s, women with such two-tone appearances were mocked for having "Fanta faces and Coca-Cola legs."[156] This jibe squarely situated skin lightening as an element of the period's broader consumer culture. Two-tone appearances were, in part, a product of the visual aesthetic promoted by black-and-white photography.

Makeba rejected skin lighteners' status as technologies of visibility and, instead, offered a different vision of beauty for fans on both sides of the Atlantic. In her autobiography, Makeba recalls growing up inundated with skin lightener ads that promised the good life. She was envious of the way white people lived but not the way they looked: "I do not want to *be* white. I will never bleach my skin, although I am dark.... As time passes I begin to discover something about myself: I am not bad-looking."[157] Makeba's disapproval of skin lighteners and pride in her natural appearance continued as she matured. Early in her career, when she joined the Manhattan Brothers, Makeba's stage name, the "Nut Brown Baby," directly referenced her medium-dark skin tone.[158] Prior to being exiled from South Africa in 1960, Makeba never appeared in skin lightener ads. Once she began performing in the United States, she refused to straighten her hair and wear makeup, and she took pleasure in being recognized as a pioneer of the "Afro" hairstyle.[159] Makeba's appearance offered an antiracist retort to the privileging of lightness in South Africa and the United States. At the height of the civil rights movement, U.S. critics and audiences alike celebrated Makeba with her natural hairstyle and melanin-rich skin as a new kind of black beauty.[160]

Makeba's autobiography also conveys the painful and complex meanings of skin color within families and communities. Describing her daughter Bongi's appearance at birth, she writes, "Her skin is light like her father's; lighter than mine. She is not like I was: She is a beautiful-looking baby."[161] Once Bongi began attending school, the light skin that Makeba admired made Bongi the

Listen to the Beauty Queens!

MISS CENTRAL,
MISS NORMA MCOYANI
SAYS

"The first step to glamour, is to have a lovely, light, smooth complexion"

"And what an easy step it is!" says Norma. "You just use the TWO Karroo beauty creams. *At night* you put on Karroo Freckle and Complexion Cream. That works against the darkening effect of our sun. *In the morning* you put on Karroo Matt Cream. It's "matt"; so it's not shiny. Karroo Matt is the perfect powder base. So there you are, the first step to glamour with the "TWO Karroo Creams"

— always use the

2 KARROO
BEAUTY CREAMS

KARROO CREAM

KARROO Cream

FIGURE 4.24. A full-color Karroo ad. In the early 1960s, with the greater use of color photography and more advanced forms of color printing, some skin lightener ads that appeared on back and inside covers began to feature a range of light brown and reddish—rather than whitish—skin tones. *Drum*, September 1961.

FIGURE 4.25. Although advances in color printing changed the look of skin lightener ads that appeared on the back and inside covers, black-and-white photography prevailed on the inside pages, leaving the whitish visual aesthetic intact. This Pond's ad exhorted consumers to use pale powder after having "lightened" with creams. *Drum* (Central and East African Edition), June 1962.

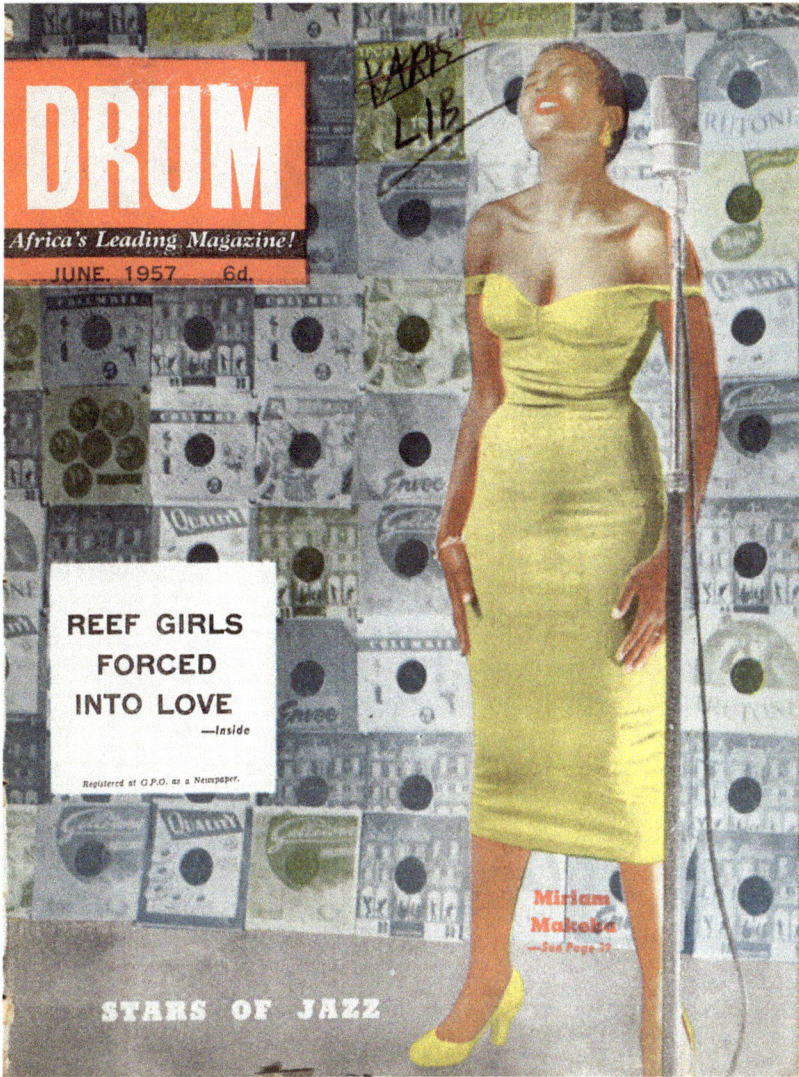

FIGURE 4.26. Miriam Makeba appeared as *Drum*'s cover girl three years before being forced into exile. This colorized photographic image drew attention to her toned physique and her brown complexion. *Drum*, June 1957. Courtesy of the Library of Congress, LC-DDSO-9859.

Jamaica parades

The Ten
Commands
of Beauty

DELIGHTFULLY diverse is the beauty of Jamaica. So recently among the relations of Joe 30th... [faded text, illegible]

1. EBONY Joy Hutton 35; 25; 40.
2. MAHOGANY Joy Drayton 34; 23; 35.
3. NUTBROWN Carmen Miller 35; 25; 36.
4. COCOA Estelle Singh 32; 24; 33.
5. COFFEE Doris Calaman 35½; 24; 37.
6. GOLDEN Doreen Madurai 33; 23½; 34.
7. PEACH Evelyn Chin 34; 24; 35.
8. CREAMY Carole Keighel 35; 22; 35.
9. MILKY Yvonne Wong 33½; 24; 34.
10. IVORY Dorothy Reid 32; 22; 34.

FIGURE 4.27. A year before Makeba's cover appearance, *Drum* ran this spread about a Jamaican beauty contest that selected winners according to ten "skin-colour and race" categories. "Nutbrown," the term used to describe the third winner from the left, also featured in Makeba's stage name, the "Nut Brown Baby," suggesting the circulation of skin tone terms across the black Atlantic. *Drum*, June 1956.

subject of taunts. Makeba writes that among Africans, those with light complexions like Bongi, presumed to be of "mixed race," were frequently denounced as "*boesman.*" Literally "bushman," *boesman* was a term of disparagement for Coloureds, signaling backwardness and racial impurity. Makeba instructed Bongi, in the face of such insults, to say that "yes, you are light, but you are beautiful."[162] The racial and aesthetic meanings of skin color were contested and contradictory. The same light brown complexion could be derided at school but exalted in families and photo magazines.

SOUTH AFRICA'S SKIN lightener boom stemmed from a conflicting set of social fantasies. Amid the growth and optimism of South Africa's postwar economy, manufacturers and media entrepreneurs—mainly white men—sought to cultivate black consumer markets. These capitalist ambitions collided early and often with the apartheid state's commitment to black disenfranchisement. It is

148   Chapter Four

noteworthy that one of their most prominent commercial successes were small luxury goods that promised to lighten young women's complexions. Apartheid's racial and gender hierarchies and economic disparities both limited *and* structured black South Africans' participation in consumer capitalism. Between the late 1940s and mid-1970s, as black wages rose, skin lighteners became increasingly affordable commodities. Products like Karroo and Bu-Tone were within the reach of many more black consumers than Apex had been in the early 1930s or specularite had been in the nineteenth century. The growth of consumer capitalism enabled people to perform elements of affluence even when they did not lead lives of material comfort. Modern girls spent some of their hard-earned cash on cosmetics because they affirmed their self-worth and helped them navigate affective worlds where even modest gradations in skin color mattered a great deal. Apartheid's keen attention to surface appearances provided fertile ground for consumer capitalism's message of the body's malleability.

Integral to the growth of consumer capitalism in South Africa, as elsewhere, was new media, often modeled after American forms. Films and photo magazines promoted a modern visual aesthetics that privileged light-colored skin and cultivated social fantasies of individual fame and success. Inundated with images of pale movie stars and beauty queens, some black consumers engaged skin lighteners as technologies of visibility, tools for gaining greater recognition within a steeply graded and finely parsed social order. Photo magazines promoted skin lightening through their cover girls, beauty contests, and omnipresent ads. In subsequent decades, skin lighteners continued to be associated with visual media in parts of Africa and the diaspora. Anthropologist Liam Buckley has documented how in postcolonial Gambia, skin lighteners, prior to their banning in 1995, were primarily sold at photography studios alongside beauty aids like hair extensions and jewelry. Photographers encouraged clients to use them to look "brightened" in portraits.[163] Similarly, Krista Thompson has examined their use in Jamaican dancehall videos during the 1990s and 2000s. People applied skin lighteners to make themselves more visible to video cameras and to garner greater attention in transnational public spheres from which they were most often marginalized.[164] Today, as we will see in the conclusion, skin lighteners' status as technologies of visibility lives on in digital media.

Yet, even in twentieth-century South Africa, not everyone embraced this aesthetic and affective regime. Makeba's position as an international glamour icon reveals that, by the early 1960s, alternative conceptions of black beauty, also forged in apartheid's cauldron, began to be recognized as modern and African. The next two chapters will explore those developments as well as growing concerns about the active ingredients in skin lighteners.

Five

ACTIVE INGREDIENTS
AND GROWING CRITICISM

In 1939, a group of African American, Mexican, and white workers at a leather factory near Chicago sued their employer after experiencing leukoderma, or depigmentation. The tannery workers rightly attributed the appearance of "milky white" patches on their arms to wearing a new type of rubber glove. When they stopped wearing the gloves, their natural skin color gradually returned. A team of medical doctors, hired by the employer's insurer, determined that their depigmentation was due to monobenzyl ether of hydroquinone (MBH), an antioxidant recently introduced to enhance the gloves' longevity.[1] The company provided the workers with a cash settlement for their damages.[2] Soon doctors elsewhere reported similar cases. Demonstrating just how closely South African practitioners followed American medical developments, two Johannesburg-based doctors published a piece in the *South African Medical Journal*, citing the Chicago case and describing six instances of occupational leukoderma among European and African employees at a factory that used the same chemical in the manufacture of rubber fabric for raincoats and mining gear.[3]

Although these medical doctors did not understand the mechanism by which MBH produced depigmentation, they quickly recognized its therapeutic and commercial potential. What seemed most striking was MBH's ability to lighten without obviously irritating or inflaming the skin or producing immediate toxic effects.[4] During discussion of the Chicago tannery case at the American Dermatological Association meetings in 1940, participants proposed that it be used to treat residual pigmentation resulting from burns and other injuries, and that it be incorporated into "bleaching or antifreckle creams."

OCCUPATIONAL LEUKODERMA

PRELIMINARY REPORT

Edward A. Oliver, M.D., Chicago; Louis Schwartz, M.D., and Leon H. Warren, M.D., Washington, D. C.

A leather manufacturing company recently reported that certain of their Negro workers who wore rubber gloves were becoming depigmented over the areas on the hands and forearms covered by the gloves. An examination of the workers showed that all of them, Negro and white, who wore a certain brand of gloves were affected not only on the arms but several of them on the covered parts of the body (figs. 1 and 2).

A similar condition was found in other tanneries, plating works, electrical apparatus manufactories and all other places investigated where that particular brand of gloves was worn.

The ingredients used in the gloves and the method of their manufacture were obtained from the company making them.

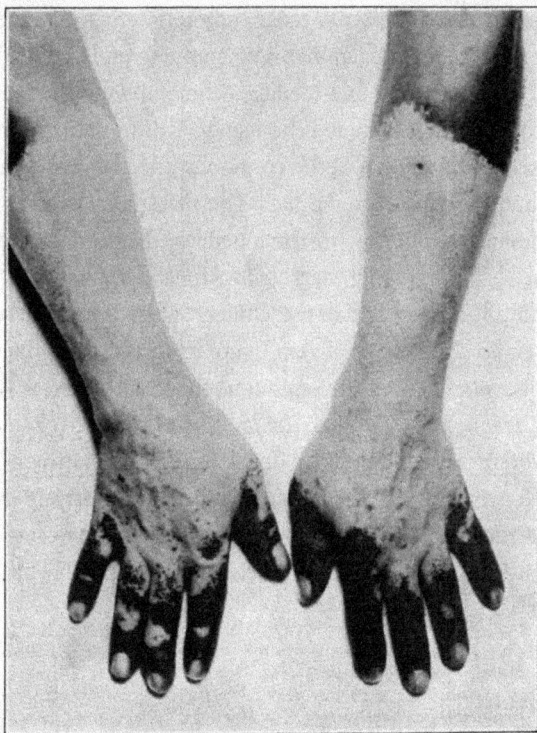

Fig. 1.—Depigmentation of forearms as a result of the wearing of rubber gloves.

FIGURE 5.1. Monobenzyl ether of hydroquinone (MBH) was identified as a depigmenting agent through an industrial accident at a tannery near Chicago. This image dramatically documents the effects on an African American worker who wore gloves treated with the chemical. *Journal of the American Medical Association*, September 1948.

A prominent dermatologist from New York, Marion B. Sulzberger, explained to his colleagues that bleaching creams were a "big industry" that catered to African Americans and others with dark—rather than freckled—complexions. Most brands contained some form of mercury and were manufactured in the American South. Many of them, Sulzberger added, were exported: "A great deal is sold all over Africa, for example."[5] This last point was more aspirational than accurate. Whereas U.S. manufacturers of skin lighteners might have imagined an Africa-wide market for their products in 1940, it would take another twenty years before commercial skin lighteners were readily available in cities beyond settler colonies in southern and eastern Africa. The newly identified depigmenting agent, in fact, would help to fuel that spread.

Over the next three decades, hydroquinone—from which MBH was derived—replaced mercury as the most common active ingredient found in skin lighteners. This chapter examines how manufacturers, regulators, and consumers contributed to this techno-medical development within rapidly changing political contexts that included the rise of African nationalism and political independence across much of the continent, and the civil rights and Black Power movements in the United States. The materiality of skin lighteners— from their chemical properties to their bodily effects—importantly shaped the expansion of skin lightener markets in Africa as well as growing criticism of their consumption there and in the United States. Attention to materiality adds new layers to the history of skin lighteners. Hydroquinone became the dominant active ingredient at the same time that South Africa's skin lightener trade reached new heights. Through the method of connective comparison, we can see how commercial and political developments in apartheid South Africa, postcolonial Kenya, and the United States both influenced and departed from one another. Crucial to this history was the growth of two distinct critiques of skin lighteners: one rooted in antiracist politics and the other, in health concerns.

Active Ingredients

The same year that the Chicago workers filed their lawsuit over MBH, the U.S. Food and Drug Administration (FDA) issued guidelines for mercurial cosmetics under the newly passed Food, Drug and Cosmetic (FDC) Act. The 1938 Act was the world's first comprehensive national law on cosmetic safety, and skin lighteners were one of its earliest targets.[6] The Act provided the FDA with the authority to restrict cosmetics deemed injurious to health or untruthful in their labeling. Rather than requiring the FDA to approve cosmetics before they went to market, the Act empowered the agency to remove dangerous and mislabeled cosmetics from the market and to penalize the companies that manufactured them. The Act also distinguished between cosmetics (articles used for "cleansing, beautifying, promoting attractiveness, or altering the appearance") and drugs (articles "intended to affect the structure or any function of the body"), while recognizing that some products slide between the two categories. The FDA classified skin lighteners, together with products like antiperspirants, sunscreens, and antiseptic lotions, as both cosmetics and drugs.[7] This dual classification made skin lighteners challenging products to regulate, and it expanded the controversies they stirred.

The 1938 FDC Act, like the 1906 Food and Drug Act that established the FDA, was the product of widespread consumer activism, much of it spearheaded by women. Cosmetic sales skyrocketed in the early twentieth-century United States as modern girls embraced makeup as part of fashionable appearances. Sales grew from less than $100,000 per year in 1900 to an estimated $125 million by the mid-1920s. Along with this dramatic rise came increasing reports of cosmetic mishaps: mascaras that caused blindness, hair products that burned the scalp, and facial compounds and creams that produced rashes and scarring. Journalists and consumer activists publicized the worst of these incidents, galvanizing public opinion in support of government regulation.[8] Concerns over mercurial skin lighteners ranged from complaints of discolored skin and lesions to cases of systemic and fatal poisoning.[9] By the mid-1930s, even some cosmetics trade journals warned that mercury was too dangerous an ingredient.[10]

Discussions surrounding the FDC Act garnered attention in South Africa. In 1934, the trade journal *South African Business Efficiency* lauded the draft bill, noting that local consumers would benefit from similar government oversight in the sale of cosmetics, foods, and patent medicines.[11] The South African government did, in fact, possess some regulatory authority in these realms. Passed in 1929, the Foodstuffs, Drugs and Disinfectants Act authorized the minister of public health to safeguard the quality and accurate labeling of a wide range of consumer products. Article 36 allowed the minister to extend the Act's provisions to "any ointment, cream, powder or similar substance for application to or use for the human skin or hair, soap."[12] In practice, officials seldom, if ever, invoked this article. Whereas old public health files housed today in the South African National Archives contain voluminous complaints and investigations related to foodstuffs and medicines, they rarely mention cosmetics.[13] Officials within the South African Ministry of Health, as late as 1959, decried the ongoing absence of adequate cosmetic labels and stated the great need for "legal standards of purity and non-toxicity" for cosmetics as existed in the United States and Canada.[14] Without their own national regulations on cosmetics safety, South African manufacturers and officials often looked to the U.S. FDA for guidance. The FDA's actions, of course, also shaped the form and content of products imported from the United States.

Rather than banning the sale of mercurial skin lighteners as cosmetics, as some consumer and medical groups urged, the FDA issued manufacturing guidelines. A 1939 notice explained that the "broad claims" made for bleach creams were misleading and their effects on "skin structures . . . harmful." To avoid violating the FDC Act, manufacturers should limit ammoniated mercury concentrations in cosmetics to 5 percent or less and apply conspicuous warning labels. The FDA advised that labels should warn against use by children while adults should be encouraged to conduct preliminary patch tests and avoid "vigorous application." Labels should also instruct users to apply only a "thin layer," to leave it on "for not more than one-half hour," and to clean it "off with some substance such as benzene or oil." These lengthy labeling guidelines suggest that, within the FDA, many concerns about ammoniated mercury remained. The notice further stipulated that claims should be limited to "such temporary lightening effect as they possess."[15] Industry insiders interpreted this last clause as prohibiting long-standing advertising claims such as "removes freckles," "removes pimples," "rid[s] skin of blemishes," acts as a "remedy for or prevents blackheads and acne," and "lightens dark skin."[16] In the immediate wake of the notice, the FDA seized batches of skin lighteners that exceeded the 5 percent threshold and worked in tandem with other federal agencies to ensure adherence to labeling and advertising guidelines.[17] Some manufacturers decreased the amount of ammoniated mercury below 5 percent, noting that 1–2 percent seemed to have the same lightening effect as higher concentrations.[18]

New guidelines and warning labels did not necessarily dissuade users and would-be manufacturers. The Tennessee-based company that manufactured Nadinola Bleaching Cream boasted that the FDA regulations had buoyed their business by increasing consumer confidence in their product.[19] Throughout the 1940s, the FDA received queries from established companies seeking to adjust their formulas and from individuals seeking to launch new brands. One unemployed woman from Arkansas asked advice on how she might mass-produce lighteners based on a recipe that had been in her family for generations.[20] A soldier, recently discharged from the Army, wrote, requesting information about "Negro Cosmetics" and a formula for a "skin bleach [that could] . . . be sold to the colored trade and also as a freckle cream for the white trade."[21] More often than not, correspondents specified that they had a black or brown clientele in mind. A businessman from Wisconsin, for instance, sought information on a skin lightener that might have "popular advertising appeal" in Latin America.[22] Such queries reveal how entrepreneurs looked to the FDA for business advice, not just industry regulations and guidelines, and how some continued to view skin lighteners as a lucrative commodity.

Although the African American press paid little attention to the FDA's heightened scrutiny of mercury-based cosmetics, MBH made the front page in the 1940s. The *Atlanta Daily World* reported that an accident at a tannery had revealed a new chemical that could turn the "skin of Negroes white."[23] The *Chicago Defender*, in turn, dismissed the story's significance, writing of "Negro indifference": "all indications are that members of the Negro race are content with the color of their skin and have no desire whatever to change it."[24] Walter White, the executive secretary of the National Association for the Advancement of Colored People (NAACP), ignited controversy a few years later by proposing MBH as a solution to America's shameful "color line." White's pale complexion, blond hair, and blue eyes had, earlier in his civil rights career, enabled him to pass as white while investigating and exposing the lynching of black men across the South. In a 1949 article in the mainstream *Look* magazine, White argued that a safe and effective form of MBH would obliterate—like an "atomic bomb"—racial prejudice by allowing people to be judged by their "ability, energy, honesty, cleanliness" rather than the color of the skin. He cited Lena Horne as sharing his optimism about this scientific fix for one of the world's great social problems.[25] Countless black leaders ridiculed White's proposition, denouncing it as "quackery," a "coward's escape," and an affront to race pride. Journalists wrote that ordinary African Americans responded to the story by expressing their love of dark skin tones.[26] The controversy, following soon after White had divorced his black wife and married a white woman, greatly weakened his leadership of the NAACP.[27] The defense of dark complexions had emerged as a decisive issue in national black politics.

Where some found political controversy, cosmetic manufacturers saw commercial opportunity. MBH was a derivative of hydroquinone, a chemical that was first used in the late nineteenth century in the development of black-and-white photos. In the 1930s, manufacturers of rubber apparel began using MBH as an antioxidant to preserve their products' pliability and durability. Soon after the accident involving the Chicago workers, medical researchers determined that MBH, like ammoniated mercury, impeded the production of melanin by interfering with the enzyme tyrosinase and the formation of melanocytes.[28] Therapeutic use of MBH, however, produced uneven and often troubling results. When applied to areas of hyperpigmentation, in concentrations ranging from 2.5 percent to 20 percent, MBH frequently produced irritation, sensitiza-tion, and uncontrolled depigmentation, making the side effects more discon-certing than the original dermatological problem.[29] While doctors struggled to hone MBH's therapeutic application, cosmetics companies developed and began selling lighteners that contained hydroquinone itself, in concentrations ranging between 1.5 and 5 percent. Their products provided moderate lighten-ing of dark spots and temporary lightening of overall skin tone with few, if any, immediate side effects. Cosmetic companies had outpaced medical researchers in harnessing hydroquinone's potential. By the mid-1960s, medical researchers concluded what companies already knew: hydroquinone made for a more reli-able lightening agent than MBH.[30]

Like medical doctors, the FDA strained to keep up with cosmetic manufac-turers' use of hydroquinone. In response to a 1960 query from a company inter-ested in learning more about hydroquinone's efficacy and safety, FDA officials explained that their preliminary investigations had not found it to be harm-ful and, thus, they were not suggesting maximum concentrations or warning labels.[31] Within a year, officials began to express more caution, advising that labels instruct consumers who developed skin irritation to stop use.[32] A few years later, they suggested that labels also include instructions about conduct-ing preliminary patch skin tests and that manufacturers keep concentrations of hydroquinone to 2 percent or less.[33] These new guidelines reflected research done by Northwestern and Harvard dermatologists who found hydroquinone in low concentrations to be a fairly effective, if temporary, agent in lightening freckles, age spots, and the overall complexion of lightly to moderately pig-mented people. Hydroquinone lightened, the researchers concluded, both by exfoliating the top layers of the skin and reducing cellular production of mela-nin by roughly half.[34] Their studies remained influential into the 1970s when the FDA appointed an independent advisory panel to consider skin lighteners as part of a broader agency review of over-the-counter drugs.[35]

Artra Skin Tone Cream was one of the earliest hydroquinone-containing skin lighteners to be marketed and the first to be sold in both the United States and South Africa. The *South African Retail Chemist* carried a promotional article in 1958 announcing the product. Hydroquinone's chemical proper-ties compelled a change in packaging. When exposed to air, hydroquinone oxidizes, both compromising its efficacy as a lightening agent and darkening creams and ointments. To minimize such oxidation, Artra was placed in tubes with narrow openings rather than wide-mouthed jars.[36] While Artra's packag-ing was fresh, its advertising claims were familiar: to lighten and brighten, to even out freckles and blemishes, to soften and smoothen the skin, to protect

FIGURE 5.2. Artra was one of the first brands of skin lightener to use hydroquinone—referred to here as "Amazing H.Q."—as an active ingredient. Most of the copy changes from figure 5.3 to this ad emphasized Artra's American origins. *Drum* (East African edition), October 1959.

FIGURE 5.3. This earlier version of the same Artra ad in figure 5.2 appeared in the African American press. Artra was a fairly prominent sponsor of black American cultural events during the 1960s. *Philadelphia Tribune*, May 1957.

it from the elements, and to provide a base for face powders.[37] A full-page Artra ad in *Drum* in 1959 announced hydroquinone as a new "miracle ingredient" that, unlike ammoniated mercury, would not cause skin "to burn, peel or break out."[38] A similar version of this ad appeared two years earlier in the African American paper *Philadelphia Tribune*.[39] Notably, almost all of the copy changes in the South African version highlighted the product's U.S. origins. For many *Drum* readers in the late 1950s, American references signaled a prosperous and glamorous consumer culture, worthy of emulation and full of promise.[40] Phrases such as "proved to be a success by beautiful American women" and "developed … in one of America's most modern laboratories" situated Artra's American and scientific provenance as selling points.[41]

Similar to Walter White's response to MBH in 1949, these Artra ads exuded an unabashed enthusiasm for techno-scientific solutions that were distinctly American. An Artra endorsement that appeared in the *Chicago Defender* (one of the papers that had ridiculed White a decade earlier) expressed a similar sentiment: "in the scientific world the development of hydroquinone as a cosmetic lightening agent marks another milestone in the astonishing achievements of research."[42] Artra gained visibility by producing some of the first American TV commercials to feature black models, awarding entertainer Diahann Carroll a lifetime achievement award, and sponsoring scholarships through the United Negro College Fund.[43] In the early 1960s, skin lighteners remained a palpable presence in African American consumer culture while manufacturers' faith in American techno-scientific achievements extended across the Atlantic.

Twins Products of Johannesburg

Around the same time that Artra arrived in South Africa, a local patent drug and cosmetics company started selling a liquid lotion that also contained hydroquinone. The company was Twins Products, founded by Solomon and Abraham Krok, the twin sons of Jewish parents who had emigrated from Lithuania to South Africa in the 1920s. Twins would eventually grow to dominate the South African skin lighteners market, helping to make the Krok brothers into some of the country's wealthiest businesspeople.

In 1953, soon after Solomon graduated from school as an accountant and Abraham, as a chemist/pharmacist, they purchased Devon Pharmacy on Noord Street in Johannesburg's Central Business District. This location placed them between the train station and a busy bus rank, leaving them well positioned to take advantage of the city's post–World War commercial boom fueled by two decades of rising black urban migration.[44] The Kroks entered cosmetics manufacturing by purchasing Super Rose, a line developed by two other Noord Street businessmen: Selman Super, an optician, and Benny Rosenberg, a doctor. In the early years of apartheid, both the government and the national pharmaceutical association continued to see the local manufacture of cosmetics and medicines that could outcompete more expensive imports as a promising realm of commercial activity. They encouraged growth of the sector by endorsing favorable tariff policies and offering business advice.[45] The original Super Rose creams targeted black consumers but did not contain a lightening agent. In an interview, Solomon Krok explained that initially sales of Super Rose were dwarfed by the "run-away seller" of the period: Karroo skin lightening cream with ammoniated mercury.[46]

Seeking a slice of this lucrative market, the Kroks began to manufacture Super Rose Freckle and Complexion Cream with ammoniated mercury. They marketed their new product by suggesting that it made "men run mad" after women, in an ad from 1956. Making themselves more attractive to men had long been one of the reasons that women gave for using cosmetics. When interviewed decades later by historian Zinhle Thwala, isiZulu-speaking women who grew up in Durban during the 1960s and 1970s explained that the desire to attract and retain desirable boyfriends and husbands was, in fact, the number one reason why women used cosmetics.[47] Yet the Kroks' cartoonish representation of that reason missed the mark. Obed Kunene, editor of the isiZulu newspaper *Ilanga*, cited it as an example of a failed effort to reach black consumers. Addressing an advertising convention in 1965, Kunene recalled that the image of a "Lothario" chasing a woman suggested that "the cream was not morally safe to use" and dissuaded women from purchasing it.[48]

Solomon Krok remembered that their "breakthrough" came when they launched an alcohol- rather than cream-based skin lightener in the late 1950s. The Kroks created Super Rose Pimple, Freckle and Complexion Lotion by adapting a formula that they found on a bottle of an anti-acne astringent lotion. To this formula, they added hydroquinone, as ammoniated mercury did not fully dissolve into the clear liquid. The Kroks aggressively marketed Super Rose by focusing all advertising resources on it and by giving out thousands of free small samples at their pharmacy and at the nearby bus and train stations.[49] An early ad for the lotion featured three overlapping photo drawings of a woman's face that became progressively lighter and pimple-free. The ad—like the very name of the lotion—alluded to the variety of reasons why black consumers might purchase skin lighteners: it "leaves a soft, smooth, alluring complexion and a lighter, brighter skin."[50] The Kroks realized their lotion was a commercial success, Solomon explained, when a shop in Witbank, an industrial town 140 kilometers east of Johannesburg, ordered ninety dozen bottles.[51] By the mid-1960s, demand was so great that they moved production to a larger factory outside of Johannesburg and opened a second factory in Durban. They employed five hundred people and generated yearly sales totaling R3 million. Twins expected that their new Durban factory would produce close to 34,000 dozen bottles of the lotion every six months.[52]

Twins marketed Super Rose Pimple, Freckle and Complexion Lotion as a less expensive complement to popular skin lightening creams. A bottle of lotion cost one-half to one-third the price of a jar or tube of cream.[53] The Kroks' strategy was to "piggyback" on Karroo's success, Krok recalled: "So I said to my

Men Run Mad

after women who
use

**SUPER
ROSE
CREAMS
and
SOAP**

**10/-
the
set**

How to gain a BRIGHTER,
LIGHTER, New Look COMPLEXION?

At night (1) Wash with Super Rose
Night Soap; (2) Apply Super Rose
Night Cream.
In the morning (3) Wash with Super
Rose Day Soap; (4) Apply Super Rose
Vanishing Cream for the day-time.
After using the Super Rose Society
Set your skin will become velvet
smooth, fresh, light and lovely. You
will then know why men go mad
about women who use these famous
Super Rose Creams.

From TWINS PRODUCTS
65 Noord Street, P.O. Box 3838,
Johannesburg.

FIGURE 5.4. An early ad for Twins Products, a company founded by Abraham and Solomon Krok. This ad became infamous as a marketing message gone awry for suggesting that the cosmetics advertised might attract untoward male attention. *Golden City Post,* November 1956.

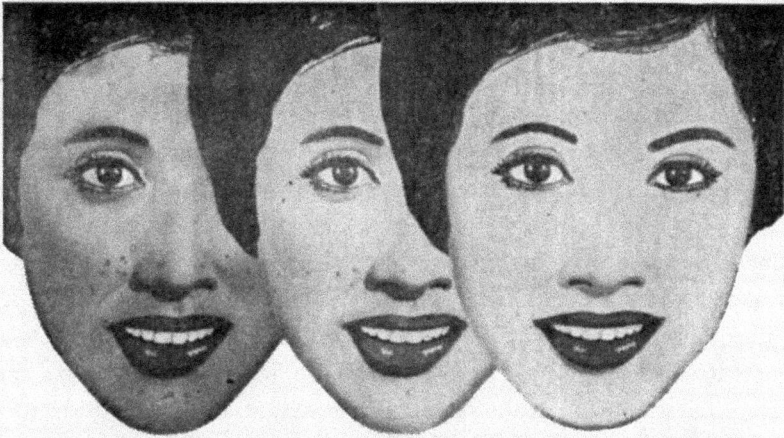

FIGURE 5.5. Super Rose Pimple, Freckle and Complexion Lotion, which contained hydroquinone, became Twins's best-selling product. Ads encouraged consumers to use it alongside of creams to make their complexions lighter and blemish-free. The lotion helped to launch the Kroks' business empire. *Bona*, May 1959.

brother we don't have to fight these guys [Karroo]....We said we don't care if you use any famous cream as long as before you use that cream you cleanse with our lotion. And it became the hottest seller in the world."[54] Krok claimed that the amount of hydroquinone in the original Super Rose lotion was 1 or 2 percent and, hence, in accordance with the U.S. guidelines.[55] Yet, by recommending that their lotion be used before applying a cream, the Kroks encouraged consumers to double their combined daily exposure to skin lightening agents. Moreover, subsequent chemical analyses revealed that, by 1980 at least, Twins skin lighteners often contained more than 2 percent and that, compared with creams and oils, alcohol significantly increased hydroquinone's penetration of the skin.[56] Twins Products enhanced consumers' exposure to hydroquinone and its ill-health effects.

In order to catch up with and, later, overtake Karroo, the Kroks adopted direct marketing strategies. Besides distributing free samples, they held demonstrations outside stores, factories, and mining compounds. They developed close working relations with storeowners and built an extensive network of itinerant sales agents or hawkers. At a 1969 conference on the urban African market, M. Mapumulo, the owner of a township shop north of Durban, described how every four months he purchased over seven thousand units of Super Rose, some of which he sold on credit to "teachers, nurses, clerks, and other professionals."[57] At the same conference, L. M. Guthrie, a manager for a local drug company, lauded Twins for passing a greater share of their profits along to sales agents.[58] Twins recruited hawkers and encouraged their own factory workers to purchase products at discounted prices and to resell them.[59] Apartheid restrictions prohibited African-owned businesses from operating in or near central business districts, which limited the businesses' ability to access loans and other forms of capital. They also prohibited African businesses from selling anything beyond essential, day-to-day commodities.[60] Such government restrictions left small township stores and hawking as among the only business opportunities open to African entrepreneurs.

During the 1970s, skin lighteners became relatively cheap and widely available commodities. Some women recall that in urban townships, like Durban's Madadeni, it was rare to find women who did not use them. Consumers included domestic workers and factory workers, nurses and stay-at-home wives. Prices were low enough that even secondary schoolgirls could afford them if they "saved their lunch money for a few weeks." Skin lighteners were more affordable than face powders and other kinds of cosmetics.[61] Twins Products helped to make them inexpensive and accessible. Solomon explained that in a deliberate strategy "to compete with ourselves so we could keep the opposition out," they multiplied their brands. Product names like Hollywood 7, Super Scott, Kool Look, Aviva, Tanlite, and Alco evoked American glamour and up-to-date style. Some, like He-Man, were promoted as "extra-strong" and specifically targeted male consumers, though women also used them.[62] Twins quickly recognized the potential of radio to reach more consumers. By the early 1970s, they spent nearly five times as much on radio than print ads.[63] Brief radio spots extolled specific brands: "Yes, more people are now using Hollywood 7 than any other skin-brightening creams."[64] By promoting their products as "brighteners" rather than lighteners, Twins used a descriptor more in line with the

FIGURE 5.6. Part of Twins's sales success lay in their recruitment of hawkers to sell their products door-to-door and in townships. This ad promised new sales agents popularity and "big money." *Bona*, May 1959.

notion of "glow" that Nimrod Mkele had insisted was the primary skin quality sought by black consumers.[65]

When interviewed in 2008, Solomon Krok provided a nuanced response to the question of why skin lighteners had been so popular. Other white businessmen involved in the apartheid-era skin lightener trade responded to this question by chuckling and providing the same pat answer: "Black people want to be white and white people want to be black."[66] This response echoed the lyrics of Taylor's "Black-White Calypso" by equating skin lightening with tanning. But whereas Taylor, like the African American journalists before him, had evoked this equation satirically to highlight the absurdity of social and political orders rooted in skin-color distinctions, these businessmen in the 2000s used it to strip skin lightening of any political meaning. Through jest, they denied that the appeal of skin lighteners related to South Africa's racial hierarchy. Solomon Krok, by contrast, offered a more subtle and substantive answer: "If a black had a light skin, they were perceived to be in a different status than a black dark person. I believe it was a status symbol that I'm lighter, I'm more educated, I'm more affluent or I'm more Westernized."[67] This explanation resonated with what anthropologists Leo and Hilda Kuper noted in their early 1960s study of the "African bourgeoisie": for middle-class women, skin lightening, together with hair straightening, had become part of cultivating glamorous and alluring appearances in a "Western idiom" with "no necessary implication of 'playing for Colored.'"[68] More so than other businesspeople, the Kroks sought to understand what animated the skin lightener trade. They consulted shoppers and hawkers and, later, hired research firms to conduct consumer surveys.[69]

Twins Products underscored the aspirational dimensions of skin lightening by expanding spokesmodels beyond beauty queens and film stars to include nurses. By the 1950s, nursing ranked as the most prestigious and respected career open to black South African women. Only a few thousand black girls in the entire country had access to the secondary school education necessary to qualify for training. Nursing was the most lucrative professional career path for black women, though their salaries lagged well behind those of white counterparts. People perceived nurses, in their white uniforms and with their highly regimented training, as those who, in the words of Shula Marks, had been most "thoroughly imbued with Western middle-class values."[70]

Nurses were also recognized as some of the first and most reputable women to use skin lighteners. In an interview, Eunice Maseko, a cosmetics sales representative, recalled that when she was growing up during the 1960s and 1970s, nurses were admired for their white uniforms, purity of purpose, and professional status. Once people discovered that some nurses were lightening their complexions, Maseko explained, the practice became "a sign of being learned" and teachers and others followed suit.[71] Nurses themselves sharply distinguished their own use of skin lighteners and other cosmetics from the very heavy use of them by *onontorotyi*, or unrespectable women who donned "tight skirts," "high heels," and "big earrings."[72] A Twins ad from 1963 sought to capitalize on nurses' prestige and respectability by featuring a testimonial from "Noreen the Nurse": Super Rose had kept her skin "bright, clean and smooth" despite the "heat and sweat of the Operation Room."[73] A decade later, another Twins advertisement similarly attributed the success of the real-life nurse Lizzie Mokoena—a nurse at Baragwanath Hospital, a debutante in Soweto, and a recent bride—to skin lightening: "I owe my happiness to Kool Look."[74] Through such testimonials, Twins depicted skin lighteners as indispensable aids to achieving the upper limits of black social mobility in apartheid South Africa while disregarding the innumerable structural obstacles that most often prevented such social fantasies from becoming realities.

First a debutante
Now a bride

That's the beautiful story of Lizzie Mokoena

When Baragwanath nursing sister Lizzie Ledwaba was chosen as one of the lovely debutantes at a glittering Soweto ball, handsome young businessman Jeffrey Mokoena could not take his eyes off her. He so admired her poise, beauty and lovely light complexion.

Jeffrey got a friend to introduce him to Lizzie and they began dating. Last week, they were married in Vereeniging at a wonderful ceremony which was attended by over 300 important guests.

Beautiful bride Lizzie, now Mrs. Mokoena, had this to say: "I owe my happiness to Kool Look. I always use Kool Look cosmetics to keep my complexion soft, light and lovely – the way Jeffrey loves it."

KOOL LOOK

Cosmetics and wigs for smart women.

FIGURE 5.7. Skin lightener spokesmodels eventually expanded beyond film stars and beauty queens to include nurses and brides. Nursing represented the most privileged career path for black women while brides had long been associated with lightened appearances. This full-page color ad featured the testimonial from a nurse-cum-bride. *Bona*, October 1973.

Having cornered much of the skin lightener market by the late 1970s, the Kroks continued to be shrewd businesspeople. They paid close attention to developments in the regional and international skin lightener trade, and they diversified. Whereas Karroo focused its energy for decades on a single product, the Kroks invested in other areas of commerce, including food, furniture, construction, engineering, and entertainment. During the 1980s, they extended their business holdings by buying subsidiaries of foreign companies as they pulled out of South Africa due to growing international condemnation of apartheid. As Solomon Krok explained to a journalist, with a frankness that would have appalled progressive activists worldwide, "Any go-ahead business-man has to take advantage of disinvestment."[75]

Alongside the growth of commercially manufactured skin lighteners during the 1960s and 1970s, *ummemezi* remained available. Herbalists and traditional healers in the Eastern Cape and Kwazulu-Natal sold truckloads of *ummemezi*, bark derived from one of a dozen or so indigenous trees, as a remedy for various skin ailments and for lightening overall complexions. Purchasers crushed the bark, mixed it with water, and then applied it to their faces in a manner reminiscent of what David Livingstone witnessed among Mokololo women in the mid-nineteenth century.[76] *Ummemezi*—meaning something that attracts attention for being shiny or bright—persisted in market stalls, beyond the purview of pharmacists and government regulators. At ten cents for a finger-sized piece of bark, it was significantly cheaper than a jar or tube of skin lightening cream. While some consumers used *ummemezi* as a less expensive alternative, others combined preparations and products in order to achieve the look they desired.[77]

East African Consumers

South African manufacturers began exporting commercial skin lighteners north of the Limpopo in the late 1950s. True to its original intent, *Drum* assisted by advertising them to African consumers far and wide. South African businesspeople saw commercial opportunity in the growth of black consumer economies in places where colonial rule was coming to an end. Take, for example, the Central and East African edition of *Drum* from June 1962. It included seven advertisements for skin lighteners, including one for Super Rose Extra Special Freckle and Complexion Cream that touted hydroquinone as the "new complexion-aid, miracle HQX" (see figures 5.8–5.14). For readers of *Drum* everywhere, images that equated lighter skin color with feminine beauty and success were inescapable.

It is difficult to know what early East African readers made of *Drum's* many skin lightener advertisements and light brown cover girls and beauty queens. As in southern Africa, anthropological evidence from some areas suggests that an aesthetic preference for young women to have brightened, smoothened, and lightened complexions might have predated colonial rule. For example, based on research in northern Tanzania in the late twentieth century, Brad Weiss found that Haya people had long linked the cultivation of clear, shiny, and "white" complexions with the oiled and secluded bodies of brides, new wives, and new mothers. People identified their radiance and lightness, he explains, with the pale and pristine skin of newborn children (rather than European whiteness). Men viewed women with radiant and light complexions as "more susceptible to the sexual control of their... husbands."[78] Along the Swahili coast, as in other parts of the continent with established Muslim communities, people often defined elite or "civilized" (*ustaarabu*) status through affiliations and appearances linked to Arab and Islamic worlds, rather than the African interior. Such appearances included dress and bodily comportment but could also extend to skin color and other physical features.[79] The advent of European colonial rule and its racial logics, in the late nineteenth century, compounded the privileging of lighter skin tones.

As in other twentieth-century European colonies, skin lighteners were cosmetics known to white settlers in East Africa. Newspapers like the *East African Standard* occasionally carried advertisements for preparations that promised to rid pale complexions of freckles and "unsightly yellow spots" caused by sun exposure. Ads specifically targeting black consumers, however, only began with the introduction of South African–made products in the late 1950s. The manufacturer of Jive skin lightening cream, in 1958, announced in *Drum* that it had appointed an agent in Kampala to distribute its product throughout Kenya, Tanganyika, Uganda, and Zanzibar.[80] Solomon Krok recalled that similarly, during the 1960s, Twins Products entered into a franchise relationship with an Indian chemist in Kampala.[81] Soon local newspapers—not just *Drum*—carried skin lightener ads. Sizable ads for a Pond's lightening cream, for example, appeared on the front page of Kenya's Kiswahili weekly *Baraza*.

FIGURES 5.8–5.14. These seven ads—four of them full-page—appeared in a single issue of the Central and East African edition of *Drum* magazine. Founded in Johannesburg in 1951, *Drum* grew to be one of the most influential publications in Africa, with regional issues published in Lagos, Accra, and Nairobi. *Drum* (Central and East African Edition), June 1962.

Here is the advice of one of the loveliest Johannesburg mannequins, Miss Linda Mhlongo. She says, "For beauty, you need a clear, light skin, and for a clear, light skin you need, of course, the Two Karroo Creams. *At night*, you use Karroo Freckle Cream, rubbing it gently into the face and neck. Soon your face becomes much lighter, bringing out your true beauty. If any pimples or spots worry you, Karroo Freckle Cream clears up those, too. *In the morning*, Karroo Matt Cream, the great non-shiny cream, protects your skin against darkening in strong sunlight. Also, it is the perfect powder base. You look so cool and smart all day, if you use Karroo Matt Cream.

KARROO MORNING, KARROO AT NIGHT—MAKES YOU LOVELY, MAKES YOU LIGHT!

"You must use the TWO KARROO CREAMS for a lighter, clearer, more lovely complexion!"

HER COMPLEXION IS FAIR AND CLEAR

Freckles have gone. Spots have cleared. Her complexion is now fair and clear because she has been using Lemon D e l p h Complexion Butter that goes deep down in the skin where the dullness forms. The natural Lemon Delph bleaching action has made her skin fair and lovely. Ask your chemist for 30c worth of Lemon Delph Complexion Butter or Lemon Delph Extra Fair and have a lovely complexion too.

FOR A LIGHTER, BRIGHTER DAY-NITE COMPLEXION

use quick acting

SUPER ROSE EXTRA SPECIAL FRECKLE and COMPLEXION CREAM

Contains the new complexion-aid, miracle HQX.

7/6 (75c) Tube

CLEANS — SMOOTHS
— CLEARS
— GETS DOWN DEEP
— AWAY GOES SPOTS,
PIMPLES, BLEMISHES

Super Rose

Obtainable from Chemists or Stores and Twins, 68 Noord Street, Johannesburg

Thank you, Bu-Tone!

says Miss Cecilie Morgan

Your wonderful Bu-Tone Vanishing Cream has given me the softest, smoothest skin a woman can desire!

"For years", says Cecilie, "I have received admiring glances from men and looks of envy from women. The reason, as I discovered, is my soft, smooth skin. Did I always have such a skin? No, I didn't. It's only since I started using Bu-Tone Vanishing Cream that my skin became so beautiful."

Your skin, too, can be as lovely

FOLLOW THIS 10-DAY BEAUTY TREATMENT

During the day: Always keep Bu-Tone Vanishing Cream handy, and apply it when you go out of doors, or before your friends come to visit you – whenever you want to look particularly attractive. Regular use of Bu-Tone Vanishing Cream will give your skin a wonderfully soft sheen . . . so smooth to the touch, so delightful to the eye. You, too, will say: "Thank you, Bu-Tone!"

At night: Before going to bed, wash with Bu-Tone Complexion Soap, and then apply Bu-Tone No. 3 Strong Cream. Bu-Tone No.3 Strong Cream is a high quality cream made from the very finest imported ingredients and does three very important things to your skin:
(1) Clears nasty spots and pimples that spoil your complexion.
(2) Makes your skin wonderfully light and attractive.
(3) Makes your skin delightfully smooth and soft.

Famous beauty consultants recommend that the following morning, after you have washed with Bu-Tone Complexion Soap, you again apply Bu-Tone No. 3 Strong Cream.

Complete your beauty treatment with Bu-Tone No. 3 Strong Cream: 3/- per Jar

and Bu-Tone Complexion Soap

Bu-Tone VANISHING CREAM

OBTAINABLE FROM ALL CHEMISTS AND STORES

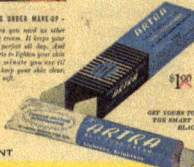

Skin · ·
Troubles.
A WONDERFUL REMEDY.

The Face, the Limbs, the Body,
freed from every kind of Skin
Complaint.

How I Got Rid of My Freckles.

Every summer my face used to be covered with unsightly yellow
spots, and my complexion was truly awful. I consulted many
doctors, but could not find anything to take out the ugly marks.
So deeply rooted did they become that even in winter time. they
could be seen, and it was obvious that as I grew older my freckles
grew worse. One day I explained my trouble to a family friend,
an eminent medical man, and he gave me the secret of a
remarkable preparation he had discovered, which, he assured
me, always succeeded, even in the most difficult cases. I was
rather incredulous, but resolved to try his treatment, and to
my surprise and delight, the first application made a distinct
difference in the depth of colour in the spots, and after a few
days they completely disappeared. My friends tried the preparation with equal success, and, desiring to make this valuable
preparation known, I will send you the preparation of Powell's
Cure for the skin trouble, 2s. 9d. Three times the quantity,
4s. 6d. Six times the quantity, 7s. 6d. Address :.

Nurse Powell's,

78 and 79, Pearl Buildings,
Portsmouth, Hants.

FIGURE 5.15. A skin lightener ad that targeted white settlers in early colonial Kenya. Like other "freckle removers" of the period, this one probably contained mercury as an active ingredient. *East African Standard* (Nairobi), October 1912.

These developments coincided with decolonization in East Africa. Tanzania and Uganda declared independence from British colonial rule in 1961 and 1962, respectively. Kenya, where the presence of a large white settler community had provoked the anticolonial Mau Mau rebellion during the 1950s, achieved political independence in 1963. That commercial skin lighteners became widely available to black East African consumers at the height of African nationalist movements helped turn these cosmetics into political lightning rods. One foreign correspondent in Nairobi pointed to the "sales boom" in skin lighteners as unequivocal evidence of colonialism's lingering effects.[82]

In postcolonial East Africa, people most commonly associated skin lightening with young women labeled modern, independent, and self-assured. This group included bar maids, sex workers, musical performers, and dancehall attendees as well as secretaries, teachers, nurses, and students.[83] A survey of

FIGURE 5.16. By the late 1960s, skin lightener ads featured prominently in Kenyan media such as this ad for a Pond's product that appeared on the front page (lower left) of a weekly Kiswahili newspaper. *Baraza* (Nairobi), August 1968.

nurses in Nairobi, from the early 1970s, found that a remarkable 95 percent of them had used or were currently using skin lighteners.[84] When Kenyan women interviewees recalled the popularity of skin lighteners during the 1960s and 1970s, they described how schoolgirls, in particular, spread knowledge of them by word of mouth. Personal recommendations and peer pressure were as influential as ads. Agnes Nyamu remembered that in the mid-1960s, schoolgirls formed a distinct social group defined by their devotion to reading and their "smart," well-scrubbed appearances. When those at boarding school came home on holiday, they often socialized together in "schoolgirl clubs." Like their peers in South Africa, they received "pocket money" from relatives and sometimes spent it on skin lighteners. Others received cosmetics as gifts from boyfriends. Nyamu recalled that while some used creams and lotions to clear pimples and smoothen their skin, others sought overall lightening.[85] Mary Gwantai, who was a secondary school student in the mid-1970s, believed that her generation, which came of age after the formal end of colonial rule, was nonetheless more attentive to skin color than her parents' generation. She explained that many of her school peers and young teachers used skin lighteners to look "brown."[86] Commercial skin lighteners had become a technology of visibility for modern girls in postcolonial East Africa as well as apartheid South Africa.

"Black Is Beautiful" and African Nationalism

As skin lighteners were taking root in East African schoolgirls and professional women's toiletries, they increasingly became the subject of political debate. During the 1960s, "Black Is Beautiful" became a rallying cry among Black Power activists in the United States and beyond. In previous decades, some black nationalist leaders, such as Marcus Garvey of the United Negro Improvement Association and Elijah Muhammad of the Nation of Islam, had urged followers to reject white standards of beauty. Such calls grew during the civil rights movement as white racism and related color hierarchies within black communities continued to disparage and discriminate against those with dark skin, full features, and tightly curled hair.[87]

Maxine Leeds Craig has insightfully argued that "Black Is Beautiful" took hold in an American context in which sociological and psychological theories of "black self-hatred" held considerable sway. Such theories were used to powerful effect in the 1954 Supreme Court case of *Brown v. Board of Education*, when "doll studies," conducted by the black psychologists Kenneth and Mamie Clark, were taken as evidence of the negative impact of school segregation on black children's self-esteem. In subsequent decades, social science research questioned the Clarks' studies, arguing that their findings were more ambiguous and that many black children retained a "positive self-image" even if they demonstrated a "white cultural orientation." Survey research from the 1940s through the 1970s, in fact, revealed that black teenagers and adults preferred "brown" skin tones to pale ones. When asked about their own complexion and that of future spouses, respondents expressed a desire for tones that were neither light nor dark but something in between. Yet studies of actual patterns of marriage found that people's words and deeds did not always align; economically successful black men were more likely to marry women with light skin tones. Within the United States where racism and colorism remained pervasive and psychological theories were influential, the affective affirmation "Black Is Beautiful" gained traction. Its declaration by African Americans of all shades, Craig writes, became a way to defy "a racial order that had held all blacks down but had granted some advantage to blacks who were physically closer to whites."[88]

Celebrities from Africa and America furthered this antiracist retort. During the late 1950s, some black women entertainers, including Abbey Lincoln, Odetta, and South Africa's own Miriam Makeba, by then an exile in the United States, began wearing "natural" hairstyles. Models from the Grandassa agency in Harlem followed suit, seeking to promote black nationalist beauty ideals that celebrated darker complexions as well as facial features and body forms deemed more African.[89] This aesthetic received an additional boost with the 1959 visit to the United States by Kenyan trade unionist and rising political star Tom Mboya. In an interview with *Ebony*, Mboya denounced the use of hair straighteners and skin lighteners as betraying "an inner question of personal worth, a sense of shame and a feeling of inferiority." He explained that while "American Negro women" might be pardoned for wanting to be "what they call glamorous," men had no excuse. With this remark, Mboya became the rare commentator to acknowledge that men too used skin lighteners. For Mboya, gender and race shaped the meaning of skin lightening. As creatures unbeholden to beauty practices, men's use of skin lighteners could signal only one thing: racial self-loathing. Mboya declared his allegiance with the words of the early twentieth-century Ghanaian educator Dr. James Aggrey: "If I could be blacker, nothing would give me more pleasure." African American journalists observed that Mboya's own "dark good looks" and those of other charismatic, anticolonial African leaders helped to make black "fashionable" in America.[90]

Black male leaders echoed the call to take pride in African appearances. The publication in the mid-1960s of *The Autobiography of Malcolm X* and the English translation of Frantz Fanon's *The Wretched of the Earth* drew attention to the psychological damage wrought by colonialism and racism, and they emphasized the power of self-awareness and personal transformation.[91] In 1962, Malcolm X, at a gathering in Los Angeles, named skin lightening as a form of self-hatred: "Who taught you to hate the color of your skin? To such an extent you bleach, to get like the white man." Three years later, he similarly urged listeners to reject the negative images of Africa instilled by European colonial powers and to embrace their "black skin, black features and black blood": "You cannot hate the root of a tree without hating the tree itself."[92] Soon after, Stokely Carmichael—a Black Power activist and Makeba's future husband—expressed a similar idea in Mississippi. After stating the need for black people to "come together" and "stop being ashamed of being black," Carmichael proclaimed, "We are black and beautiful." Thereafter "Black Is Beautiful" became both a common chant at Black Panther demonstrations and a refrain in the alternative press.[93]

James Brown expressed the sentiment to a much wider audience with his 1968 hit song "Say It Loud—I'm Black and I'm Proud." Around the same time, Toni Morrison wrote *The Bluest Eye* (1970), a novel that tells the tragic story of Pecola, a young African American girl who faces violent abuse and constant disparagement about her dark skin color. To this day, Morrison's novel remains a widely read account of the destruction wrought by the "internalization" of white beauty standards and media images.[94] These cultural productions coincided with the declining promotion of skin lighteners within African American publications.[95] Many in the United States understood "Black Is Beautiful" as a statement of solidarity with African nationalist movements and a return to African beauty standards.

The apparent contradiction between those sentiments and the continent's skin lightener "boom" was not lost on people in East Africa. Ten years after Mboya denounced skin lighteners and hair straighteners in the United States, they became the object of condemnation by nationalists in East Africa. In October 1968, the Tanzania Youth League, an arm of the ruling party, banned "women's bleaches" along with miniskirts, wigs, and "tight male trousers." Known as Operation Vijana, the campaign aimed to protect the country's youth from the "moral decadence" of the West and to forge a national culture that was socialist and African. On the one hand, the ban on skin lighteners and wigs resonated with the antiracist politics of "Black Is Beautiful." On the other, the fashion prohibitions encompassed styles, like bell-bottomed trousers and short skirts, often worn by Black Power activists and other black nationalist groups in the United States. Tanzanian officials distanced themselves even further from contemporary African American political and aesthetic sensibilities in 1969 by

FIGURE 5.17. Party officials in Tanzania display images of fashions and practices prohibited under Operation Vijana, a campaign to fight corrupting foreign influences. The second placard from the right depicts skin lightening. *Standard* (Dar es Salaam), December 1968.

banning "soul music," including the work of James Brown. As Audrey Wipper and Andy Ivaska have insightfully argued, Tanzania's Operation Vijana and other bans cast urban youth as a national problem and situated party leaders as the nation's puritanical and authoritarian fathers. Enforcement of the prohibitions on dress, in particular, resulted in humiliating and sometimes violent attacks on urban young women.[96]

Kenyan politicians entered the fray over skin lighteners just a month after Tanzania's ruling party. On the floor of the Kenyan National Assembly, Member of Parliament (MP) Martin Shikuku complained that schoolgirls were straightening their hair and using "skin-whitening creams" to "look like Europeans," and that in pursuit of "such luxury" some had gotten into "trouble," a reference to the socially vexed issue of "schoolgirl pregnancies."[97] According to Shikuku, the desire for such appearances stemmed from an "inferiority complex" that

African schools were obliged to remedy. The psychologizing discourses that informed discussions of skin color and "Black Is Beautiful" in the United States also took root in East Africa. Responding on behalf of the Kenyatta administration, Minister of Education Dr. Julius Kiano agreed that some people still suffered from "a terrible colonial mentality" and then shared a saying he had heard while studying in the United States: "If you are white, you are all right; if you are brown, stick around; but if you are black stay back."[98]

Kiano's response displayed a cosmopolitan familiarity with U.S. racial politics. It also suggested that disparagement of dark skin tones was an international and American problem, and not just a colonial and African one. Shikuku and other MPs called for the government to ban hair straightening and skin lightening, arguing that they conflicted with the nation's stated commitment to African socialism. Kiano demurred, explaining that beauty was a personal pursuit and, hence, difficult to legislate.[99] By not instituting prohibitions on certain fashions and cosmetics, the Kenyatta government displayed its more liberal political leanings and broke ranks with Tanzania's ruling party and soon-to-appear promulgations by regimes in Malawi, Uganda, and Swaziland.[100]

Kenyan politicians, nonetheless, continued to comment on skin lighteners. Discussion arose during debates over the Affiliation Act, a law passed at the end of the colonial era that granted single women the right to sue the biological fathers of their children for paternity support. Opponents of the Act argued that women used the support payments not to provide for their children but instead to buy wigs, miniskirts, and skin lighteners, enabling them to "attract" new boyfriends. In accusing women of misusing affiliation payments to purchase clothing and cosmetics that would enable them to appear "Western" and secure more suitors, MPs portrayed women as vain betrayers of "African culture." To the dismay of women's and welfare organizations, the all-male National Assembly repealed the Affiliation Act, absolving men of financial responsibility for children born outside of wedlock and casting the mothers of such children as predators and selfish consumers.[101]

When the National Assembly discussed skin lighteners for a third time, in 1971, the focus turned from users to the ads for one specific brand, Ambi. MP Samuel Kivuitu asked Assistant Minister for Information and Communication Ombese Makone if the government would ban "immediately" ads currently showing in cinemas that abused "the dignity of Africans" by claiming that the "new Africans" were "light skinned Africans who used Ambi." Makone responded that he shared his colleagues' concern and that his ministry had already spoken with the company and it had agreed to remove the ads from newspapers, radio, and cinema. In the discussion that ensued, Grace Onyango, the first woman MP elected to Kenya's postindependence legislature, pointedly asked her male colleagues what women will do if they are "forbidden to use Ambi" given "the fact that many men are in favour of brown women." The assistant minister clarified that the government was only discouraging certain ads, not banning products, but he then ignored Onyango's query that shifted the gendered responsibility for skin lightener use from women to men.[102]

Ambi's history highlights links between postcolonial Kenya and apartheid South Africa's skin lightener trade, and it demonstrates how those links often passed through the prism of the United States. Ambi was an American brand of skin lightener that contained hydroquinone. It arrived in southern Africa in 1963 when a pharmacist, named Atkinson, in Harare (then, Salisbury, Rhodesia) purchased the southern and possibly eastern African license from the product's U.S. owner. Initially, Atkinson struggled to launch Ambi as the market was so dominated by other brands that retailers and wholesalers refused to stock it. In a last-ditch effort, he decided to give away Ambi in a "massive sampling campaign." Township shop owners distributed free Ambi samples to customers who purchased staples like mealie meal. According to an industry insider, this tactic and the "whispering campaign" that ensued proved highly effective in spreading news about skin lighteners beyond "the more sophisticated Bantu" and to the "masses." By 1969, Ambi, Karroo, Bu-Tone, Artra, and Super Rose were the five major brands of skin lighteners sold in South Africa.[103] Over the following three decades, Ambi was sold across southern and eastern Africa as progressively larger companies—culminating in the U.S. multinational Sara Lee—gained control of the license.[104]

Ambi ads became notorious in both Kenya and South Africa. Some featured the slogan "successful people use Ambi" along with images of a light-toned nurse and doctor attending to a patient with a markedly darker complexion. A marketing researcher used the ads' blatant messaging to study black South Africans' perceptions of advertising models. Three hundred men and women surveyed in Soweto described the nurse and doctor as educated, attractive, respectable, and wealthy, and the kind of the people they hoped their children and grandchildren would become.[105] South African doctors who later campaigned against skin lighteners used the same ads to illustrate the insidious marketing messages employed by industry.[106] Forty years later, some still remembered the ads as especially offensive. Fatima Dike, a South African playwright who became a Black Consciousness activist, recalled her anger at seeing skin lightening so nakedly associated with succeeding in life.[107] For postcolonial Kenyan

FIGURE 5.18. Ambi, a brand first developed in the United States, became popular in southern and eastern Africa in the 1970s. Black Consciousness activists and some African nationalists criticized ads like this one for equating light-toned skin with success and modern achievements. *World* (Johannesburg), January 1970.

audiences, Ambi localized its message by hailing "modern Africans" (*Waafrika wa kisasa*) and using Kiswahili. Kenyan politicians were unimpressed. Although they might tolerate the sale of skin lighteners, they would not allow pronouncements—especially in the modern, urbane space of cinemas—that equated lightened skin color with belonging to a new African nation. The

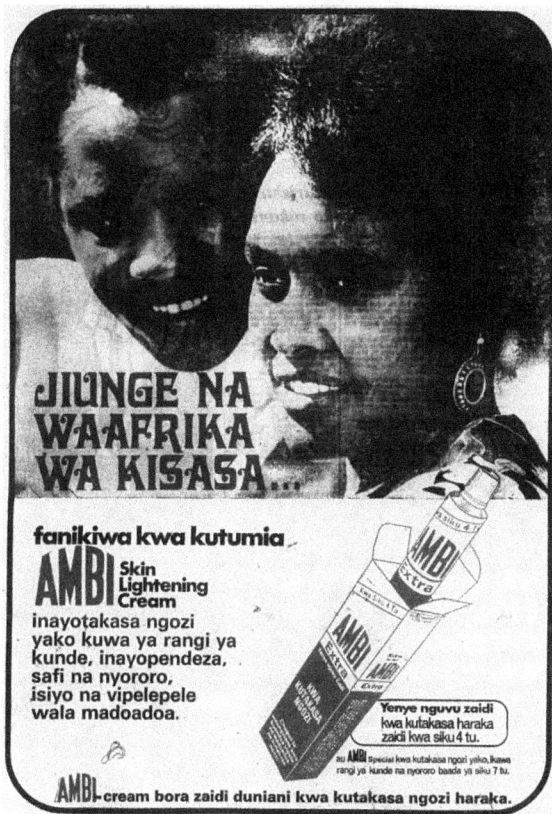

JIUNGE NA WAAFRIKA WA KISASA...

fanikiwa kwa kutumia

AMBI Skin Lightening Cream

inayotakasa ngozi yako kuwa ya rangi ya kunde, inayopendeza, safi na nyororo, isiyo na vipelepele wala madoadoa.

Yenye nguvu zaidi kwa kutakasa haraka zaidi kwa siku 4 tu.

au AMBI Special kwa kutakasa ngozi yako, ikawa rangi ya kunde na nyororo baada ya siku 7 tu.

AMBI-cream bora zaidi duniani kwa kutakasa ngozi haraka.

FIGURE 5.19. Kenyan politicians protested ads like this one that identified "the new Africans" as those who used Ambi. The Kenyatta government eventually barred such ads from newspapers, magazines, the cinema, and the radio. *Baraza* (Nairobi), March 1971.

marketing messages surrounding skin lighteners could generate greater political ire than their actual use.

Soon after Kenya's parliamentary discussion, Ambi changed its slogan. The new slogan, "the Ambi Look, the Clear, Natural look," downplayed the product's lightening effects. Accompanying images featured romantic, rather than professional success. These Ambi ads, in yellow and brown hues, conjured an earthy aesthetic, distinct from the striving ambition of the "new Africans" campaign. As Tanisha Ford has argued regarding similar ads in the United States and South Africa, they evoked elements of the then-current "soul style" that promoted "natural appearances" and black pride to sell products that many regarded as, in fact, the antithesis of that ethos.[108] Ambi remained a popular brand in Kenya well into the 1990s. The fact that it contained hydroquinone rather than ammoniated mercury helped to ensure its survival through the 1970s when medical professionals and government officials focused increasing attention on skin lighteners' active ingredients.

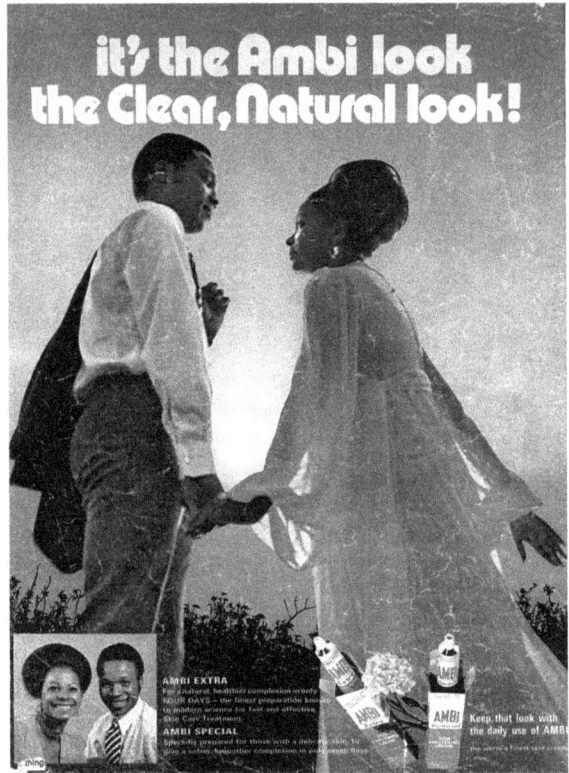

it's the Ambi look
the Clear, Natural look!

AMBI EXTRA
For a natural, healthier complexion in only
FOUR DAYS — the finest preparation known
to modern science for fast and effective
Skin Care Treatment.
AMBI SPECIAL
Specially prepared for those with a delicate skin, to
give a softer, smoother complexion in only seven days.

Keep that look with
the daily use of AMBI
the world's finest skin cream

FIGURE 5.20. Following protests, Ambi changed its advertising message and aesthetic. The new ads emphasized the product's ability to clear blemishes rather than to lighten. Through more advanced color printing techniques, the ads used saturated hues to evoke the era's embrace of "natural appearances." *Trust* (Nairobi), 1972.

Medical Problems and Government Regulations

When East African politicians condemned the use of skin lighteners, they never raised health concerns. Instead, they stuck close to the script of postcolonial nationalism, defending African values and appearances, and disparaging women who seemingly betrayed them.[109] Yet, at Kenyatta National Hospital—just a few kilometers away from the Kenyan National Assembly—dire health consequences had begun to surface. In 1972, a team of internists and pathologists from Glasgow University and the University of Nairobi published, in the prestigious *British Medical Journal*, the first refereed journal article on the ill-health effects of skin lightener use in Africa. They were alerted to the problem when a number of "young sophisticated African women"—many of them secretaries and nurses—presented with nephrotic syndrome or kidney damage. That some of the women worked in such close proximity to the doctors helped to render the problem visible.[110] After inquiries and tests, the team realized that the women had used one of two creams that contained 5–10 percent ammoniated mercury. Once the patients stopped using the creams, half experienced, after a few months, complete remission while the other half struggled with the long-term effects of kidney damage. The Nairobi doctors and researchers concluded that the situation was "entirely avoidable" by prohibiting mercury from cosmetics.[111]

Their findings attracted attention. The *Sunday Nation* carried a feature story and, four days later, a cosmetics company published a statement in the *Daily Nation* explaining that their creams contained no mercury.[112] Soon Ambi placed a similar disclaimer in one of its "Natural look" ads.[113] Researchers at Kenyatta Hospital soon undertook a follow-up study, enlisting fifty-six healthy female African nurses, a group deemed easy to track. All but three had used or were currently using a skin lightening cream. The study found the health effects of mercurial creams to be unpredictable. Although current users had high levels of mercury in their urine, none exhibited signs of kidney damage. From this, the researchers concluded that nephrotic syndrome was an "idiosyncratic response to mercury" that affected "only a few of the individuals" exposed.[114] Such variability helps explain why some users fell deathly ill while many others did not.

Two medical doctors involved in the Kenyatta studies, Drs. Alfred Kungu and Malaki Owili, recalled, when interviewed in 2004, that skin lighteners had been "very popular like mini-skirts." They explained that women used them to remove dark spots and make their faces "shine and look nice." According to Kungu, it was easy to identify patients who used the creams as when they undressed for medical exams, their faces would be a few shades lighter than the rest of their bodies. Clinicians kept a tube of Bu-Tone, the most commonly used mercurial cream, on hand so patients could identify whether it was the product they used. Owili recalled that Bu-Tone had an especially pleasant smell and texture. Whereas early postcolonial politicians had denounced skin lighteners as evidence of "racial shame" and a persistent "colonial mentality," Owili and Kungu insisted that women used them to achieve lighter, reddish complexions that were rare in the region, and had been coveted since precolonial times.[115]

In 1975, the Kenyan news magazine the *Weekly Review* ran an exposé on mercury poisoning and cosmetics. The article made no mention of the earlier criticism of skin lighteners by nationalist politicians. Rather, it chronicled the shocking death from kidney failure of "Ruth," a single mother of three in her mid-twenties, and described the Ministry of Health's indifference to doctors' various pleas to ban the cosmetics used by Ruth and other "modern girls." The article then presented research findings from the Chief Government Chemist Mr. N. Muraguri that revealed which brands contained the highest levels of mercury: Bu-Tone No. 3 skin lightener contained 10.2 percent ammoniated mercury and Metamorphosa Night Cream, 7.1 percent. Explaining his findings, Muraguri noted that Kenya lacked a regulatory body, like the U.S. FDA, that could safeguard the public against harmful cosmetics. He then used the press to exhort his own employer, the Kenyan government, to require skin lightener manufacturers to declare active ingredients and their amounts on packaging, and to ban all cosmetics containing more than 0.2 percent mercury.[116] Muraguri's exhortations, like those of the Kenyatta Hospital researchers, did little to stir regulatory action.

By the time Muraguri made his recommendations, the U.S. FDA had already adopted a tougher stance toward mercurial skin lighteners. This new stance was the culmination of years of complaints and investigations. During the 1960s, scientists identified mercury as a major environmental problem. Some of the earliest evidence came from Japan. An epidemic of severe mercury poisoning tied to industrial wastewater from a chemical factory in the city of Minamata revealed that micro-organisms could convert various forms of mercury into the highly toxic compound methyl mercury. Waterways then distributed mercury toxins into fish and throughout the food chain. The most disturbing cases of what became known as Minamata disease entailed insanity, paralysis, coma, death, and congenital disorders.[117] News of such calamities prompted consumers like Sallie Buckley of New York to write to the FDA asking whether face creams with 2–4 percent ammoniated mercury were safe to use: "I have heard and read that mercury is poison."[118] The FDA also received anxious queries from consumer groups and members of Congress.[119]

At the same time that scientists were raising concerns about mercury pollution, the U.S. federal government was turning greater attention to drug safety. Industrial and pharmaceutical developments after World War II had unleashed thousands of new chemicals and products into all aspects of American life, overwhelming the FDA's approval and regulatory mechanisms.[120] The thalidomide tragedy that resulted in thousands of cases of children born worldwide with malformed limbs and other physical impairments prompted Congress to pass the Kefauver-Harris Amendment of 1962 aimed at strengthening drug standards. The amendment propelled the FDA, ten years later, to launch a review of all over-the-counter drugs by independent advisory panels. Commercial skin lighteners—officially classified as "skin bleaching drug products"—were subject to review.[121] But rather than wait for the panel's findings, the FDA chose to ban mercurial skin lighteners immediately, effective January 1973.[122] Skin lighteners containing hydroquinone remained within the panel's purview. Those deliberations would stretch on for decades—and up to the present day—with manufacturers contesting evidence of hydroquinone's health risks.

In banning mercury, the FDA stated that it was a "known hazard" and had "questionable efficacy" as a bleaching agent. To support these statements, the FDA mustered evidence from numerous medical authorities, including the American Medical Association, as well as a new investigation by two of the agency's own toxicologists, F. N. Marzulli and Daniel W. C. Brown.[123] Their investigation acknowledged, like the second Kenyatta study, that individual susceptibility to mercury exposure was variable but then documented that chronic users of mercurial bleach creams routinely absorbed dangerous levels of mercury into their bodies, levels at least twenty times that derived from daily food intake. Over time, these levels could produce the notoriously wide-ranging signs of mercury poisoning including nervousness, numb limbs, weakness and loss of bodily control, and difficulties with speech, vision, hearing, and kidney functioning. After studying the hospital records of six chronic users, Marzulli and Brown worried that physicians' lack of awareness about mercury's ability to penetrate the skin meant that some patients were "being dismissed or misdiagnosed as psychotic" rather than being treated for systemic poisoning. Marzulli and Brown directed their findings to industry insiders by publishing in the *Journal of the Society of Cosmetic Chemists*.[124] The FDA further justified the ban by noting that they had never received "well controlled studies" documenting the effectiveness of mercurial skin lighteners.[125]

The South African government followed the lead of the FDA. Around the same time the U.S. ban came into effect, officials in Pretoria instructed manufacturers who still relied on ammoniated mercury to find a replacement ingredient or stop producing skin lighteners.[126] In 1975, the government added legal weight to this administrative action by passing a national regulation banning cosmetics containing mercury, lead, or MBH.[127] This regulation came into effect under the relatively new Foodstuffs, Cosmetics and Disinfectants (FCD) Act of 1972 that appointed inspectors to ensure that cosmetics did not include harmful ingredients or carry deceptive labeling.[128] In its broad scope, South Africa's FCD Act mimicked the U.S. FDC Act, while outpacing the United Kingdom's adoption of national cosmetics standards by six years.[129]

Despite the new regulation, confusion reigned. Mercurial creams continued to be "freely available" in South Africa while manufacturers scrambled to find a replacement ingredient.[130] An "epidemic" of leucomelanoderma—the dramatic loss of pigmentation in localized patches—resulted when a popular brand, most probably Karroo, introduced MBH to its product a few years prior to the banning. The manufacturer used MBH rather than hydroquinone because the latter oxidized in their signature wide-mouthed jars. Over a six-month period, dermatologists at two Johannesburg hospitals saw 347 cases of leucomelanoderma. One in eight cases involved men, revealing that women were not the sole users. Doctors also documented a case of a white patient who seemed from a bygone era. Whereas whites "generally prefer bronzed to pale faces," the patient was an eighty-two-year-old English woman who had never taken up tanning and instead "preserved her lily-white complexion for over 50 years" with a mercurial cream. When the manufacturer substituted MBH for ammoniated mercury, she too developed leucomelanoderma.[131]

South Africa's banning of mercury directly benefited manufacturers like Twins Products who already relied on hydroquinone as their lightening agent. Solomon Krok recalled that the ban proved Karroo's death knell as they were never able to develop a successful replacement formula.[132] In 1974, a Twins representative, seeking to learn more about U.S. regulations, sent a query to the Society of Cosmetic Chemists. The society forwarded the query to the FDA where an officer responded that hydroquinone had replaced mercury, and that skin lighteners were considered both a cosmetic and a drug, and therefore were subject to various guidelines.[133] By the mid-1970s, those guidelines included keeping concentrations of hydroquinone to 2 percent or less, and providing warning labels. Twins likely looked to the United States to learn whether more regulations might be in the pipeline.

Through the early 1980s, the FDA set the international standards for many drugs and cosmetics. In his wide-ranging history of U.S. pharmaceutical regulations, Daniel Carpenter argues that the FDA's framework was a "primary institutional export of the United States" in the second half of the twentieth century. In so many other realms of domestic policy that potentially encroached on business, the American federal government lagged behind counterparts in Europe and Asia. When it came to drug regulation, however, the FDA employed, in the 1970s, "more scientists and more heavily trained personnel" than "all the world's other drug regulators combined." Other countries often mimicked its institutional procedures and specific regulations.[134] The FDA's reputation for high standards extended to cosmetics even though such products did not require the agency's approval before being marketed. To ensure safety, the FDA largely relied on the cosmetic industry to self-regulate by voluntarily following agency guidelines.[135] When it came to skin lighteners, not all manufacturers adhered to the 2 percent guideline on hydroquinone. For example, one manufacturer continued through the early 1980s, at least, to use concentrations of up to 4 percent.[136] Some countries, like South Africa, modeled their skin lightener regulations on FDA guidelines while in others the FDA's influence worked more informally. The Kenyan government did not ban mercury but the country's manufacturers nonetheless proclaimed their products mercury-free and in line with FDA guidelines.[137] During the 1980s, as we shall see, the FDA's position at the forefront of cosmetics safety weakened considerably. As the over-the-counter drug-review panels faced considerable resistance from manufacturers and became bogged down in multistage procedures and underfunding, a number of product categories, including skin lighteners containing hydroquinone, remained without definitive regulations.[138]

A New Politics of Skin Color

Regulatory discussions of skin lighteners during the 1960s and 1970s rarely referenced race. The FDA's review panel, for instance, never noted that all four brands of skin lighteners submitted for consideration—Nadinola, Ambi, Artra, and Golden Peacock—were mainly marketed to African American consumers.[139] As Michelle Murphy has argued in her study of sick building syndrome and the Environmental Protection Agency, federal agencies in Washington, D.C., have been highly racialized workplaces. During the 1970s and 1980s, almost all scientists and professional staff were white whereas the agencies' secretarial, security, and custodial staff were predominantly African American. White privilege, Murphy argues, not only shaped power dynamics within federal workplaces but also operated as a "regime of imperception," blocking some issues from regulators' field of vision.[140] In the case of the FDA and skin lighteners, white privilege and imperceptions were likely compounded by liberal unease about explicitly discussing race and skin color. FDA officials, in their public deliberations at least, largely ignored how a consumer's racial identity or skin tone might influence why and how they used skin lighteners. Years later, a dermatologist criticized the FDA on this very point. He argued that because most FDA officials were of "northern European ancestry and have fair skin," they had little appreciation for conditions common in melanin-rich skin, including forms of hyperpigmentation that might prompt skin lightener use.[141]

In contrast to the FDA's public stance of "color blindness," racialized discussions of skin color suffused press coverage of an American doctor who treated white and black patients suffering from the depigmenting disorder vitiligo. Dr. Robert Stolar, a white dermatologist based at Georgetown University in Washington, D.C., courted attention for his therapeutic use of MBH to treat the mottled complexions produced by vitiligo. At the 1960 meeting of the American Medical Association (AMA), Stolar described his efforts, since the mid-1940s, to ease the tremendous social and psychological strains his patients felt. He then, quite dramatically, presented to his audience a light-complexioned nurse, one of sixteen "Negro" patients who now passed for white. To achieve this effect, Stolar explained, patients applied creams containing between 5 and 15 percent MBH over their entire bodies for two to three years.[142]

Stolar's announcement attracted queries and controversy. He reportedly received letters from African Americans, Indians, and Pakistanis with no dermatological problems, asking whether they too could receive the treatment. He also received "outraged phone calls," mainly from whites, who denounced him for committing "an injustice, because ... no one would be able to tell who was who." Others lauded him for solving "the race problem." Stolar responded, "My ointment method is just too slow and too tedious to affect a major part of the Negro population."[143] The African American press greeted Stolar's work, as they had Walter White's earlier embrace of MBH, with doubt and derision. The *Philadelphia Tribune* reported that black dermatologists found MBH to be an unreliable and unsafe agent.[144] The Baltimore *Afro-American* chided Stolar by pointing to a new politics of skin color in the era of African decolonization: "With the increasing importance in world affairs of the emerging nations of Africa, he should experiment with reversing the present results of his concoction. ... [Soon] there will be a tremendous market among white people who may no longer find it economically or socially profitable to remain so."[145] The commentator teased that African independence and geopolitical realignments might just make dark complexions preferable to pale ones.

By the late 1960s, the cultural influences of the African nationalist and Black Power movements challenged narratives that linked skin lightening to scientific progress. A 1968 article in *Esquire*, a mainstream U.S. news magazine, began with this anxious lead-in: "An ointment has turned fifty-five Negroes white, and there may soon be a pill that can do the job more effectively— presuming, of course, that by then there is still some advantage in *being* white." This is likely the article on skin lighteners that the young Barack Obama encountered in the U.S. Embassy library in Jakarta around 1970 and that, by his own account, sparked his racial awareness.[146] The article showcased the work of Stolar and a Yale dermatologist. It situated two of Stolar's patients, the nurse he presented at the AMA meeting (later identified as Doris Morris) and a young woman named Juana Burke, as the inverse of John Griffin, the white journalist who authored *Black Like Me* (1961). Griffin had taken the drug psoralen, also used to treat vitiligo, to turn his light skin dark, enabling him to pass as a black man in the Deep South. Like Griffin, Morris and Burke experienced white racism from a new perspective. Passing for white, they obtained better jobs and

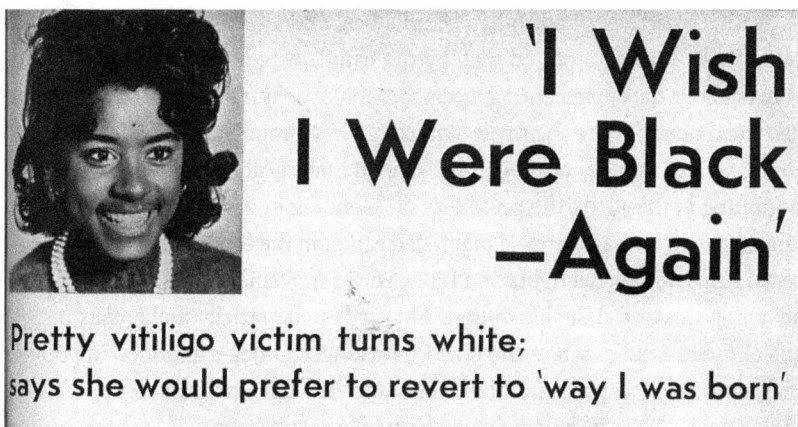

FIGURE 5.21. This *Ebony* article told the story of Juana Burke, an African American woman who had undergone treatment with MBH for her vitiligo. The larger photo shows Burke with her mother while the smaller one is of Burke as a teenager, before her complexion changed. The headline quote from Burke affirmed black pride, a message found elsewhere in the magazine. *Ebony*, December 1968.

new social opportunities; Burke was even invited by a coworker to a Ku Klux Klan meeting in Maryland. The *Esquire* article speculated that if a pill version of MBH became available, it would appeal to those who still used commercial skin lighteners—a market estimated at $14 million per year—but would be scorned by advocates of black pride.[147]

Antiracist activists had shifted the political and affective resonances of skin color. Stolar himself reported that, by the early 1970s, he received far fewer inquiries about his depigmenting research. Moreover, those he treated for vitiligo described how, despite their pale skin color, they proudly identified as black.[148] In her history of racial passing in the United States, Allyson Hobbs argues that, beginning in the 1950s, the possibility of "blending in with the white world" no longer carried the same appeal that it had earlier in the century. The political and social gains of the civil rights and Black Power movements made passing a less advantageous and desirable option. Although some racially ambiguous people still chose to pass for white, the practice no longer garnered attention in popular magazines, newspapers, and films. For many African Americans, it appeared as "either a relic of the past or the worst form of racial treachery."[149] In some regards, skin lighteners followed a similar path. By the late 1960s, skin lightener ads featured less prominently in African American publications, and black leaders rarely felt the need to comment on their use. Amid declarations of black pride and black beauty, skin lighteners seemed to be artifacts from another era, overdetermined evidence of racial shame and self-hatred. Such unsettling associations were sufficiently strong and transnational to be felt by the nine-year-old son of a white American mother and a black Kenyan father living in Southeast Asia.

During the 1970s, skin bleaches largely stopped being sold as such in the United States. Marketing surveys found that many consumers took offense at the term "skin bleaching"—with its connotations of "whitening"—and preferred the language of lightening and toning. Advertising appeals promised to fade dark spots and even out skin tone rather than lighten overall complexions. Revamped brand names reflected the new emphasis: "Dr. Fred Palmer's" went from being a "Bleaching Cream" to an "Ultra Bleach and Tone Cream" while "Bleach 'N Glow" became "Ultra Glow." Surveys found that consumers mainly used these products "to lighten unusually dark patches of skin in order to produce a more even tone." This desire was fairly commonplace. A 1974 study that included interviews with 250 black women about hair and skin-care products found that 38 percent of them had used or were currently using a "skin-toning" product.[150] Skin lighteners had not disappeared from American store shelves and toiletries, but the discourses and meanings surrounding them had shifted significantly. These shifts would make the FDA's regulatory mission all the more challenging.

DURING THE 1960S AND 1970S, skin lighteners became increasingly contested things on both sides of the Atlantic. One line of opposition centered on medical concerns. These critiques focused attention on skin lighteners' material properties and bodily effects, and the slippery distinction between cosmetics and drugs. The identification of hydroquinone as a new depigmenting agent was one episode in the much broader expansion of industrial and pharmaceutical production in the decades surrounding World War II. Cosmetics manufacturers in the United States and South Africa quickly incorporated hydroquinone into their products, hailing it as a safe alternative to mercury and yet another American scientific breakthrough. Such optimism, however, soon ran headlong into growing concerns about the environmental and bodily toxins unleashed by science and industry. Those concerns prompted the FDA to ban mercurial cosmetics and to launch a review of all over-the-counter drugs, including those with hydroquinone. Manufacturers, government officials, and medical doctors in Africa tracked these American developments. Through research publications, Kenyan and South African doctors helped make the health dangers of mercurial and, later, hydroquinone-based products visible both nationally and internationally.

The second line of opposition was rooted in antiracist politics that ricocheted across Africa and the diaspora. Postcolonial leaders rejected skin lighteners' status as technologies of visibility, condemning their use as a betrayal of African values and appearances. Civil rights and Black Power activists in the United States similarly criticized skin lightening as a misguided and shameful practice. They interpreted skin lightening through psychological and racialized idioms of inferiority complexes and colonial mentalities, and they embraced the retort "Black Is Beautiful." Such political and affective appeals altered some people's practices and changed marketing messages. Promises of touch up replaced those of overall transformation.

Throughout this period, condemnation of skin lighteners on medical grounds and on political grounds remained strikingly distinct. Medical researchers and government regulators focused on the impact of chemical agents on physical bodies, scarcely acknowledging that black and brown people were the main consumers. Antiracist activists approached the body from a very different perspective. They paid little heed to health effects but instead insisted that bodily surfaces—and how one thought and felt about them—were integral to personal and national liberation. In South Africa, beginning in the late 1970s, these two lines of critique became entangled, producing novel results.

Six

BLACK CONSCIOUSNESS
AND BIOMEDICAL OPPOSITION

At a marketing conference held in Durban in 1969, one presenter, Mr. A. Tiley, expressed an abiding optimism in South Africa's skin lightener trade. Tiley explained that another business consultant, a recent immigrant—likely from the United States—had offered a "misguided" prediction: political independence elsewhere in Africa and the U.S. Black Power movement with its affirmation "Black Is Beautiful" signaled the trade's long-term demise. Tiley insisted that South Africa's market was too strong and too distant from those political movements to feel their effect. Mockingly, he asked whether Stokely Carmichael (by then, Miriam Makeba's husband) and Rap Brown, another Black Power activist, could really change "purchasing patterns in the Republic of South Africa?" Tiley answered his own question by arguing that skin lighteners carried a "sex[ual]" rather than "political connotation."[1] Tiley was right that desires to look attractive and sexy spurred skin lightener sales. What he missed was how those desires had long been shaped by cultural and political ties that crisscrossed the Atlantic, and by racial and gender inequities. Over the course of the 1970s and 1980s, as resistance to apartheid grew, Tiley's question would appear more naïve than the newcomer's prediction.

The same year that Tiley and other businessmen attended the marketing conference in Durban, students at the nonwhite medical school across town founded the South African Student Organization (SASO), the all-black group from which Black Consciousness thought emerged. Steve Biko (the leader of the group) and his fellow students were influenced by the work of Black Power activists like Carmichael and Brown as well as African nationalism, Marxism, liberation theology,

Négritude, and the writings of Frantz Fanon. Black Consciousness activists combined and reworked these transnational influences to craft a political ideology that addressed the exigencies of life under apartheid by imagining new ways of thinking and being. Those exigencies included a barrage of images and messages that equated power and beauty with lightness and whiteness. Activists embraced "Black Is Beautiful" and condemned skin lighteners, as they sought to transform an older politics of racial respectability into one of racial self-respect.

During the 1980s, Black Consciousness thinking intersected with growing medical concerns about hydroquinone to affect skin lightener manufacturing and marketing. This chapter examines how and why political and health critiques that had previously remained distinct became intertwined. Broad and powerful alliances forged at the height of the anti-apartheid movement enabled grassroots consumer and women's groups to join forces with biomedical professionals and turn opposition to skin lighteners into an issue with widespread appeal. These alliances fundamentally altered industry and regulatory discussions of skin lighteners in South Africa and internationally. Their effects on everyday practices, by contrast, have remained more elusive.

Black Consciousness

In early 1970s South Africa, "Black Is Beautiful" circulated through popular media and was often taken as a direct retort to the pervasive presence of skin lighteners. For example, in 1971, *Bona*, the government-subsidized alternative to *Drum*, reported that Ginyindlovu Sigcau, the wife of the paramount chief of the Eastern Transkei, endorsed the motto. The pro-government press initially interpreted Black Power sensibilities as supportive rather than subversive of apartheid's principle of separate development.[2] Asked whether she endorsed the motto, Sigcau stated, "I think anybody is very proud of his colour. . . . I think Black is REALLY BEAUTIFUL." She also expressed her preference for cosmetics that do not "destroy [her] colour or complexion."[3] That same year, two social scientists noted that while "Black Is Beautiful" was heard in South Africa, its impact was negligible. Michael G. Whisson and William Weil, in a study of domestic workers, described how most people, regardless of skin color, believed that "light skins are better than dark skins." This belief, they explained, had "given rise to a large cosmetics industry aimed at making skins lighter, with advertisements emphasizing that light-brown girls are considered more beautiful and light-brown men more competent and likely to succeed in life."[4] Black Power ideas had yet to alter South African thinking.

SASO activists set about to change that. The organization initially assumed the state's racial categories, defining itself as a nonwhite student organization. But in 1970, SASO members rejected the term, amending their constitution to replace "non-white" with "black." "Non-white," they argued, denied "self-respect to the majority of South Africa's people." By using "black" to reference all disenfranchised by apartheid, SASO activists, like antiracist activists in Britain, expanded the concept of blackness rooted in African ancestry and espoused by many African nationalists and U.S. Black Power activists.[5] By defining those classified as "Coloured" and "Indian" as well as "African" as black, SASO sought to forge an intellectual and political community rooted in apartheid's racial exclusions.[6] In the early 1970s, a number of liberal publications and organizations, including *Drum, Rand Daily Mail*, and the South African Institute for Race Relations, followed suit, replacing "non-white" with "black." Other, more conservative media, did not alter their terminology, sometimes citing Indian and Coloured discomfort.[7]

SASO activists insisted that blackness was as much a way of thinking and feeling as a way of looking. Whereas previous African nationalists often presumed the masses, by virtue of their experiences, already understood the injustices of colonialism and just needed to be mobilized, SASO activists, living through the political quiescence that followed the 1960 Sharpeville massacre and the state's repression of anti-apartheid organizations, called for consciousness raising. Being conscious meant rejecting feelings of impotence and inferiority and believing in black strength and self-worth. It also meant not collaborating with the ruling regime. In a paper for a SASO training course, Biko wrote that "being black is a reflection of a mental attitude" and explained that it was still possible for a dark-skinned person to be "non-white": "Any man who calls a white man 'Baas,' any man who serves in the police force or Security Branch is *ipso facto* a non-white. Black people—real black people—are those who can manage to hold their heads high in defiance rather than willingly surrender their souls to the white man."[8]

This definition of blackness that emphasized psychical and affective dimensions, in addition to bodily features, owed much to Fanon. SASO activists encountered Fanon's ideas both by reading works like *The Wretched of the Earth* (1961; English translation, 1963) and especially *Black Skin, White Masks* (1952; English translation, 1967), and by hearing them refracted through the words of U.S. Black Power activists.[9] A black psychiatrist from Martinique who trained in France, worked in Algeria, and was influenced by the Négritude movement and existential philosophy, Fanon theorized colonialism as a system of oppression that entailed psychological as well as economic and political domination.

Racism functioned, according to Fanon, by co-opting blacks through their internalization or, in his reworking of psychoanalytic terminology, "epidermalization" of white culture including beauty standards. *Black Skin, White Masks* explored the position of the *evolué*, the "black man" who, despite his mastery of the French language and schooling system, was denied recognition within white society. Through discrimination and objectifying—if desiring—looks, the *evolué*'s "white mask" was shattered, leaving him black and "emasculated." Fanon, as Stuart Hall has explained, recast psychoanalysis's Oedipus complex from a familial to societal drama, positioning white colonizers as the father and black colonial subjects as the son. In so doing, he argued that pervasive racism was the product of not only laws and personal interactions but also media ranging from nursery rhymes and schoolbooks to movies and advertisements.[10]

As South African *evolués*, SASO activists identified with Fanon's writings and borrowed heavily from them. Yet as Mark Sanders and Dan Magaziner have argued, they did not apply his ideas wholesale but rather translated them to fit political conditions in South Africa. Within *Black Skin, White Masks*, Fanon evoked apartheid South Africa to illustrate the coexistence of structural racism and modern industrialization in sub-Saharan Africa.[11] When SASO activists read *Black Skin, White Masks*, fifteen or more years after it was published in the original French, the apartheid government remained one of the world's most formidable regimes of state-sponsored racism. By the early 1970s, it showed few signs of weakness and had a proven track record of banning, imprisoning, and exiling political opponents. Operating within these constrained circumstances, SASO activists directed their energies to consciousness raising rather than confronting government authorities. In contrast to Black Power activists in the United States and the revolutionaries called forth by Fanon in his later work, SASO activists' early intellectual and political project was less concerned with making political demands in the present than, in the words of Magaziner, ascertaining "how one should live in service of the future."[12]

Fanon's analysis of the psychological damage wrought by racism lent support to interpretations of skin lightening both as an expression of self-hatred and as the product of inferiority complexes and colonial mentalities. The very title *Black Skin, White Masks* points to a misalignment between appearances and projections. It also seems an apt description of the two-tone look of those who used skin lighteners only on their faces, leaving the rest of their bodies a few shades darker. Writing from Algeria in the early 1950s, Fanon did not discuss skin lighteners per se. He did, however, mention scientific investigations under way to develop medicines that could remove pigmentation: "For several years certain laboratories have been trying to produce a serum for 'denegrification';

with all the earnestness in the world, laboratories have sterilized their test tubes, checked their scales, and embarked on researches that might make it possible for the miserable Negro to whiten himself and thus to throw off the burden of that corporeal malediction."[13] Students and activists, who read these words in the late 1960s and early 1970s, may have felt he was describing the experiments that gave rise to the products that they saw all around them. Some skin lightener ads (see figures 5.2 and 5.3, lower right corner) had even included test tube–wielding scientists in white lab coats. For those who embraced Fanon's writings, black people's use of skin lighteners appeared as a concrete manifestation of the "epidermalization" of white beauty standards.

Not all southern Africans who encountered such psychological arguments were persuaded by them. In 1970, Abel Muzorewa, a Methodist bishop who had recently returned from studying in the United States, raised the topic with his parishioners in Harare (Salisbury). Muzorewa would go on to become a prominent political figure in Zimbabwe: he served as prime minister for a few months during the 1979 political transition and, in the 1990s, launched a campaign to unseat President Robert Mugabe. More than twenty years earlier, Muzorewa urged his parishioners to shake their "inferiority complex" and to stop using skin lighteners. His own wife, meanwhile, confided to a local journalist that she still used them, explaining they were simply cosmetics and part of "being modern": "If we don't do this, then we are bound to look like men, and this is bad."[14] For Mrs. Muzorewa, skin lightening was a gendered, not racialized, practice that helped to distinguish sophisticated feminine appearances from masculine ones.

In South Africa, SASO activists sided with her husband's interpretation. The earliest Black Consciousness condemnation of skin lighteners in print dates to 1972. That year, James Matthews, a prominent writer from a working-class and mainly Coloured neighborhood in Cape Town, published a poem denouncing "my sister" whose face is "smeared with astra cream / skin paled for white man's society" as a "schemer and a scene-stealer"; for her, "'black is beautiful' has become as artificial as the wig she wears." In contrast to this cosmetics-using, wig-wearing figure, Matthews described his naturally beautiful and regal woman: "her blackness a beacon among the insipid / faces around her / proudly she walks, a sensuous, black lily / swaying in the wind / This daughter of Sheba."[15] A couple of years later, Matthews once again evoked skin lighteners as evidence of blacks' self-destructive emulation of whites:

white syphilization
taints blacks
makes them

carbon copies...
the women
faces smeared
skin bleached
hair straightened

wake up
black fools![16]

Such poetry cast lightening as a female bodily practice that along with wearing wigs and straightening hair demonstrated a misplaced desire to appear white. By interpreting these practices through the racial binary of white and black, Matthews implicitly rejected, as a kind of false consciousness, alternative explanations of skin lightening centered on eliminating blemishes, removing tanned skin, looking modern, or cultivating a brown complexion.

Steve Biko too viewed black beauty as meriting political attention. At a conference of religious and political leaders in 1971, Biko pointed to soul music and specifically James Brown's song "Say It Loud! I'm Black and I'm Proud" as illustrating the emergence of a "modern black culture," defined by "defiance, self-assertion and group pride and solidarity."[17] Whereas some East African nationalists saw soul music, like bell-bottom trousers, miniskirts, and skin lighteners themselves, as an affront to African respectability and banned it, Biko viewed Brown's lyrics and rhythms as beckoning a way forward.[18] Black Consciousness aesthetic sensibilities aligned more closely with those of U.S. Black Power activists than African nationalists to the north. Apartheid officials increasingly recognized this alignment as a political threat. In 1975, the government banned T-shirts emblazoned with "Black Is Beautiful" and featuring a strong stoic woman with a large Afro hairstyle.[19]

Biko offered his most extensive recorded comments on black beauty in 1976, the year before he was murdered in police custody. Testifying at a trial for a group of Black Consciousness activists charged with terrorism, he explained their use of the term "black." The popular association of "whiteness" with positive things like "angels...God, beauty" produced a "feeling of self-censure within the black man." This comment prompted the state's advocate, David Soggot, to ask Biko whether the phrase "'black is beautiful'...fit in with the Black Consciousness approach." Biko responded "yes."

Now in African life especially it also has certain connotations...on the way women prepare themselves for viewing by society, in other words the way they dream, the way they make up and so on, which tends to be

FIGURE 6.1. The South African government banned this T-shirt design in 1973 on the grounds that it would harm "race relations" and threaten law and order. *Die Burger,* April 1975.

a negation of their true state and in a sense a running away from their co-lour; they use lightening creams, they use straightening devices for their hair and so on. They sort of believe I think that their natural state which is a black state is not synonymous with beauty and beauty can only be approximated by them if the skin is made as light as possible and the lips are made as red as possible, and their nails are made as pink as possible and so on. So in a sense the term "black is beautiful" challenges exactly the belief which makes someone negate himself.[20]

Despite concluding his explication with the male pronoun, Biko, like Matthews, grouped skin lightening with a range of female bodily practices. including hair straightening and wearing lipstick and nail polish. Black Consciousness use of the phrase "Black Is Beautiful," he explained, specifically sought to counter these practices that expressed African women's psychological rejection of their natural appearances.

A SASO *Newsletter* article singled out beauty products in analyzing the "cultural imperialism" perpetrated by advertising. "In a racist and capitalistic society, such as S.A.," the author wrote, "advertisements are used to reinforce the exploitation and oppression of black people." As all the country's newspapers were owned by the white capitalist "ruling class," their contents inevitably reflected their views. Citing skin lighteners and hair straighteners as some of the most heavily advertised products, the author argued that these ads instilled "an inferiority complex into the Black man" by linking success to a changed "physical appearance."[21] For these activists, the popularity of these products demonstrated not just the need to promote racial pride. It also embodied the pernicious intertwining of racism and capitalism, and the need to develop black-controlled media and commerce.[22]

Efforts to promote pride in black appearances were part of other Black Consciousness initiatives. In 1974, an organizer of the Black Renaissance Convention, a gathering of black leaders partly inspired by Black Consciousness principles, announced plans to hold a "Miss Black" competition. This was not the first time that activists had sought to use a beauty contest to convey an anti-apartheid message. One group's plan to hold a "multi-racial beauty competition" in 1961 as part of a youth festival resulted in the venue owner withdrawing permission for the entire event.[23] The Black Consciousness effort, more than a decade later, sought to deemphasize skin color: "the criterion will not be the *colour* of the skin, because our definition of *Black* does not refer primarily to the colour of the skin." The organizer chided, "Those who may have lighter skins than the 'darkies' ought not to be disheartened."[24] This remark poked fun at the routine bias toward light-toned contestants in other beauty competitions. In an interview, Cynthia Malgas, who was selected "Miss Cape Town" in 1976, explained that in contests open to all "non-Europeans," it took enormous courage and confidence for young African women like herself to compete against Coloureds with lighter skin and longer hair.[25] Malgas and other former beauty queens described how "Black Is Beautiful" became a powerful maxim for darker-skinned contestants and fashion models during the 1970s because it directly challenged previous preferences.[26]

Black Consciousness discussions of beauty products and skin lighteners situated women as their exclusive users. Yet, by the mid-1970s, as we have seen, manufacturers targeted men with brands like "He-Man" and "Alco Extra-Strong."

At dermatology clinics, men accounted for between 10 to 20 percent of skin lightener users presenting with problems.[27] Black men in southern Africa had long expressed a keen interest in their own appearance by using aromatics and medicines, styling their hair, and wearing smart clothing to make themselves attractive. The early black press reflected these concerns by paying due regard to male fashions. By the mid-1940s, *tsotsi*, the word used for narrow-bottomed male trousers, had become synonymous with stylish urban young men. In response to its first beauty contest, *Drum* received a flood of male submissions, compelling a "Mr. Africa" to be crowned (see chapter 4). Consumer surveys conducted in subsequent decades revealed that men continued to devote significant resources to clothing, haircuts, and personal grooming products.[28] Black Consciousness, nonetheless, ignored men's beauty practices, including the use of skin lighteners. This erasure fit with the movement's overarching gender politics. As a growing number of scholars of Black Consciousness and Black Power have argued, in combating white racism's emasculation of black men, these movements often reinforced patriarchal relations between black men and black women, and heteronormative roles for both.[29] In apartheid South Africa too, activist efforts to survive and combat disenfranchisement could fuel brittle forms of black masculinity.

In some regards, women played prominent roles within Black Consciousness. Deborah Matshoba and Mamphela Ramphele were among the more visible spokespeople featured in the press. The self-assertive and Afro-modern style of these young black women activists fascinated observers, reminding them of the international icon Angela Davis.[30] When Black Consciousness activism moved beyond university campuses, as Leslie Hadfield has demonstrated, women often comprised the organization's leadership and rank-and-file.[31] Yet, at the Durban medical school and other campuses where Black Consciousness thought developed, women struggled to be accepted as equal to male activists. Apart from elaboration of "Black Is Beautiful," Black Consciousness writers paid little attention to the particular conditions of black womanhood in South Africa.[32] Rather, they, like Fanon, focused on the emasculated subject.

Inattention to women's issues coincided with Black Consciousness's rejection of contemporary feminist thought. Ramphele, who in the 1990s went on to earn her PhD in social anthropology and become the vice-chancellor of the University of Cape Town, reflected on her earlier experiences in the movement as a leader, medical student and doctor, and Biko's partner. She explained that "gender as a political issue was not raised at all." She both felt "genuine comradeship" with her male counterparts and faced sexist treatment as they dismissed women as "little girls" and assigned them cleaning and cooking responsibilities at group functions. To combat such treatment, Ramphele and other women activists sought "honorary male status" by spending late nights drinking and smoking with "the boys" and becoming, as Ramphele put it in 1991, "assertive, to the point of arrogance." Even the Black Women's Federation, an organizational offshoot founded in 1975 to mobilize women, gave "scant regard" to sexism. According to Ramphele, second-wave feminism had little influence on Black Consciousness because state censorship prohibited many writings from entering the country but, more importantly, because activists dismissed feminism as a "'bra-burning' indulgence of bored, rich white Americans" that was irrelevant to black South Africans.[33] In 1971, SASO activists specifically rebuffed a proposal by leaders of the University Christian Movement, a then allied organization, to engage political insights from South Africa's emerging feminist movement. As Daniel Magaziner and Kopano Ratele have argued, Black Consciousness's masculinist politics were not simply a "product of the times" but a deliberate choice.[34] SASO activists insisted on the primacy of race over gender.

Yet women activists also recall that the one Black Consciousness issue explicitly gendered female—beauty—was decisive in attracting women to the movement. It was also the one issue that pointedly linked psychological transformation to the physical body. Ramphele has written that the assertion of "Black Is Beautiful" had a significant impact on black South African women by challenging their self-doubt: "For the first time many black women could fall in love with their dark complexions, kinky hair, bulging hips and particular dress style.... The skin-lightening creams, hot-oil combs, wigs, and other trappings of the earlier period lost their grip on many women." Such transformations, according to Ramphele, "liberated black women from being defined in terms dictated by dominant white culture." This critique of white beauty standards was not directly informed by the writings of black and white feminists in the United States. Whereas Ramphele recalled reading Fanon, Malcolm X, and the Black Panthers, she was unfamiliar then with *The Black Woman* and *Sisterhood Is Powerful*, both anthologies published in 1970 that explored the twinned forces of racism and sexism in black women's lives.[35] The feminist impulses that lay behind some women's turn to "natural" aesthetics in the United States did not travel across the Atlantic and gain traction among SASO activists.

Like Ramphele, other former women leaders in SASO recalled the importance of "Black Is Beautiful" to their involvement in the movement. Nkosazana Dlamini-Zuma explained its influence. A medical doctor who married (and divorced) future South African president Jacob Zuma, Dlamini-Zuma has held various cabinet posts in the post-apartheid period and ran unsuccessfully in 2017 for the African National Congress's top leadership post. Reflecting in the

FIGURE 6.2. Steve Biko and Mamphela Ramphele outside of the magistrate's court in East London, South Africa, in January 1977. Courtesy of Gallo Images/Daily Dispatch.

late 1980s on her involvement with SASO in the 1970s, Dlamini-Zuma described how at that time "there was a lot of emphasis commercially" on skin lightening and hair-straightening products. Black Consciousness activists interpreted their popularity as evidence of how "white people have actually made us feel that even the way we look is not right." Such feelings, according to Dlamini-Zuma, prompted SASO to prioritize "restoring pride and confidence" before undertaking any other sort of activism: "It was seen that there was really nothing substantial we can do to try and organize politically in a people who psychologically don't think they are of any value. And the first to do would be to make people feel they have a value and they are good as they are. They don't have to imitate anyone else." Rejecting skin lighteners and hair straighteners became a prerequisite for political action.[36] Similarly, Deborah Matshoba, who became SASO's literacy director and was later imprisoned and tortured for her activism, explained how female Black Consciousness activists distinguished themselves from those outside of the movement by abandoning "Ambi skin lighteners," lipsticks, and hair straighteners, and embracing afros, dashiki shirts, hot pants, and platform shoes.[37] Raising consciousness entailed encouraging black compatriots to value their bodies in new ways and to cast some beauty practices in explicitly and exclusively racial terms.

In her 1989 autobiography, *Strikes Have Followed Me All My Life*, Emma Mashinini, a prominent labor activist, explains the damage caused by associating light skin with beauty. Mashinini describes how she and other African women working in factories around Johannesburg during the 1970s used skin lighteners "to compete with the fair-skinned, so-called 'coloured,' women who ha[d] better status socially and at work." These women used skin lighteners to negotiate apartheid's hierarchies of color and privilege, motivated by a desire to look beautiful and to pass for a lighter shade of black. Attesting to the power of an antiracist ideology to rework everyday bodily practices, Mashinini attributed her and other African women's abandonment of skin lighteners to Black Consciousness: "[It] saved us from hating the colour of our skin."[38]

For some Black Consciousness activists, the disavowal of skin lighteners was a first step toward political awareness. When interviewed in 1989, Malusi Mpumlwana explained: "Some people's conscientization will only lead them to stop using skin lighteners. For some people it would give them commitment to political activism. And for yet others it would give them the commitment to the armed struggle."[39] Like Mashinini, these activists understood that skin lightener usage was especially entrenched among those who sought to compete for jobs reserved for those classified as Coloured. In an interview in 1985, Mpumlwana together with Thoko Mbanjwa and Mamphela Ramphele cited the continued use of skin lighteners by some in the predominantly Coloured Western Cape as evidence of the need for further "conscientization" in that area.[40] Consumer surveys suggested that although African households in the heavily populated areas of Johannesburg and Pretoria accounted for the greatest share of the country's total expenditure on skin lighteners, "nonwhite" residents of Cape Town spent the largest percentage of their personal care budgets on skin lighteners.[41] Reflecting in the early 1990s on the uneven impact of the sentiment "Black Is Beautiful," Ramphele wrote, "Those in rural areas, the poor and those in the Western Cape exposed to the extra burdens of the Coloured Labour Preference policy which privileged 'coloureds' above 'Africans,' remain vulnerable to an inferiority complex. The material benefits of being 'slightly coloured,' compared to being proudly African, are too real for those at the lower socio-economic strata to ignore."[42] Apartheid's minutely regulated racial hierarchies structured the economic terrain upon which "Black Is Beautiful" and its attendant rejection of skin lighteners gained traction in South Africa.

Even though many prominent Black Consciousness activists during the 1970s were medical students and doctors, none of them raised concerns about the effects of skin lighteners on the physical body. Of all the critics discussed here, only Mashinini, the labor activist, mentioned that skin lighteners damaged skin. And that statement was written in the late 1980s, after political and medical organizations teamed up to lobby for a government ban on them. Black Consciousness activists were, no doubt, familiar with the noticeable damage often caused by skin lighteners. But what made skin lighteners the object of political critique was not their harmful effect on the skin but what their widespread usage demonstrated about how structural racism had impacted black people's self-esteem and self-valuation.

During the mid-1970s, manufacturers and marketers began to express concern about the possible impact of Black Consciousness's critique on skin lightener sales. Despite their divergent politics, market researchers shared with activists an interest in psychology: what motivated people to purchase certain products and to identify with certain advertising messages? In 1975, the Bureau of Market Research at the University of South Africa conducted a study to answer these questions. The study took place in the immediate wake of the South African government's ban on mercury and in the year prior to the Soweto Uprising. Researchers showed a skin lightener ad to three hundred men and women in Soweto and asked if they thought people would purchase the product. Most responded that black consumers would buy the product, mainly because the model was attractive and "Blacks want to be lighter." Roughly 15 percent explained that consumers would not purchase the product because "Blacks want to be Black" while another 6 percent stated people would not buy the product because it caused "skin disease" or was "bad for skin."[43] Although skin lighteners remained popular, the Black Consciousness critique and, to a lesser extent, health concerns were beginning to make inroads.

"Hi-Lite treats your skin easy,"

says Grace Sekese
of Vosloorus, Boksburg.

"I was one of those who did not care for my complexion. But as a factory worker, I was jealous of some of the girls' complexions. They were smooth, light and beautiful. One day my friend said, "Grace, try Hi-Lite Extra Complexion Cream". So I used it almost everyday. It was just wonderful to see how my complexion improved with Hi-Lite. Within a weeks' time I was light in complexion and smooth at the same time. Hi-Lite doesn't burn your skin, it treats your skin easy."

This is an extract from just one of the thousands of letters from satisfied Hi-Lite users.

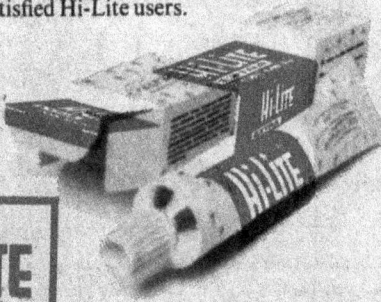

Hi-LiTE

HI-LITE EXTRA COMPLEXION CREAM.
Contains completely safe Hydroquinone

FIGURE 6.3. In 1975, market researchers showed this Twins ad to people in Soweto to assess their views of skin lighteners. While most said that black consumers would purchase the product, some said they would not due to health concerns or pride in black appearances. *Bona,* September 1976.

A study of consumer expenditures further suggested that the skin lightener market was beginning to change. Approaching the market through apartheid's racial categories, the study found that Coloured spending on skin lighteners had declined in some areas between 1970 and 1975 while Indian spending, especially in Durban, had increased. What prompted these shifts is difficult to determine, especially as they occurred against the backdrop of an overall increase in black purchasing power.[44] A sociological study done in 1973 found that Coloureds now disapproved of "passing" for white in greater numbers than they had done twenty years earlier. This finding mirrored the declining appeal of passing among African Americans in the postwar United States. The South African study concluded that greater pride in being Coloured did not, though, necessarily translate into a willingness to forge political alliances under the banner of Black Consciousness as poor Coloureds, in particular, worried about the larger African population "swamping" them.[45] The Soweto Uprising of 1976 unsettled this perspective. In its wake, Black Consciousness ideas increasingly informed young people's protests in Coloured townships and schools, encouraging some to question the political legitimacy of the category of Coloured itself.[46]

Manufacturers responded to this changing political terrain. In 1977, Twins Products, operating on "a hunch that the concept 'black is beautiful' would now catch on in Soweto," introduced a new product, Tanlite, with the slogan "For the Young, the Black and the Beautiful." The brand name, like earlier plays on tanning, situated skin-color preferences as unconnected to racial distinctions. The slogan co-opted the period's foremost antiracist retort. Unrelenting in their self-promotion, the Kroks declared Tanlite their "greatest success yet."[47]

Biomedical Concerns

As skin lightener manufacturers adjusted their advertising strategies in the hope of preserving their market, biomedical researchers in South Africa produced some of the most in-depth studies of hydroquinone's health effects undertaken anywhere in the world. Such studies blurred the distinction between commercial interests and therapeutic concerns. Between 1969 and 1975, the local manufacturer of Ambi, Nicholas Research Laboratories, supported two dermatologists based at the University of Natal, B. Bentley-Phillips and Margaret A. H. Bayles, to investigate the efficacy of cosmetic lighteners. Nicholas Laboratories provided the hydroquinone preparations used in the study and helped to organize 840 volunteers to receive patch tests. Based on the tests, Bentley-Phillips and Bayles concluded that 3 percent hydroquinone was relatively effective while higher percentages often produced irritation followed by hyperpigmentation.[48] Limiting concentrations of hydroquinone, they argued in the *South African Medical Journal*, could help place the country's sizable skin lightener market on safer footing.

Alongside their medical findings, dermatologists offered varying explanations for why people used skin lighteners that differed from those of Black Consciousness activists by not naming structural racism. Bentley-Phillips and Bayles wrote that many Africans and Coloureds used skin lighteners to improve their social standing and appearances, and to achieve a highly coveted "smoothening" effect.[49] They explained that consumers preferred a preparation that "'stings or burns'" and that they often applied creams of "higher and higher strengths [of hydroquinone] ... frequently and vigorously until a good contact dermatitis has appeared." Painful medicines were powerful medicines. When irritation turned to hyperpigmentation, users visited dermatology clinics to demand "yet another and more powerful 'lightener.'"[50] Researchers at the University of Pretoria, led by the dermatologist G. H. Findlay, attributed the appeal of skin lighteners to the "strange allurement of tradition, aesthetics, advertising, money and power" and a preference for light brown over dark brown skin tones. Users sought to replace "dull, drab, dusty, or scaly" skin with bright skin.[51] By highlighting the desire for smooth and light brown skin and radically different conceptions of medical efficacy, dermatologists' explanations pointed away from racism and toward cultural preferences and practices.

Dermatologists were not alone in largely ignoring Black Consciousness interpretations while recognizing skin lighteners' disfiguring effects. In her book, *Beauty: A Black Perspective*, Nakedi Ribane, a former Miss Soweto, recalls that skin lightener use in the 1970s was fueled by the commonplace notion that "lighter" was "better." The "danger," Ribane writes, "was that, initially, they seemed to work. They did a good job of 'taking away the Blackness' and making you look good. On first application, the skin would become smooth and yellowish, giving a lovely complexion, all pimples and blemishes vanishing like magic." With greater use, the lightening and clarifying effects of hydroquinone turned to darkening as people developed *chubabas*—darker or purpled patches of skin on the cheeks and below the eyes. Such results did not deter all users. As one woman told Ribane years later, "'Anybody who knew anything used those creams. If you don't have *chubabas*, then you were not an "it" girl of the moment!'"[52] But, *chubabas* also worked as a term of derision, a source of humiliation and shame. The term came from the Setswana word for a "burn mark on the skin" (*tshubaba*) and carried the connotation of "moral weakness."[53] Ribane recalls that young women concealed the disfigurement by wearing large,

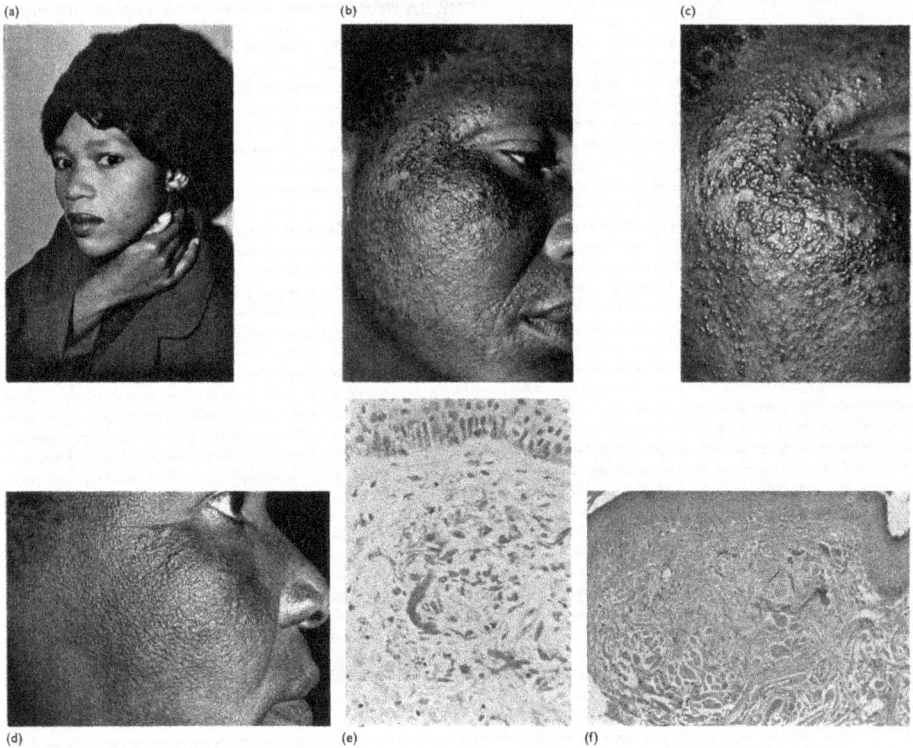

FIGURE 6.4. These photos accompanied a medical journal article on hydroquinone-induced exogenous ochronosis in South Africa. The image in the upper left shows the contrasting skin tones of a woman who used skin lighteners on her face but not her hands. The other images illustrate how exogenous ochronosis appeared on the body's surface and under an electron microscope. *British Journal of Dermatology*, 1975.

round sunglasses and applying thick foundation.[54] At some point, Ambi began selling "Chubaba Cover Cream," to help hide the damaging effects caused by their own products.[55]

In isiZulu, *chubabas* became *amashubabe* and part of a children's taunt. When children living in Durban's townships spotted a woman with dark patches, they would sing "You have *amashubabe* on your face (three times) / Take cream and apply them," before bursting into laughter. The taunt drew attention to the woman and mocked her failed quest for beauty. For some, such mockery was louder than the voices of Black Consciousness activists. In her history of skin lightener use in Madadeni, Zinhle Thwala found that women who were middle-aged during the 1970s and 1980s did not feel that Black

Consciousness had much of an impact. Women who used skin lighteners "carried on as usual" and were more likely to be dissuaded by the products' disfiguring effects than political ideologies. Younger women, however, who were students in the 1970s and 1980s, recalled learning about "Black Is Beautiful" from teachers and others. A number of them chose not to use skin lighteners as a result.[56]

What were popularly known as *chubabas*, Findlay and his colleagues at the University of Pretoria identified as an epidemic of exogenous ochronosis and colloid milium. In 1974, they reported in the *British Journal of Dermatology* on patients presenting with faces marred by patches of bluish-black hyperpigmentation and caviar-like clusters of darkened papules. Although some initially blamed the disfigurement on the women's use of hormonal birth control pills, the researchers suspected skin lighteners. Their study involved thirty-five African women, between the ages of thirty and thirty-nine, who had used hydroquinone-containing creams for up to eight years. Dermatologists had long known that phenol compounds, such as those found in fuels, could cause exogenous ochronosis (as opposed to endogenous ochronosis caused by metabolic disorders). Findlay and his colleagues were the first to identify hydroquinone as another trigger for the condition. They dated the origins of South Africa's exogenous ochronosis epidemic to 1966, when a number of manufacturers increased concentrations of hydroquinone from 3 percent to upward of 8 percent. By the mid-1970s, nearly 30 percent of the African patients seeking treatment at dermatology clinics did so for exogenous ochronosis. The condition proved difficult to treat; the disfigurement appeared to be long-term and possibly permanent, and it seemed to be aggravated by sun exposure.[57] The publication of these findings in a top medical journal made Findlay and his colleagues into the world's foremost medical authorities on hydroquinone-induced exogenous ochronosis.

Their research figured prominently in the deliberations of the U.S. Food and Drug Administration (FDA) about hydroquinone. In 1978 and again in 1982, the agency's advisory panel on skin bleaches reviewed the existing medical literature and solicited testimony from researchers, manufacturers, and consumers. Panelists singled out Findlay and his colleagues' study as decisive in reaching two of their key conclusions: hydroquinone concentrations of higher than 2 percent put consumers at risk for developing exogenous ochronosis, and exposure to ultraviolet radiation heightened that risk. The panel recommended that the FDA's already existing guideline of 2 percent hydroquinone be made into a regulation. It also recommended that products include sunscreens and that labels carry more extensive warnings.[58] American manufacturers pushed back hard on these recommendations. They questioned the FDA's scientific evidence and bristled at the panel's descriptions of their products as "bleaches" and "lighteners" rather than "toners."[59] Manufacturers' coordinated resistance combined with procedural delays and underfunding of the FDA to prevent the recommendations from becoming regulations. Instead, they remained voluntary guidelines.[60]

While regulatory deliberations languished in the United States, more and more South African medical professionals began to voice concern over the widespread use of hydroquinone. Dermatologists at Baragwanath Hospital in Soweto and Ga-Rankuwa Hospital in Pretoria reported a related rise in skin disorders including dermatitis, leucomelanoderma, melanosis, colloid milium, and ochronosis. The "aesthetic embarrassment" caused by these chemically induced conditions, they explained, left young women "emotionally disturbed." The researchers urged the government to test skin lighteners for safety and to strengthen manufacturing regulations.[61] Others argued that medical professionals could not wait for government action. In 1978, Lee Cornwell, who worked at a hospital dispensary in Pretoria, published a letter in the *South African Pharmaceutical Journal* deriding the ethics of retail pharmacists. The skin lightener trade preyed on "under-educated" and "impressionable" consumers by associating all manner of success with fair-colored complexions: "Is it proper for the pharmacist to exploit this sort of advertising and to sell a product which may well cause irreparable damage?"[62] For Cornwell, false consciousness and capitalist greed had produced an intolerable situation.

By 1980, Findlay sought to draw broader attention to the country's growing skin lightener problem. He recognized that his earlier study had been "too academic" and had had little practical impact. He wrote that cases of exogenous ochronosis could still be seen "everywhere on the streets." Manufacturers had succeeded in undermining proposals for greater regulation. More detailed knowledge of the products and market dynamics, Findlay decided, might make a difference. Together with a clinical assistant, he collected and analyzed thirteen brands, publishing the results in the *South African Medical Journal*. One company, they discovered, manufactured seven of the thirteen the brands tested, including the two that contained the very highest concentrations of hydroquinone of between 6.5 and 7.5 percent. The researchers had stumbled across Twins's singular role in the skin lightener trade.[63]

Medical researchers now understood skin lighteners as a complex issue where health concerns collided with commercial interests, and where political awareness might transform aesthetic preferences. Findlay hoped that black consumers would realize that they did not need cosmetic skin lighteners. He found cause for optimism in recent developments. Some manufacturers reported that political ideas spread by the Soweto Uprising had stalled, if not decreased, sales while one women's magazine had stopped carrying skin lightener advertisements, citing the damage they caused.[64] Political and medical critiques of skin lighteners were gaining ground and beginning to reinforce each another. An advertising guide, for one, noted that "increasing Black consciousness" together with greater awareness of health risks had turned many consumers away from skin lighteners.[65] Nimrod Mkele, the advertising man who twenty-three years earlier had insisted that women used skin lighteners to achieve a glowing and "titivating" appearance, concurred. In an editorial, Mkele lauded medical professionals for raising alarm bells and credited Black Consciousness for altering how black beauty was judged.[66]

An Anti-Apartheid Corollary

The convergence of political and medical opposition to skin lighteners began to achieve noticeable results. In 1980, the Department of Health turned the U.S. FDA's guidelines on hydroquinone into a South African regulation by limiting the maximum concentration to 2 percent and requiring brief warning labels.[67] This regulation, however, did not satisfy medical professionals who believed that, even at lower concentrations, hydroquinone was dangerous. Findlay, for one, surmised that the duration and intensity of use likely mattered more than the percentage of hydroquinone. The fact that South African consumers tended to use skin lighteners multiple times per day and for extended periods of time while experiencing some of the most intense sun exposure in the world made the U.S. guidelines insufficient.[68] Black organizations joined dermatologists in calling for a complete ban. The organizations ranged from the Azanian People's Organization, the leading Black Consciousness group, to the more conservative Inkatha Women's Brigade. Condemnation of skin lighteners garnered support across the spectrum of black politics. The largest manufacturers—namely, Twins Products, Nicholas Laboratories, and Adcock Ingrams Laboratories (by then, the manufacturer of Bu-Tone)—fought back. They argued that the 2 percent limit was the international gold standard and sufficient for safeguarding South Africans.[69]

In 1983, the Department of Health, under pressure from activists and medical professionals, required manufacturers to include sunscreens, limit product claims, and attach additional warnings. Once again, South African authorities imbued FDA guidelines with the force of law. The new regulations mandated that labels explain that products might not be effective on dark skin and that they should be discontinued if lightening did not occur within two months. The new regulations also required manufacturers to refrain from claiming that products could render skin healthier, younger, brighter, or clearer, or that they could "fade spots on skin."[70] These restrictions prohibited many long-standing advertising appeals. They also demonstrated the greater willingness of South African authorities, compared to their American counterparts, to intervene in marketing messages.[71]

In the early 1980s, the coalition of activists and medical professionals also convinced *Drum* to stop carrying skin lightener ads. For three decades, the magazine had featured countless ads that helped to make light-toned models and beauty queens iconic figures across much of the subcontinent. Although the number of skin lightener ads in *Drum* had declined over the 1970s, they still represented a significant source of revenue.[72] When announcing its decision to drop the ads, *Drum* pointed to health concerns over hydroquinone and pressure from political groups who considered the ads "an affront to the dignity of Black people." At the forefront of pressuring *Drum* was the adult literacy magazine *Learn and Teach*.[73] Founded by a young white anti-apartheid activist, Marc Suttner, in 1981, *Learn and Teach* sought to raise political awareness through articles on topics of popular interest, written in easy-to-read English. The magazine affirmed the Black Consciousness slogan "Black Is Beautiful," reported on the dangers of skin lighteners, and featured graphic photos of consumers who had been disfigured by them. It also challenged newspapers and magazines to stop advertising them.[74] When *Drum* heeded that challenge in 1983, it reportedly forsook R50,000 in annual revenue.[75]

As *Learn and Teach*'s campaign suggests, skin lighteners had become an issue embraced by white leftists. Criticism of a practice born of consumer capitalism appealed to their often Marxian politics. Furthermore, activism on this issue demonstrated a practical concern for Africans' well-being and an appreciation for the political insights of Black Consciousness.[76] Some Black Consciousness activists, in fact, chided white and "integrationist" organizations for taking so long to recognize and condemn the destruction wrought by skin lighteners.[77] Beginning in the early 1980s, such condemnation became increasingly common. For instance, Geoff Budlender and colleagues at the Legal Resource Center in Johannesburg set out to bring a class action lawsuit against the manufacturers. After encountering some difficulty in recruiting a "named plaintiff," they enlisted a domestic worker from Johannesburg who had suffered disfigurement. The case fell apart, though, once it became clear that she and other consumers had used numerous products over many years, making it difficult to target a specific company.[78] Skin lighteners also attracted the attention of white intellectuals inspired by feminist and critical media studies. In publications aimed at reaching wider audiences and linking their academic

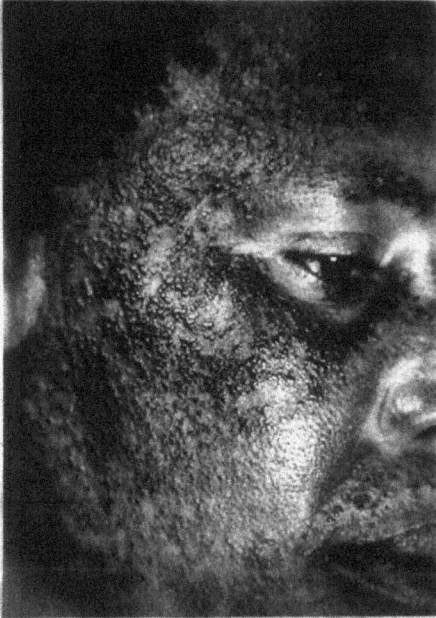

SAY GOODBYE TO SKIN LIGHTENING CREAM

The Health Department may ban skin lightening creams later this year. They may ban skin lightening creams because these creams can poison your skin.

In March this year, The Health Department sent out forms to skin doctors. The Health Department wants to know what skin doctors think of skin lightening creams.

Some doctors have sent the forms back. Other doctors will send back the forms soon. "We will decide what to do after we get all the forms back", says Dr Piet Swanepoel from the Health Department.

Learn and Teach decided to find out what skin doctors think of skin lightening creams. We spoke to 11 skin doctors from all over South Africa. We spoke to skin doctors who help black people.

Ten doctors said the Health Department must ban skin lightening creams. Only one doctor said the Health Department must not ban skin lightening creams.

The doctors say shops must only sell skin lightening creams to people with a doctor's note. They say only skin doctors must decide who can use skin lightening creams. Doctors sometimes give skin lightening cream to people with skin diseases. But doctors only give skin lightening creams to a few people.

Please turn the page

This person has hydroquinone poisoning. This person got hydroquinone poisoning from skin lightening cream. LEARN AND TEACH 1982 2

These are some skin lightening creams which are made with hydroquinone. LEARN AND TEACH 1982 3

FIGURE 6.5. This spread that featured a close-up of exogenous ochronosis appeared in an anti-apartheid adult literacy magazine that actively campaigned to have all skin lighteners banned in South Africa. *Learn and Teach* (Johannesburg), 1982.

work to political struggle, they evoked skin lightening as evidence of advertisers' ability to create false needs and called on African women to develop confidence in "their blackness."[79]

Ethnographic research undertaken by Mamphela Ramphele revealed just how difficult it was for poor women to heed that call. When studying Cape Town's migrant labor hostels in the mid-1980s, Ramphele found skin lightening to be an integral part of single women's competition for male partners. Where definitions of beauty often centered on skin color and attractiveness was a "matter of survival," women considered it "suicidal to stop using skin-lightening creams." Those who gave them up would be "dumped," one woman explained, in favor of those who were "nice and pink." For those barely able to make ends meet, skin lighteners remained technologies of visibility. The damage evident on older women's faces was no deterrent: "Let that day come when it comes; for now I can't stop and take the risk of losing out. In any case it might happen when I am too old to bother about my looks." Ramphele observed that once a woman's skin became "ugly, rough, dark," she often turned to stronger creams with higher concentrations of hydroquinone or to other products including bleach, shoe polish, and cortisone cream. Such desperate attachment to skin lightening, Ramphele concluded, was the result of a "racist environment that denigrates anything that is not white" and the "sexual objectification of women's bodies, turning them into play-things owned by men."[80] Skin lightening was rooted in racial, gender, and class inequities.

Epidemiological research confirmed that skin lightening was more deeply entrenched among poor and less-educated consumers, and that its physically damaging effects were more widespread than previously presumed. In 1985 and 1986, researchers randomly surveyed 195 patients seeking nondermatological treatment at two hospitals in Pretoria. Nearly half reported that they had used skin lighteners, mainly for reasons of achieving a lighter and "more beautiful" complexion or for fixing skin problems. A remarkable one-third of all those surveyed (15 percent of the men and 42 percent of the women) had exogenous ochronosis. Of the four demographic variables recorded (age, sex, employment, and education), low levels of education correlated most closely with ochronosis. Whereas approximately 15 percent of those with six or more years of schooling had ochronosis, it was around 50 percent for those with five years or less. Suggesting that ochronosis was a cumulative condition and that anti–skin lightener messages might have begun to take root with young people, ochronosis rates were highest among thirty- to forty-nine-year-olds while no teenagers reported using skin lighteners.[81] Two other surveys likewise indicated that one-third of black women in the Pretoria and Johannesburg area had exogenous ochronosis. The researchers behind those surveys surmised that the 2 percent limit on hydroquinone and extensive warning labels had done little or nothing to stem the epidemic, especially among those with limited literacy.[82]

Growing concern about skin lighteners dovetailed, in the mid-1980s, with increasing resistance to apartheid. The United Democratic Front, founded in 1983 to protest political reforms that continued to exclude those classified as African, grew into a broad anti-apartheid coalition of labor, civic, church, and student organizations. Their protest activities included boycotting the government's new tricameral parliament, and staging large demonstrations, stay-aways, and strikes. The government responded to these and other protests by declaring a partial state of emergency in 1985 and a more comprehensive one the following year that resulted in thousands of detentions, disappearances, and deaths. With mass gatherings banned, curfews imposed, and arrests and detentions widespread, some activists turned to alternative tactics including consumer boycotts. More and more South Africans felt compelled to take some sort of stand against apartheid.[83] Lobbying for a complete ban on skin lighteners emerged as one relatively safe yet symbolically powerful way for a range of consumer, medical, and women's groups—including even the Housewives' League of South Africa—to demonstrate a commitment to political change.[84] Opposition to skin lighteners had become a corollary of the anti-apartheid movement that both leftist and liberal organizations could embrace.

By 1987, the National Black Consumer Union (NBCU) and a group of dermatologists led the campaign. Ellen Kuzwayo, a leader of the African National Congress Youth League in the 1960s, was now president of the NBCU, bringing political clout to the organization's work. Hilary Carman, one of the dermatologists who teamed up with the NBCU, explained in an interview in 2004 that she joined the campaign to turn her medical knowledge to activist ends. Carman was a member of the National Medical and Dental Association, a professional group formed in 1982 to oppose apartheid policies in health-care services. Kuzwayo, Carman, and others gave presentations to community groups, and urged the government to ban skin lighteners. Consumers, they argued, still seemed to disregard warning labels, and manufacturers seemed unwilling or technically incapable of controlling hydroquinone concentrations.[85] While one newspaper reported that skin lightener sales were declining by 10 percent each year, others emphasized that the market was still sizable. Estimates of total sales varied widely, ranging anywhere between R30 million to R94 million per year.[86] One study found no fewer than fifty-eight brands of skin lighteners for sale in Johannesburg shops.[87] Feeling that officials were ignoring their pleas, the NBCU and dermatologists took their case to the country's supermarket chains. In May 1987, Checkers and Pick n Pay dropped all products containing hydroquinone from store shelves.[88] A cross-racial alliance of consumer and health groups had achieved a significant victory.

Around the same time, the apartheid government announced a draft regulation to ban all skin lighteners. Activists welcomed the announcement but worried that manufacturers might foil the plan. Twins, which reportedly controlled 70 percent of the market, took the lead in denouncing the proposed regulation. One spokesperson, Tony Bloom of the Premier Group, which owned half of Twins, argued that skin lighteners should be treated like cigarettes: although they can have damaging effects, consumers should have the right to buy them. Citing the U.S. FDA declaration that hydroquinone was safe at 2 percent or less, Bloom insisted that skin lighteners were only harmful when "overused" or used in combination with household products. Abe Krok also warned of dire consequences if the proposed ban were implemented.[89] Despite Twins's lobbying efforts, the parliament passed the regulation in December 1987 with an implementation date of July 1, 1988, so as to allow retailers and manufacturers time to clear stock and adjust operations. The regulation both prohibited all depigmenting agents, including hydroquinone in any amount, from over-the-counter products and prohibited all cosmetics purporting to be a "skin bleacher, skin lightener or skin whitener." Regardless of the ingredients they used, companies would no longer be allowed to market cosmetics under any of these claims.[90] A week before the July deadline, the minister of health, Dr. W. A. van Niekerk, shocked observers by deferring implementation of the regulation for another two and a half years. Van Niekerk attributed his decision to "certain legal, economic and health implications."[91]

Medical associations, activists, and even mainstream politicians expressed outrage about the decision. The head of the dermatological society called it a "national disgrace." Another leading dermatologist, Dr. Mary Ann Sher, urged officials to reconsider the postponement as the latest research indicated that preparations with even 1 percent hydroquinone could be harmful. As South African opponents of a ban continued to evoke FDA guidelines to defend their position, one doctor in Pretoria wrote to American officials asking whether, given the accumulating medical evidence, it was not time for them to reconsider their position. The NBCU vowed to launch an even more aggressive campaign.[92] The health spokesperson for the Progressive Federal Party, the main parliamentary opposition to the governing National Party, stated that blacks now referred to the damage caused by skin lighteners as "apartheid disease" because they believed that "if white women developed the same symptoms, the product would be banned immediately." Another medical professional explained that the government's inaction demonstrated, once again, how the "interests of industry and capitalism superseded the health and wellbeing of individuals."[93] Although activists already understood the country's skin lightener problem as the product of state racism and corporate capitalism, the minister's sudden postponement seemed to reveal a more explicit collusion. Representatives from a black-owned businesses' association reportedly told President P. W. Botha that if he failed to heed popular pleas on skin lighteners, he would not have "credibility on wider issues."[94] By 1990, opposition to skin lighteners had become a litmus test for the country's highest political leader.

Twins's fingerprints appeared all over the postponement. Soon after it was announced, Ian Ellis, the general manager of Twins, threatened that the company would sue anyone who continued to make "unsubstantiated allegations" about the harmful effects of skin lighteners. He argued that the postponement would protect consumers from "unscrupulous backstreet operators." Undercutting this strident defense, Ellis further explained that the company would comply when the ban eventually came into effect in January 1991 by registering its products as medicines rather than cosmetics. Activists viewed the company's threat of a lawsuit as unacceptable and a sham.[95] Some, in fact, suspected that the Kroks had bribed the minister to defer the ban.[96] Responding to rumors, van Niekerk insisted that he had made a "thorough investigation" and handled the issue with "great care."[97]

Changes in political leadership made a difference. In April 1990, in the period between Nelson Mandela's release from prison and the start of public negotiations with the African National Congress, the National Party government returned to the issue. By this point, the Department of Health was led by Dr. Rina Venter, a social worker by profession. Her appointment made her the first female cabinet member in South African history. As part of newly elected President F. W. de Klerk's cabinet, Venter was charged with beginning to desegregate health services and directing greater attention to the health needs of the country's majority population.[98] After meeting with leaders of the NBCU, black business groups, and medical associations, Venter accelerated the ban. Despite a last-minute legal challenge by Twins, the importation, manufacture, and sale of cosmetic skin lighteners became illegal on August 10, 1990. South Africa banned hydroquinone and all other depigmenting agents from cosmetics. Moreover, it became the first—and remains the only—country in the world to prohibit all cosmetic claims to bleaching, lightening, or whitening.[99] This combination bears witness to the broader antiracist political movement that fought for the regulations.

After nearly a decade of campaigning, activists and their allies celebrated their victory. The NBCU congratulated Venter for taking the final step while Sher stated that the Dermatological Society was ecstatic.[100] Others pointed to Black Consciousness's pivotal role in changing people's minds by promoting "Black Is Beautiful" and bolstering peoples' "confidence and pride." Journalist Farieda Khan described the ban as a "barometer" of the times, a product of increased political assertiveness by black grassroots organizations. Khan also expressed caution: the desire for light skin had deep historical roots that could not be "legislated out of existence."[101] An NBCU spokesperson suggested the difficulty of separating that desire from the universal longing to look good. Anastasia Thula explained that, as a young nurse during the 1970s, she used creams with hydroquinone not to appear "whiter" but to be "beautiful." The disfigurement they produced had left her and many other women with "grave psychological damage." In contrast to Black Consciousness thinkers, Thula situated psychological problems as the consequence rather than the cause of cosmetics use. She also underscored their affective appeal, stating that "any person will always want to have a beautiful face."[102]

The 1990 regulations did not extinguish consumer desires but they did have an immediate effect on commercial manufacturing. Stuck with an inventory worth R13 million, Twins was reportedly "very unhappy" with the situation. They considered exporting their remaining stock to neighboring countries where similar bans did not exist. Twins had earlier promised to develop new skin lightening products that did not contain hydroquinone.[103] By prohibiting that entire category of cosmetics, however, the regulations made that plan moot and Twins halted their manufacturing operations for lighteners.

Meanwhile, former users and dermatologists worked to heal the many cases of exogenous ochronosis that remained. Darkened and scarred patches on peoples' faces served as a visible testament to heavy and prolonged hydroquinone use. Some turned to over-the-counter creams to fix or conceal the patches. Others secured prescriptions from doctors and pharmacists for creams containing more hydroquinone or topical corticosteroids.[104] During the 1990s, corticosteroids—purchased over-the-counter in low dosages or in higher dosages by prescription and on the black market—were repurposed as skin lighteners in many African cities. Normally used to treat a variety of skin irritations, corticosteroids lighten skin by restricting blood flow and slowing the production of melanocytes or pigment cells. When used over a prolonged period and at greater strengths, they can produce rashes and skin thinning and invite fungal infections.[105] Unscrupulous health professionals supplied traders with prescription-only topical corticosteroids such as Lenovate and Persivate.[106] While the use of corticosteroids produced new problems, South African dermatologists recall that, over the 1990s, they saw fewer and fewer cases of hydroquinone-induced ochronosis in their clinics and on the streets. Many peoples' damaged skin slowly recovered and the earlier epidemic largely faded from view.[107] At least in the short term, the 1990s regulations produced tangible results.

With hydroquinone products relatively difficult to obtain, demand for *ummemezi* spiked. In the mid-1990s, Farieda Khan, together with a group of environmental researchers from the University of Cape Town, investigated the trade in bark from indigenous, and often endangered, trees. Although herbalists sold *ummemezi* for a variety of skin conditions, the majority of consumers surveyed said they purchased it to achieve a lighter and more beautiful skin color. Such complexions, they insisted, enhanced their job prospects and success in attracting and retaining boyfriends. The reasons for skin lightening seemed unchanged from the apartheid era. Khan also explained that demand for *ummemezi* was damaging the country's forests.[108] Sale of botanical preparations for skin lightening had survived and even thrived across the country's dramatic political changes.

South Africa's Regulatory Influence Elsewhere

As South Africa's new skin lightener regulations produced uneven effects at home, they helped ignite fresh debate abroad. News of them reached Washington, D.C., just as FDA officials were beginning to ask whether hydroquinone might be carcinogenic. New York City officials picked up on those concerns and the South African regulations to publicly urge the FDA to stop the sale of skin lighteners until their safety could be assured. Consumer Affairs Commissioner Mark Green, a white Democratic Party activist, and Ritashona Simpson, an African American research associate, garnered attention in the *New York Times* and *Los Angeles Times*. Their report documented the industry's flagrant disregard for the FDA's 1982 guidelines and blamed the Reagan and Bush administrations' deregulatory agenda for stalling federal action. Green and Simpson pressed the FDA to move against an industry that garnered $44 million in annual sales and placed hundreds of thousands of consumers—mainly African Americans—at risk.[109]

Their call sparked a heated response from industry representatives and, less predictably, black political organizations. The Nonprescription Drug Manufacturers Association (NDMA) dismissed the new evidence against hydroquinone as flawed and irrelevant to American consumers. The NDMA presented the FDA with a chart comparing the U.S. and South African situations: many more skin lighteners were sold in South Africa (25 million units per year in South Africa versus 10–15 million per year in the United States) with much higher concentrations of hydroquinone (6–8 percent in South Africa versus 1–2 percent in the United States), often in alcohol solutions, and with little appropriate labeling or the inclusion of sunscreens.[110] The NDMA ignored Green and Simpson's finding that manufacturers often disregarded the FDA's guidelines.[111] The Congressional Black Caucus, the National Urban League, and Women in the National Association for the Advancement of Colored People (NAACP) soon added their voices to hydroquinone's defense. Their responses were closely timed and appeared coordinated with one another and with industry. They too dismissed evidence from "developing countries" while charging the FDA with failing to consult black physicians and dermatologists. For over fifty years, they argued, millions of African American consumers had safely and effectively used "fade creams" as a "low cost option" for treating various forms of hyperpigmentation resulting from acne, insect bites, razor bumps, and other skin irritations.[112] These organizations were strong allies of the anti-apartheid movement but on the issue of skin lightener regulation, they did not see eye to eye.[113]

One African American leader voiced support for greater FDA oversight. Dr. Denese Shervington was chairwoman of the International Coalition of Women Physicians. In a letter to the FDA, she explained that while more black experts should be involved in the agency's deliberations, scientific integrity must be maintained: hydroquinone's safety should be addressed "scientifically, and not in a political reactionary manner." African Americans deserved health policy rooted in "accurate and sound medical evidence." These statements resonated with FDA officials' sense of their own mission. In an unusually forthright and enthusiastic response, a senior official told Shervington that he "fully agree[d]" and then shared her letter with the National Urban League and the NAACP.[114] Feeling pressure from black political organizations and aware that FDA deliberations on skin lighteners had been a largely white affair, this official saw Shervington's letter as a useful piece of support.

Over the 1990s, the FDA debated whether greater restrictions should be placed on hydroquinone. In May 1992, officials held a meeting with the NDMA's "Hydroquinone Task Force," a group of industry leaders and eminent dermatologists, including from Harvard and Howard, a historically black university. These dermatologists testified that hydroquinone was a safe and indispensable drug for treating hyperpigmentation for both clinical and over-the-counter uses. Nonetheless, they acknowledged the labeling abuses documented by Green and Simpson and advocated new guidelines to remedy them.[115] Officials worried that labeling guidelines alone were insufficient to address their ongoing concerns. At the FDA's urging, industry promised, in 1999, to adopt stricter warnings and to conduct further tests regarding hydroquinone's safety.[116] Results from those tests never materialized.

In the meantime, a number of other countries altered their regulations. Zimbabwe adopted the first round of South African regulations in 1983 by making 2 percent hydroquinone the legal limit, mandating expansive warning labels, and restricting advertising claims.[117] Reminiscent of African nationalist measures of the late 1960s and early 1970s, the military ruler of the Gambia, in 1995, banned all skin lighteners, declaring them decadent and un-African. He also noted that they were harmful to health.[118] Physicians in the United Kingdom took note of South Africa's 1990 ban with some calling for more careful scrutiny of hydroquinone.[119] Newspapers in a variety of countries carried reports of skin lighteners being manufactured in Europe and illegally imported to South Africa.[120] In 2001, the European Union (EU) issued the directive that the U.S.

FDA had contemplated. They barred hydroquinone from skin lightening cosmetics, citing the chemical's "harmful secondary effects."[121] That same year, the Japanese government added more complexity to international standards by actually loosening their restrictions. Since the development of hydroquinone as a depigmenting agent in the 1940s and 1950s, the Japanese government had limited its use to prescription by doctors. Beginning in 2001, however, a broad deregulation of cosmetics made it easier for Japanese companies to include ingredients like hydroquinone without undergoing an extensive and expensive approval process. Subsequently, a number of Japanese companies introduced hydroquinone into their cosmetics products.[122]

A number of other African governments followed the lead of South Africa, the Gambia, and the EU. As we have seen, skin lighteners had been the subject of significant debate and discussion in Kenya since the 1960s. Although the early postcolonial government, unlike neighboring regimes, did not ban skin lighteners outright, it did bar certain advertisements and condemned the sale of mercurial cosmetics. During the 1980s and 1990s, debate continued as Kenyan newspapers and magazines routinely ran features, editorials, and letters to the editor promoting the sentiment "Black Is Beautiful" and documenting the ill health effects of skin lighteners. A few months after the EU passed its directive in 2001, the Kenya Bureau of Standards issued a public notice banning cosmetics containing mercury, hydroquinone, and topical corticosteroids. The notice listed fifty-three products currently on the market that contained those ingredients.[123] Uganda and Tanzania soon passed similar regulations. Whereas thirty years earlier, they had banned skin lighteners on political grounds, their opposition was now rooted in naming harmful ingredients and outing specific brands.[124]

THE FACT THAT SOUTH African regulations prohibit skin lightening ingredients and any claims in advertising to bleaching, lightening, or whitening has much to do with the country's late twentieth-century status as the foremost bastion of state-sponsored racism. Political opposition to skin lighteners there, as elsewhere, stemmed from antiracist efforts to embrace blackness and the beauty of melanin-rich complexions. Black Consciousness activists denounced skin lightening as evidence of the psychological damage wrought by racism and capitalism. At the same time, dermatologists raised concerns about the damage done to physical bodies. Through the broader anti-apartheid movement, these critiques became conjoined. Together, political activists, consumer and women's groups, and health professionals turned hydroquinone into a household word and highlighted yet another way in which inequality produced ill health. It was the very entanglement of political and medical concerns that made their campaign so efficacious in the waning months of apartheid. By banning skin lighteners in August 1990, the National Party government sought to address a charged public health issue and gain political credibility.

Regulatory victories proved easier than dissuading all users. When interviewed at the time, people explained that they used skin lighteners to fix skin problems, and to make themselves look more modern, more beautiful, and more attractive to sexual partners. Such explanations often situated the body's surface outside the racialized binary of white versus black. Instead, interviewees pointed toward gender politics and material pressures. While manufacturers had long promoted their products as the preserve of beauty queens and nurses, heavy skin lightener use was, by the 1980s, most common among poor and less-educated women. Female hostel dwellers' forthright account of skin lightening as a survival strategy reveals how, for some struggling to get by, it had become an indispensable beauty practice. A luxury was now a necessity, explaining why health warnings could go unheeded.

In as much as South African debates over skin lighteners were borne of apartheid's particularities, they were also tethered to transnational developments. Like the popular culture and commercial forces that gave rise to the trade, opposition to it emerged from a transatlantic traffic. Black Consciousness activists took inspiration from Black Power mottos and anthems while dermatologists successfully lobbied for FDA guidelines to become the letter of South African law. By the mid-1980s, South African regulations had eclipsed those in the United States. The FDA proved incapable of acting on the recommendations of its own review panels in an era of government deregulation. South Africa set a new international benchmark that a number of other countries followed. A political coalition had proven more effective at instituting regulatory change than the world's largest agency dedicated to consumer safety.

Conclusion

SEDIMENTED MEANINGS
AND COMPOUNDED POLITICS

Johannesburg's Apartheid Museum opened in 2001 to critical acclaim and some questioning of the motivations and moral standing of those who financed it. Beneath the museum's celebrated surface lay a dubious commercial enterprise. The founders of Twins Products bankrolled the project. By the mid-1990s, the Kroks ranked among the country's wealthiest families. Partly inspired by the United States Holocaust Memorial Museum, Abraham and Solomon Krok sought to build a museum dedicated to those who lived and died under apartheid as part of a larger entertainment complex that would include a casino and amusement park. To design the museum, the Kroks hired distinguished architects, artists, and academics. This team's efforts were well received. National and international critics alike applauded the building's dignified modern aesthetic and the exhibits within for effectively conveying apartheid's inhumanity and courageous struggles against it.[1] Yet some questioned whether it was appropriate to locate the somber memorial within a lighthearted entertainment complex. Others drew attention to the enterprise that made the Kroks wealthy enough to sponsor such a project. They saw a profound irony in the fact that a museum dedicated to documenting the racism of apartheid was underwritten by a family fortune generated from the sale of skin lighteners.[2]

That irony and the Kroks' brazen business style stuck with people. When, more than a decade ago, I began researching skin lighteners, the Kroks often came up. Almost invariably, whenever I explained my topic to South African academics, businesspeople, and medical professionals, they asked, "Have you ever heard of the Krok brothers?" For these interlocutors, the Kroks were the most memorable figures associated with the country's skin lightener trade. On the one hand, the question rightly pointed me to the Kroks' importance. By the late 1970s, they dominated the South African trade, manufacturing some of the most popular and potent products. When medical authorities and activists identified their damaging effects, the Kroks fiercely defended them and did their best to prevent the 1990 regulations. On the other hand, by associating skin lighteners so closely with the Kroks, the question pointed to their manufacture and sale rather than their use, suggesting a trade driven more by supply and mass production rather than demand and affective consumption. It also cast skin lighteners as products of a bygone era, something that disappeared along with the shuttering of Twins's manufacturing operations and the end of apartheid.

Recent developments have made clear that skin lighteners and the issues they raise do not belong to a bygone era. They are very much with us today. South Africa's post-apartheid constitution is often hailed as the most progressive in the world, with a bill of rights that bars discrimination on grounds including race, color, and sexual orientation and that guarantees social rights to education, health care, and a clean environment. These expansive rights, like the 1990 regulations regarding skin lighteners, were a product of the hard-fought struggle against apartheid and the diversity of groups who ultimately participated in that struggle. Today, South Africa is as notable for the righteousness of its legal principles and political ideals as its difficulties in upholding them. Past injustices loom large in the post-apartheid present. At the same time, South Africa's new leaders—in their policies and ethical conduct—often stray far from the political future envisioned by anti-apartheid activists.

The appeal of skin lighteners in South Africa and elsewhere stems from sedimented layers of history. Some layers include gendered beauty ideals that, over centuries, have been buffeted by institutional and everyday practices of racism and colorism. Others encompass the international spread of consumer capitalism and the transnational movement of new forms of visual media and new active ingredients. In the twenty-first century, these layers continue to compound, expanding the trade in skin lighteners to include people across the globe and, once again, white women.

A New Millennium

Less than a decade after the South African government passed the world's most expansive regulations on skin lighteners, reports of commercially manufactured skin lighteners in South Africa resurfaced. A government raid on a wholesaler in Johannesburg found a large cache of hydroquinone-containing creams that had been manufactured in England and routed through a distributor in Kenya. Other seized products were manufactured in the United States, Taiwan, and Zambia. Bu-Tone, a brand developed by a Jewish pharmacist in Johannesburg in the 1940s, was now produced in Ndola, Zambia, and smuggled southward in travelers' suitcases.[3] The end of apartheid coincided with the increasing liberalization of the country's economy, reducing restrictions on international trade and encouraging the influx of cheap goods, including skin lighteners, from abroad. The implementation of neoliberal trade policies across Africa and elsewhere had made it more difficult for regulators and customs officers to track a wide range of prescription and nonprescription drugs.[4] South African officials complain that they had an insufficient number of investigators to monitor all imports.[5] Government corruption and apathy further hamstrung enforcement efforts.

During the 1990s and 2000s, additional health and political issues emerged that impinged on efforts to combat skin lightening. Dermatologists were on the front lines of the region's HIV/AIDS epidemic. Those ill with AIDS often first presented with skin conditions, like Kaposi's sarcoma and thrush, that preyed on their weakened immune systems. Caring for these cases and coming to terms with the epidemic's devastating reach consumed much of the attention of those working in South Africa's public hospitals. For those who secured AIDS treatment and battled back from opportunistic infections, doctors sometimes recommended skin lighteners to lessen the visibility of the scars and marks left behind. The HIV/AIDS epidemic drew scrutiny away from skin lighteners and introduced new reasons for using them.[6] Xenophobia introduced even more. Immigrants and refugees from other parts of the continent are often stereotyped as having darker complexions. To protect themselves from day-to-day discrimination and outbursts of anti-foreigner violence, some people with melanin-rich skin tones—regardless of whether they are South African citizens or not—have turned to lighteners.[7]

In the new millennium, skin lightening also returned as a practice tied to stardom. South African TV personalities, entertainers, and prominent figures, including Sorisha Naidoo, Nomasonto "Mshoza" Mnisi, and even Winnie Madikizela-Mandela, appeared in public with noticeably lighter complexions and endorsed new products that skirted the 1990 regulations by promising "brighter" and more even-toned skin. One newspaper commentator dubbed them the "lite brigade" while some used the isiZulu saying "money washes" (imali iyagezana) to chide black celebrities whose complexions faded once they gained wealth and fame.[8] These celebrity consumers are more akin to the glamorous entertainers and beauty queens who had promoted products during the 1950s and 1960s than the poor and unnamed women associated with skin lightening during the 1980s. Some document their transformations by posting dramatic before-and-after photos to Facebook and Instagram.

Digital platforms have become the latest forms of visual media where skin lighteners are deployed as technologies of visibility, tools to gain greater recognition. South Africa critics, in turn, use these same platforms to condemn high-profile consumers of skin lighteners for bending to racist beauty ideals, endangering their health, and serving as poor role models. These debates echo those that surrounded some American celebrities, including baseball player Sammy Sosa and performers like Beyoncé and Lil' Kim. Whereas in some cases, lightened appearances reflect advertisers' airbrushing of images, in others, they are the result of chemical compounds.[9] Similar to previous publicity surrounding Michael Jackson, these discussions sensationalize the practice and can raise questions about the celebrity's state of mind.[10] By presenting skin lightening as an individual pathology, they occlude the deeper histories and broader social processes that animate the practice.

Skin lightening reappeared on the cover of *Drum* in 2011. That cover featured before-and-after photos of Mshoza, a popular musician, whose face, chest, and arms had been transformed from light brown to pale peach, and carried the provocative subtitle "I was tired of being ugly."[11] Dermatologists and other observers guessed that Mshoza's new look was the result of intravenous infusions of glutathione and vitamin C. Around 2004, scientists in Korea, Thailand, India, Japan, and the Philippines began investigating the capacity of glutathione, an antioxidant naturally found in human cells, to reduce melanin. Soon high-end spas, beauty salons, and clinics in a variety of countries were offering glutathione infusions and capsules as skin lightening treatments despite the fact that long-term health effects are unknown. Like mercury and hydroquinone, elevated levels of glutathione seem to interfere with the enzyme tyrosinase.[12] When queried by the press and startled fans about why she markedly lightened her skin, Mshoza defended her actions by stating that skin lightening was a matter of "personal choice," no different from breast implants, nose jobs, or tanning.[13] This remark resonated with how some businessmen had long defended the skin lightener trade and how some satirists had long chided its racial politics. It also resonated with some feminists' arguments. A few scholars of black Atlantic popular culture, most recently Shirley Anne Tate, have pointedly challenged the idea that skin bleaching should be seen as any more pathological or any more racialized a practice than tanning, a beauty practice that also can produce bodily harm.[14] When another South African singer, Khanyi Mbau, faced criticism for skin lightening, she declared that "beauty" was limited only by the size of one's "wallet."[15] Mbau's declaration

FIGURE C.1. In 1982, *Drum* magazine, responding to pressure from political and medical groups, agreed to drop all skin lightener ads. Nearly thirty years later, skin lighteners returned to the cover of *Drum* in a feature story about Mshoza, a popular South African musician, who defended her decision to dramatically lighten her skin tone. *Drum*, November 2011.

conveyed an underlying principle of consumer capitalism: money makes the body's surface malleable.

Mshoza's and Mbau's statements were a piece of the consumer revolution that accompanied the end of apartheid. White support for the dismantling of apartheid was, in part, driven by a desire to join an increasingly consumerist global economy.[16] For many blacks, who had long suffered material deprivations as well as the denial of political rights, the possibility of frequenting shopping malls, earning higher salaries, and enjoying luxury goods helped to define post-apartheid freedom. Assuming state power at the height of the "Washington Consensus," Nelson Mandela's African National Congress faced significant international pressure to adopt free-market policies. Such policies, as we have seen, increased the influx of foreign goods, including illicit skin lighteners. Faith in the free market also inspired a mix of domestic initiatives. One of the most visible post-apartheid initiatives was Black Economic Empowerment, a program that resulted in a very small number of black entrepreneurs becoming very rich, fueling new forms of conspicuous consumption.[17]

Mshoza was part and parcel of post-apartheid's "bling" culture, a form of consumer culture that embraced and flaunted the promise of a supposedly postracial and more equitable society. Born into a family of modest means in Soweto in 1983, Mshoza rose to fame as a *kwaito* musician in the late 1990s. She became renowned in the tabloid press and on social media for her expensive tastes, her tumultuous personal life, and, after 2011, for dramatically lightening her skin. She now sells her own line of skin lighteners. Mshoza's initial response that skin lightening was just another cosmetic practice and that she had always "dreamt of having a lighter complexion" was similar to explanations that South African women offered in the 1960s and early 1970s.[18] What was different forty years later was the public reaction. Mshoza faced immediate and vocal charges of betraying her blackness and suffering from "low self-esteem." She replied by partly accepting the diagnosis, popularized by Black Consciousness activists, that skin lightening stemmed from psychological unease. She nonetheless rejected the notion that racial affinities could be read from surface appearances: "Yes, part of it is a self-esteem issue and I have addressed that and I am happy now. I'm not white inside, I'm not really fluent in English, I have black kids. I'm a township girl, I've just changed the way I look on the outside."[19] These remarks evinced a kind of freewheeling agency, unaccountable to prior histories and enduring political structures while at the same time laying claim to racial and gender authenticity. Although earlier activists did not end the practice of skin lightening, they did bequeath a powerful antiracist retort to which Mshoza was compelled to respond.

It is a retort that black feminists have resurfaced and reimagined on a global stage. In 2014, the Mexican-Kenyan actress Lupita Nyong'o used an award acceptance speech in Hollywood to share the story of how she came to see beauty in her own "night-shaded skin." She described that, recently, she had received a letter from a girl explaining that her success had given the girl hope and "saved" her from purchasing a skin lightener marketed by a West African pop star. Nyong'o recounted that, when she was young, she too had felt "unbeautiful" and had prayed to God each night to make her a "little lighter." Growing up in Nairobi in the 1980s and 1990s, she was surrounded by advertisements that equated pale skin with success. In second grade, a teacher chided Nyong'o that she would never find a man darker than herself to marry. Such remarks, Nyong'o explained, fed a "self-hate." Those feelings were not upended by the political ideals of male African nationalists or Black Power activists. Rather, it took the visual presence and words of women: Oprah Winfrey's and Whoopi Goldberg's performances in *The Color Purple*, and her own mother's insistence that beauty was not something to "acquire or consume" but something that resided within. Moreover, seeing the Sudanese-British model Alek Wek, a woman "who looked so much like me," celebrated as beautiful made Nyong'o feel "more seen, more appreciated by the far away gatekeepers of beauty." Images of Wek helped Nyong'o to recognize herself in new ways and as part of wider worlds and conceptions of beauty. Nyong'o hoped that now her own presence on screens and in magazines would do the same for others.[20]

Nyong'o and Wek are the latest in a series of African figures who have moved back and forth across the Atlantic to challenge impoverished beauty ideals. These figures reveal how the transnational and diasporic movement of people and images has worked to unsettle and recast national and personal aesthetic sensibilities.[21] In the 1930s, Rilda Marta returned from studying at a beauty school in New Jersey to open one of the first hair salons in South Africa's Eastern Cape for black women. Two decades later, Kenyan politician Tom Mboya condemned skin lighteners on a visit to the United States where he was admired for his own "dark good looks." A couple of years after that, South Africa's Miriam Makeba, with her natural hairstyle and deep brown complexion, became part of a cohort of black women entertainers who stretched dominant American conceptions of beauty. As Nyong'o's story suggests, such role models, coupled with the words of a loving mother, could provide powerful antidotes to marketing messages and personal barbs. Other African women are conveying these same sentiments through alternative media. Mixing animation and documentary styles and interweaving family conversations, Kenyan artist Ng'endo Mukii, in her 2012 short film *Yellow Fever*, has offered a poignant meditation

FIGURE C.2. A still from Ng'endo Mukii's award-winning film, *Yellow Fever* (2012), that foregrounds the hands of a hairstylist who uses skin lighteners. Mukii's film explores how the ubiquity of white beauty ideals shapes African girls' and women's understandings of themselves and their appearances.

on the beauty ideals and affective desires that encourage some to turn to skin lightening.[22] Somali-American activist Amira Adawe alerted public health officials in Minneapolis to the toxic products being sold there, prompting them to take action. Through her weekly radio program, Adawe warns members of the Somali diaspora of the dangers of skin lighteners and urges them to reconceive what counts as beauty.[23]

Yet alongside the popular circulation of ever-more varied images of black beauty, skin lighteners persist as technologies of visibility. In the age of social media and selfies, when many young women feel the perpetual need to be camera-ready, cosmetics sales, in general, have soared. Millennials have propelled the stocks of makeup companies to record highs.[24] And according to industry analysts, skin lighteners represent one of the fastest growing segments of the global beauty trade. The key multinational manufacturers include Beiersdorf, Shiseido, Hindustan Unilever, L'Oreal, and Procter & Gamble. Their products tend to contain either low percentages of hydroquinone or more recently identified compounds, like vitamin B3 (niacinamide), that have mild lightening effects. Marketing reports, compiled in the United States, point to Japan, China, and India as the largest and most lucrative markets for skin lighteners, followed by the United States, Southeast Asia, and Europe. Such reports pay less attention to African countries, noting that while demand is strong, overall purchasing

Obsession With Lighter Skin Tones in Asia, the Middle East & Africa Drives Opportunities in the Global Skin Lighteners Market

Published: June 2017

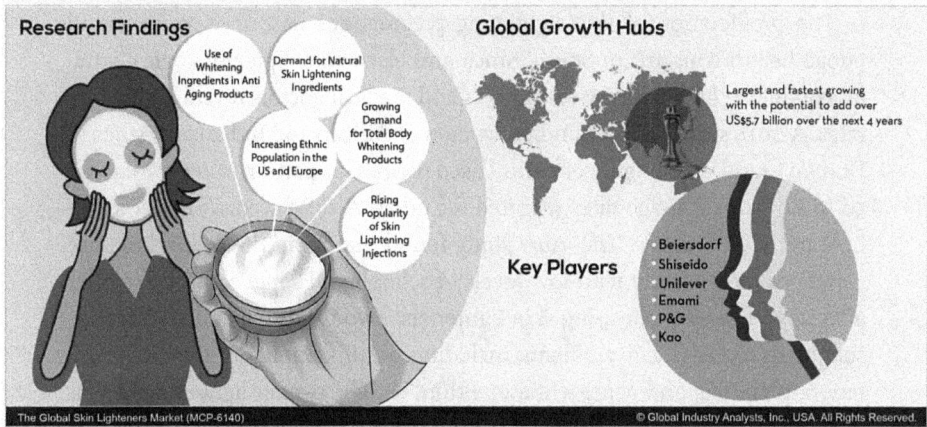

Research Findings

Use of Whitening Ingredients in Anti Aging Products

Demand for Natural Skin Lightening Ingredients

Increasing Ethnic Population in the US and Europe

Growing Demand for Total Body Whitening Products

Rising Popularity of Skin Lightening Injections

Global Growth Hubs

Largest and fastest growing with the potential to add over US$5.7 billion over the next 4 years

Key Players
- Beiersdorf
- Shiseido
- Unilever
- Emami
- P&G
- Kao

The Global Skin Lighteners Market (MCP-6140)

FIGURE C.3. An image from a marketing research website that analyzes the global trade in skin lighteners. It features a model with relatively pale skin. The analysis highlights the market's growth and profitability, as well as the varied ways people consume skin lighteners, including in anti-aging products and through injections. Global Industry Analysts, Inc., http: //www.strategyr.com/MarketResearch/Skin _Lighteners_Market_Trends.asp (last modified March 2018).

power is weak.[25] Nonetheless, Beiersdorf recently launched an advertising campaign for its Nivea line of skin lightening products in West Africa while Unilever's Fair & Lovely can be found throughout eastern and southern Africa.[26]

Trading stalls and store shelves in African cities and towns now carry a wide range of skin lighteners. Products manufactured by multinational companies reach them through the diasporic networks of traders and shopkeepers. There they sit alongside other, often lower-end products, made locally or in nearby countries. Cosmetic traders operating in African cities, along sidewalks and near bus and train depots, also mix their own lightening preparations, promising to tailor them to meet clients' specific skin needs. In South Africa, these traders are often immigrants from other parts of the continent, especially francophone central and West Africa, while, in Kenya, they often hail from coastal areas. Their preparations—*mkorogo* or mixture in Kiswahili—usually combine cosmetic creams and lotions with illegally obtained prescription products like topical corticosteroids and hydroquinone in concentrations over 2 percent. They can also include household ingredients—both harmless and highly caustic—like toothpaste, milk, bleaching detergent, and brake fluid.[27] Avid consumers of skin lighteners produce similar concoctions in their own sitting rooms and share them with friends.

The proliferation of skin lightening preparations has, once again, raised public health concerns in South Africa and elsewhere. Epidemiological studies conducted by university researchers and medical doctors reveal high usage rates. A 2014 survey of six hundred women of African and Indian ancestries in Durban found that roughly one-third used them. This portion is lower than the 50 to 80 percent usage rates reported for urban African women under apartheid but is still sizable. The same study found that, as in the 1980s, high use correlates most closely with low levels of schooling. People continue to offer a variety of reasons for using skin lighteners. Two-thirds explained that they sought to remedy skin problems, including postinflammatory hyperpigmentation, melasma, and acne, while one-third sought overall lightening.[28] This diversity of reasons poses a challenge to explanations of skin lightening that focus solely on racism and colorism. Studies suggest that the very highest rates of usage on the continent are in West Africa. In Nigeria and Senegal, between 60 to 70 percent of women reportedly use skin lighteners.[29] These are places that, compared with South Africa and Kenya, included far fewer white settlers during the colonial era and where, historically, racial hierarchies were a less pronounced element of everyday life.[30] They are also, not coincidentally, places where organized opposition to skin lighteners is a more recent development. To understand the appeal of skin lighteners in West Africa today, we need accounts that, in addition to analyzing colonial and global politics of beauty, explore precolonial conceptions of beauty and how those conceptions were shaped by the cultural and commercial influences of Islam, and trading networks that crossed the Sahara Desert as well as the Atlantic Ocean.

For contemporary public health campaigns to make inroads, they will need to attend to the complex and varied reasons why people use skin lighteners. Like the South African protests during the 1980s, they will need to combine antiracist activism with close attention to the health effects of specific active ingredients and mobilize greater resources for underfunded regulatory agencies. They will also need to address skin lighteners' dual status as cosmetics and drugs, a status that has long hinged on the slippery distinction between beauty preparations and therapeutic treatments. As I learned during a grand rounds session in Seattle, dermatologists themselves debate the ethics of responding to patient requests for lightening prescriptions in order to enhance social and professional opportunities. Dermatologists of African descent have been at the forefront of pointing to the ethical issues raised by requests that can leave white dermatologists, partly because of their racial privilege, feeling either determined or ill-positioned to deny them. Some dermatologists argue that acquiescing to requests for overall lighteners makes doctors complicit in perpetuating racism by providing the medical profession's stamp of approval. Others counter that given the well-documented real-life effects of colorism, meeting such requests provides patients with a beneficial service.[31] If white patients can request and purchase a variety of procedures to alter their appearances, why should not patients of color be allowed to do the same? Here, as with some forms of plastic surgery, the distinction between the aesthetic and the therapeutic is contested. Skin lighteners exist as slippery things for dermatologists as well as consumers and regulators.

The ongoing debate over hydroquinone only adds to the confusion. In 2006, the Food and Drug Administration (FDA) proposed that hydroquinone be prohibited from all over-the-counter products and that prescription formulations be required to undergo new drug approval. The FDA's proposal was prompted by new reports of hydroquinone-induced exogenous ochronosis— bluish-black hyperpigmentation—in the United States and other countries and preliminary data suggesting that hydroquinone might impair fertility and could be carcinogenic. The agency invited comment on its proposal.[32] This time, dermatologists—including African American dermatologists—took the lead in opposing the FDA. Many of the most vocal critics had commercial interests at stake. They either served as consultants for companies that would be impacted by the new regulations or offered lightening treatments as part of their cosmetic practice. These dermatologists argued that hydroquinone was mainly prescribed for discoloration, not overall lightening, and that they had rarely, if ever, observed negative health effects. They insisted that the FDA had underappreciated the chemical's benefits, especially for black and brown consumers of modest means. Far from producing purely cosmetic outcomes, hydroquinone was a cheap and highly effective treatment for conditions that caused "tremendous psycho-social distress."[33] Testimonials from users conveyed that distress. One woman with melasma wrote to the FDA, explaining that hydroquinone helped her to avoid "looks and laughter" and to "feel good" about herself. Banning hydroquinone would only compel her and others to turn to more expensive and harsher treatments like facial peels and laser surgery. People should be informed of the risks involved but then allowed to choose "the risks" they take. Reminding FDA officials of the gender issues at play, she wrote, "Life is hard enough in a society based on the beauty of women."[34]

This response from consumers, medical experts, and industry groups compelled the FDA to again withhold action on hydroquinone and request additional laboratory studies with rats and mice. More than a decade later, the government has yet to release new findings on hydroquinone's reproductive toxicity and carcinogenicity.[35] The agency that pioneered cosmetics regulations worldwide has been waylaid by its own multistage review process, political demands for deregulation, and coordinated pushback from trade and medical groups. A central part of that pushback has been dismissal of evidence from Africa. In 2007, the leading U.S. cosmetics trade organization singled out South Africa as a place where hydroquinone had been "*mis*used to lighten large surface areas of the skin."[36] While earlier studies did indeed suggest that South African consumers tended to use skin lighteners more extensively and for longer durations of time, this statement denied that people in both countries used skin lighteners in a variety of ways and that some in the United States used them for overall lightening. An editorial in a leading dermatology journal went so far as to state that "very different standards of beauty prevailed" in Africa.[37] This statement missed how contemporary conceptions of beauty—especially as they relate to skin color—had been forged through currents that have criss-crossed the Atlantic for centuries.

The commercial stakes of the hydroquinone debate have been heightened by manufacturers' repackaging of skin lightening formulations as so-called anti-aging products. Around the same time that the FDA issued its proposal to ban hydroquinone from over-the-counter preparations, *Newsweek* and the *New York Times* reported on a supposedly new beauty trend originating in Japan: skin whiteners and lighteners. Cosmetic manufacturers had just released a torrent of products to help middle-aged white women and others fade the age spots and wrinkles produced through years spent in the sun, often in determined pursuit of deep tans.[38] The reporting missed how such products had long been available to U.S. consumers, if, in recent decades, largely confined to the "ethnic beauty care" sections of drug stores and hair salons and small shops frequented by immigrants from Asian, Latin American, Caribbean, and African countries. In their efforts to cling to youthful appearances, baby boomers have brought skin lighteners full circle from nearly a century ago. Whereas white women in the 1920s and 1930s swapped skin lighteners for the healthy glow of sun-kissed skin, their granddaughters were picking them back up to combat tanning's long-term effects. These skin lighteners—packaged as "toners," "illuminators," and "brighteners"—are sold at high-end department stores and beauty boutiques. Amina Mire has argued that marketing campaigns that situate skin lightening as a solution for aging appearances carry "troubling racial overtones." The campaigns occlude the vexed and racialized history of skin lighteners, harkening back to older, colonial discourses that valorized fair complexions and disparaged dark ones while promoting newer discourses that insidiously conflate aging and darkening with ugliness.[39] Like so many other cosmetic appeals in the past and present, they also cast the aging of women as a form of disfigurement and something that money might fix.

Expanding demand for skin lighteners paired with persistent concerns about their health effects has stirred a scramble for alternative depigmenting agents. Glutathione infusions and capsules and vitamin B3 are not the only new preparations to appear in recent years. Industry insiders classify these new skin lightening preparations as cosmeceuticals, signaling, once again, their slippery status between cosmetics and pharmaceuticals. While this slipperiness has been a challenge for the U.S. FDA and other regulatory agencies to manage, it has proven highly lucrative for manufacturers. Cosmeceuticals cater to consumer demand while largely sidestepping the costly and time-consuming regulatory testing required of pharmaceuticals.[40] Skin lightening cosmeceuticals include compounds like mequinol, retinoids, and azelaic acid that temporarily interfere with the enzyme tyrosinase, though, from the perspective of many dermatologists, less effectively than hydroquinone, still considered the "gold standard." Other new products, often developed in Japan and in response to consumer concerns about safety, contain botanical or naturally occurring lightening agents, including arbutin, kojic acid, aleosin, licorice extract, ascorbic acid or vitamin C, and soy proteins.[41] The incentive for manufacturers to continue developing alternative agents is strong as market analysts predict demand to increase from men and for total-body whitening products.[42] Skin lighteners remain a highly profitable enterprise.

Amid the scramble for new agents, an old one—mercury—returned. More than twenty years after being banned from cosmetics in most countries, mercury resurfaced as a common active ingredient found in low-end skin lightening creams and soaps. In the late 1990s, Japanese researchers investigating possible mercury contamination around Lake Victoria from small-scale mining operations were surprised to find that it was not Tanzanian and Kenyan gold miners or fishers who possessed the highest levels of mercury but rather women who used mercurial soaps to lighten and clarify their skin. The Japanese researchers had run headlong into an illicit transnational trade and governments' half-hearted efforts to stop it.[43] In 2011, the World Health Organization drew attention to the global problem of mercurial skin lighteners, explaining that the health dangers extended beyond immediate users. As the inorganic mercury is discharged into the ecosystem through wastewater, it transforms into the more lethal organic compound, methylmercury, accumulating in fish that are then consumed by humans.[44] Here is a visceral instance of the environmentalist Rachel Carson's insight that small, domestic choices are making the world uninhabitable.[45]

Mercurial cosmetics pool in places where regulations are lax and consumers are poor. Recent studies by South African researchers found that over 40 percent of over-the-counter skin lighteners sold illegally in Durban and Cape Town contain mercury, though it rarely appears on labels.[46] Within the United States, mercurial cosmetics can be found in salons and shops that serve black and brown immigrant communities. Products containing upward of 20 percent hydroquinone can be found alongside them. Brands that are popular, if dangerous, in countries where migrants originate follow them to places where they face new, if readily recognizable, forms of colorism and racism. Highly toxic skin lighteners are currently available in most American cities but exist largely beyond the purview of more affluent consumers. As Imani Perry aptly describes the segmented market for skin lighteners, "the whitening of the world's wealthy is a much safer affair than that of its poorer, and blacker, populations."[47] With the loosening of trade and other regulations, class now appears as a more effective bulwark against dangerous products than national boundaries.

Class also shapes ongoing debates about race, beauty, and belonging that extend beyond the realm of skin lightening. In 2016, black students at some of South Africa's most elite girls' high schools took to the pavement and social media to protest policies that prohibited them from wearing Afros, dreadlocks, and braids, and compelled them to straighten their hair with chemical relaxers. Their antiracist protests garnered the support of thousands online, as well as government ministers, and received international press coverage. Their protests were partly inspired by the #BlackLivesMatter movement that began in the United States and spread elsewhere, and calls to decolonize higher education. The secondary schools at the center of the storm were, for most of their histories, exclusively white institutions. They only began admitting black students in the early 1990s as the legal apparatus of apartheid was dismantled. The post-apartheid reputations and financial solvency of such schools, in large part, have depended on recruiting a racially diverse student body while claiming to uphold the highest educational standards, standards closely associated with whiteness. Attending formerly white high schools enhances black students' chances for garnering university admission and achieving class mobility. It also exposes them to subtle and not-so-subtle forms of racism, extending from receiving unequal treatment from some staff to being discouraged from speaking African languages.[48] That the antiracist protests that erupted at these schools in 2016 centered on hair policies reveals how, in contemporary South Africa, concerns over what might appear to be just surface appearances speak viscerally and powerfully to peoples'—and especially girls' and women's—everyday experiences of racism. The protests, in their affinities with social justice movements elsewhere, also reveal that the process of apprehending and acting on those experiences continues to emerge through political and cultural conversations that stretch far beyond South African borders.

THE HISTORY OF SKIN lighteners is a layered history, one stacked with sedimented meanings and compounded politics. In some parts of the world, the ability to avoid outdoor labor and escape the sun's darkening and roughening effects was long a sign of elite status. From, at least, the development of the transatlantic slave trade and European colonial conquest across much of the globe, the privileging of pale and smooth complexions became yoked to processes of racial formation and a core element of white supremacist beauty ideals. In some places, the privileging of lightness was a wholesale innovation. In others, like parts of southern Africa, it confronted already-existing ideals that associated beauty with shiny and luminescent bodily surfaces and that encouraged some young women to prepare for marriage by using botanical lighteners. Through time, these various conceptions of beauty and skin color became entangled as new layers of meaning and politics deposited on older forms.

Such accretions continued over the many years of colonial, segregationist, and apartheid rule in South Africa where the ideal of light skin came to reflect political inequities and carry material consequences. Paler skin tone, usually combined with other social markers such as straighter hair, more European-looking facial features, or a whiter accent, could help a person secure better educational and economic opportunities, pass for a more entitled racial classification, or attract a more desirable lover or spouse. The sale of commercial skin lighteners took off in apartheid South Africa as manufacturers and visual media promoted lighteners as indispensable technologies of visibility and promoted the capitalist mantra that commodities could improve how black consumers looked and felt. "Black Is Beautiful," as an antiracist retort, challenged the logic of such marketing campaigns by celebrating melanin-rich skin and framing the rejection of skin lighteners as a measure of political authenticity. This framing added new layers of meanings and strengthened the visceral reactions that skin lighteners could provoke. It lessened but did not eliminate their appeal. Rather, for some consumers, older meanings and politics remained visible through newer layers.

The bodily effects that people have sought from skin lighteners have often exceeded racialized conceptions of skin color. While some consumers and patients have sought overall lightening, others have aimed to heal scarred tissue or even out skin tone. The variety of skin lighteners' active ingredients and the multiplicity of their effects have made them slippery things to regulate and to render obsolete. This slipperiness, in turn, adds other facets, other layers, to their history. Medical and regulatory concerns accumulated alongside large-scale manufacturing and glitzy marketing campaigns. These layers compounded the issues at stake. They turned the work of pharmacists, doctors, and FDA officials as well as chemicals and cosmetic formulas into matters of public scrutiny and debate.

The persistence of skin lightening in the present day reminds us that surfaces matter. The unrelenting presence of beauty practices in our globalized world stems from their ability to play on and reproduce a range of inequalities while, at the same time, offering hope and stirring feelings of self-worth. The deep and contentious history of skin lightening, as told from South Africa, demonstrates how the political and affective dimensions of beauty derive from processes that stretch far back in time and across vast distances. Contemporary beauty practices are rooted in sedimented meanings and compounded politics, some of which are affirming and some of which are disturbing. Those layers include the privileging of whiteness and lightness that flourished through European institutions of slavery and colonial rule. They also include precolonial bodily practices and gender inequities as well as the transnational—and often diasporic—traffic in new forms of commerce, media, and medicine, and new forms of protest politics. The weight of time and struggle have compressed these layers, rendering them difficult to peel apart.

That difficulty suggests the danger of quick judgments and easy dismissals. Understanding practices that have been shaped by histories of subjection requires humility and empathy. It requires apprehending the world in ways that are more generous and more nuanced. Too often, people have turned to Africa's past in search of simple origin stories or stark narratives of oppression versus resistance. A layered history offers a different approach, an approach that recognizes composite meanings and unexpected conjunctures. Unearthing more subtlety and surprise in the past might just help us to envision less predictable and more liberatory futures.

Notes

INTRODUCTION: A LAYERED HISTORY

1. Global Industry Analysts, *Skin Lighteners*, accessed March 21, 2017, http://www
.strategyr.com/MarketResearch/Skin_Lighteners_Market_Trends.asp.

2. For example, Helene Cooper, "Where Beauty Means Bleached Skin," *New York Times*, November 26, 2016, accessed March 9, 2010, https://www.nytimes.com/2016/11/26/fashion/skin-bleaching-south-africa-women.html?_r=0.

3. Burns, "Useable Past," 362.

4. For work, most often by literary scholars, on the importance of attending to surfaces and especially skin, see Ahmed and Stacey, *Thinking through the Skin*; Janelle Taylor, "Surfacing the Body Interior"; Cheng, *Second Skin*; Nuttall, "Surface, Depth and the Autobiographical Act"; Hurst, *Surface Imaginations*; Lafrance, "Skin Studies."

5. Modern Girl Around the World Research Group, *Modern Girl Around the World*; L. Thomas, "Love, Sex, and the Modern Girl in 1930s Southern Africa."

6. For more information about the Karroo brand, manufactured in the Karoo region of South Africa, see chapter 3. J. D. Mweli Skota Correspondence, Historical Papers Research Archive, Library, University of Witwatersrand, Johannesburg AD2781, letters from Zilpah T. D. Skota to J. D. Mweli Skota, October 10, 1936, April 17, 1941, May 2, 1941, and June 30, 1942. I thank James Campbell for directing me to the following unpublished paper and rich archival source: J. Campbell, "T. D. Mweli Skota," 30–31. For more on Skota and the *African Yearly Register* (1930), see Couzens, *New African*, 3–14; Erlmann, *Music, Modernity, and the Global Imagination*, 53–58.

7. Jablonski, "Evolution of Human Skin and Skin Color"; Jablonski, *Skin*, esp. chaps. 4–6; Jablonski, *Living Color*, esp. 159–62. Also see Gibbons, "How Africans Evolved a Palette of Skin Tones."

8. Elphick and Giliomee, *Shaping of South African Society*; Keegan, *Colonial South Africa*; Magubane, *Bringing the Empire Home*.

9. West, "Genealogy of Modern Racism"; Mbembe, "African Modes of Self-Writing," 245–46; Nuttall, *Beautiful/Ugly*; Camp, "Black Is Beautiful."

10. Denton, Lerner, and Fitzpatrick, "Inhibition of Melanin Formation by Chemical Agents"; Swiderski, *Quicksilver*, 162–90; Bennett, "Mercolized Wax."

11. Appadurai, *Social Life of Things*. Another important contribution in this vein that appeared the year before was Mintz, *Sweetness and Power*.

12. Within African studies, this work included Burke, *Lifebuoy Men, Lux Women*; B. Weiss, *Sacred Trees, Bitter Harvests*; Presholdt, *Domesticating the World*; Stein, *Plumes*. Also see Ramamurthy, "Feminist Commodity Chain Analysis."

13. For recent work on science and technology in African studies, see Larkin, *Signal and Noise*; Storey, *Guns, Race, and Power*; Hecht, *Being Nuclear*; Osseo-Asare, *Bitter Roots*; Breckenridge, *Biometric State*; Breckenridge and Hecht, "Confronting African Histories of Technology." For two reviews of the anthropology of pharmaceuticals that aptly chart the shift from a biography of objects approach to an STS approach focused on the materiality of things, see van der Geest, Whyte, and Hardon, "Anthropology of Pharmaceuticals"; Hardon and Sanabria, "Fluid Drugs." On the analytical shift from objects to things as enabling attention to the "circulations of materials on which life depends," see Ingold, "Toward an Ecology of Materials."

14. Wipper, "African Women, Fashion, and Scapegoating."

15. Burke, *Lifebuoy Men, Lux Women*, 189–90.

16. Modern Girl Around the World Research Group, "Modern Girl as Heuristic Device," 22.

17. L. Thomas, *Politics of the Womb*, esp. 17–20.

18. Modern Girl Around the World Research Group, "Modern Girl as Heuristic Device," 2–3. This method resonates with Gillian Hart's "relational comparison" elaborated in "Denaturalizing Dispossession." *Histoire croisée* offers a somewhat similar approach. See Werner and Zimmermann, "Beyond Comparison."

19. Tsing, *Friction*, 5. In her contribution to "AHR Conversation: On Transnational History," Isabel Hofmeyr similarly notes the problematic tendency for antiglobalization critiques to "flatten" Third World complexities.

20. On the long history of connections and comparisons between the United States and South Africa, see Fredrickson, *White Supremacy*; Cell, *Highest Stage of White Supremacy*; Hull, *American Enterprise in South Africa*; Nixon, *Homelands, Harlem and Hollywood*; von Eschen, *Race against Empire*; J. Campbell, *Songs of Zion*; J. Campbell, "Americanization of South Africa"; Magubane, *Bringing the Empire Home*, chap. 7; Vinson, *The Americans Are Coming!*; *Safundi: The Journal of South African and American Studies*, founded in 2000.

21. On dress, see Brooks, "Signares of Saint Louis and Gorée"; Hendrickson, *Clothing and Difference*; K. Hansen, *Salaula*; Fair, *Pastimes & Politics*; Motsemme, "Distinguishing Beauty, Creating Distinctions"; R. Ross, *Clothing*; Allman, *Fashioning Africa*; Ivaska, *Cultured States*; Hansen and Madison, *African Dress*; M. Brown, *Khartoum at Night*.

22. Boone, *Radiance from the Waters*. Also see Guyer and Belinga, "Wealth in People," esp. 115–16; L. Thomas, *Politics of the Womb*; Popenoe, *Feeding Desire*.

23. For thoughtful overviews of those debates, see Felski, "'Because It Is Beautiful'"; Camp, "Black Is Beautiful."

24. Barnard, "Contesting Beauty," 345. Also see Ebrahim-Vally, "Beauty and Race in the South African Context"; Magubane, *Bringing the Empire Home*, esp. chap. 2. For a nuanced account of the importance of beauty to animating art and everyday life under apartheid, see Magaziner, *Art of Life in South Africa*.

25. Erasmus, "Hair Politics," 392, 383–84. Also see Erasmus, *Race Otherwise*, esp. chap. 3.

26. Jarrín, *Biopolitics of Beauty*, 198, 11. For related approaches to the study of beauty, see Nguyen, "Biopower of Beauty"; Edmonds, "Biological Subject of Aesthetic

Medicine"; Ochoa, *Queen for a Day*. For early statements on the importance of affect to African gender history, see Thomas and Cole, "Introduction"; Hunt, "Affective, the Intellectual, and African Gender History."

27. Rodney, *How Europe Underdeveloped Africa*; Comaroff and Comaroff, *Of Revelation and Revolution*. Consumption is also important to Jean-François Bayart's argument that, over the *longue durée*, African leaders have retained power through "strategies of extraversion." Bayart, "Africa in the World."

28. Iliffe, *Emergence of African Capitalism*, 21.

29. Comaroff and Comaroff, "Occult Economies and the Violence of Abstraction"; Ferguson, *Expectations of Modernity*; Mbembe, "African Modes of Self-Writing"; Hyslop, "Shopping during a Revolution"; B. Weiss, *Street Dreams and Hip Hop Barber-shops*; Cole, *Sex and Salvation*; Lewis and Hames, "Gender, Sexuality and Commodity Culture"; James, *Money from Nothing*; Posel and van Wyk, *Conspicuous Consumption in Africa*.

30. Colson and Scudder, *For Prayer and Profit*; Crush and Ambler, *Liquor and Labor in Southern Africa*; Akeyeampong, *Drink, Power and Cultural Change*; J. Willis, *Potent Brews*; Mager, *Beer, Sociability, and Masculinity in South Africa*. Two notable exceptions to the focus on alcohol and men are Burke, *Lifebuoy Men, Lux Women*; Murillo, *Market Encounters*. On the relative paucity of historical studies of consumer capital-ism in the Global South, see Woodward, "Consumer Culture."

31. Vinikas, *Soft Soap, Hard Sell*, 59; Ramphele, *Bed Called Home*, 80.

32. Peiss, *Hope in a Jar*; Modern Girl Around the World Research Group, "Modern Girl Around the World"; Sutton, *Globalizing Ideal Beauty*; Jones, *Beauty Imagined*.

33. On that entanglement more broadly, see Negri, "Value and Affect"; Zelizer, *Pur-chase of Intimacy*; Illouz, *Cold Intimacies*; Berlant, *Cruel Optimism*; Illouz and Benger, "Emotions and Consumption"; Illouz, *Emotions as Commodities*. For a pioneer of this perspective, see Marchand, *Advertising the American Dream*. On plastic surgery as also depending on the belief that small differences in appearance can produce significant differences in how people feel, see Hurst, *Surface Imaginations*.

34. Obama, *Dreams from My Father*, 29–30, 51–52, 193.

35. Lasker, "Whiter Shade of Black." Journalists first pointed out this discrepancy and also noted that Obama would have likely already learned about racial prejudice from children in his Jakarta neighborhood who teased him for his big size and "black features." Kirsten Scharnberg and Kim Barker, "The Not-So-Simple Story of Barack Obama's Youth," *Chicago Tribune*, March 25, 2007. An Obama critic, Jerome R. Corsi, made much of this misremembering in his best-seller, *The Obama Nation* (see 65–66).

36. Taraborrelli, *Michael Jackson*, 435–37, 521; J. Harris, "Did Michael Jackson Have Vitiligo?"

37. Obama, *Dreams from My Father*, 193, 52.

38. The sociologists Michael Omi and Howard Winant developed the concept of *racial formation* in *Racial Formation in the United States*, first published in 1986. Early theorists of intersectionality include hooks, *Ain't I a Woman*; Spelman, "Gender & Race"; Crenshaw, "Mapping the Margins."

39. Holt, "Marking."

40. Nuttall and Michael, *Senses of Culture*, 11–12. For an earlier, intellectual history of racism, see Dubow, *Scientific Racism in Modern South Africa*.

41. Powell, *Different Shade of Colonialism*; Glassman, *War of Words, War of Stones*; El Hamel, *Black Morocco*; B. Hall, *History of Race in Muslim West Africa*; Lee, *Unreasonable Histories*; Ray, *Crossing the Color Line*; Shadle, *Souls of White Folk*; Lindsay, *Atlantic Bonds*. For a pointed, recent critique of the absence of attention to race within African studies, see Pierre, *Predicament of Blackness*.

42. Morrison, *Bluest Eye*, 122. Also see the discussion of racial beauty in Toni Morrison's foreword to the 2007 edition.

43. Camp, "Black Is Beautiful," 677. On the centrality of aesthetics to European racial thinking, see West, "Genealogy of Modern Racism"; Fredrickson, *Racism*, 59–60; Nuttall, *Beautiful/Ugly*.

44. S. White and G. White, *Stylin'*, chap. 7; Craig, *Ain't I a Beauty Queen?*; S. Walker, *Style & Status*; Baldwin, *Chicago's New Negroes*, chap. 2; Modern Girl Around the World Research Group, "Modern Girl Around the World"; Baldwin, "From the Washtub to the World"; Gill, *Beauty Shop Politics*; Ford, *Liberated Threads*.

45. Rooks, *Hair Raising*; Craig, "Decline and Fall of the Conk"; Peiss, *Hope in a Jar*, 41; Banks, *Hair Matters;* Craig, *Ain't I a Beauty Queen?*, chaps. 2, 6; P. Russell, "Styling Blackness."

46. See, for instance, Craig, *Ain't I a Beauty Queen?*, 26; S. Walker, *Style & Status*, 68. Similarly, in *A Chosen Exile*, Hobbs makes no mention of skin lightening and, in general, pays little heed to the kinds of material and bodily practices that might have aided some racially ambiguous people in their efforts to pass for white.

47. Peiss, *Hope in a Jar*, chap. 7.

48. Amina Mire, "The Emerging Skin-Whitening Industry," *Counterpunch*, July 28, 2005, accessed March 9, 2019, https://www.counterpunch.org/2005/07/28/the-emerging-skin-whitening-industry/; Dorman, "Skin Bleach and Civilization."

49. A. Walker, "If the Present Looks Like the Past." Walker specifically defined "Colorism" as "prejudicial or preferential treatment of same-race people based solely on their color," and she pointed to black African women writers like Buchi Emecheta, Ama Ata Aidoo, and Bessie Head as the hope for challenging this form of oppression along with racism, sexism, and classism. For examples of mid-twentieth-century social science research that paid attention to ideas about skin color and inequality, see Herskovits, "Some Physical Characteristics of the American Negro Population"; Parrish, "Color Names and Color Notions." For a pioneering study of colorism in the late twentieth century, see Russell, Wilson, and Hall, *Color Complex*.

50. Herring, Keith, and Horton, *Skin Deep*; Ronald Hall, *Empirical Analysis of the Impact of Skin Color*; Margaret Hunter, *Race, Gender, and the Politics of Skin Tone*; Kerr, *Paper Bag Principle*; Hochschild and Weaver, "Skin Color Paradox and the American Racial Order"; Jablonski, *Living Color*; R. E. Hall, *Melanin Millennium*, 19–38; Norwood, *Color Matters*; Monk, "Cost of Color"; "Global Perspectives on Colorism."

51. A. Harris, "Introduction," 2; Glenn, "Consuming Lightness"; L. Thomas, "Skin Lighteners in South Africa." For more on the global trade, see Perry, "Buying White Beauty"; Jablonski, *Living Color*, 169–81; Jha, *Global Beauty Industry*.

52. Blay, "Yellow Fever"; Blay, "Ahoofe Kasa!," 53, 63, 69, 72; Pierre, "'I Like Your Colour!'"; Blay, "Skin Bleaching and Global White Supremacy"; Pierre, *Predicament of Blackness*, 101–22. Blay edited a special issue of *JENdA: A Journal of Culture and African Women Studies* 14 (2009) on skin bleaching. She also coedited with Christopher Charles a special issue of *Journal of Pan African Studies* 4, no. 4 (2011), on the same topic. Charles's individually authored contribution to the *JENdA* special issue provides another powerful critique of the "self-hatred" thesis: "Liberating Skin Bleachers." For a wide-ranging study that both draws on decades of dermatological expertise treating the ill effects of skin lighteners in Nigeria and argues that women mainly use skin lighteners to attract and retain marriage partners, see Olumide, *Vanishing Black African Woman*. On health effects, see Mire, "Skin-bleaching."

53. For an African American's surprise that skin lighteners were among the most popular cosmetics in Indonesia in the 1950s, see Marguerite Cartwright, "A Teacher Talks: Brown-Skinned by Choice," *Pittsburgh Courier*, November 12, 1955, p. SM6.

54. Saraswati, *Seeing Beauty*, 62. For a similar interpretation that emphasizes shame and dignity, see Shevde, "All's Fair in Love and Cream."

55. Friedman, "Political Economy of Elegance," esp. 171 and 175. Friedman's analysis is an explicit refutation of Fanonian and Manonian interpretations of skin lightening as well as what he views as Bourdieu's hyper-rationalization of consumption through the concept of *social distinction*. For another take on skin lightening in Africa as not being about racial whiteness, see White, "Sex, Soap, and Colonial Studies," esp. 484.

56. Barnes, *Cultural Conundrums*, 102–14; Brown-Glaude, "Fact of Blackness?"; Hope, "Fashion Ova Style"; Tate, *Black Beauty*, 125–28; Brown-Glaude, "Don't Hate Me 'Cause I'm Pretty." Tate has, more recently, extended these arguments across the black Atlantic world in *Skin Bleaching in Black Atlantic Zones*.

57. K. Thompson, *Shine*, 1–46, 112–68. Thompson's interpretation of skin bleaching has additional layers. She also argues that bleachers' skin becomes "a new form of photographic surface" that is more sensitive to light and that skin bleaching is "an example of what we might describe as a body of photography, the result of and transference of the effect of photographic technologies on the body and part of a broader creation of a social body through vision, light, and visual media" (22–23).

58. Illouz, "Toward a Post-Normative Critique of Emotional Authenticity," in *Emotions as Commodities*, 208. For recent studies of beauty and bodily practices that use a similar approach, see Herzig, *Plucked*; Nelson, *Social Life of DNA*.

59. Carolyn McGibbon, "Blooming Trade May Be Nipped in Bud," c. May 1987, TimesMedia clippings files, TimesMedia House, Johannesburg.

60. hooks, *Black Looks*, 9–20.

I. COSMETIC PRACTICES AND COLONIAL CRUCIBLES

1. Monica Hunter, *Reaction to Conquest*; A. Bank, "'Intimate Politics' of Fieldwork."

2. Hutchings et al., *Zulu Medicinal Plants*, 18–19; U.S. Environmental Protection Agency, "Citronella (Oil of Citronella) (021901) Fact Sheet."

3. Monica Hunter, *Reaction to Conquest*, 169–70, 214. For this use of Tambookie grass roots, also see de Lange, "Some Traditional Cosmetic Practices," 91.

4. Henshilwood, d'Errico, and Watts, "Engraved Ochres"; Balter, "Early Start for Human Art?"; Watts, "Pigments from Pinnacle Point Cave"; Henshilwood et al., "100,000-Year-Old Ochre-Processing Workshop." I appreciate Francesco d'Errico explaining this research to me on July 27, 2012.

5. Campbell, Robbins, and Taylor, *Tsodilo Hills*, 93. Also see Robbins, "*Sebilo*"; Livingstone, *Missionary Travels and Researches*, 122, 298, 205.

6. Jablonski, *Living Color*, 49–50, 62–63; Tobias, "Biology of the Southern African Negro."

7. R. Ross, *Concise History of South Africa*, 7–8; Landau, *Popular Politics*, chaps. 1, 2; Simon Hall, "Farming Communities."

8. Raven-Hart, *Cape Good Hope*, 8, 463; A. Bank, "Liberals and Their Enemies."

9. Raven-Hart, *Cape Good Hope*, 19, 56, 68, 84, 219, 264, 291, 331, 347, 404–5.

10. Raven-Hart, *Cape Good Hope*, 68, 264, 382, 433. On European descriptions of Khoekhoe skin color, see Steinmetz, *Devil's Handwriting*, 108.

11. Moffat, *Missionary Labours*, 287, cited in Comaroff, "Empire's Old Clothes," 22; Comaroff, "Medicine, Colonialism," 224–25.

12. Burke, *Lifebuoy Men, Lux Women*, 24–25.

13. Raven-Hart, *Cape Good Hope*, 16, 343.

14. Soga, *Ama-Xosa*, 413–14; A. Bank, "'Intimate Politics' of Fieldwork," 76. Also see de Lange, "Some Traditional Cosmetic Practices," 88.

15. Raven-Hart, *Cape Good Hope*, 127, 241; S. Kay, *Travels and Researches in Caffraria*, 177, 372; Kirby, *Andrew Smith and Natal*, 106; de Lange, "Some Traditional Cosmetic Practices."

16. Jacobson-Widding, *Red-White-Black*.

17. Soga, *Ama-Xosa*, 413–14; Monica Hunter, *Reaction to Conquest*, 6, 101; Mayer with Mayer, *Townsmen or Tribesmen*, 21, 25–26; Broster, *Tembu*, 3.

18. Ngubane, *Body and Mind*, 126–27, 156. Also see Berglund, *Zulu Thought-Patterns*, 160–61.

19. Soga, *Ama-Xosa*, 255; Schapera, *Married Life*, 257; Mayer with Mayer, *Townsmen or Tribesmen*, 25; Broster, *Tembu*, 87, 96; Berglund, *Zulu Thought-Patterns*, 134–35; Comaroff, *Body of Power*, 85–118. For similar uses of white clay elsewhere in Africa, see Richards, *Chisungu*, 88–90, 124, 137; Boone, *Radiance from the Waters*, 18–23; Ferme, *Underneath of Things*, 187–95; Blay, "Yellow Fever," chap. 7.

20. Colenso, *Zulu-English Dictionary*, 163.

21. Doke and Vilakazi, *Zulu-English Dictionary*, 381.

22. Ngubane, *Body and Mind*, 113–15. Also see Krige, *Social System*, 370–71.

23. J. Tom Brown, *Secwana Dictionary*, 73, 103, 249; Matumo, *Setswana English Setswana Dictionary*, 116.

24. Ferme, *Underneath of Things*, 188–89.

25. Dlova et al., "Chemical Analysis."

26. B. Weiss, "Dressing at Death," 148. For South Africa, see Krige and Krige, *Realm of a Rain-Queen*, 114; Van der Vliet, "Growing Up," 230–31. For elsewhere in Africa,

see Adamson, *Peoples of Kenya*, 98, 106, 108, 328, 338; Kratz, *Affecting Performance*, 123 and plate 31; Hunt, *Colonial Lexicon*, 300, 409n23; Popenoe, *Feeding Desire*, 99, 117–19, 145, 203n6.

27. Monica Hunter, *Reaction to Conquest*, 329.

28. De Lange, "Some Traditional Cosmetic Practices," 86.

29. Monica Hunter, *Reaction to Conquest*, 105.

30. H. Callaway, *Nursery Tales*, 182; Webb and Wright, *James Stuart Archive*, 3:151–52 (also see 4:339).

31. In *The Realm of the Word*, Landau argues that Setswana speakers generally referred to early European missionaries and travelers not as "whites" but as "reds" in reference to sunburned hues (13n31).

32. Stuart and Malcolm, *Diary of Henry Francis Fynn*, 81.

33. Livingstone, *Missionary Travels and Researches*, 26, 203–5, 210.

34. Mini, *Greater Dictionary of Isi Xhosa*, 330–31; Earle, "Can the Nubian Change"; Khan, "Beauty, Myths and Trees." Trees used for *ummemezi* include *Pretorhus longifolia*, red beech; *Cassine croceum*, saffron wood; *Curtisia dentate*, assegaaihout; *Bersama tysoniana*, bastard sneezewood; *Rapanea melanophloeos*, cape beech; *Olea capensis*, black ironwood; *Cassipourea flangenii*, onion wood; *Vepris undulata*, bastard ironwood; *Calodendron capense*, cape chestnut; *Pappea capensis*, wild plum; and *Sideroxylon inerme*, white milkwood. Thanks to Sinfree Makoni and Ana Deumert for helping me to trace the meanings of *ukumemeza*, via email correspondence, January 29 and February 3, 2018.

35. Muholland et al., "Non-toxic Melanin Production Inhibitors."

36. On linguistic borrowing in South Africa, see Mesthrie et al., "Language Contact 1."

37. Livingstone, *Missionary Travels and Researches*, 203–4.

38. Landau, *Popular Politics*, chap. 1, quote from 12. I am grateful for personal correspondence with Paul Landau, March 27 and 31, 2017, in helping me to understand the *métis* world that Livingstone described. Also see Monica Hunter, *Reaction to Conquest*, 6–7.

39. Wilner, "Roman Beauty Culture"; Wallace, "Color in Homer," 19–20; Diamandopoulos, Kolonas, and Grapsa-Kotrotsou, "Use of Lead Cosmetics"; Pointer, *Artifice of Beauty*, 15, 35–38; B. Thomas, "Constraints and Contradictions"; McCoskey, "Naming the Fault." Also see Blay, "Skin Bleaching and Global White Supremacy."

40. Kelly, "Cosmetics in Roman Antiquity." On lead as historically the most important white pigment in painting, see Gettens, Kühn, and Chase, "Lead White."

41. Pointer, *Artifice of Beauty*, 73–79.

42. For ongoing debates over Elizabeth I and Venetian ceruse, see Riehl, "'Let Nature Paint Your Beauty's Glory'"; Karim-Cooper, *Cosmetics in Shakespearean and Renaissance Drama*.

43. Gunn, *Artificial Face*, 76–77, 85, 90; Oumeish, "Cultural and Philosophical Concepts"; Pointer, *Artifice of Beauty*, 96–98, 103–4, 110.

44. Gunn, *Artificial Face*, 76–77; Blanco-Dávila, "Beauty and the Body"; Pointer, *Artifice of Beauty*, 92–96. Mercury was also common in rouges. Martin, "Doctoring Beauty," esp. 357.

45. Wagatsuma, "Social Perception," esp. 407–12; Modern Girl Around the World Research Group, "Modern Girl Around the World: Cosmetics Advertising," 40; author's personal correspondence with Dorothy Ko, November 2, 2011; Saraswati, *Seeing Beauty*, chaps. 1, 2.

46. Jordan, *White over Black*, chap. 1; Erickson, "'God for Harry'"; Korhonen, "Washing the Ethiopian White."

47. K. Hall, *Things of Darkness*, 1–24; Pointer, *Artifice of Beauty*, 101; K. Brown, *Foul Bodies*, 42–43.

48. K. Hall, *Things of Darkness*, chap. 2; Pointer, *Artifice of Beauty*, 112; Gwilliam, "Cosmetic Poetics"; Festa, "Cosmetic Differences"; Iyengar, *Shades of Difference*, 130–36.

49. Schama, *Embarrassment of Riches*, 165, 375–97, 403–4.

50. Martin, "Doctoring Beauty"; Martin, *Selling Beauty*, intro., chaps. 1, 5; Festa, "Cosmetic Differences."

51. "Among the Variety of Cosmetics," *Times* (London), 270, November 5, 1785, 3.

52. Mintz, *Sweetness and Power*. Also see Smith, *Consumption and the Making of Respectability*; Berg, *Luxury and Pleasure*; Yang, *Performing China*.

53. Jordan, *White over Black*; Stuurman, "François Bernier"; Camp, "Black Is Beautiful." On the politics of complexion still being quite fluid in England before the 1780s, see Nussbaum, "Women and Race"; Wheeler, *Complexion of Race*.

54. Vail, *History of Cosmetics in America*, 76, 78, 100; K. Brown, *Foul Bodies*, 132–33.

55. Coleman, "Janet Schaw," 178, 173. On white women tanning and whitening in the West Indies, see Gwilliam, "Cosmetic Poetics," 152–58; Nussbaum, "Women and Race," 82.

56. Strutt, *Fashion in South Africa*, 22, 52, 75, 120, 136; Guelke, "Freehold Farmers and Frontier Settlers"; Armstrong and Worden, "Slaves."

57. Sopher, "Indigenous Uses of Turmeric"; Decary, *Mœurs et Coutumes*, 81–82; Modern Girl Around the World Research Group, "Modern Girl Around the World," 40–41; Patkar, "Herbal Cosmetics"; author's personal correspondence with historians Jean Gelman Taylor, October 23, 2011, and Purnima Dhavan, October 15, 2011.

58. Strutt, *Fashion in South Africa*, 52, 166, 211, 241, 285; Worden, Van Heyningen, and Bickford-Smith, *Cape Town*, 49, 101, 93, 97, 123; Jean Taylor, *Social World of Batavia*, 40–41, 62; Jean Taylor, "Painted Ladies of the VOC"; R. Ross, "Sumptuary Laws in Europe," 382–89; B. Schmidt, "Collecting Global Icons."

59. Elphick and Shell, "Intergroup Relations," 215; Keegan, *Colonial South Africa*, 23–24.

60. R. Ross, *Status and Respectability*, 11.

61. Bickford-Smith, "Black Ethnicities"; Worden, Van Heyningen, and Bickford-Smith, *Cape Town*, 89, 112. Ian Goldin notes that prior to the early twentieth century, some officials used "coloured" to encompass all non-Europeans in the Cape, including Bantu-speaking Africans. See *Making Race*, xxvi, 12. Also see Erasmus, *Coloured by History*.

62. Bird and Colebrooke, *State of the Cape of Good Hope*, 165–66, cited and discussed in R. Ross, *Status and Respectability*, 134–35.

63. Gordon, *Letters from the Cape*, 83–84, cited and discussed in R. Ross, *Status and Respectability*, 84–85. On Victorian dressing tables, see Pointer, *Artifice of Beauty*, 138–39.

64. Kalydor ads, *Graham's Town Journal*, November 24, 1842, 4; *Rand Daily Mail*, October 21, 1905, 3; Strutt, *Fashion in South Africa*, 211, 346, 385–96. For chemical analyses of Kalydor, see "Poisonous Cosmetics," *New Remedies*, March 1, 1874, 168; James P. Tuttle, "Cosmetics: Their Constituents and General Effects, with a Few Special Cases Other Than Saturnism," *Medical Record* 25, March 8, 1884, 257–59; "Notes and Queries: Kalydor," *Druggists' Circular and Chemical Gazette*, December 1, 1892, 277.

65. Peiss, *Hope in a Jar*, chaps. 2, 3; Pointer, *Artifice of Beauty*, 152.

66. Tuttle, "Cosmetics," 259. Tuttle cites Dr. W. E. Chandler's report "Dangerous Cosmetics" (1870) as an earlier warning delivered to the New York Metropolitan Board of Health. Others include Caroline Lee Mentz, "The Fatal Cosmetic," *Boston Cultivator*, November 24, 1849, 373; "Poisonous Soaps and Perfumery," *Lancet Medical News*, July 1861, 123; "Cosmetics," *Bistoury: A Quarterly Medical Journal, Devoted to the Exposition of Charlatanism in Medicine*, January 1, 1871, 206. For a photographer's warning, see Rodgers, *Twenty-Three Years*, 189–201.

67. Fenner, *Fenner's Twentieth Century Formulary*, 1385; Richard Von Foregger, "Oxygen Toilet Preparations," *American Druggist and Pharmaceutical Record*, February 12, 1906, 61–62; Chilson, *Modern Cosmetics*, 113.

68. For critical articles, see "Poisonous Cosmetics," *Scientific American*, August 3, 1861, 80; X. Apothecary, "The Cosmetic Case," *Druggists' Circular and Chemical Gazette*, February 1, 1894, 27. For recipes, see query "(42)," *Scientific American*, March 20, 1875, 187; X. Apothecary, "Quackery and Cosmetics," *Druggists' Circular and Chemical Gazette*, October 1, 1892, 219. For a recipe containing mercury that noted it was "very poisonous," see "Selected Formulas," *American Druggist and Pharmaceutical Record*, October 1, 1921, 47.

69. For example, Valeska Suratt, "How to Make Big and Little Wrinkles Disappear," *Washington Post*, October 19, 1913; "Beauty: Its Cultivation and Protection," *South African Lady's Pictorial and Home Journal*, November 1930, 56; "Beauty Hints," *Afro-American*, April 30, 1932, 24.

70. Electrolysis ad, *Rand Daily Mail*, October 7, 1902, 2; Madame Lydiard ad, *Cape Times*, February 10, 1913, 4.

71. For example, Ayer's Sarsaparilla ad, *Rand Daily Mail*, February 17, 1903, 8; Dr. Williams' Pink Pills ad, *Cape Times*, September 4, 1913, 4; Feluna Pills ad, *Cape Times*, September 6, 1913, 15.

72. For example, Cuticura Soap ad, *Standard and Diggers' News*, October 3, 1899, 6; Fauldings Solyptol Soap ad, *Rand Daily Mail*, February 3, 1903, 11; Pomeroy Skin Food ad, *Cape Times*, November 4, 1913, 11. On protecting white settler bodies, see Wells, "Sun Hats, Sundowners."

73. Telmo-Double Strength ad, *South African Pictorial*, February 8, 1919, 18.

74. Downing, "Cosmetics—Past and Present"; Cramp, *Nostrums and Quackery and Pseudo-Medicine*, 30.

75. James Bennett, "Cosmetics and Skin: Mercolized Wax," http://cosmeticsandskin.com/aba/mercolized-wax.php (accessed January 23, 2012); Greenberg and Lester,

Handbook of Cosmetic Materials, 47. Stillman's, another U.S.-made skin lightener with mercury, was also sold in South Africa. Stillman's Freckle Cream ad, *Cape Times*, September 1, 1913, 4.

76. Alice Brewer Ross, letter to Sallie, August 11, 1912, http://grandtour1913. wordpress.com/2008/04/17/13/ (accessed January 23, 2012). Ross's words echoed the product's slogan, "complexion soft and clear as baby's." Mercolized Wax ad, *South African Pictorial*, October 16, 1920, 22.

77. "Enforcing the Poison Law," *Druggists' Circular and Chemical Gazette*, February 1, 1891; "Virginia Company Barred: Accused of Advertising a Compound That Would Make Negroes' Skin White," *Washington Post*, June 8, 1905, 5. The earliest known state regulation that mentions cosmetics was enacted by Massachusetts in 1886. Hutt, "History of Government Regulation," 3.

78. Cramp, *Nostrums and Quackery: Articles on the Nostrum Evil*; "Curb on Cosmetics Urged by Doctors," *New York Times*, May 17, 1927, 7.

79. "Poisonous Cosmetics," *British Medical Journal*, August 26, 1893, 480–81; "Poison in a Cosmetics," *Druggists' Circular and Chemical Gazette*, October 1, 1893; "German Paternalism," *Urn*, April 25, 1893; "House & Health," *Christian Observer*, September 4, 1895.

80. Curran, "British Food and Drug Law."

81. Wells, "Eva's Men."

82. Scully, *Liberating the Family?* , chap. 1; Groenewald, "Slaves and Free Blacks."

83. Van Onselen, "Witches of Suburbia"; Ally, *From Servants to Workers*, chap. 1; Gaitskell et al., "Class, Race and Gender"; Cock, "Domestic Service"; Mayer with Mayer, *Townsmen or Tribesmen*, 245.

84. Cock, "Domestic Service"; Comaroff and Comaroff, *Of Revelation and Revolution*, chaps. 5, 6.

85. See, for example, Killie Campbell Library, Makhanya Papers, file 10: Principal, Sibusisiwe Secondary School, Umbumbulu, Natal, "Sibusisiwe Secondary School, Umbumbulu," c. 1971.

86. De Lange, "Some Traditional Cosmetic Practices," 89.

87. Burke, *Lifebuoy Men, Lux Women*, chaps. 2–4; Comaroff and Comaroff, *Of Revelation and Revolution*; R. Ross, *Status and Respectability*, 111–21.

88. McClintock, *Imperial Leather*, 207–31. On the centrality of black domestic workers to colonial commodity fetishism, see Ally, "'Ooh, eh eh.'" For another analysis of commodity fetishism and soap, see Blay, "Yellow Fever," chap. 9.

89. Erlmann, *African Stars*, 21–53; J. Campbell, *Songs of Zion*; Vinson, *Americans Are Coming!*

90. Monica Hunter, *Reaction to Conquest*, 2–8, 108–10, 174–79.

2. MODERN GIRLS AND RACIAL RESPECTABILITY

1. Mitchell, *New Girl*, 3.

2. Modern Girl Around the World Research Group, "Modern Girl as Heuristic Device," 11.

3. "Matters for Women: The Modern Girl," *Rand Daily Mail*, May 31, 1909, 2; Ella Hepworth Dixon, "The New Girl: Strong and Merciful," *Rand Daily Mail*, January 4, 1910, 2. On girls as part of "the great white race," see Joan Ford, "The Ideal Girl for South Africa," *South African Lady's Pictorial*, June 1930, 63.

4. Duke University, Rare Book, Manuscript, and Special Collections Library (hereafter, Duke Collection), J. Walter Thompson Collection, reel 225, Marketing Reports, South Africa, Port Elizabeth, J. Walter Thompson Co. (Pty.) Ltd., "Report for Lehn & Fink," (Sept. 1931), 45; U.S. Department of Commerce, *Advertising in the Union of South Africa*, 13.

5. Manoim, "Black Press 1945–1963," 40–42.

6. Switzer, *"Bantu World,"* 189–212, quote from 190–91; South African Institute of Race Relations Collection, Historical Papers Archive, the Library, University of Witwatersrand, Johannesburg (hereafter, WHP, SAIRR), AD843 RJ AA3.3.2 1, Correspondence on the Black Press, J. D. Rheinallt Jones's letter to R. Muir, September 16, 1931; Couzens, "Short History of 'World.'" *Bantu World's* early circulation figures were double those of contemporary African papers and, by 1946, had climbed to 24,000 per week.

7. Switzer, *"Bantu World,"* 198. For subtle analyses of *AmaRespectable* ideology, see Couzens, *New African*; B. Peterson, *Monarchs, Missionaries and African Intellectuals*; B. Peterson, "Bantu World"; Mokoena, *Magema Fuze*.

8. This conception of respectability bridges those developed by previous Africanist and African Americanist scholars. Wilson and Mafeje, *Langa*; Bickford-Smith, *Ethnic Pride and Racial Prejudice*; Willan, *Sol Plaatje*; Bickford-Smith, van Heyningen, and Worden, *Cape Town in the Twentieth Century*, 43; Iliffe, *Honour in African History*, 246; Goodhew, *Respectability and Resistance*; Marks, "Patriotism, Patriarchy and Purity"; Marks, *Not Either an Experimental Doll*, 1–55; Higginbotham, *Righteous Discontent*; Wolcott, *Remaking Respectability*, 1–10; K. Gaines, *Uplifting the Race*.

9. "The Son of Africa," "Great Progress! The Bantu World Calls to the Women of the Race," and "Competition," *Bantu World* (hereafter, BW), October 22, 1932, 10.

10. For ethnographic and erotic photography of African women in this period, see C. Williams, "Erotic Image Is Naked and Dark"; Stevenson and Graham-Stewart, *Surviving the Lens*, 19–21; Bradford, "Framing African Women." For some of the earliest extant examples of African women commissioning their own photos, see the National Library of South Africa, Cape Town, Special Collections, Grey Ethnological Album 167, INIL 14165 and 14210; Schoeman, *Face of the Country*, 68. For key works on the reappropriation of photography, see Hayes and Bank, *Kronos* ("Special Issue: Visual History"); Landau and Kaspin, *Images and Empires*; Pinney and Peterson, *Photography's Other Histories*; D. Willis, *Posing Beauty*; Campt, *Image Matters*; Feyder, "Portraits of Resilience."

11. S. Kay, *Travels and Researches in Caffraria*, 165; Isaacs, *Travels and Adventures in Eastern Africa*, 51, 56, 88, 107, 179, 190–91, 221, 265, 289, 291; Stuart and Malcolm, *Diary of Henry Francis Fynn*, 73, 164, 293; Hanretta, "Women, Marginality and the Zulu State."

12. Webb and Wright, *James Stuart Archive*, 3:151–52, 4:339.

13. Schapera, *Married Life in an African Tribe*, 46–48; Monica Hunter, *Reaction to Conquest*, 222–6.

14. Schapera, *Married Life in an African Tribe*, 46; Monica Hunter, *Reaction to Conquest*, 222.

15. Krige, *Social System of the Zulus*, 375.

16. Harries, "Photography and the Rise of Anthropology"; Hofmeyr, *Portable Bunyan*, 185.

17. Mofokeng, "Black Photo Album"; Mofokeng, "Trajectory of a Street-Photographer." Also see Mofokeng, *Black Photo Album/Look at Me*.

18. Cohen, Wilk, and Stoeltje, "Introduction," esp. 3–4.

19. Kracauer, *Mass Ornament*, 57–58.

20. *South African Pictorial: Stage and Cinema*: "Found in a Beauty Contest," March 5, 1920, 5; "Searching for 'Stars,'" April 24, 1920, 4; "'Beauty and Talent' Contest," May 15, 1920, 5.

21. For accounts of Africans enjoying foreign magazines and hanging photos of film stars on their walls, see Hellmann, "Native Life in a Johannesburg Slum Yard," 40; R. Phillips, *Bantu in the City*, 105; Sachs, *Black Hamlet*, 148–50.

22. On the need for a "magazine for Natives," see SAIRR AD843 RJ AA33.2 1, Rheinallt Jones letter to Muir, September 16, 1931.

23. Couzens, "'Moralizing Leisure Time'"; J. Campbell, "T. D. Mweli Skota"; Bunche and Edgar, *African-American in South Africa*; Kemp, "'Up from Slavery' and Other Narratives"; Kemp and Vinson, "'Poking Holes in the Sky'"; Vinson, *Americans Are Coming!*

24. South African National Archive Repository (hereafter, SAB) NTS 1681, file 2/276 vol. 1, Protector of Natives at Kimberley to Secretary for Native Affairs, September 24, 1924; SAB, NTS 1877, file 75/278, Magistrate at Butterworth to Chief Magistrate at Umtata, June 6, 1928.

25. On the political innovations of *Negro World*'s women's pages, edited by Amy Jacques Garvey, see Adler, "'Always Leading Our Men in Service and Sacrifice.'"

26. By the time of *Bantu World*'s contest, African American beauty contests were no longer so demure. The first bathing-beauty contest took place in 1926. S. White and G. White, *Stylin'*, 201; Craig, *Ain't I a Beauty Queen?*, 46–55.

27. J. Campbell, "T. D. Mweli Skota," 6. On debate in the contemporary African press over these terms, see Bunche and Edgar, *African American in South Africa*, 350n22.

28. "Bantu World Beauty Competition Entrants," *BW*, February 18, 1933, 10.

29. Cohen, Wilk, and Stoeltje, "Introduction."

30. Modern Girl Around the World Research Group, "Modern Girl Around the World: Cosmetics Advertising and the Politics of Race and Style," esp. 28.

31. "The Son of Africa," "Competition," *BW*, October 22, 1932, 10.

32. Modern Girl Around the World Research Group, "Modern Girl Around the World: Cosmetics Advertising and the Politics of Race and Style," 37–38.

33. It is possible that Ndobe's clothing, particularly the tippet, was a prop that belonged to the studio photographer. On props in African studio photography, see Pivin, "Icon and the Totem," 28; Mofokeng, "Black Photo Album," 69.

34. SAB, NTS 7725, file 180/333, Commissioner of Police to Sec. for Native Affairs, August 25, 1931, and November 25, 1931, and Sec. for Native Affairs to B. Ndobe, October 23, 1931; Roux, *Time Longer Than Rope*, x, 204, 230–43; Simons and Simons, *Class and Colour in South Africa*, 426–33; Drew, *Discordant Comrades*, 105–6. In October 1931, one year before Flora entered the competition, the South African government deemed Bransby an "undesirable inhabitant" and deported him to Basutoland, his birth place.

35. "Bantu Women and the Community," *BW*, March 25, 1933, 4.

36. "Tommy," "Pink-Cheeked Lady and Tom: Daughters of Ham Take to Powdering Their Faces," *BW*, February 11, 1933, 3.

37. Dyer, *White*, 82–142. On how Josephine Baker defied Hollywood's "cult of light," identified by Dyer, and instead conveyed "sheen," "shine," and "plasticity," see Cheng, *Second Skin*, 111–21.

38. Peiss, *Hope in a Jar*, 45–48; Conor, *Spectacular Modern Woman*, 143. For photographers' opinions on cosmetic use, see Rodgers, *Twenty-Three Years under a Sky-Light*, 189–201; Robinson, *Studio*, 117.

39. Fan Tan ad, *Chicago Defender*, August 3, 1935, 6. In another demonstration of the close association between cameras and skin care, see this promotion from a Coloured newspaper that enabled consumers who purchased three bars of soap to get a free studio portrait: "Erasmic Herb Toilet Soap," *Sun*, July 7, 1933, 6.

40. Duke Collection, Thompson, reel 225, "Report for Lehn & Fink," 10.

41. Couzens, *New African*, 42–81.

42. L. Thomas, "Love, Sex, and the Modern Girl in 1930s Southern Africa."

43. L. T. Baleni, "Unnecessary Expense Incurred by Women Striving for Beauty," *BW*, September 30, 1933, 10.

44. Peiss, *Hope in a Jar*, 4, 26–31, 53–60.

45. Duke Collection, Thompson, reel 225, "Report for Lehn & Fink," 2, 9. Also see "Correct Behavior for Business Girls," *South African Business Efficiency*, June 1935, 198.

46. Ntantala, *Life's Mosaic*, 74.

47. Editress, "Disappointing Make-Ups," *BW*, June 23, 1934, 12; "Over the Tea Cups: Arabelle and Isabel," *BW*, April 3, 1937, 9.

48. S. H. D. Lee Mnyandu, "Jo'burg Ladies," *BW*, September 17, 1938, 12. Also see his "Use of Cosmetics by Women," *BW*, October 1, 1938, 11; "'Basuto Ladies Are Smart,'" *BW*, November 2, 1938, 12.

49. Dhlomo, *African Tragedy*.

50. Population figures are from South Africa, Office of Census Statistics, *Official Year Book of the Union and of Basutoland, Bechuanaland Protectorate, and Swaziland*, 1056. On interwar Johannesburg, see Bonner, "'Desirable or Undesirable Basotho Women?'"; Bozzoli, *Women of Phokeng*; Berger, *Threads of Solidarity*; Marks, *Divided Sisterhood*; Burns, "Reproductive Labors"; Coplan, "You Have Left Me Wandering About."

51. Hellmann, "Native Life," 40; Hellmann, *Rooiyard*, 78.

52. Kuper, *African Bourgeoisie*, 113.

53. Bonner, "Transvaal Native Congress"; Eales, "Patriarchs, Passes, and Privilege"; Marks, "Patriotism, Patriarchy and Purity"; Ballantine, *Marabi Nights*, 46–50, 82–83; Kemp, "'Up from Slavery,'" chaps. 2, 3; Erlank, "Gender and Masculinity in South African Nationalist Discourse."

54. Miss Roamer, "Beautiful Bantu Women Need No Lipstick or Powder to Aid Nature," BW, March 4, 1933, 10; R. R. R. D., "True Beauty," BW, September 29, 1934, 12; Israel Mhlambi, "'Behavior of Girls,'" BW, October 5, 1935, 12; Editress, "Weak Women," BW, March 20, 1937, 9; Dimbane, "A Word in Season," BW, March 27, 1937, 12; "Over the Tea Cups: Arabelle and Isabel," BW, April 3, 1937, 9; Editress, "A Terrible Sight!" BW, January 29, 1938, 10. Also see L. Thomas, "Love, Sex, and the Modern Girl."

55. Modern Girl Around the World Research Group, "Modern Girl as Heuristic Device."

56. M. P., "Powder and Lipstick for the Africans?" BW, May 2, 1936, 11.

57. Peiss, *Hope in a Jar*, 41–43; Rooks, *Hair Raising*; Banks, *Hair Matters*; Craig, *Ain't I a Beauty Queen?*

58. S. White and G. White, *Stylin'*, 188–91, quote from 188; S. Walker, *Style and Status*, 67–70, quote from 68.

59. Miss Roamer, "Beautiful Bantu Women Need No Lipstick or Powder to Aid Nature," BW, March 4, 1933, 10; R. R. R. D., "True Beauty," BW, September 29, 1934, 12; Editress, "Disappointing Make-Ups," BW, June 23, 1934, 12; "Over the Tea Cups: Arabelle and Isabel," BW, April 3, 1937, 9. Also see "What R. Roamer Hears about Town," BW, September 23, 1933, 8; "R. Roamer Talks to the People," BW, May 19, 1934, 6; Editress, "Weak Women," BW, March 20, 1937, 9; Editress, "A Terrible Sight!" BW, January 29, 1938, 10; Editress, "Why Put That Stuff on Your Face?" BW, June 18, 1938, 9. On white men wearing blackface, see L. White, "Precarious Conditions."

60. M. F. Phala, O. F. S. Koffiefontein, "The Bantu and Colour," BW, December 29, 1934, 8. For other letters of complaint, see A. L. J. Rabotapi, "Mr. R. Roamer Blunders Now: Some Women Behave Disgracefully in the Streets," BW, April 21, 1934, 10; "Mok Tedi," "Ladies Must Choose Their Types," BW, April 23, 1938, 10; A. A. Mgoblo, "Ladies and Cosmetics," BW, September 17, 1938, 12; Erasmus Ngcabetsha, "Cigarette Smoking by Women," *Umlindi we Nyanga*, February 15, 1939.

61. Messrs. D. Mogoje and P. J. G. M., "Swanee Should Be Supported: Powder and Lipsticks Disfigure Bantu Women," BW, June 19, 1934, 10. On *imbola*, see Pinnock, *Xhosa*, 28.

62. "The Son of Africa," "Great Progress!"

63. L. N. Msimang, "'Girls Despised by Men,'" BW, October 5, 1935, 12.

64. "Swanee," "Women Should Not Use Lip-Sticks and Powders as Toilets," BW, May 19, 1934, 12. The biting wit of this letter combined with the pseudonym suggest R. Dhlomo's authorship.

65. S. Ngcobo, "Articles on Lipsticks Dance, Dresses and Love Become Boring," BW, September 29, 1934, 15.

66. "Powdered Face," "Women Want Good Constructive Advice from Their Critics," BW, June 28, 1934, 10. The style of this letter combined with the fact that R. Dhlomo

later used "Powdy Face" as a stock character in his fictional writing in *Ilanga* also suggest that the "editress" himself may have penned this letter.

67. "R. Roamer Talks to the People," *BW*, June 9, 1934, 8; also see column on August 4, 1934, 8. The letters were authored by Miss I. R. E. of Maseru and S. W. Y. of Zeerust, respectively.

68. S. M. Harden, "The Effect of Education upon the Negro: Particularly the West African," *Lagos Standard*, December 22, 1909, 5–6. Several years later, an editorial in another Lagos newspaper, the *Lagos Weekly Record*, castigated the values of a rival paper, *Nigerian Pioneer*, by chiding that it "should import from America some skin-whitener and endeavour to pass off for white, in order to be true to its cherished tradition." "The Nigerian Pioneer and the Majestic Bravery of Idolised Ignorance," *Lagos Weekly Record*, December 24–31, 1921, 5–6. Thanks to Lisa Lindsay for sharing these references with me.

69. Peiss, *Hope in a Jar*, 108–9. For a nineteenth-century discussion about African American women inappropriately wearing white face powder, see Rooks, *Hair Raising*, 37. Levine, *Black Culture and Black Consciousness*, 284–93, examines how "brown" was consistently valued over "yellow" and "black" in popular culture. Also see S. Walker, *Style and Status*, 81.

70. S. White and G. White, *Stylin'*, 189. Also see Rooks, *Hair Raising*; Craig, *Ain't I a Beauty Queen?*; S. Walker, *Style and Status*; Baldwin, *Chicago's New Negroes*, chap. 2; Baldwin, "From the Washtub to the World"; Gill, *Beauty Shop Politics*; Ford, *Liberated Threads*.

71. Peiss, *Hope in a Jar*, 203–24, 113. For the Garveys' critique of skin lighteners, see M. Garvey, "'Colored' or Negro Press"; A. Garvey, "I Am a Negro—and Beautiful," 57–58. In an effort to raise revenues, the Garveys' newspaper *Negro World* began carrying frequent skin lightener and hair straightener advertisements in 1923. Digby-Junger, "*Guardian, Crisis, Messenger*, and *Negro World*," esp. 271; "The Marcus Garvey and Universal Negro Improvement Association Papers Project," http://www.international.ucla.edu/africa/mgpp/ (accessed August 24, 2018).

72. Parrish, "Color Names and Color Notions"; Peiss, *Hope in a Jar*, 207–8; Walters, "Negro Press," esp. 40; Gatewood, *Aristocrats of Color*, chap. 6; Hill and Burger, "Aristocrats of Color"; Kerr, *Paper Bag Principle*; Dorman, "Skin Bleach and Civilization."

73. Schuyler, *Black No More*; Peiss, *Hope in a Jar*, 113, 207–13. For Schuyler praising Walker, see George S. Schuyler, "Madam C. J. Walker," *Messenger* 6, August 1924, 251–66.

74. H. I. E. Dhlomo, "An Experiment in Colour," *African Observer* 3, no. 4 (August 1935): 67–80. Republished with an English translation of the Afrikaans phrase in Visser and Couzens, *H. I. E. Dhlomo*, 489–500. Lovedale Press rejected an earlier version of the story and, when it was finally published, it carried this disclaimer: "the author's views are not necessarily those of *The African Observer*." Dhlomo's story drew inspiration from Sir Arthur Keith's research on the role of "glandular action and secretions" in determining "racial character." Couzens, *New African*, 181–85. More than a decade before, *Umteteli wa Bantu* reported on a Brazilian doctor who claimed to have developed a pill that could "make black men white," noting that "there will be

no stampede of South African Natives anxious to be bleached." "White from Black," *Umteteli wa Bantu*, April 8, 1922, 3.

75. The value of U.S. imports totaled about one-third of those from the United Kingdom. Other countries from which South Africa imported goods were, in ranked order, Germany, Canada, Japan, British India, Belgium, and France. U.S. Department of Commerce, *Advertising in the Union of South Africa*, 1–2.

76. Apex ad, *BW*, July 15, 1933, 10; "The Opening of Vast Unexplored Market," *BW*, May 26, 1934, 1.

77. J. Barnard Belman, "Garvey 'Great King' in South Africa," *Negro World*, October 24, 1925, 10; "Jack Barnard's Well-Known Book Shop" ad, *Worker's Herald*, March 27, 1926, 6; "Notice to Johannesburg Readers," *Sun*, March 25, 1938, 10. For a photo of Barnard in front of his bookshop, see Vinson, *Americans Are Coming!*, 58. Describing himself as a "good friend of the Natives," Barnard advertised for a "native with capital" to become his business partner. "Wanted: Partner," *Worker's Herald*, November 30, 1928, 6. Thanks to Robert Vinson for sharing this information with me.

78. Apex ad, *New York Amsterdam News*, June 1932.

79. Barthes, "Rhetoric of the Image," esp. 200.

80. Apex ads in *BW*: August 26, 1933, 15; September 2, 1933, 14; September 16, 1933, 15. Thanks to Lorato Chwene for the translation from Sesotho: "Ke Mafura a sueufats-ang letlalo la motho. A tlosa diso le ditshila tse ding letlalong. A etsa gore motho a be motle, a dira letlalo la gagoe boleta gamogo le sefahlogo sa gagoe."

81. Rooks, *Hair Raising*, 81–85.

82. "Remarkable Business Acumen of Negro Woman Shown in Her Work," *BW*, November 11, 1933, 10.

83. "Opening of Vast Unexplored Market," 1. A "Bantu Exhibition" was also advertised in *Umteteli wa Bantu* in April 1933.

84. Couzens, "Short History of 'World,'" 77. Cosmetics—including soaps, dyes, toothpastes, shaving equipment, and razors and razor blades as well as hair and skin products—accounted for about 10 percent of all items advertised in *Bantu World* during the 1930s. Health products and services dominated *Bantu World* advertising, accounting for just over 30 percent of all items. Switzer, "*Bantu World*."

85. Editress, "Advertisements in Your Paper," *BW*, May 5, 1934, 11. For women's accounts of their visit to the exhibition, see "Woman Visitor to Bantu World Show Writes about It," *BW*, May 20, 1933, 10; "A Woman Correspondent," "Bantu World Trade Exhibition Promises to Surpass Last Year's," *BW*, March 3, 1934, 10.

86. "R. Roamer Talks to the People," *BW*, June 2, 1934, 8.

87. "Offices," *Apex News*, June/July 1936, 6; L. Herbert Lekhethoa, "South Africa.... Past and Present," *Apex News*, January 1940, 11; "News from Abroad," *Apex News*, September 1939, 30.

88. Valmor ad, *BW*, February 22, 1936, 17. This same Valmor ad appeared in a 1935 issue of the *Gold Coast Independent*, a West African newspaper, suggesting a broader effort by the company to tap African markets.

89. Bunche and Edgar, *African-American in South Africa*, 177. Peiss similarly argues that the rise of Valmor with its cheaper products, more aggressive marketing, and

sexualized advertising appeals marked, by the late 1930s, the end of the race pride era of black cosmetic companies. See *Hope in a Jar*, 237.

90. For examples, see "Bleacho" ad, *Sun*, February 1, 1935, 4; "American Straight-O" ad, *Sun*, March 25, 1938, 4.

91. During the 1930s, African American missionaries also noted how black South Africans admired their appearance and especially their curled and marcelled hair. A. White and L. White, *Dawn in Bantuland*, 79, 198–99; Wright, *Beneath the Southern Cross*, 47–50. Thanks to James T. Campbell for directing me to these sources.

92. "Miss Rilda Marta's Trip to the United States Full of Excitement," *BW*, June 29, 1935, 12; "Miss Rilda Marta's Trip to United States of America Full of Interest," *BW*, July 6, 1935, 12; "Miss Rilda Marta's Trip to America," *BW*, July 13, 1935, 12. For more on Marta in the United States and her African American guardian who was also a beauty specialist, Lida Broner, see "Miss Rilda Marta Honored at Tea in Newark, N.J.," *New York Age*, December 9, 1933, 2; Clarke, *Activist Collector*.

93. "Miss Rilda Marta's Trip to United States of America Full of Interest"; "Miss Rilda Marta's Trip to America."

94. Kemp, "'Up from Slavery,'" 6, 156; Berger, "African American 'Mother of the Nation.'"

95. James R. Korombi, Johannesburg, "Hair Straightening," *BW*, March 4, 1939.

3. LOCAL MANUFACTURING AND COLOR CONSCIOUSNESS

1. Blay, "Yellow Fever," 424–25.

2. Karroo ad, *Sun*, January 19, 1934, 4. An earlier Karroo ad appeared in September 1933. Politically, the *Sun* was progressive, supporting the Coloured African People's Organisation and the white United Party. Switzer and Switzer, *Black Press in South Africa and Lesotho*.

3. Steenkamp, "Bantu Wages in South Africa," 96, table II; "Servant Problem in Cape Town," *Cape Argus*, March 17, 1930; email communication with Wayne Dooling, July 22, 2019. Between 1825 and the declaration of the Republic of South Africa in May 1961, South Africa used the British system of pounds, shillings, and pence as its currency, with a pound worth twenty shillings and a shilling worth twelve pence. After May 1961, a new currency based on rand and cents was introduced, with one rand worth 100 cents. The initial exchange rate against the British sterling was two rand to the pound. Feinstein, *Economic History of South Africa*, xx. Also email communication with Keith Breckenridge, July 28, 2008; with T. Dunbar Moodie, September 17, 2009.

4. Interviews with Francois Roux by Lynn M. Thomas and Sarah Espi-Sanchis, Middleburg, July 14, 2008; with Phillip Rolfe, July 29, 2008.

5. One pharmacist, for instance, complained about colleagues who "employ native touts and travelers, who diagnose and supply the chemist's mixtures in the locations." E. Gordin, letter to the editor, *South African Pharmaceutical Journal*, February 1935, 33.

6. Union of South Africa, *Sixth Census of the Population of South Africa*, 11.

7. In nineteenth- and early twentieth-century South Africa, as in Germany and Britain, "chemist" referred to those who had undergone an entrance examination in

chemistry and botany and had served an initial apprenticeship, while "pharmacist" was reserved for those who had also passed advanced examinations in chemistry and botany and had served an additional apprenticeship. While lay South Africans have often and still do use "chemist" and "pharmacist" interchangeably, within the trade "pharmacist" denotes someone with the license to dispense medicines while "chemist" refers to someone with only the right to prepare medicines. Ryan, *History of Organised Pharmacy in South Africa*, 31, 73; interview with Gerald Schap by Lynn M. Thomas and Sarah Espi-Sanchis, Cape Town, July 22, 2008.

8. "Ysabel" Skin Whitening Lemon Cold Cream ad, *South African Pharmaceutical Journal*, October 1934, 1.

9. Peiss, *Hope in a Jar*, 71; Jones, "Blonde and Blue-Eyed?," esp. 128.

10. The chains were Lennon Limited, Sive Brothers and Karnovsky, and Publix. Ryan, *History of Organised Pharmacy in South Africa*, 36, 97–99. By 1934, South Africa had 1,250 registered chemists and druggists. South African National Archive Repository, Pretoria (hereafter, SAB), HEN, 617, 85, vol. 1, Secretary for Commerce Industries to Secretary to the High Commissioner for the Union of South Africa, London, December 14, 1934.

11. Flint, "Competition, Race, and Professionalization," 213. On the apprenticeship system, see Ryan, *History of Organised Pharmacy in South Africa*, 38, 35–36.

12. South Africa, "Medical, Dental and Pharmacy Act No. 13 of 1928," 180–293; Flint, "Competition, Race, and Professionalization," 216–17; Ryan, *History of Organised Pharmacy in South Africa*, 25–26, 69–70, 115.

13. South Africa, "Act No. 5 of 1937 (Medical, Dental and Pharmacy Act)," 24–31; SAB, HEN, 618, 85/29/750, "Section 76 of the Medical, Dental and Pharmacy Act No. 13 of 1928 as amended by Section 2 of Act No. 5 of 1937"; SAB, HEN, 617, 85, vol. 1, A. Kramer, News Editor, Misc. Enquiries Section, S. A. Pharmaceutical Journal to Mr. C. O. Lawrence, North Shields, England, August 17, 1944.

14. H. R. Hudson, "Manufacture of Toilet Preparations," *South African Pharmaceutical Journal*, June 1935, 43; Duke University, Rare Book, Manuscript, and Special Collections Library, J. Walter Thompson Collection (hereafter, Duke JWT Collection), reel 225, Marketing Reports, South Africa, Port Elizabeth, J. Walter Thompson Co. (Pty.) Ltd., "Report for Unguentine" (1929), 1, 5; Ryan, *History of Organised Pharmacy in South Africa*, 100.

15. Interview with Schap, July 22, 2008.

16. Duke JWT Collection, reel 225, Marketing Reports, South Africa, Port Elizabeth, J. Walter Thompson Co. (Pty.) Ltd., "Report for Lehn & Fink," September 1931, 9, 11, 13. Thompson opened its Port Elizabeth office as part of an agreement the company had with General Motors (GM) to have an office in each country where GM had a manufacturing or assembly facility. Subsequent offices were opened in Cape Town (1930), Johannesburg (1932), and Durban (1935). Duke JWT Collection: Young Papers, Box 2, File "Notes on Billing, 1927–29," "International Offices," January 8, 1957; Sidney Berstein Papers, Box 5, File "International Office Histories, South Africa, January 1964," "Report for J.W.T.'s 100th Anniversary Book, New York: J. W. T. in Southern Africa."

17. It grew from thirty-six manufacturers to 125 importers in 1944. SAB, CSO 2, file S02/10, "Local Manufacturers—Toilets & Cosmetics" and "Importers—Toilets

& Cosmetics," May 9, 1944. A 1931 listing included sixteen manufacturers of toilet preparations and requisites; some of these, such as Lever Bros. (S.A.) Ltd., were South African subsidiaries of foreign companies. South African Federated Chamber of Industries, *National Directory of Manufacturers 1931*, 139.

18. Feinstein, *Economic History of South Africa*, 116–19. Also see Palmer, "Some Aspects of the Development of Secondary Industry"; Houghton, *South African Economy*, 112–18; Kaplan, "Politics of Industrial Protection in South Africa"; Marais, "Structural Changes in Manufacturing Industry." By as late as 1936, the U.S. government considered South African customs tariffs to still be quite low. U.S. Department of Commerce, *Advertising in the Union of South Africa*, 1.

19. The Customs Amendment of 1923 placed a 40 percent duty on perfumery and toilet preparations. Act No. 23 of 1923, *Statutes of the Union of South Africa 1925*, 204–22, perfumery rate listed on 220; "Annexure 'I': Principal Increases in Customs Duties since 1920," in South Africa, Board of Trade and Industries, *Report No. 282: Investigation into Manufacturing Industries in the Union of South Africa*, 168. Previously, these items had been taxed at 25 percent. Ryan, *History of Organised Pharmacy in South Africa*, 79.

20. SAB, HEN, 617, 85/2/1, W. F. McMullen, Secretary for Commerce and Industries to the First Secretary, Legation of the Union of South Africa, Rome, October 31, 1934. For foreign cosmetics companies' requests for reduction in the tariff rate in 1937–38, see SAB, RHN, 906, 85/9/3.

21. "Annexure 'I': Principal Increases in Customs Duties since 1920," 168.

22. SAB, RHN, 907, 85/12/1: "Proposed Excise Duty on Cosmetics," Secretary for Commerce and Industries to Acting Secretary, Board of Trade and Industries, Cape Town, February 15, 1941; "Proposed Excise Duty on Cosmetics," Acting Director, Office of Census and Statistics to Secretary for Commerce and Industries, Pretoria, February 27, 1941. SAB, HEN, 617, 85/2/1, "Vervaardiging an Kosmetiek in Die Unie," Direkteur Van Sensus En Statistieke, Pretoria to F. W. Quass, Sekretaris Van Handel En Nywerheid, June 20, 1950.

23. Fieldhouse, "Unilever in South Africa."

24. Peiss, *Hope in a Jar*, 98.

25. Bozzoli, "Origins, Development and Ideology of Local Manufacturing."

26. "Kaffir products" was tied to "Kaffir trade" and "Kaffir truck," phrases used throughout southern Africa to refer to the itinerant traders who sold cheap manufactured goods to Africans living in rural areas. Burke, *Lifebuoy Men, Lux Women*, 66–67; *Dictionary of South African English*, 342–50.

27. The amount of imported toiletries dipped to its lowest levels of under £64,000 in 1943 and 1944 but quickly rebounded to over £438,000 in 1945. SAB, HEN, 617, 85, vol. 1, "War-Time Controls: Toilet Preparations," B. J. Joubert, Acting Secretary for Commerce and Industries to Federal Agency Executive, Central News Agency, Ltd., Johannesburg, June 20, 1956. For an elaborate plea for the value of imported and domestically produced cosmetics for maintaining wartime morale, see SAB, HEN, 617, 85/2/1, Dermacult, Cape Town to Minister of Commerce and Industries, Pretoria, August 19, 1942.

28. SAB, HEN, 617, 85, vol. 1, N. V. Lang (PTY) Ltd., Representing Leading Overseas and South African Factories, Cape Town to Secretary, Board of Trade, Pretoria, June 11, 1945.

29. SAB, HEN, 617, 85, vol. 1, "Toiletries," P. D. Oliver, Durban to Department Head, Trade Department, South Africa House, London, July 1947.

30. South Africa, Board of Trade and Industries, *Report No. 282*, 168. A decade later, a "Buy South African" campaign was launched. "Why the 'Buy South African' Campaign Is Important," *African Market*, April 1955, 15. Beginning in the mid-1950s, light and intermediate consumer goods were increasingly produced locally. Bloch, "Room at the Top?," 50.

31. X. Apothecary, "Quackery and Cosmetics," *Druggists' Circular and Chemical Gazette*, October 1, 1892, 219; Fenner, *Fenner's Twentieth Century Formulary*, 1385; Richard Von Foregger, "Oxygen Toilet Preparations," *American Druggist and Pharmaceutical Record*, February 12, 1906, 61–62; Chilson, *Modern Cosmetics*, 113; Cook, LaWall, and Remington, *Remington's Practice of Pharmacy*, 780, 1989–2020.

32. SAB, HEN, 4516, 822, vol. 1, "Mercury," for Chairman, Board of Trade and Industries to W. J. Stevens, Esq. , Cirencester Mine, Eastern Transvaal, June 13, 1930. For a skin lightener from 1945 that specifically names mercury as the active ingredient, see "Diana Special Cream" ad, *Imvo Zabantsundu Bomzantsi Afrika*, April 7, 1945, cited in Khan, "Fanta Face, Coca-Cola Body," 2–3.

33. Interview with Roux and factory employees, July 14, 2008. A government survey from 1941 identified Karroo as a mid-level cosmetics manufacturer with an annual output of £5,500. SAB, RHN, 907, 85/12/1, "Proposed Excise Duty on Cosmetics," Secretary for Commerce and Industries, Department of Commerce and Industries to Acting Secretary, Board of Trade and Industries, Cape Town, February 15, 1941.

34. Karroo ad, *Die Huisgenoot*, October 18, 1946, 73. I am indebted to Emile Coetzee for translating this ad and some others from Afrikaans to English. Personal correspondence, March 27, 2012. Other Karroo ads appeared in *Die Huisgenoot* on October 4, 1946, 48; October 25, 1946, 79; November 8, 1946, 70; October 29, 1948, 85.

35. Interview with Roux and factory employees, July 14, 2008. The name *Skewe Sewe* originated from the men's drunken walking style following the rugby matches they attended on weekends. The name stuck when one member developed a spinal condition that caused him to walk with a limp. Interview with Joe Vorster by Lynn M. Thomas and Sarah Espi-Sanchis, Mossel Bay, Western Cape, July 23, 2008.

36. Keppels ad, *Rand Daily Mail*, December 20, 1938, 11.

37. SAB, RHN, 907, 85/11, H. S. Coaker, Manager, Keppels Cosmetic Laboratories, Ladybrand to Secretary, Board of Trade and Industries, Pretoria, November 29, 1937; August 14, 1939; August 24, 1939; February 8, 1940.

38. Keppels ad, *Bantu World*, April 1, 1939, 17. A few years later, Keppels ran an ad campaign in the *Cape Times* that claimed its cosmetics could remedy the harmful effects of "our South African climate." *Cape Times*, July 3, 1945, 8; July 10, 1945, 8.

39. U.S. Department of Commerce, *Advertising in the Union of South Africa*, 14, 11–12, 47; "Harrow," "Critical Commentaries on Current Advertising—No. 11," *South African Business Efficiency*, October 1934, 302–8, esp. 304.

40. Duke JWT Collection, reel 225, Marketing Reports, South Africa, Port Elizabeth, J. Walter Thompson Co. (Pty.) Ltd., "'Unguentine' in the South African Market," (1929), 1; U.S. Department of Commerce, *Advertising in the Union of South Africa*, 11.

41. "The Native Trade: The Non-European Market Provides the Chemist with a Valuable but Difficult Business," *South African Retail Chemist*, February 1953, 31–32.

42. Interview with Solomon Krok by Lynn M. Thomas, Johannesburg, August 12, 2008. Krok recalled that Arenband's pharmacy was located in Doornfontein and that he later immigrated to Israel. For L. Arenband as director, see SAB, HEN, 618, 85/29, P. Segal, Secretary, Crowden Products [PTY] Ltd. to Department of Commerce and Industries, Pretoria, March 7, 1961.

43. Bu-Tone ad, *Die Huisgenoot*, April 7, 1944, 31; Bu-Tone ad, *Cape Times*, July 10, 1945, 6.

44. Bu-Tone ads, *Sun*, March 4, 1949, 5.

45. For another fascinating African healer and entrepreneur who operated in the interwar period, see Burns, "Louisa Mvemve."

46. Flint, *Healing Traditions*, 136, 143; "South Africa's Richest African," *Drum*, December 1954, 21–23.

47. SAB, GES, 1788, 25/30M, Israel Alexander pamphlet (c. 1940), cited in Flint, *Healing Traditions*, 135. Thanks to Karen Flint for sharing Alexander's pamphlet with me together with a preliminary translation of the Be-A-Beauty ad. I am indebted to Tumishang Leta and Natasha Erlank for providing a more literal translation from Sesotho. Email correspondence, February 2012.

48. Xaba, "Witchcraft, Sorcery or Medical Practice?," 92–95.

49. J. D. Mweli Skota Correspondence, Historical Papers Research Archive, the Library, University of Witwatersrand, Johannesburg, AD2781, letter from Zilpah T. D. Skota to J. D. Mweli Skota, April 17, 1941.

50. Bozzoli with Nkotsoe, *Women of Phokeng*, 102. For another account from this study that admiringly describes a light-colored complexion and compares it to that of a Coloured person, see Mrs. Mekgwe: "In those days Aunt Naomi was a real beauty, so light in complexion that she looked Coloured, and yes, she had an eye for clothes, that one" (101).

51. Ribane, *Beauty*, 105, 12. "*Tswang, tswang, tswang, le boning, ngwana o tshwana le le Coloured!*" See another account of the same Sotho song translated as "Gather ye all, gather ye all. Behold a child so beautiful she resembles a coloured," in Bafana Khumalo, "Marrying In, Marrying Out," *Cosmopolitan*, February 1996, 96–99, cited in Khan, "Fanta Face, Coca-Cola Body," 2.

52. Goldin, *Making Race*, 36–47; Adhikari, "Predicaments of Marginality," esp. x.

53. Posel, "Race as Common Sense," 97.

54. Findlay, *Miscegenation*; Watson, *Passing for White*, 18–19; Goldin, *Making Race*, 80; personal communication with Robert Ross and Wayne Dooling, July 2019.

55. L. Green, *Outspan*, November 17, 1950, 19, cited in Watson, *Passing for White*, 18, 27n12.

56. Adhikari, *Not White Enough*, 11–14.

57. "Shifting the Colour Bar," *A.P.O.*, March 11, 1922, 6. By contrast, for an early twentieth-century protest over another South African magazine's use of "black" to refer to "coloured people," see "What Are You, Anyhow?" *South African Spectator*, June 29, 1901, 5. For the magazine's defenses of its usage, see the July 13, 1901, issue.

58. Henry C. A. Cloete, "The Dress of Non-European Girls," letter to the editor, *Sun*, March 2, 1934, 5. For an incisive historical analysis of how poverty and fragile class divides shaped respectability politics in early twentieth-century South Africa, see Dooling, "Poverty and Respectability."

59. "Two Domestic Servants of Wynberg," "Dress and Habits," letter to the editor, *Sun*, March 9, 1934, 7; Francis C. Rousseau, "Re: The Dress of Non-European Girls," letter to the editor, *Sun*, April 6, 1934, 5. Also see Andrew Mackrill, "Women's Dress," *Sun*, May 25, 1934, 7.

60. Henry C. A. Cloete, "Dress and Habits," *Sun*, March 16, 1934, 2; Henry C. A. Cloete, letter to the editor, *Sun*, April 20, 1934, 6. For someone who agreed with Cloete's criticism of scanty clothing, see "Modesty," letter to the editor, *Sun*, April 20, 1934, 6.

61. "Pageant Progress," *Cape Standard*, February 2, 1936, 2; "Pageant Queens," *Cape Standard*, December 28, 1936, 6; "Pageant Plans Complete," *Cape Standard*, December 28, 1936, 7. Compared to the *Sun*, the *Cape Standard* was more outspoken in its condemnation of racial discrimination and, based on examination of available issues, appears not to have carried skin lightener and hair straightener ads. Switzer and Switzer, *Black Press in South Africa and Lesotho*.

62. "Why Coloureds Pass as White: Economic and Moral Urge Involved," *Cape Standard*, July 2, 1940, 7.

63. "Race Consciousness," *Sun*, June 21, 1935, 3; "Will They?," *Sun*, March 3, 1938, 3; J. H. Pitt, "Pride and Prejudice," letter to the editor, *Sun*, January 18, 1935, 5.

64. "No Permission," "Old Age Versus Youth," *Cape Standard*, July 9, 1940, 2.

65. Feldman, Pike, and Adams, *Vitamin D*, 18; Segrave, *Suntanning in 20th Century America*, chaps. 2, 3; Jablonski, *Living Color*, 74–79. On the distinction between "heliotherapy" and "phototherapy," see Woloshyn, "Soaking Up the Sun's Rays."

66. "The Isipongo Recovery School," *Child Welfare* 6, no. 1 (June 1927): 4–5. Thanks to Sarah Duff for this reference.

67. Segrave, *Suntanning in 20th Century America*, chaps. 2, 3; D. Hansen, "Shades of Change," chaps. 2–4; Modern Girl Around the World Research Group, "Modern Girl Around the World: Cosmetics Advertising and the Politics of Race and Style," esp. 46–50; Lindsley, "Girl Pictures," chap. 1.

68. "Peace and War: A Study in Contrast," *Stage and Cinema: The Dramatic Sporting and Social Journal of South Africa*, May 26, 1917, 5. Soon after this issue, the title changed to *South African Pictorial: Stage and Cinema*.

69. "Bathing-Photo Competitors, Please Note!," *South African Pictorial: Stage and Cinema*, December 16, 1922, 11.

70. See *South African Pictorial: Stage and Cinema* from December 23, 1922, through February 10, 1923. For a beauty column that proposed remedies for restoring the "soft white lustre" lost through too much "bathing" and "sunning" on the beach,

see "Beauty: Its Cultivation and Protection," *South African Lady's Pictorial*, November 1930, 56.

71. "Sunburn," *South African Lady's Pictorial and Home Journal*, February 1, 1925, 8.

72. Duke JWT Collection, reel 225, Marketing Reports, South Africa, Port Elizabeth, J. Walter Thompson Co. (Pty.) Ltd., "Report for Unguentine" (1929), foreword and p. 27. For an early locally manufactured sunscreen, see "Torch Brand Sunban" ad, *South African Pharmaceutical Journal* 1, no. 3 (December 1934): cover.

73. Karroo ad, *Die Huisgenoot*, October 18, 1946, 73; Keppels ad, *Cape Times*, July 3, 1945, 8. Also see Bu-Tone and Keppels ads, *Cape Times*, July 10, 1945, 6 and 8.

74. Marie Du Bois, "What Is Sun-Tan Doing to Cosmetics?," *Advertising and Selling*, June 12, 1929, 19–20, 62, 64. Also see Marie Du Bois, "The Sun-Tan Mode Arrives," *Advertising and Selling*, May 1, 1929, 28, 76.

75. Donald S. Cowling, "Will the Vogue for Tan Last?," *Printers' Ink Monthly*, August 1929, 31–32, 82, 84. This discussion of the Cowling quote and other material in this paragraph draws on the Modern Girl Around the World Research Group's interpretation in "Modern Girl Around the World: Cosmetics Advertising and the Politics of Race and Style," 46–48. Similarly, a beauty advice column from 1900 noted that a popular expression for referring to deeply tanned white skin was "as black as an Indian." Grace Peckham Murray, "The Summer Girl's Complexion," *Harper's Bazaar*, June 16, 1900, 444.

76. For an important exploration of tanning as white racial privilege, see Weinbaum, "Racial Masquerade." Also see Williamson, "Woman Is an Island"; Ahmed, "Animated Borders," esp. 61; Perry, "Buying White Beauty," 586.

77. Berry, *Screen Style*, chap. 3; D. Hansen, "Shades of Change," chap. 3.

78. For example, "Doris Interprets the Mode," *Washington Post*, December 4, 1929, 16; Elsie Pierce, "How to Be Beautiful," *Sun*, August 27, 1936, 8; "Beauty and the Elements . . . Sun, Wind, and Water," *Vogue*, May 15, 1941, 34–41. Also see D. Hansen, "Shades of Change," chap. 3.

79. Daggett & Ramsdell's Perfect Cold Cream ad, *New York Times*, September 1, 1918, 61; Helena Rubinstein ad, *Spur*, September 15, 1926, 107; Gervaise Graham Lotion Face Bleach ad, *McClure, the Magazine of Romance*, July 1927, 97.

80. In both cases, the author of the advice column responded that time in a temperate climate would naturally return the writer's original skin color. H. G. L., Cuba, "Tropical Climate," *Hygeia*, February 1926, 119; K. T., Idaho, "Face Bleacher," *Hygeia*, March 1927, 162. Cited and discussed in D. Hansen, "Shades of Change," 41–42.

81. National Archives and Records Administration, College Park, Maryland (hereafter, NARA), FDA, RG 88, General Subject Files, 1942, 581.1: Mrs. J. Mott Buck, La Salle Hotel, Chicago, Illinois to FDA, Agriculture Dept., November 12, 1942; H. Wales, Acting Chief, Interstate Division, FDA to Mrs. Buck, November 23, 1942.

82. "Sun Tan," *Afro-American*, August 24, 1929, 6.

83. J. A. Rogers, "Europe's Sun Tan Fad," *New York Amsterdam News*, August 21, 1929, 20. Virtually the same article appeared under a different title as J. A. Rogers, "Berlin's Fashion Decrees Dark Skin Color," *Afro-American*, August 17, 1929, 5.

84. Alfred Smith, "Adventures in Race Relations," *Chicago Defender*, May 3, 1947, 15.

85. Tan-Off ad, *Baltimore Afro-American*, 1928; Fan Tan ad, *Baltimore Afro-American*, October 26, 1929, 20; Peiss, *Hope in a Jar*, 113. This discussion of Tan-Off and Fan Tan draws on the Modern Girl Around the World Research Group's interpretation in "Modern Girl Around the World: Cosmetics Advertising and the Politics of Race and Style," 48–49; Berry, *Screen Style*, 94. Interestingly, Tan-Off did not contain mercury until the early 1940s. NARA, FDA, RG 88, General Subject Files, 1942, 581.1: "Memorandum of Interview" involving Mr. Buck, Plough Chemical Co., Memphis, Tennessee and, from the FDA, Mr. G. F. Larrick, November 26, 1940.

86. "Dangers of Sunburn: Hints for Holiday-makers," *Cape Standard*, January 4, 1938, 10. For examples of similar advice in the white British and U.S. press, see "The Summer Complexion," *Times* (London), July 7, 1939, 19; Klein, *How to Suntan for Health and Fun*. In Zoe Wicomb's 2006 novel about passing in apartheid South Africa (*Playing in the Light*), some characters use "tannie" interchangeably with "Coloured."

87. Keppels ad, *Cape Times*, July 3, 1945, 8; Bu-Tone ad, *Cape Times*, July 10, 1945, 6. References to complexions "ravage[d]" by South Africa's "cruel" climate and "harsh winds and searing sun" may have also served as euphemisms for skin that was naturally brown.

88. Duke JWT Collection, reel 53, Investigations, "Pond's" (1931), 15–20, 1–3. This list notably excluded a number of products regularly advertised in the African American press.

89. Chilson, *Modern Cosmetics*, 113.

90. "Sunburn Preparations," *Drug and Cosmetic Industry*, 34, March 1934, 237–38; "Sun Tan Lotion," *Drug and Cosmetic Industry*, 41, July 1937, 131; Duke JWT Collection, reel no. 233, Marketing Research Reports: "Test of Pond's New Sun Tan Powder," April 1936, "Skol Company, Incorporated; Consumer Investigation on Sunburn Preparations," September 1937, "Skol Company, Incorporated; Second Consumer Investigation on Sunburn Preparations," October 1937, and "Trend in Sales of Sun Tan Lotions, Creams and Pads in Drug, Department and Variety Stories," August 1938; Duke JWT Collection, reel no. 712: Pond's Extract Co., "Information on Tinted Foundation and Creams," April 1941.

91. Segrave, *Suntanning in 20th Century America*, chap. 6; D. Hansen, "Shades of Change," chap. 8.

92. The poem's title ironically referenced the biblical Song of Solomon. Jeffreys also published a six-part series entitled "How White Are the Whites?" in *Drum* magazine in 1959–60. Hamsi (Marie Kathleen Jeffreys) with introduction by Samuelson, "Though I Am Black, I Am Comely."

4. BEAUTY QUEENS AND CONSUMER CAPITALISM

1. "The Native Trade: The Non-European Market Provides the Chemist with a Valuable but Difficult Business," *South African Retail Chemist*, February 1953, 31–32. The Cape Town chemist featured in this piece named Karroo as the top seller, and Bu-Tone and Metamorphasa as other popular brands.

2. Langschmidt, "Some Characteristics of the Urban Bantu Market," 21. This study listed skin lightener purchases behind those of soap and detergent, tea, and tinned and powdered milk.

3. Makeba with Hall, *Makeba*, 111.

4. "Petty apartheid" referred to racial segregation of public and private amenities as well as prohibitions on "mixed" marriages, whereas "grand apartheid" referred to the racial segregation and "separate development" of residential areas, in terms of both rural homelands and urban neighborhoods. Louw, *Rise, Fall, and Legacy of Apartheid*, 50, 58–59.

5. On the 1950s, in particular, as a remarkable period of "romantic self-construction" and self-stylization, see Coplan, *In Township Tonight!*; Samuelson, "Urban Palimpsest."

6. Marchand, *Advertising the American Dream*.

7. Norval, *Quarter of a Century of Industrial Progress*; Bloch, "Room at the Top?"; R. Ross, *Concise History of South Africa*, 106–19; Feinstein, *Economic History of South Africa*, 151–57.

8. See, for example, R. Brennun, "The African as an Industrial Worker: Bring Him into Industry and You Make Him into a Consumer," *South African Advertising and Selling*, November 1945, 17–19. *Selling* began as *South African Advertising* in 1936, changed to *Selling* in 1946, and continued as *Advertising and Selling* from 1951 to 1957.

9. For more, see Horwitz, *Expand or Explode*. Like *Selling*, *Selling Age* underwent a number of confusing name changes. It began in 1953 as *South African Packaging and Sales Promotion*, changed to *South African Sales Promotion and Packaging: The Journal for the Selling Age* in 1955, continued as *Selling Age* from 1956 to 1962, and reverted back to *South African Sales Promotion and Packaging* in 1962. For an excellent discussion on post–World War II marketing to black consumers, see Manoim, "Black Press."

10. Bantu Press (Pty.) Ltd., *Black Gold!*, 3. Bantu Press remained under the management of Bertram Paver. On the coterminous development of the consumer consciousness and the black commercial press in South Africa, see Laden, "Who's Afraid of a Black Bourgeoisie?"

11. Bantu Press (Pty.) Ltd., *Approach to Bantu Press Advertising*, back cover.

12. Crankshaw, "Class, Race and Residence in Black Johannesburg," 363; South Africa, Bureau of Census and Statistics, *Population Census, 1960, Sample Tabulation, No. 3*, 29; South Africa, Bureau of Census and Statistics, *Population Census, 1960, Sample Tabulation, No. 5*, 54–55; Gaitskell, Kimble, Maconachie, and Unterhalter, "Class, Race and Gender."

13. Bantu Press (Pty.) Ltd., *Approach to Bantu Press Advertising*, back cover; Mayer with Mayer, *Townsmen or Tribesmen*, 245.

14. Ginsburg, *At Home with Apartheid*, 59.

15. "The African Market: Potentialities of the Middle-Class Families," *Selling Age*, June 1959, 15–19. Also see "The Tremendous Progress of the African Socially and Economically," *African Market*, January 1960, 9–10.

16. Eiselen, "Elasticity of the Bantu Consumer Market." A summary for wider audiences was published in "Second Success: The Advertising Convention Improved on Last Year's Achievements," *Selling Age*, October 1959, 15, 19–21.

17. Mqotsi and Mkele, "Separatist Church."

18. Mkele, "Advertising to the Bantu." Mkele's presentation was also summarized in "European Standards," *Selling Age*, October 1959, 20, and "Advertising to the African," *Selling Age*, November 1959, 22–23, 25. For other analyses of these presentations, see Burke, "'Fork Up and Smile'"; Burke, *Lifebuoy Men, Lux Women*, chap. 5; R. Ross, "Politics of African Household Budget Studies," esp. 222. For more on Mkele, see Bank, "Witchcraft and the Academy," esp. 232–33.

19. Mkele, "Advertising to the Bantu," 127.

20. Eiselen, "Elasticity of the Bantu Consumer Market," 105; Mkele, "Advertising to the Bantu," 129.

21. Mkele, "Advertising to the Bantu," 129.

22. "Growing Demand for Metamorphosa Face Cream and Soap: Introduction of New Wonder Cream," *South African Retail Chemist*, July 1955, 21; "'Jive' Cosmetic Range for the Non-European Trade," *South African Retail Chemist*, January 1958, 37; "'Top-flight Skin Cream of Unusual Quality': Big Campaign to Launch Artra Skin Tone Cream," *South African Retail Chemist*, July 1958, 29.

23. South African National Archives Repository, Pretoria (hereafter, SAB), RHN, 177, 2/101/6/4, various responses including Chemist, Paarl to Secretary, Board of Trade and Industries, September 22, 1960; W. B. Lamb, Queenstown to Secretary, Board of Trade and Industries, September 1, 1960; A. White, Cape Town to Secretary, Board of Trade and Industries, November 4, 1960.

24. Personal communication and email correspondence with Gill Hart, October 7, 2005, and June 2008.

25. Mkele, "Advertising to the Bantu," 118. Also see Tiley, "Problems of Retailing," 41.

26. "Who Spends the Money in African Homes in South Africa?" *African Market*, March 1960, 5. Also see Western Cape Provincial Archives and Records Service, Cape Town (hereafter, WCPA), 3/CT 4/1/5/1256: J. B. Cook and Son, Ndabeni Trading Stores, Maitland to Chairman, Native Affairs Committee, City Council, Cape Town, February 11, 1932, and December 28, 1932; J. B. Cook and Son, Ndabeni Trading Stores, Maitland to Town Clerk, Cape Town, May 16, 1934.

27. Tiley, "Problems of Retailing," 42.

28. Interview with Don Vaphi, Leticia Vaphi, and Primrose Coki by Lynn M. Thomas and Lulama Moss, Langa, July 20, 2008.

29. "Coloured People Who Pass as White," *Sun*, January 13, 1950, 2; Jessie Hertslet, "The Cape Coloured People," *Sun*, April 14, 1950, 3.

30. George Manuel and Gerard Van de Haer, "Playing White," *Drum*, August 1952, 6–7. For a powerful fictional meditation on "play-whites" as a disturbing "misnomer" of people's profoundly serious efforts to pass for white under apartheid, see Wicomb, *Playing in the Light*, 123.

31. Dr. Richard Van Der Ross, "Stop This Snobbery," *Drum*, September 1961, 40–41.

32. Whisson and Weil, *Domestic Servants*, 36.

33. Goldin, *Making Race*, chaps. 4, 5, quote from 88.

34. Posel, "Race as Common Sense," 107. Also see Posel, "What's in a Name?," 60; Stone, *When She Was White*, 94–96. Such cases are described as "borderline" in Horrell, *Survey of Race Relations in South Africa, 1958–9*, 40.

35. Watson, *Passing for White*; Unterhalter, "Changing Attitudes to 'Passing for White'"; Ntantala, *Life's Mosaic*, 129–30; Adhikari, *Not White Enough*, 10, 108.

36. Posel, "Race as Common Sense," 107.

37. On the need for analysts of skin lightening to take more seriously practitioners' desire to look beautiful, see Buckley, "Portrait Photography in a Postcolonial Age," esp. 296.

38. "You Ask, We Answer," *Bona*, January 1965, 29; Violet Ngwenya, "Your Beauty Column," *Bona*, July 1968, 53, and January 1971, 49.

39. "Aunt Thandi," *Zonk!*, January 1954, 47; Violet Ngwenya, "Your Beauty Column," *Bona*, August 1967, 67. Some "blood purifying pills" and laxative preparations were even marketed as cures for acne and other blemishes. See, for example, Puritone Blood Purifier ad, *Zonk!*, May 1954, 54; Metamorphosa skin lightener ad, *Zonk!*, March 1956, 2.

40. Kuper, *African Bourgeoisie*, 116, 94.

41. Musuva, *Peeping through the Reeds*, 2–3.

42. Van Der Ross, "Stop This Snobbery," 40–41.

43. C. Ross, "Skin Disease in the Venda," 303. On schoolgirls as vexing cultural figures, see L. Thomas, "Gendered Reproduction."

44. Ramphele, *Across Boundaries*, 40–41.

45. Interview with Joyce Molefe and Notumato Tyeku (pseudonyms) by Moss Lalama and Lynn M. Thomas, Langa, July 10, 2008.

46. Thwala, "Bleaching to Become Beautiful?," 66.

47. Mkele, "Advertising to the Bantu," 135. Makeba, in her autobiography, uses "bright" as a synonym for "light" when describing the skin tone both of Africans who pass for Coloured and of Coloureds who pass for white. *Makeba*, 63.

48. Interview with Vaphi, Vaphi, and Coki by Thomas and Moss.

49. R. Ross, "Politics of African Household Budget Studies," 222–24. On apartheid's "welfare paternalism," also see Bozzoli, *Theatres of Struggle*; Mark Hunter, *Love in the Time of* AIDS, esp. chap. 4; Mark Hunter, "Bond of Education." For fond reflections on the richness of black life under apartheid, see Dlamini, *Native Nostalgia*.

50. Moolman and Loubser, "Market Potentials," A11, A24–25, A37–38, A50–51, A63–64, A76–77, A89–90, A102–3, A115–16, A127–28, A141–42, A154–55, A167–68, A180–81, and A193–94.

51. J. Walter Thompson, *African Market Division 1973*, 18.

52. Steenekamp, *Changes in the Income and Expenditure Patterns*, 27; J. Walter Thompson, *African Market Division 1974*, 24.

53. Van der Reis, *Motivational Factors*, 16, 18, 20, 68–69, quote from 55.

54. Horrell, *Survey of Race Relations in South Africa, 1967*, 136–37; seventy-five cents from Artra ad, *Bona*, June 1965, 1; fifty cents from Tru-Glam ad, *Bona*, March 1964, 50; eighty-six cents from Ambi Extra Strength for Men (large tube) ad,

Drum (April 1965). Average domestic worker wages rose nationwide by 58 percent between 1958 and 1968. Whisson and Weil, *Domestic Servants*, 4, 49.

55. "How Trust Built Furniture Sales to Natives into a Thriving Business," *Selling Age*, October 1956, 31, 63; "The African Market: Potentialities of the Middle-Class Families," *Selling Age*, June 1959, 15–19.

56. "In Search of an Ideal Home for Two," *Drum* (East and Central African edition), May 1962, 75–88. Skin lighteners generally cost more than other face creams. For example, see Jive ad (four shillings and nine pence for Bleaching Complexion Cream and three shillings for Vanishing and Cold Creams), *South African Retail Chemist*, January 1958, 13; Super Rose ad (five shillings for Freckle and Complexion Cream and two shillings and six pence for Vanishing Cream), *Zonk!*, February 1960, 62.

57. On consumption as vital to notions of citizenship in the post–World War II United States, see L. Cohen, *Consumers' Republic*. On beauty contests as drawing young women into new circuits of consumer citizenship, see Cohen, Wilk, and Stoeltje, "Introduction."

58. Langschmidt, "Some Characteristics of the Urban Bantu Market," 27. In 1968, the top seven product groups were nonalcoholic beverages comprising 14.4 percent of advertising revenues amounting to R569,000; medicines, 13.6 percent (R537,000); household stores and services, 12.4 percent (R489,000); alcoholic beverages, 8.1 percent (R319,000); beauty preparations, 7.9 percent (R312,000); tobacco and associated products, 6.3 percent (R248,000); and toiletries and personal care, 5 percent (R199,000).

59. South African Institute of Race Relations Collection, Historical Papers Archive, the Library, University of Witwatersrand, Johannesburg (hereafter, WHP, SAIRR), J. D. Rheinallt Jones's letter to R. Muir, September 16, 1931; Editress, "Articles on Love," *Bantu World*, August 1, 1936, 9. Although one black magazine, *Umlindi we Nyange* (The watchman), was launched in the 1930s, its content resembled that of most contemporary newspapers, privileging text over photos and emphasizing political and educational issues rather than entertainment and human interest stories. On plans for the *Cape Standard* to launch a "Coloured illustrated monthly magazine" in 1940, see "A Pictorial Monthly," *Cape Standard*, February 6, 1940, 6.

60. Manoim, "Black Press," chaps. 4, 5. On the didactic and aspirational qualities of these magazines, see Laden, "Who's Afraid of a Black Bourgeoisie?"

61. Mkele, "Advertising to the Bantu," 127; Eiselen, "Elasticity of the Bantu Consumer Market," 104.

62. Manoim, "Black Press," 62–65; Coplan, "African Musician"; Jaji, *Africa in Stereo*, 111–46. Also on *Zonk!*, see Laden, "'Making the Paper Speak Well.'"

63. "Backstage," *Ebony*, November 1945, 2; "Backstage," *Ebony*, December 1946, 4, in M. Williams, "'Meet the Real Lena Horne.'"

64. Responding to previous progressive scholarship, especially Frazier's *Black Bourgeoisie*, that dismissed *Ebony* as escapist and elitist, Adam Green (*Selling the Race*) provides an insightful rereading of the magazine as contributing to the creation of a "black national community . . . [that] made new notions of collective interest—and politics—plausible" (132).

65. Lena Horne photo and message, *Zonk!*, August 1949, 4.

66. Jaji, *Africa in Stereo*, 120–21.

67. See, for example, a Dr. Fred Palmer's Skin Whitener ad, *Chicago Defender*, June 8, 1935, 24.

68. Manoim, "Black Press," 66–77. Brooks remained as the editor and only original shareholder and board member until 1962. The new board, apart from Brooks, comprised senior members of the Afrikaner establishment, including Mr. Jan Victor, Dr. Ben Havenga, and Dr. Albert Hertzog.

69. Manoim, "Black Press," 181–86, quote from *Zonk!* advertising rate card reproduced on 181.

70. Manoim, "Black Press," 218–20, quotes from 220.

71. Vinikas, *Soft Soap, Hard Sell,* 7; Manoim, "Black Press," 38–40.

72. "Readers' Letters to the Editor: All for Sixpence," *Zonk!*, February 1954, 7; "Readers' Letters to the Editor: Help to Make It Bigger," *Zonk!*, January 1954, 7. Also see "Readers' Letters to the Editor," *Zonk!*, October 1957, 5. After the currency change in 1961, the cover price changed to seven and a half cents.

73. Manoim, "Black Press," 72, including note 46.

74. Van der Reis, *Motivational Factors*, 27, 37.

75. Brooks launched *Hi Note* in 1954. Due to limited commercial success, he folded it into *Zonk!* three years later. Manoim, "Black Press," 72.

76. Karroo ad and "What Make a Beauty Queen?," *Zonk!*, December 1956, inside cover and 21.

77. Manoim, "Black Press," 80–82. While Robert Crisp, a white South African war and cricket hero actually initiated African Drum Publications, he resigned from the board in 1952, and by 1954, Bailey was the sole owner. Bailey estimated *Drum's* potential South African readership as "55 percent African, 20 percent Indian, 20 percent Coloured and 5 percent white." Manoim, "Black Press," 129.

78. "Danger of Losing the African Market," *Cape Argus*, July 8, 1946; J. Walter Thompson, *Markets to the North*; Alfred Beit, "Trade in Southern Africa: An Analysis of Pan-African Economy," *African Market*, June 1947, 4–6; "A Short Account of the Gold Coast: Where One Can Sell Anything, from a Safety Pin to a Bulldozer," *African Market*, February 1948, 39.

79. Fleming and Falola, "Africa's Media Empire"; Mutongi, "'Dear Dolly's' Advice"; Odhiambo, "Inventing Africa." From the 1950s through the 1970s, *Drum* variously established satellite offices and contacts also in Tanganyika, Rhodesia, Sierra Leone, Liberia, Ethiopia, Congo, Nyasaland, and Uganda. Fleming and Falola, "Africa's Media Empire," 140.

80. Soyinka, *Art, Dialogue and Outrage*, 115, cited in Fleming and Falola, "Africa's Media Empire," 156.

81. *Press, Advertising and Radio Review*, May 1956, cited in Manoim, "Black Press," 83. A government commission on the press reported *Drum's* 1955 sales within South Africa as 73,657. South Africa, *Report of the Commission of Inquiry into the Press*, 96.

82. Manoim, "Black Press," 75; Fleming and Falola, "Africa's Media Empire," 140, 163. Clowes, in "'A Modernised Man?," writes that by the late 1950s, *Drum* reported selling

250,000 copies per month and claimed to reach 3.5 million readers in South, Central, East, and West Africa.

83. Manoim, "Black Press," 83–87; R. Ross, *Things Change*. Soon after the West African edition was launched in 1953, *Drum* offered free advertising in that edition to those who advertised in the South African edition. *Drum* ad, *Advertising and Selling*, April 1953, 34.

84. Anthony Sampson, quoted in Manoim, "Black Press," 82.

85. Driver, "*Drum* Magazine (1951–9)."

86. Nixon, *Homelands, Harlem and Hollywood*, 20.

87. Ballantine, "Gender, Migrancy, and South African Popular Music," 392–94.

88. Meyerowitz, "Women, Cheesecake, and Borderline Material," 9, 19–20. For more on debates over African American cover girls and pin-ups, see M. Williams, "'Meet the Real Lena Horne,'" esp. 126–28; Buszek, *Pin-Up Grrrls*, 248–55, esp. 253; Green, *Selling the Race*, 151–55. On the ethics of engaging with power-laden images of women, see Hayes, "Introduction."

89. For example, see Frances Majeke, "Admiration," *Zonk!*, October 1957, 7.

90. Hamisi Osman, "More Madondo," *Zonk!*, June 1962, 7.

91. Manoim, "Black Press," 127.

92. Personal Papers of Irwin Manoim, Big Media, Johannesburg (hereafter, Manoim papers), "Drum Style Sheet," no date, 1. I am grateful to Manoim for providing access to these papers in August 2008.

93. Manoim, "Black Press," 169, 224, 226; Driver, "*Drum* Magazine (1951–9)"; Mutongi, "'Dear Dolly's' Advice"; Clowes, "'Modernised Man?'"; Clowes, "'Are You Going to be MISS (or MR) Africa?'"; Rauwerda, "Whitewashing *Drum* Magazine," esp. 394 and 400–402.

94. A full-page ad cost £45 per issue when *Drum* was first launched and increased to £85 by the mid-1950s. Drum ad, *Advertising and Selling*, August 1951; Drum ad, *Advertising and Selling*, April 1953, 34.

95. Bu-Tone ad, *Drum*, August 1958, 46–47. The thirteen countries or colonies were South Africa, Basutoland, Swaziland, Bechuanaland, Southern and Northern Rhodesia, Nyasaland, Portuguese East Africa, Kenya, Uganda, Tanganyika, Ghana, and Nigeria. The ad mentioned that Bu-Tone products would soon be available in three more: Belgian Congo, French Equatorial Africa, and Ethiopia.

96. Bunting, *Who Runs Our Newspapers?*, 2–3. *Bantu World*'s black editors and staff criticized apartheid's harshest policies but, within the spectrum of black opposition politics, they espoused a relatively conservative Africanist political position that was critical of the African National Congress's alliance with other groups, especially Communists. Manoim, "Black Press," 155–65.

97. "Album of Advertisements which appeared in African Newspapers, 1953–1957," Historical Papers Archive, the Library, University of Witwatersrand, Johannesburg, 2A427.

98. The *Post* became the first black publication to break the circulation figure of 100,000. Manoim, "Black Press," 88–94; South Africa, *Report of the Commission of Inquiry into the Press,* 307; various issues of *Golden City Post*, 1956–71.

99. By 1959, *Bona* had a circulation of 94,000 copies per month with at least one-third of those being purchased and distributed to schools by the government. Bunting, *Who Runs Our Newspapers?*, 5–6; Manoim, "Black Press," 73–74.

100. For announcements regarding the "Miss Bona" competition, see *Bona*, May 1956, 13, and June 1956, 16–17. Like the 1932 *Bantu World* competition, readers elected "Miss Bona" based on photos published in the magazine.

101. Ads for many other products, including Karroo's Snellerin tablets, were exclusively in isiXhosa, suggesting manufacturers' preference for keeping cosmetic ads, in particular, in English.

102. "Hazel Makes a Film," *Zonk!*, March 1956, 19.

103. "Joburg Girl Makes Hit in First African Cinemascope Film!," *Bona* (Xhosa edition), October 1958, 32. For an ad that featured Nkonyeni as Miss Bu-Tone, see Bu-Tone ad, *Bona*, July 1959, 59.

104. "The Native Trade: The Non-European Market Provides the Chemist with a Valuable but Difficult Business," *South African Retail Chemist*, February 1953, 31–32.

105. Hayman and Tomaselli, "Ideology and Technology"; Tomaselli and Tomaselli, "Between Policy and Practice in the SABC"; Hamm, "'Constant Companion of Man'"; Lekgoathi, "Bantustan Identity, Censorship and Subversion"; Coplan, "South Africa Radio in a Saucepan." On the limited availability of radio in the 1930s, see U.S. Department of Commerce, *Advertising in the Union of South Africa*, 31.

106. Langschmidt, "Some Characteristics of the Urban Bantu Market," 26.

107. Van der Reis, *Motivational Factors*, 27.

108. "Folk Song a Hit in South Africa: Parody by Oxford Graduate Spreads to Other Lands," *New York Times*, July 22, 1962, 56; Jeremy Taylor, *Ag Pleez Deddy!*, 7–10; email correspondence with Jeremy Taylor, July 16, 2017. For the song lyrics and an audio performance, see "Black-White Calypso," 3rd Ear Music's Hidden Years Archive Project, http://www.3rdearmusic.com/lyrics/calypso.html (accessed July 7, 2017); "Black and White Calypso (Live)," https://www.youtube.com/watch? v=NKXE5rbwoSM (accessed February 12, 2018). Thanks to Helen Lunn and Simphiwe Ngwane for directing me to this song.

109. Barnard, "Contesting Beauty," 349.

110. Alegi, "Rewriting Patriarchal Scripts," 31.

111. Ashforth, "Weighing Manhood in Soweto," 56–57. For more on South African beauty contests, see Johnson, "'Talking the Talk and Walking the Walk"; J. Kennedy, dir., *Cinderella of the Cape Flats*, video (Johannesburg, Film Resource Unit, 2004); Ribane, *Beauty*, 39–54, 91–102; Alegi, "Rewriting Patriarchal Scripts."

112. "She Sent Up Newspaper Circulations," *Selling Age—South African Sales Promotion and Packaging*, November 1956, 26.

113. "Congratulations Penny—We Expected It!" and "The Girl You Helped to Choose Is Miss World Now," *Sunday Times*, October 19, 1958, 12 and 13.

114. Ribane, *Beauty*, 5–6; Barnard, "Contesting Beauty," 351.

115. "S. Africa Has Biracial Entries for 'Miss World,'" *Jet*, November 19, 1970, 27. The strategy of sending two contestants lasted until 1978 when South Africa was finally banned from "Miss World."

116. Ribane, *Beauty*, 54–59.

117. Beauty-contest announcement, *Zonk!*, February 1951, 35.

118. Clowes, "'Are You Going to Be MISS (or MR) Africa?" For requests for "cover guys," see letter to the editor, *Zonk!*, June 1959, 5; Ralph Themba Mesatywa, "The Cover Page," *Bona*, November 1964, 8.

119. Morel, "It's Gotta Be Cash for a Cookie." For other accounts of the physical threats felt by female performers, see "Even the Animals Stared When Lovely Mary Came to Town," *Zonk!*, January 1951, 13–15; "What Makes a Beauty Queen?," *Zonk!*, December 1956, 21; "Wolf-Wolf," "Beauties Take Care!" in Readers' Letters to the Editor, *Zonk!*, October 1957, 7; Makeba with Hall, *Makeba*, 46–47; Ballantine, "Gender, Migrancy, and South African Popular Music."

120. Interview with Molefe and Tyeku. By contrast, a successful beauty contestant from a poor family in the mid-1970s, Cynthia Malgas, recalled that her grandmother, with whom she lived, was proud of her success and grateful that she could contribute earnings to their household. Interview with Cynthia Malgas by Lynn M. Thomas, Cape Town, July 21, 2008.

121. Bu-Tone ad, *Drum*, October 1957.

122. Mkele, "Advertising to the Bantu," 128. Woodson's *Drum: An Index* corroborates Mkele's claim that by the late 1950s, the focus on black Americans had declined: most of the references to features about African Americans (indexed under "U.S.; Blacks") date from between 1951 and 1955.

123. Miller, *Capitalism*, chap. 3 and 196.

124. Interview with Molefe and Tyeku.

125. Cohen, Wilk, and Stoeltje, "Introduction," 1–11.

126. Marchand, *Advertising the American Dream*, xix.

127. "What Makes a Beauty Queen?," *Zonk!*, December 1956, 21.

128. "Eat More Fish" ad, *Bona*, December 1957, ii. For the use of beauty queens in the promotion of other noncosmetic products, see Venoid's ad, *Zonk!*, December 1956; BB Tablets ad, *Bona*, August 1967, 8.

129. Wright Moshabesha, "Beauty Pays . . . ," *Drum*, June 1953, 12; M. S. P. Mkhonza, "Not-So-Beautiful," *Drum*, May 1953, 12. Also see P. M., Big Bend, "Go Ahead," *Bona*, December 1965, 43.

130. Letters to the editor, *Zonk!*, July 1951, 5–6; A Reader, "Can't All Be Perfect," *Zonk!*, May 1963, 5.

131. "Even the Animals Stared When Lovely Mary Came to Town," *Zonk!*, January 1951, 13–15.

132. See, for example, Elijah M. Nkomo, "Take Some Stopping," *Zonk!*, January 1963, 5; "Bikinis, Western Dress or the Traditional?," *Bona*, November 1964, 15, 17.

133. Herman Negro Molla, "Beauty Competition," *Zonk!*, April 1951, 4.

134. "Aunt Thandi Replies to Correspondents," *Zonk!*, April 1952, 33.

135. "Golden Girl 1954 Competition," *Zonk!*, May 1954, 17.

136. "African Beauty Queen," *Jet*, April 24, 1952, 16–20, quotes from 17 and 20.

137. John Banks, "Beauty Bouquet!," *Drum*, August 1953, 42.

138. Manoim papers, "Drum Style Sheet," no date, 3. Similarly, a marketing study found that the size and use of color in advertisements were the most crucial factors in determining their effectiveness. Van der Reis, *Motivational Factors*, 62.

139. Jaji, *Africa in Stereo*, 128; Samuelson, "Urban Palimpsest."

140. Interview with Abigail Khubeka by Lynn M. Thomas, Soweto, May 21, 2009. Khubeka explained this technique after being shown photos of very pale-faced beauty queens reproduced in Brandel-Syrier, photo inset in *"Coming Through,"* after 166. For skin lightener ads that featured Khubeka, see Karroo ad, *Zonk!*, December 1962, back cover; Hollywood Super 7 ad, *Bona*, May 1973, 4–5.

141. Dyer, *White*, 82–142. For more on pale skin as the presumed norm in photography, see Winston, "Whole Technology of Dyeing"; Roth, "Looking at Shirley." For an argument for how portrait photography of Josephine Baker defied Hollywood's "cult of light," identified by Dyer, and instead conveyed "sheen," "shine," and "plasticity," see Cheng, *Second Skin*, 111–21.

142. Berry, *Screen Style*, 94–141; Modern Girl Around the World Research Group, "Modern Girl Around the World: Cosmetics Advertising and the Politics of Race and Style," 48.

143. Darker-toned African American actors did appear in early films but in supporting rather than starring roles. As Jane Gaines explains, "Light-skinned blacks could not find work in white motion pictures" because on film they "looked white" whereas the makers of films produced specifically for all-black audiences (i.e., "race films") preferred light-skinned blacks in their leads. Gaines, *"Scare of Shame,"* 75. Also see Ralph Matthews, "Too Light for the Movies," *Afro-American*, March 25, 1933, 8.

144. Vilakazi, *Zulu Transformations*, 59–60. A beautician who was a contemporary of Vilakazi's expressed an alternative view. She stated that "special herbs" had, in fact, long been used to lighten complexions in Zululand. See Kuper, *African Bourgeoisie*, 113.

145. Krige, *Social System of the Zulus*, 375.

146. Van der Reis, *Some Aspects of the Acceptability of Particular Photographic Models*, esp. 25, 44, 50, 60, 62, 63, 65, 72, 76, and 78.

147. For a rich analysis of young black women's engagement with studio photography in this period, see Feyder, "Space of One's Own."

148. Winston, "Whole Technology of Dyeing," 107; Roth, "Looking at Shirley."

149. Mashinini, *Strikes Have Followed Me All My Life*, 9. For a fictional account of such photographic "touch-up," see Wicomb, *Playing in the Light*, 173. For photographers lightening clients' complexions during the development process in Peru and Jamaica, respectively, see Poole, *Vision, Race, and Modernity*, 207–8; K. Thompson, *Developing Blackness*, 11.

150. Wendl, "Entangled Traditions," 81. Wendl describes other retouching efforts aimed at producing a "cool" appearance, including erasing wrinkles and furrows, lighting the whites of the eyes, and inserting "fat wrabbles" on necks.

151. "There's a Story in the Cover" and "Which Cover Did You Like? Guineas for Best Letters," *Zonk!*, July 1951. Thanks to Julie Graber and Danny Hoffman for their help in interpreting this image, via email correspondence, May 10, 2016. For another

discussion of South African photographers using dodging to lighten complexions, see Feyder, "Portraits of Resilience," chap. 2.

152. For discussion of the "reddening" of color photos to make complexions look lighter after skin lightening cosmetics were banned in the Gambia in 1995, see Buckley, "Portrait Photography in a Postcolonial Age," 303–9.

153. Pond's ad, *Drum* (Central and East African Edition), June 1962, 70.

154. Johnny Seboni, "'Skirts and Scandals!' 'Use Cosmetics Sensibly!,'" *Africa*, April 1955, 59; Johnny Seboni, "'Skirts and Scandals!' Pretty Goes with Plain!" *Africa*, May 1955, 59. The second piece was partly a response to Milton Macauley, "Mrs. Dube's Diary," *Africa*, April 1955, 35.

155. Makeba with Hall, *Makeba*, 49.

156. Burke, *Lifebuoy Men, Lux Women*, 190. Also see Agnes Ndibi, dir., "Fantacoca" (23 mins.) on *Africa, Africas* (New York, Distributed by Women Make Movies, 2001).

157. Makeba with Hall, *Makeba*, 19–20; Feldstein, *How It Feels to Be Free*, 51–83.

158. Makeba with Hall, *Makeba*, 48; "Jamaica Parades the Ten Commands of Beauty," *Drum*, June 1956, 40–41.

159. Makeba with Hall, *Makeba*, 86, 135. Makeba appeared in a cigarette ad in *Zonk!*, 1960.

160. Feldstein, *How It Feels to Be Free*, esp. 75–76.

161. Makeba with Hall, *Makeba*, 36–37. Makeba explained that while Bongi's father was classified as African, his mother was classified as Coloured because her father was Italian and her mother was African.

162. Makeba with Hall, *Makeba*, 62. For another discussion of African contempt for Coloureds as "mixed breeds," see Adhikari, *Not White Enough, Not Black Enough*, 24–25.

163. Buckley, "Portrait Photography in a Postcolonial Age," 303–9. On Senegalese women's interest in cultivating elegant portraits, see Mustafa, "Portraits of Modernity"; Buggenhagen, "Snapshot of Happiness."

164. K. Thompson, *Shine*, 112–68.

5. ACTIVE INGREDIENTS AND GROWING CRITICISM

1. Oliver, Schwartz, and Warren, "Occupational Leukoderma: Preliminary Report"; Oliver, Schwartz, and Warren, "Occupational Leukoderma."

2. "News Note," *Chicago Defender*, December 18, 1948, 1; Walter White, "Has Science Conquered the Color Line?," *Look*, August 30, 1949, 94–95.

3. Lockhart and Loewenthal, "Occupational Leukoderma."

4. Oliver et al., "Occupational Leukoderma," esp. 1010–13; Schwartz, "Occupational Pigmentary Changes in the Skin."

5. Oliver et al., "Occupational Leukoderma," 1010.

6. Hutt, "History of Government Regulation," 6, 20.

7. Sec. 201 of the "Drug and Cosmetic Provisions of the Federal Food, Drug, and Cosmetic Act"; Clark, "Federal Food Drug, and Cosmetic Act"; Hutt, "Legal Distinction in the United States between a Cosmetic and a Drug." The Wheeler-Lea Act of

1938 granted the Federal Trade Commission the authority to regulate truthfulness in advertising. See Werble, "Federal Trade Commission."

8. Lamb, *American Chamber of Horrors*; Copeland, "Protection for the Public"; G. Kay, *Dying to Be Beautiful*, 6.

9. See, for example, "The Toxicology of Toilet Preparations," *Medical Record*, December 4, 1915, 964; Antoinette Donnelly, "The Case against Cosmetics," *Washington Post*, July 27, 1924, 10; Dr. Irving S. Cutter, "Face Bleachers Often Injurious as Beauty Aid," *Washington Post*, April 30, 1936, 13.

10. "Removing Freckle," *Drug and Cosmetic Industry* 31, no. 5 (1932): 440; "The Compounders' Corner," *Drug and Cosmetic Industry* 37, no. 5 (1935): 673; "Readers' Questions: Skin Bleaches," *Drug and Cosmetic Industry* 39 (1937): 382.

11. "Stricter Control of Advertising?," *South African Business Efficiency*, November 1934, 330–31.

12. "Application of Certain Provisions to Soap, Tobacco and Certain Other Articles" to "Food, Drugs and Disinfectants Act No. 13 of 1929," *South African Government Gazette*, March 28, 1930, 759. The 1929 Act replaced previous provincial legislation on food and drugs. On the complex history of South African efforts to regulate medicine, see Parle, "'A Drug, Like a Scalpel.'"

13. For example, see South African National Archive Repository, Pretoria (hereafter, SAB): GES, 1562, 52/26H; GES, 1727, 40/28; GES, 1732, 55/28A; LTD, 249, R2368; LTD 250, R2368.

14. SAB, GES, 1732, 55/28B, "Drugs and Disinfectants Act No. 13 of 1929," Chief Regional Health Office, Department of Health, Cape Town to Secretary for Health, Pretoria, December 3, 1959.

15. "Notice to Manufacturers of Mercury Bleach Creams," reproduced in Ozier, "Skin Lighteners and Bleach Creams," 215–16. The notice was issued in May 1939 but only came into effect in January 1940 in order to provide manufacturers with time to comply.

16. "A Legal Issue," *Drug and Cosmetic Industry* 46, no. 5 (1940): 537–51, 563. Not all skin lightener manufacturers agreed with the FDA's assessment of mercury's potential dangers. Ozier, "Skin Lighteners and Bleach Creams," 216.

17. "May Require Badges," *New York Times*, April 7, 1939, 39; "Mercolized Wax Stopped," *Drug and Cosmetic Industry*, September 1939, 325; "Freckle Ointment Cited," *Drug and Cosmetic Industry* 46, no. 1 (1940): 65; National Archives and Records Administration, College Park, Maryland (hereafter, NARA), FDA, RG 88, General Subject Files, 1940, 581.1–.23: W. G. Campbell, Chief, FDA to Chief, Central District, FDA, November 13, 1940; G. P. Larrick, Acting Commission, FDA to Chief, Central District, FDA, November 13, 1940.

18. NARA, FDA, RG 88, General Subject Files, 1945, 581.1–.10, W. A. Queen, Chief, Division of State Cooperation to Mr. J. W. Forbes, Chief, Food and Drug Section, State Department of Health, New Orleans, Louisiana, January 17, 1945; D. F. Nealon, "Analysis of Consumer Complaints," *Drug and Cosmetic Industry* 56, no. 1 (1945): 34–35, 116–17.

19. D. F. Nealon, "Ammoniated Mercury and the Skin," *Drug and Cosmetic Industry* 52, no. 2 (1943): 159–62; Nealon, "Analysis of Consumer Complaints"; Nealon, *Report of Studies on Nadinola Bleaching Cream*.

20. NARA, FDA, RG 88, General Subject Files, 1950, 581.1–.10: Mrs. Valara E. Gregory, Little Rock, AR, to Federal Pure Food Law, March 16, 1940; G. P. Larrick, Acting Chief, FDA to Mrs. Gregory, April 1, 1940.

21. NARA, FDA, RG 88, General Subject Files, 1945, 581.1–.10: L. Matt, Wyoming, OH, to Dept. of Agriculture, Washington, DC, March 4, 1941.

22. NARA, FDA, RG 88, General Subject Files, 1950, 581.1–.10: David J. Syvestson, West Salem, WI, to FDA, Washington, DC, April 1, 1950.

23. "Discovers Chemical That Will Turn Skin of Negroes White," *Atlanta Daily World*, February 6, 1941, 1.

24. "New Chemical Turns Skin White but Negroes Don't Want to Change Color," *Chicago Defender*, October 16, 1943, 1.

25. W. White, "Has Science Conquered the Color Line?"; W. White, *Man Called White*.

26. "Leaders Ridicule White's Solution of Race Problem through Bleach," *Afro-American*, August 27, 1949, 12; Lilian Scott, "Walter White's Skin Bleach Ideas Fail to Get Favorable Reception," *Chicago Defender*, August 27, 1949, 27; S. W. Garlington, "Walter White, 'Loses Face' with Wanna-Be-White Story," *New York Amsterdam News*, August 27, 1949, 2.

27. Anderson, *Eyes Off the Prize*, 158–59.

28. Peck and Sobotka, "Effect of Monobenzyl Hydroquinone"; Lorincz, "Studies on the Inhibition of Melanin Formation"; Denton, Lerner, and Fitzpatrick, "Inhibition of Melanin Formation by Chemical Agents"; Forman, "Note on the Depigmentation Properties."

29. Pollack, "Hyperpigmentation Improved"; E. Kelly, "Pigmented Skin Lesions"; Ito, "Monobenzylether-Hydroquinone Leucomelanderma"; Canizares, Jaramillo, and Vegas, "Leukomelanoderma Subsequent"; Dorsey, "Dermatitic and Pigmentary Reactions"; Becker and Spencer, "Evaluation of Monobenzone"; "Skin Research: Skin Bleaching," *Drug and Cosmetic Industry* 90 (June 1962): 761. In 1957, the Japanese government banned MBH from cosmetic products. *Tokyo Cosmetic Industry Association Bulletin* no. 10 (1957): 14.

30. Spencer, "Hydroquinone Bleaching"; Arndt and Fitzpatrick, "Topical Use of Hydroquinone." The commercial brands tested in these studies included Nadinola and Artra.

31. NARA, FDA, RG 88, General Subject Files, 1960, 581.1: Harold F. O'Keefe, Assistant to the Director, Division of Administrative Review, Bureau of Enforcement, FDA to Donald Edwards Pharmaceutical Company, January 27, 1960.

32. NARA, FDA, RG 88, General Subject Files, 1960, 581.1: G. Robert Clark, Direction, Division of Cosmetics, FDA to Kolar Laboratories, Inc., September 9, 1960; NARA, FDA, RG 88, General Subject Files, 1953, 520. Q05: Dr. J. H. Draize to Mr. Hoeting, Division of Pharmacology, August 18, 1961.

33. NARA, FDA, RG 88, General Subject Files, 1964–65, 581.1: R. E. Hamilton, FDA to Detroit District, Division of Case Supervision, March 10, 1965; Juanita P. Horton, Advisory Opinions Branch, Division of Industry Advice, Bureau of Education and Voluntary Compliance, FDA to Miss Enid Molyneaux, New York, September 17, 1965.

34. Spencer, "Hydroquinone Bleaching"; Arndt and Fitzpatrick, "Topical Use of Hydroquinone"; Spencer, "Topical Use of Hydroquinone."

35. U.S. FDA, Proposed Rules, "Skin Bleaching Drug Products, Establishment of a Monograph," *Federal Register* (November 3, 1978); U.S. FDA, Proposed Rules, "Skin Bleaching Drug Products for Over-the-Counter Human Use, Tentative Final Monograph," *Federal Register* (September 3, 1982); Hutt, "Legal Distinction in the United States between a Cosmetic and a Drug," 433–35.

36. Dogliotti, Caro, Hartdegen, and Whiting, "Leucomelanoderma in Blacks," esp. 1556; U.S. FDA, "Skin Bleaching Drug Products," 43, no. 214 *Federal Register* (November 3, 1978): 51533; U.S. FDA, "Skin Bleaching Drug Products," 47, no. 172 *Federal Register* (September 3, 1982): 39110.

37. "'Top-flight Skin Cream of Unusual Quality': Big Campaign to Launch Artra Skin Tone Cream," *South African Retail Chemist*, July 1958, 29.

38. "Artra Skin Tone Cream" ad, *Drum* (East African edition), October 1959, 72.

39. On Artra and other ads from the 1950s and 1960s, see S. Walker, *Style and Status*, 109–10, 156–59.

40. Manoim, "Black Press," 26–32.

41. For more on American science as a selling point in post–World War II cosmetic ads, see Modern Girl Around the World Research Group, "Modern Girl Around the World: A Research Agenda and Preliminary Findings," 280.

42. "Hydroquinone Is Answer for Lovelier Complexion," *Chicago Defender*, May 24, 1958, 15.

43. "Negroes Breaking into TV Advertising This Fall," *New York Amsterdam News*, September 15, 1962, 19; "Diahann Carroll Receives Artra Top Award," *Atlanta Daily World*, February 19, 1964, 8; "In Key Roles," *New York Amsterdam News*, April 23, 1966, C1; "Artra Scholarship Award," *Atlanta Daily World*, February 19, 1970, 2.

44. Beavon, *Johannesburg*, chap. 2.

45. SAB, GES, 1781, 21/30D: F. N. Lock for Secretaries, South African Pharmaceutical Manufacturers' Association to Minister of Health, Pretoria, "Representation on Pharmacy Board," May 22, 1956; SAB, HEN, 620, 86/2/1: A. Immelman, Secretary for Commerce and Industries to Charge d'Affaires, Legation of the Union of South Africa, Rio de Janeiro, Brazil, "Establishment of Industry," June 30, 1956; B. Gaigher, Secretary for Commerce and Industries to Secretary for Health, Pretoria, "Production of Morphine, Etc. in South Africa," November 11, 1961.

46. Interviews with Solomon Krok by Lynn M. Thomas, Johannesburg, August 8 and 12, 2008.

47. Thwala, "Bleaching to Become Beautiful?," chap. 3. A study of beauty-preparation ads in the mid-1960s also found that 97 percent claimed that their products made consumers more attractive to the opposite sex whereas 60 percent conveyed the message of "identification with 'Western way of life'" and 24 percent, "health of self and family." Van der Reis, *Motivational Factors in Bantu Buying Behaviour*, 41.

48. "Avoiding Pitfalls in the Bantu Advertising Field," *Press, Advertising and Radio Review*, January 1965, 2.

49. Interviews with S. Krok, August 8 and 12, 2008.

50. Super Rose ad, *Bona*, May 1959, 73.

51. Interview with S. Krok, August 8, 2008.

52. Interviews with S. Krok, August 8 and 12, 2008; "Business Achievers of the Month," *Herald Times*, July 31, 1987, 6; SAB, RHN, 906, 85/9/3: Messrs. Twins Products Natal, Durban to I. L. Blignaut, Director of Imports and Exports, "Establishment of Industrial Expansion," August 25, 1966. This application for import licenses for raw materials included a request to import hydroquinone.

53. A regular-size bottle of Super Rose lotion sold for thirty cents while a double-size bottle sold for fifty cents and a tube of Super Rose cream sold for seventy-five cents. Super Rose ads, *Bona*, May 1963, 30, and July 1963, 30. Other skin lightener creams sold for similar prices.

54. Interview with S. Krok, August 8, 2008.

55. Interview with S. Krok, August 12, 2008.

56. Findlay and De Beer, "Chronic Hydroquinone Poisoning"; Levin and Maibach, "Exogenous Ochronosis."

57. Mapumulo and Legwate, "Problems of Retailing to the Bantu Market."

58. Guthrie, "Successes and Failures in Marketing," 68.

59. Interview with Lorato Mosweu (pseudonym) by Lynn M. Thomas and T. Mpho, Thembisa, May 18, 2009.

60. Crankshaw, "Class, Race and Residence," esp. 361–62.

61. Thwala, "Bleaching to Become More Beautiful?," 68, 105, and chaps. 3–5 more generally.

62. Interviews with S. Krok, August 8 and 12, 2008.

63. "Founding Affidavit of Abraham Krok," in vol. 1, *Hollywood Curl* (PTY) *Limited (First Appellant)*, 16.2.

64. Letter from Ian Snelling, Media Manager, Becker Dissel Schreuder Trull Vinjevold (Pty.) Ltd. to Mr. Reid, Twins Products, Isando and attached radio transcripts in vol. 1, *Hollywood Curl* (PTY) *Limited (First Appellant)*, AK6.

65. Mkele, "Advertising to the Bantu," 135.

66. Interviews with Francis Roux by Lynn M. Thomas and Sarah Espi-Sanchis, Middelburg, July 14, 2008; Gerald Schap by Lynn M. Thomas and Sarah Espi-Sanchis, Cape Town, July 22, 2008; Phillip Rolfe by Lynn M. Thomas and Sarah Espi-Sanchis, July 29, 2008.

67. Interview with S. Krok, August 8, 2008.

68. Kuper, *African Bourgeoisie*, 112–13.

69. *Hollywood Curl* (PTY) *Limited and The International Hollywood Curl Hairdressers Suppliers and Training Centre v. Twins Products* (PTY) *Limited*, vol. 3, BB1, pp. 388–416.

70. Marks, *Divided Sisterhood*, 10.

71. Interview with Eunice Maseko by Lynn M. Thomas, August 4, 2008, Johannesburg.

72. Kuper, *African Bourgeoisie*, 228.

73. Super Rose ad, *Zonk!*, May 1963, 58.

74. Kool Look ad, *Bona*, October 1973, 7.

75. "Krok Brothers: Mixing a New Brew," *Financial Mail*, April 3, 1987, 31–32.

76. D. Livingstone, *Missionary Travels and Researches in South Africa*, 203–5.

77. Earle, "Can the Nubian Change His Skin," 8; Thwala, "Bleaching to Become Beautiful?," 78.

78. B. Weiss, "Dressing at Death," 147–49.

79. Glassman, *War of Words, War of Stones*, 87–88, 133–34, esp. notes 39 and 40 on 326 and note 101 on 340; K. Lewis et al., "Historical and Cultural Influences of Skin Bleaching in Tanzania." For the complex status of skin color within racial thought elsewhere in Muslim Africa, see B. Hall, *History of Race in Muslim West Africa*, esp. 30–36.

80. Jive ad, *Drum*, July 1958, 3.

81. Interview with S. Krok, August 8, 2012.

82. Stanley Meisler, "Africa Rejects Missionaries: Indelible Mark Left on People Who Now Seek Own Salvation," *Washington Post*, June 3, 1967.

83. Ivaska, *Cultured States*, 60–61, 101, 200–201; Callaci, *Street Archives and City Life*, chap. 3.

84. Barr, Woodger, Path, and Rees, "Levels of Mercury in Urine."

85. Interviews with Agnes Nyamu by Lynn M. Thomas and Patricia Nyamu, Langata, Nairobi, May 28 and June 1, 2009.

86. Interview with Mary Gwantai by Lynn M. Thomas, Meru School, Meru, June 8, 2009. Also interview with Bibi by Patricia Nyamu, Stella Bosire, and Lynn M. Thomas, Antonio's Café, Nairobi, June 17, 2009; L. Thomas, *Politics of the Womb*, 114.

87. Craig, *Ain't I a Beauty Queen?*, 78–80.

88. Craig, *Ain't I a Beauty Queen?*, 23–44, quote from 42.

89. Davis, "Afro Images"; Craig, *Ain't I a Beauty Queen?*, 78–100; S. Walker, *Style and Status*, chap. 6; Feldstein, *How It Feels to Be Free*, 76–78; Ford, *Liberated Threads*, chaps. 1–3.

90. Lerone Bennett Jr., "Message from Mboya: African Leader Stresses the Need for Self-Respect," *Ebony*, August 1959, 34–36, 38, 40, 43. Reported on in "'We Want More Negro Action,' Says Mboya," *Tri-State Defender* (Memphis, TN), August 1, 1959, 16. Also see Craig, *Ain't I a Beauty Queen?*, 81.

91. Craig, *Ain't I a Beauty Queen?*, 90.

92. "Malcolm X Speech in Los Angeles (May 5, 1962)"; Malcolm X, "After the Bombing," 168–69.

93. Craig, *Ain't I a Beauty Queen?*, 93, 94.

94. J. Brown, "Say It Loud"; Morrison, *Bluest Eye*. On Morrison's and other black women writers' playful and inventive descriptions of skin color as ways to individualize their characters and to convey a sensual aesthetics, see Benthien, *Skin*. On readers' inability to also recognize "loving blackness" in Morrison's novel, see hooks, *Black Looks*, 9–20.

95. By the late 1950s, the *Afro-American*, a newspaper published in Baltimore, that had previously carried numerous such ads in each issue, only occasionally included

them. I thank Kristy Leissle for surveying skin lightener ads at five-year intervals of the *Afro-American* from 1920 through 1965.

96. Wipper, "African Women, Fashion, and Scapegoating"; Ivaska, *Cultured States*, 60–85. Also see Burgess, "Cinema, Bell Bottoms, and Miniskirts"; Callaci, *Street Archives and City Life*, chap. 1. The international press also took note of Operation Vijana. Callaci, in chapter 4 of *Street Archives and City Life*, explains that the Tanzanian government banned *Drum* in 1972, as part of its seizure of all newspapers and media, but that it remained popular and continued to circulate clandestinely.

97. L. Thomas, "Gendered Reproduction."

98. Kenya, *National Assembly Debates* (November 28, 1968): 3660–61.

99. Kenya, *National Assembly Debates* (November 28, 1968): 3660–61. Also see Kenya, *National Assembly Debates* (April 4, 1968): 1589–90 for another attempt to ban some Western fashions and cosmetics.

100. Mazrui, "Discourse on Mixed Reactions to—Miniskirts"; Mamdani, *Imperialism and Fascism in Uganda*, 54; Kambili, "Ethics of African Tradition"; Decker, *In Idi Amin's Shadow*, 60–74.

101. L. Thomas, *Politics of the Womb*, esp. 161.

102. Kenya, *National Assembly Debates* (March 30, 1971): 1376–79.

103. Guthrie, "Successes and Failures in Bantu Marketing," 63–74; Burke, *Lifebuoy Men, Lux Women*, 180, 263n38; interview with Don Vaphi, Leticia Vaphi, and Primrose Coki by Lynn M. Thomas and Lulama Moss, Langa, July 20, 2008.

104. In recent years, Sara Lee has been owned by the U.S. multinational companies Sara Lee and Johnson & Johnson; it is unclear who owned it in 1963.

105. Deppe, "Comparative Study of Motives Observed," 25–33, 73.

106. Findlay and De Beer, "Chronic Hydroquinone Poisoning."

107. Interview with Fatima Dike by Moss Lulama and Lynn M. Thomas, Cape Town, July 7, 2009.

108. Ford, *Liberated Threads*, 173, 179.

109. A few women at the time recognized skin lighteners as both a political and health problem. "Mali Women Hit Skin Lighteners," *Washington Post*, January 2, 1975, B2; Wipper, "African Women," 349.

110. On the persistent invisibility of uranium's toxicity to African mineworkers, see Hecht, *Being Nuclear*, chaps. 6, 8.

111. Barr et al., "Nephrotic Syndrome in Adult Africans in Nairobi"; interview with Dr. Alfred Kungu by Lynn M. Thomas, Nairobi Hospital, June 16, 2004. For a piece in the African American press that reported on this study and noted that the prior debate over skin lighteners in Kenya was "cultural" and "not medical," see "Skin Lighteners Scored in Kenya," *Bay State Banner* (Massachusetts), July 13, 1972, 6.

112. Saffron statement and ad, *Daily Nation*, April 20, 1972.

113. Ambi ad, *Daily Nation*, April 28, 1972.

114. Barr et al., "Levels of Mercury in Urine." In South Africa too, doctors investigating the potentially harmful effects of skin lighteners would soon use nurses as their research subjects. Bentley-Phillips and Bayles, "Cutaneous Reactions." In the United

States as well, nurses have often been the subject of health surveys. See http://www
.nurseshealthstudy.org/about-nhs/history (accessed January 24, 2018).

115. Interviews with Dr. Malaki Owili by Lynn M. Thomas, Aga Khan Hospital,
June 16, 2004; Kungu, June 16, 2004. Kungu was a pathologist and coauthor on the
first Kenyatta study while Owili was a medical resident at the time the research was
done and went on to become a dermatologist.

116. Ngoima wa Mwaura, "Mercury Poisoning Threat Posed by Some Cosmetics,"
Weekly Review, October 13, 1975, 16–17. For a case of mercury poisoning in Uganda
similarly attributed to "Butone Extra-Strong Night Cream," containing 10–15 percent
ammoniated mercury, see Kibukamusoke, Davies, and Hutt, "Medical Memoranda."
For an insightful ethnography of toxicologists working in postcolonial Senegal that
mentions mercurial lighteners as among their concerns, see Tousignant, *Edges of
Exposure*, esp. 10.

117. George, *Minamata*; B. Walker, *Toxic Archipelago*; NARA, FDA, RG 88, General Subject Files, 1969, 520 Mercury: Glenn W. Kilpatrick, Acting Director, Office of
Legislative and Governmental Services, FDA to Mr. Ichinose, First Secretary, Scientific,
Washington DC, November 21, 1969. The Japanese government banned mercurial
cosmetics in 1974, one year after the United States. See the Japanese Ministry of Environment web page at http://www.env.go.jp/chemi/tmms/tobira/riyo.html (accessed
January 24, 2018). Thanks to Kazumi Hasegawa (email correspondence, November 14,
2017) and Azusa Tanaka (email correspondence, December 18, 2017) for locating and
translating this information for me.

118. NARA, FDA, RG 88, General Subject Files, 1970: Sallie M. Buckley, Springfield
Garden, NY, to FDA, November 22, 1970; Dr. Mervyn F. Silverman, Director, Office of
Consumer Affairs, FDA to Miss Buckley, December 23, 1970. Also see "Mercury Found
in Cosmetics," *Sun*, September 16, 1970, A7.

119. NARA, FDA, RG 88, General Subject Files, 1970: Dr. Mervyn F. Silverman,
Office of Consumer Affairs, FDA to Mr. Christian S. White, Associate, Public Interest Research Group, Washington, DC, October 26, 1970; M. J. Ryan, Director, Office
of Legislative Services, FDA to Hon. Harrison A. Williams Jr., Committee on Labor
and Public Welfare, U.S. Senate, Washington, DC, December 23, 1970; Patsy T. Mink,
presentation on "Mercury in Cosmetics," 92nd U.S. Cong., *Congressional Record* 117
(July 1, 1971): 23311–18.

120. Nash, "From Safety to Risk," esp. 4.

121. G. Kay, *Dying to Be Beautiful*, 124; Bruch and Larson, "Early Historical Perspective on the FDA's Regulation of OTC Drugs"; Palm and Toombs, "Letter to the Editor,"
122.

122. FDA, Regulation, "700.13 Use of Mercury Compounds in Cosmetics Including Use as Skin-Bleaching Agent in Cosmetic Preparations Also Regarded as Drugs."
This regulation also banned the use of mercurial preservatives in cosmetics, except in
certain eye-area cosmetics. Hutt, "History of Government Regulation," 22, 26. For press
coverage of the impending ban, see Nancy L. Ross, "Ban on Mercury," *Washington
Post*, July 1, 1972, D2.

123. FDA, Proposed Rule Making, "Use of Mercury in Cosmetics," 12967–68; FDA, Rules and Regulations, "Use of Mercury in Cosmetics Including Use as Skin-Bleaching Agent in Cosmetic Preparations Also Regarded as Drugs," 853–54.

124. Marzulli and Brown, "Potential Systemic Hazards of Topically Applied Mercurials." For press coverage of this study, see Edwin Kiester Jr., "Ugly Truths about Today's Beauty Aids," *Today's Health,* submitted by Hon. Member Patsy Mink for inclusion in presentation on "Mercury in Cosmetics," 92nd U.S. Cong., *Congressional Record* 117 (July 1, 1971): 23316–17.

125. FDA, Proposed Rule Making, "Use of Mercury in Cosmetics," 12967; FDA, Rules and Regulations, "Use of Mercury in Cosmetics," 854.

126. Bentley-Phillips and Bayles, "Butylated Hydroxytoluene as a Skin Lightener"; Dogliotti et al., "Leucomelanoderma in Blacks"; Bentley-Phillips and Bayles, "Cutaneous Reactions."

127. No. R. 740, "Regulation of Cosmetics" under the Foodstuffs, Cosmetics and Disinfectants Act, 1972 (Act 54 of 1972), Department of Health, No. 4668 *South African Government Gazette* (April 18, 1975): 3. The proposed regulation was posted in the gazette five months earlier, and interested persons were invited to send comments to the Secretary of Health in Pretoria. No. R. 2185, "Regulation of Cosmetics" under the Foodstuffs, Cosmetics and Disinfectants Act, 1972 (Act 54 of 1972), Department of Health, No. 4512 *South African Government Gazette* (November 22, 1974): 13.

128. Republic of South Africa, "Foodstuffs, Cosmetics and Disinfectants Act No. 54 of 1972," *Government Gazette* 84, no. 3530 (June 2, 1972): 2–31.

129. On the United Kingdom's act, see *The Cosmetic Products Regulations 1978,* statutory instrument no. 1354; Robin Young, "New Regulations to Outlaw Cosmetics Harmful to Health," *Times* (London), August 4, 1978; Friedel, "Regulation of Cosmetics in the Common Market."

130. Saffer, Tayob, and Bill, "Correspondence," 1499. Saffer and his neurology staff colleagues at Baragwanath Hospital in Soweto reported on nine instances of patients presenting with "bizarre movement disorders" caused by chronic mercury intoxication from skin lighteners.

131. Dogliotti et al., "Leucomelanoderma in Blacks." Some of these patients were treated with topical corticosteroids. Also see Bentley-Phillips and Bayles, "Cutaneous Reactions," 1391.

132. Interview with S. Krok, August 8, 2008.

133. NARA, FDA, RG 88, General Subject Files, 1974, 581.1: Dr. Leonard J. Trilling, Assistant Director for Medical Review, Division of Cosmetics Technology, Dept. of Health, Education, and Welfare to H. Wulffhart Wins Products (PTY) Limited, Johannesburg, South Africa, March 6, 1974.

134. Carpenter, *Reputation and Power,* 20–22.

135. Hutt, "History of Government Regulation."

136. U.S. FDA, "Skin Bleaching Drug Products," Docket FDA-1979-N-0023 at https://www.regulations.gov/docket? D=FDA-1978-N-0023: Richard N. Hurd, Elder Pharmaceuticals to Office of the Hearing Clerk, FDA, "Establishment of a Monograph; Notice

of Proposed Rulemaking, Skin Bleaching Drug Products for Over-the-Counter Human Use," January 24, 1979.

137. "Skin Scrum: Manufacturers Hotly Deny Minister's Claim," *Weekly Review*, October 31, 1980; "No Final Word: Mercury Issue Continues," *Weekly Review*, November 7, 1980, 43. Officials in India also noticed the FDA's ban on mercury. NARA, FDA, RG 88, General Subject Files, 1973, 580.2: Dr. S. S. Nishat, Director, Hygienic Research Institute, Bombay, India to Secretary, Association of Official Analytical Chemists, Washington, DC, July 21, 1973.

138. Janet Woodcock, "Modernizing the Other Side of the Counter: FDA Oversight of Nonprescription Drugs," *Health Affairs Blog*, June 9, 2016, http://www.healthaffairs .org/do/10.1377/hblog20160609.055243/full/ (accessed November 3, 2017); Califf, McCall, and Mark, "Cosmetics, Regulations, and the Public Health."

139. FDA, "Notice of Proposed Rulemaking," *Federal Register* (November 3, 1978): 51546–55. Around the same time, anti-apartheid activists in the United States protested plans by one of the last remaining small black-owned cosmetic companies to sell skin lighteners and hair straighteners in South Africa. Linn Washington, "Mississippi Cosmetics Firm Makes Deal to Sell Skin Lightener Products to S. African Blacks," *Philadelphia Tribune*, October 19, 1976, 5.

140. Murphy, *Sick Building Syndrome*, chap. 5.

141. Nordlund, "Hydroquinone," esp. 284.

142. Nate Haseltine, "D.C. Dermatologist Tells Doctors He Has Turned 16 Negroes 'White,'" *Washington Post*, December 2, 1960, A3; Stolar, "Induced Alterations of Vitiliginous Skin."

143. Lasker, "Whiter Shade of Black," 63. For the sensationalist response, in the early twentieth century, to the possibility of X-ray experiments turning patients from black to white, see De la Pena, "'Bleaching the Ethiopian.'"

144. Malcolm Poindexter, "Can Drugs Change Skin from Black To White?" *Philadelphia Tribune*, December 17, 1960, 11. Also see "Medical Mixologist," *Chicago Defender*, December 17, 1960, 6.

145. "Suggestion for Stolar," *Afro-American*, December 17, 1960, 4.

146. Obama, *Dreams from My Father*, 29–30, 51–52, 193.

147. Lasker, "Whiter Shade of Black." The nurse's identity was revealed in Evelyn Irons, "Blacks with White Skin," *Sun*, January 31, 1971, D1.

148. Irons, "Blacks with White Skin"; "Black Is Beautiful, So Fewer Blacks Want to 'Bleach' Skin Nowadays," *Jet*, June 7, 1973: 44–45; "'I Wish I Were Black—Again,'" *Ebony*, December 1968, 119–20, 122, 124; Ron Harris, "The Man Who Turned White," *Ebony*, November 1978, 165–66, 168, 170; A. Wright, *Color Me White*.

149. Hobbs, *Chosen Exile*, 263.

150. U.S. FDA, "Skin Bleaching Drug Products," Docket FDA-1979-N-0023 at https:// www.regulations.gov/docket? D=FDA-1978-N-0023: Richard Serbin, Regulatory Counsel, Norcliff Thayer Inc., Tuckahoe, NY, to FDA, "RE: DOCKET NO. 78N-0065," January 31, 1979; Kleinfeld, Kaplan and Becker, Counsel for Nicholas Products, Ltd., Washington, DC, to FDA, "RE: Docket No. 78N-0065, Skin-Bleaching Drug Products," February 1, 1979; Andrew C. Inglis, Marketing Director, Keystone Laboratories, Inc.,

Memphis, TN, to FDA, "RE: Skin-Bleaching Drug Products," October 26, 1982; Mario de la Guardia, President, Carson Products Company, Savannah, GA, to FDA, "RE: Skin-Bleaching Drug Products," November 1, 1982; Kenneth R. Johannes, Director Regulatory Affairs, Plough Inc., Memphis, TN, to FDA, "Re: Docket No. 78N-0065," November 2, 1982.

6. BLACK CONSCIOUSNESS AND BIOMEDICAL OPPOSITION

1. Tiley, "Problems of Retailing to the Bantu Market," 37–38.
2. Gerhart, *Black Power in South Africa*, 267–69.
3. "Queen Mother Gives Advice to the Women of Today," *Bona*, January 1971, 17, 19.
4. Whisson and Weil, *Domestic Servants*, 35–36.
5. Stuart Hall, "What Is This 'Black' in Black Popular Culture?"
6. Gerhart, *Black Power in South Africa*, 277–81; Fredrickson, *Black Liberation*, 302; Magaziner, *Law and the Prophets*, chap. 3.
7. Magaziner, *Law and the Prophets*, 205–6n17. Also see "Why Not Call Us 'South Africans?' Ask Coloured People," *Argus*, July 19, 1972; Adhikari, *Not White Enough*.
8. Biko, "Definition of Black Consciousness," 48–49; Gerhart, *Black Power in South Africa*, 273–76; Fredrickson, *Black Liberation*, 301–2.
9. Ranuga, "Frantz Fanon and Black Consciousness"; Sanders, *Complicities,* chap. 5; Magaziner, *Law and the Prophets*, 204n79.
10. Stuart Hall in *Frantz Fanon*, dir. Isaac Julien. On media, see Fanon, *Black Skin, White Masks*, 32, 127, 131, 151. This interpretation of *Black Skin, White Masks* builds on Bergner, "Who Is That Masked Woman?"; Sanders, *Complicities*, 179–86.
11. Fanon, *Black Skin, White Masks*, 67, 161.
12. Magaziner, *Law and the Prophets*, 9. Also see Sanders, *Complicities*, 179–88.
13. Fanon, *Black Skin, White Masks*, 90.
14. "Inside Rhodesia: Skin Lighteners Popular," *Chicago Daily Defender*, August 15, 1970, 12.
15. Matthews and Thomas, *Cry Rage!*, 48, 69. Also see Magaziner, *Law and the Prophets*, 111.
16. Matthews, *Black Voices Shout!*, 29. On Matthews as a Coloured and Black Consciousness intellectual, see Adhikari, *Not White Enough*, 135–46.
17. Biko, "Some African Cultural Concepts," 46. On this essay, see Veriava and Naidoo, "Remembering Biko from Here and Now"; Magaziner, *Law and the Prophets*, 45–46.
18. Black Consciousness activists likely knew of the East African campaigns from *Drum* and other media. Ford, *Liberated Threads*, 174.
19. "Black Is Beautiful," *Die Burger*, April 30, 1975. The government also banned T-shirts bearing the Black Power fist. Magaziner, *Law and the Prophets, 47.
20. Biko, "What Is Black Consciousness?" For a discussion of Biko advising women activists not to use skin lighteners, see *A Blues for Tiro*, dir. Steve Kwena Mokwena.
21. "Advertisements as Affecting Black People," SASO *Newsletter*, November/December 1975, 11–12.

22. On the need to develop black businesses, see Biko, "White Racism and Black Consciousness," 71; Motsuenyane, "Black Consciousness and the Economic Position of the Black Man."

23. South African Institute of Race Relations Collection, Historical Papers Archive, the Library, University of Witwatersrand, Johannesburg (hereafter, WHP, SAIRR), AD1912 Box 122, "Immorality Act, 1942–1959": "Multiracial Beauty Contest Next Week," *Star*, December 8, 1961; "Multi-Racial Youth Rally Called Off," *Rand Daily Mail*, December 16, 1961; "Food for 2,000," *Star*, December 16, 1961.

24. Karis-Gerhart Collection, Historical Papers Archive, the Library, University of Witwatersrand, Johannesburg (hereafter, WHP, Karis-Gerhart), A2675, Part III, Folder 289: Rev. Smangaliso Mkhathshwa, Ad Hoc Organizing Secretary, Steering Committee, "black renaissance convention," *Pro Veritate*, November 1974, 24. Also see Magaziner, "Pieces of a (Wo)man," 57. For another critique of beauty contests, see "Mechanisms for Cultural Alienation and the Need for Cultural Liberation," *Azania News* 18, no. 6 (June 1982): 22.

25. Interview with Cynthia Malgas by Lynn M. Thomas, Cape Town, July 21, 2008.

26. Interviews with Malgas and Dia Sydo by Sarah Espi-Sanchis and Lynn M. Thomas, Athlone, July 22, 2008. Also see Ribane, *Beauty*, 51. On the African National Congress's surprising embrace of beauty contests in the 1990s, see Barnard, "Contesting Beauty," 356.

27. Dogliotti et al., "Leucomelanoderma in Blacks"; Dogliotti and Leibowitz, "Granulomatous Ochronosis."

28. Manoim, "Black Press," 122; Glaser, *Bo-Tsotsi*, 50–52, 68–70; Clowes, "'Are You Going to be MISS (or MR) Africa?"

29. Springer, *Living for the Revolution*; R. Williams, "Black Women, Urban Politics": Springer, "Black Feminists Respond"; Ward, "Third World," 79–104, 105–18, 119–44.

30. Davis, "Afro Images."

31. Hadfield, *Liberation and Development*.

32. D. Lewis, "Women and Gender"; Gqola, "Contradictory Locations"; Ratele, "Men and Masculinities"; Magaziner, "Pieces of a (Wo)man"; Noble, *School of Struggle*, 230–33.

33. Ramphele, "Dynamics of Gender," 215, 216, 221. Also see Ramphele, *Across Boundaries*, esp. 71. On the Black Women's Federation, see Hassim, *Women's Organizations and Democracy*, chap. 2.

34. Magaziner, "Pieces of a (Wo)man"; Ratele, "Men and Masculinities."

35. Ramphele, "Dynamics of Gender," 217; Ramphele, *Across Boundaries*, 57–58; Bambara, *Black Woman*; Morgan, *Sisterhood Is Powerful*.

36. WHP, Karis-Gerhart A2675, Part I, Folder 41, interview with Nkosazana Dlamini-Zuma, London, July 3, 1988.

37. Alexander and Mngxitama, "Interview with Deborah Matshoba," esp. 275, 280.

38. Mashinini, *Strikes Have Followed Me All My Life*, 9. On Coloured labor preferences, see Goldin, *Making Race*.

39. WHP, Karis-Gerhart A2675, Part I, Folder 26, interview with Malusi Mpumlwana, Uitenhage, August 7, 1989.

40. WHP, Karis-Gerhart A2675, Part III, Folder 289, interview with Malusi Mpuml-wana, Thoko Mbanjwa, and Mamphela Ramphele, Cape Town, August 7, 1989.

41. Steenekamp, "Inkomste- en bestedingspatrone," table 15; Moolman and Loubser, "Market Potentials . . . in 1970," A11, A24–25, A37–38, A50–51, A63–64, A76–77, A89–90, A102–3, A115–16, A127–28, A141–42, A154–55, A167–68, A180–81, and A193–94.

42. Ramphele, "Dynamics of Gender," 217. On job advertisements for "slightly co-loured," also see Farieda Khan, "Creams That Are Destroying Black Beauty," *Weekend Argus,* August 25, 1990, 15.

43. Deppe, "Study of the Attitudes," 45–47, 74, 79.

44. Moolman and Loubser, "Market Potentials . . . in 1970," A11, A24–25, A141–42, A193–94; Loubser, "Market Potentials . . . in 1975," 17, B16, B37, B58, B79, B100, B121, B142, B163, B184, B205, B226, B247, B268.

45. Unterhalter, "Changing Attitudes."

46. Adhikari, *Not White Enough,* 144.

47. Tony Koenderman, "Twins Agree: Black's Beautiful," *Sunday Times,* July 3, 1977.

48. Bentley-Phillips and Bayles, "Cutaneous Reactions."

49. Bentley-Phillips and Bayles, "Correspondence," 233.

50. Bentley-Phillips and Bayles, "Butylated Hydroxytoluene," 216; Bentley-Phillips and Bayles, "Correspondence," 233.

51. Findlay, Morrison, and Simson, "Exogenous Ochronosis," 614; Findlay, "Ochrono-sis," 1093.

52. Ribane, *Beauty,* 51–54.

53. Matumo, *Setswana English Setswana Dictionary,* 436. *Tshubaba* derives from the verb "to set fire to" or "burn up" (*tshuba*). Today, *chubabas* is a term mainly used by Setswana and Sesotho speakers around Johannesburg and can refer either to ochronosis or melasma. Personal correspondence with Ncoza Dlova, October 12, 2017. In Ghana, the Akan phrase used for similar disfigurement, *"Ne nso Oben?"* ("Why would you do a thing like that?"), conveys both disbelief and dismay. Blay, "Yellow Fever," 64.

54. Ribane, *Beauty,* 51–54.

55. In June 2008, small containers of Ambi Chubaba Cover Cream, manufactured by Johnson & Johnson, could be purchased from cosmetic shops at the Cape Town train station.

56. Thwala, "Bleaching to Become Beautiful?," 81, 100–103. In isiZulu, the taunt went *"Unamashubabe' bsweni* [three times] / *Thathu cream uwugcobise."* According to Thwala (62), *amashubaba* could also reference sunburns.

57. Findlay, Morrison, and Simson, "Exogenous Ochronosis"; Findlay and De Beer, "Chronic Hydroquinone Poisoning"; "New Skin Disease Identified in the Republic," *Medical Chronicle,* October 1975, 24.

58. U.S. FDA, Proposed Rules, "Skin Bleaching Drug Products, Establishment of a Monograph," *Federal Register* (November 3, 1978); U.S. FDA, Proposed Rules, "Skin Bleaching Drug Products for Over-the-Counter Human Use, Tentative Final Mono-graph," *Federal Register* (September 3, 1982); O'Donoghue, Lynfield, and Derbes, "Letter to Editor."

59. For letters of concern submitted to the FDA by companies in 1979 and 1982, see U.S. FDA, "Skin Bleaching Drug Products," Docket FDA-1978-N-0023 at regulations .gov (hereafter, "Skin Bleaching Drug Products" at regulations.gov). The companies include Elder Pharmaceuticals, Chettem, Inc. (manufacturer of Nadinola), Norcliff Thayer Inc., Nicholas Products, Ltd. (manufacturer of Ambi), Plough, Inc., the Proprietary Association, Keystone Laboratories, Inc., Carson Products Co. (manufacturer of Dr. Fred Palmer's), Revlon Health Care Group, and the Cosmetic, Toiletry and Fragrance Association, Inc.

60. Hutt, "History of Government Regulation"; Woodcock, "Modernizing the Other Side of the Counter"; Califf, McCall, and Mark, "Cosmetics, Regulations, and the Public Health"; phone interview and email correspondence with Peter Hutt, November 2, 2017.

61. Dogliotti and Leibowitz, "Granulomatous Ochronosis"; Schulz, "Skin Disorders in Black South Africans."

62. Cornwell, "Letter to the Editor."

63. Findlay and De Beer, "Chronic Hydroquinone Poisoning"; Findlay, "Ochronosis Following Skin Bleaching," 1093.

64. Findlay and De Beer, "Chronic Hydroquinone Poisoning"; Findlay, "Ochronosis Following Skin Bleaching," 1093.

65. Personal Papers of Irwin Manoim, Big Media, Johannesburg (hereafter, Manoim papers), Planning and Research Department of Grey-Phillips, Bunton, Mundel and Blake, "Communicating with the Black Consumer: A Research Overview and SABC Guidelines for the Introduction of TV2" (1980/81), 26.

66. Nimrod Mkele, "My View: The Threat to Black Beauty," *Star*, September 16, 1982, 20.

67. Republic of South Africa, No. R. 1023, "Regulation Governing the Use of Hydroquinone, Mercury and Lead in Cosmetics," *South African Government Gazette* 6999 (May 16, 1980): 3–4.

68. Findlay and De Beer, "Chronic Hydroquinone Poisoning"; Findlay, "Ochronosis Following Skin Bleaching."

69. Bob Kennaugh, "State Warns on Skin Lighteners," *Star,* February 18, 1980, 4; Nat Diseko, "Skin Cream Rumpus Is Growing," *Sunday Times*, September 12, 1982, 1; "Skin Lightening Creams a Danger," *Star,* September 24, 1982, 13; Schulz, "Skin Disorders in Black South Africans."

70. Republic of South Africa, No. R. 2083, "Regulations Governing the Sale of Cosmetics Containing Hydroquinone, Mercury and Lead," *South African Government Gazette* 8900 (September 23, 1983): 7–9. This regulation also banned mercurial creams known as Blue Butter, Blue Ointment, and, in Afrikaans, Blou Botter. Such creams were often used to treat gonorrhea and syphilis infections. Swiderski, *Quicksilver*, 34.

71. U.S. FDA, Proposed Rules, "Skin Bleaching Drug Products for Over-the-Counter Human Use, Tentative Final Monograph," *Federal Register* (September 3, 1982).

72. They declined from an average of seven per issue in the mid-1960s to two to three by the mid-1970s. Khan, "Fanta Face, Coca-Cola Body," 13.

73. "Drum to Ban All Ads for Skin Lightening Creams," *Rand Daily Mail*, September 8, 1982; "Drummed Out (and Here's Why): Magazine Bans Ads for Skin-Lightening Creams," *Sunday Tribune*, September 12, 1982, 2; "Skin-lightener Ads to Go," *Citizen*, September 25, 1982, 9. Ads for "toners" continued in *Drum*. For example, see the Future Look ad, *Drum*, January 1983, 4–5; Clear Tone ad, *Drum*, February 1983, 100.

74. "Skin Lightening Creams: A Big New Problem," *Learn and Teach* 2, no. 5 (1982): 1–3; M. Dumila, "Letter," *Learn and Teach* 2, no. 4 (1982): 35; "The Learn and Teach Challenge," *Learn and Teach* 2, no. 5 (1982): 4; "If the Health Department Keeps Its Promise," *Learn and Teach* 2, no. 3 (1982): 2–4.

75. Martin Feinstein, "Drum to Ban All Ads for Skin Lightening Creams," *Rand Daily Mail*, September 8, 1982; "Drummed Out! (and Here's Why)."

76. For a trenchant analysis of the challenges that Black Consciousness posed to white intellectuals, see Ally, "Oppositional Intellectualism as Reflection."

77. "What Is Wrong with Black Consciousness? (Some Common Questions and Answers)."

78. Phone interview with Geoff Budlender by Lynn M. Thomas, Cape Town, July 25, 2008.

79. Frederikse, Tomaselli, Muller, and Anderson, *Culture and the Media*, 21–23; Vukani Makhosikazi Collective, *South African Women on the Move*, 167–68.

80. Ramphele and Boonzaier, "Position of African Women," 160; Ramphele, *Bed Called Home*, 80.

81. Hardwick et al., "Exogenous Ochronosis."

82. Carman, "Memorandum on the Use of Skin Lightening Creams"; Weiss, del Fabbro, and Kolisang, "Cosmetic Ochronosis."

83. Morobe, "Towards a People's Democracy"; Mufson, *Fighting Years,* 106–9; Van Kessel, *"Beyond Our Wildest Dreams,"* 33–34.

84. Personal Papers of Hilary Carman, Johannesburg (hereafter, Carman papers): press conference by Dr. E. Kuzwayo and Dr. Hilary Carman, "Ban of Hydroquinone and Other Harmful Ingredients in Skin Lighteners," March 9, 1988; J. Tatham, Vice President, the Housewives' League of South Africa to Director General, Foodstuffs, Cosmetics and Disinfectants Act, "Banning of Skin Lighteners," March 16, 1988.

85. Wroughton, "Action Plea on Skin Lighteners," *Pretoria News,* May 15, 1987, 7; Carman papers, press conference by Kuzwayo and Carman; Carman papers, Dr. C. Isaacson, Professor and Head, Department of Anatomical Pathology, University of Witwatersrand, to Dr. Stevens, National Health and Population Development, Pretoria, May 25, 1987; Legal Resources Centre Collection, Historical Papers Archive, the Library, University of Witwatersrand, Johannesburg (hereafter, WHP, LRC), AG 3199 5.7.1, files on Cosmedicae, P. I. Folb, "Report to the Ministry of Health on Aspects of the Safety and Scheduling Status of Hydroquinone Preparations," April 12, 1989; interview with Hilary Carman by Lynn M. Thomas, Johannesburg, August 15, 2004; email correspondence with Hilary Carman, July 2012.

86. "Cosmetics: Skin Lightener Sales Still Strong," *Finance Week*, April 6, 1989; Hardwick et al., "Exogenous Ochronosis"; Yvonne Grimbeek, "Postponing

of Skin Lighteners' Ban Slammed by City Pharmacists," *Natal Witness*, July 15, 1988; Tania Levy, "Ban on Hydroquinone Surprises Twins," *Business Day*, April 24, 1990.

87. Phillips, Isaacson, and Carman, "Ochronosis in Black South Africans."

88. Carman papers, Vita Palestrant, Consumer Affairs Manager, Checkers South Africa Limited, Johannesburg, to Ellen Kuzwayo, President, the National Black Consumers Association, Johannesburg, March 30, 1987; "'White Skin' Creams under Fire," *Sowetan*, May 18, 1987; "Skin Lighteners: New Regulation Likely Soon," *Citizen*, May 21, 1987, 8; Juliette Saunders, "National Chain Acts against Skin Lighteners," *Eastern Province Herald*, June 25, 1987; "Two Firms Ban Sale of Skin Lighteners," *Citizen*, June 25, 1987; "Beyond the Pale," *Herald*, June 26, 1987, 14.

89. "Cosmetics: Skin Lightener Sales Still Strong"; Carolyn McGibbon, "Blooming Trade May Be Nipped in Bud," c. May 1987, found in TimesMedia clippings files, TimesMedia House, Johannesburg; "Lipworth Profit Warning," *Citizen*, June 24, 1987; "Draft Regulations Regarding Skin Lightening Cosmetics," *Salos* 10, no. 4 (June-July 1987).

90. Republic of South Africa, No. R. 2892, "Regulations Prohibiting the Use of Hydroquinone, any Active or Potentially Active Depigmenting Ingredient," *South African Government Gazette* 11086 (December 31, 1987): 56–57; Carman papers, press conference by Kuzwayo and Carman.

91. Republic of South Africa, No. R. 1227, "Regulations Prohibiting the Use of Hydroquinone, any Active or Potentially Active Depigmenting Ingredient," *South African Government Gazette* 11360 (June 24, 1988): 38–39; Carman papers, "Press Announcement: The Skin Lightening Industry," June 26, 1988.

92. Presbury, "Hydroquinones: A National Disgrace!"; Carman papers, Dr. Mary Ann Sher, Chairman, Dermatological Society of South Africa, to Prof. Louise Tager, Chairman, Business Practice Committee, Parklands, "Re: Reversal of the Ban on the Sale of Cosmetic Bleaching Creams Containing Hydroquinone," July 6, 1988; Carman papers, Sher to Dr. C. E. M. Viljoen, Secretary General, Medical Association of South Africa, "Banning of Hydroquinone," November 29, 1988; "MASA Bulletin"; Schulz and Sher, "Rescinding of Legislation to Ban Hydroquinone-Containing Bleaching Creams"; "Skin Bleaching Drug Products," regulations.gov; Prof. R. S. Summers, Head, School of Pharmacy, Medunsa, South Africa to Dockets Management Branch, FDA, "Comments on Tentative Final Monograph: Skin Bleaching Products for O-T-C Human Use," December 15, 1988; Sy Makaringe, "Anger over Skin Cream Move," *Sowetan*, July 25, 1988, 2; Simpiwe Ncwana, "Red Faces over Skin Lighteners," *City Press*, July 31, 1988, 3.

93. "Cosmetics: Skin Lightener Sales Still Strong"; Mokgadi Pela, "Skin Lighteners Do Damage," *Sowetan*, April 27, 1989.

94. Ruth Bhengu, "The Facts about Skin Lighteners," *Drum*, April 1990, 86, 90. Perhaps hoping to buoy their own political credibility, homeland authorities in the Ciskei went ahead and banned skin lighteners in June 1989. "Ciskei Prohibits Skin-Lighteners," *Daily Dispatch*, June 27, 1989, 9.

95. Carman papers, "Press Announcement"; Bhengu, "Facts about Skin Lighteners."

96. In print, dermatologists pointed to a certain "deputation from the companies" as decisive to the minister's postponement but stopped short of stating that he had been bribed. Such accusations nonetheless circulated by word of mouth. Presbury, "Hydroquinones: A National Disgrace!"

97. WHP, LRC, AG 3199 5.7.1, files on Cosmedicae: Dr. W. A. van Niekerk, MP, and Minister of National Health and Population Development to D. Dalling, MP, Marshalltown, August 21, 1989.

98. Albrecht, "Introducing Dr. Rina Venter"; Gastrow, "Elizabeth Hendrina Venter"; Van Niekerk, "Evolution of Health and Welfare Policies in South Africa."

99. Janette Bennett, "Cut Off Date of Controversial Skin Lighteners under Debate," *Sunday Tribune*, April 22, 1990; Asha Singh, "Skin Creams Face Ban," *Sowetan*, April 24, 1990; "Battle against Skin Lighteners Ends," *Sowetan*, August 30, 1990, 8; Republic of South Africa, No. R. 1861, "Regulations Prohibiting the Use of Hydroquinone, Any Active or Potentially Active Depigmenting Ingredient—Amendment," *South African Government Gazette* 12700 (August 10, 1990).

100. "Consumers Union Welcomes Ban," *Sowetan*, April 25, 1990; Anthony Barker, "End of 10-Year Battle to Ban Skin Lighteners," *Business Day*, August 30, 1990, 8.

101. Pela, "Skin Lighteners Do Damage"; Khan, "Creams That Are Destroying Black Beauty."

102. "Battle against Skin Lighteners Ends."

103. Barker, "End of 10-Year Battle"; Pat Sidley, "Now-banned Skin-Lighten Cosmetics to Be Sold Outside SA," *Weekly Mail*, August 17–19, 1990, 1; "Pharmacists Slam Reports," *Pretoria News*, August 25, 1990; "The Dark History," *Sunday Times*, December 12, 1999.

104. WHP, LRC, AG 3199 5.7.1, files on Cosmedicae: Matthew Walton, Legal Resources Centre, to William Kerfoot, "Memorandum on Essence of Ivory: Cosmetic Care," September 30, 1992; R. Lakha, "Skin Lighteners: The Abuse Continues," *True Love*, July 1996, 44–45, 55.

105. Malangu and Ogunbanjo, "Predicators of Topical Steroid Misuse."

106. Schulz, Summers, and Summers, "Correspondence"; Fernandes, "Hydroquinone."

107. Interviews with Hilary Carman by Lynn M. Thomas, August 15, 2004, and May 20, 2009; interview with Dr. Jameela Aboobaker by Lynn M. Thomas, July 19, 2007, Durban; email correspondence with Ncoza Dlova, November 8, 2017.

108. Khan, "Beauty, Myths and Trees"; Khan, "Black Beauty, White Mask"; Glenda Daniels, "Skin-deep Beauty Remains Elusive for Many SA Women," *Star*, June 19, 1997, 13; Khan, "Fanta Face, Coca-Cola Body."

109. "Skin Bleaching Drug Products," regulations.gov: Mark Green and Ritashona Simpson, Department of Consumer Affairs, City of New York, "A Study in Hype and Risk: The Marketing of Skin Bleachers" (February 1992); Mark Green, Commissioner, Department of Consumer Affairs, New York, to David A. Kessler, Commissioner, FDA, February 11, 1992. Also see Warren E. Leary, "Mislabeling and Health Risks Tied to Skin Lightener Creams," *New York Times*, February 26, 1992; Robin Abcarian, "Skin Whiteners, Faded Beauties—and Racism," *Los Angeles Times*, April 17, 1992.

110. "Skin Bleaching Drug Products," regulations.gov: R. William Soller, Senior Vice President, NDMA, to Paul Botstein, Acting Director, Office of OTC Drugs, FDA, February 11, 1992; Soller to David A. Kessler, Commissioner, FDA, February 14, 1992; Soller to Gilbertson, May 11, 1992; Hydroquinone Task Group, NDMA, Washington, DC, "Salient Observations from the Published Literature on Exogenous Ochronosis Reportedly Associated with Skin Discoloration Fade Products" and "Chronic Health Effects Testing for Hydroquinone," May 12, 1992.

111. In addition to the frequent lapses in labeling that Green and Simpson identified, some consumers reported using over-the-counter cosmetics containing more than 2 percent hydroquinone long after the 1982 guidelines were issued. See, for instance, "Skin Bleaching Drug Products," regulations.gov: Debra L. Bowen, Director, Division of OTC Drug Products, FDA, to Lilly Johnson, Georgia, October 16, 1996.

112. Skin Bleaching Drug Products," regulations.gov: Frances D. Hooks, National Co-ordinator, WIN (Women in NAACP), to David A. Kessler, Commissioner, FDA, May 14, 1992; Ed Towns, Chairman, Congressional Black Caucus, to David A. Kessler, Commissioner, FDA, May 18, 1992; William J. Haskins, Vice President, National Urban League, Inc., to David A. Kessler, Commissioner, FDA, May 18, 1992.

113. For earlier criticism by U.S. anti-apartheid activists of an African American cosmetics company's willingness to defy the economic boycott and sell products in South Africa, see Linn Washington, "Mississippi Cosmetics Firm Makes Deal to Sell Skin Lightener Products to S. African Blacks," *Philadelphia Tribune,* October 19, 1976, 5.

114. "Skin Bleaching Drug Products," regulations.gov: Denese O. Shervington, Chair-person of Board of Directors, International Coalition of Women Physicians, to William Gilbertson, Director, Monograph Review Division, FDA, May 12, 1992; Gilbertson to Shervington, June 3, 1992; Gilbertson to Frances D. Hooks, National Coordinator, WIN, June 24, 1992; Gilbertson to William J. Haskins, Vice President of Programs, National Urban League, Inc., June 24, 1992.

115. "Skin Bleaching Drug Products," regulations.gov: "Memorandum of Meeting between FDA Representatives and NDMA Hydroquinone Task Force Representa-tives, May 20, 1992, Parklawn Building"; Statement of Mark Green, Commissioner of Consumer Affairs, New York City, "The Safety of Skin Bleach Products for Over-the-Counter Human Use," May 20, 1992; Hydroquinone Task Group, NDMA, "Voluntary Labeling Guidelines," May 1992.

116. "Skin Bleaching Drug Products," regulations.gov: "OTC Hydroquinone Meet-ing, July 10, 1996"; "Carcinogenicity Assessment Committee, Open Public Meeting—Hydroquinone (OTC monographed ingredient, December 4, 1996"; Debra L. Bowen, Acting Director, Division of OTC Drug Products, FDA, to R. William Soller, Senior Vice President, NDMA, December 7, 1998; Lorna C. Totman, Director of Scientific Affairs, Consumer Healthcare Products Association (formerly, NDMA), to Debra L. Bowen, Acting Director, Division of OTC Drug Products, FDA, April 13, 1999.

117. Drugs Control Council, Zimbabwe, "Notice: Skin-Lightening Cosmetics," *Herald* (Harare), May 21, 1983. The Zimbabwean regulations came into effect on October 1, 1983, a month after South Africa's 1983 regulations. Controversially, they limited the

sale of all skin lighteners to pharmacies only. Thanks to Susan Ziki for tracking down this information.

118. "Gambia Bans Skin-Bleaching," *Daily Nation* (Nairobi), January 2, 1996; Buckley, "Portrait Photography in a Postcolonial Age," esp. 293.

119. H. Williams, "Skin Lightening Creams Containing Hydroquinone."

120. Chris Erasmus, "Alert over Bleaching Ointments," *Daily Nation*, December 13, 1999; Corinna Schuler, "Africans Look for Beauty in Western Mirror," *Christian Science Monitor*, December 23, 1999.

121. European Communities, "Twenty-Fourth Commission Directive"; Jesitus, "Distant Decisions."

122. *Hokkaido* newspaper (morning Zendo edition), June 11, 2003, 19; email communications with Katsuo Matsumoto, January 22 and 29, 2018. Thanks very much to Katsuo Matsumoto, Asuza Tanaka, Kazumi Hasegawa, and Mikiko Soga for translating sources and helping me to understand the history of hydroquinone in Japan.

123. "Public Notice: Product Ban—Beware of Those Beauty Products," *Daily Nation*, May 11, 2001.

124. N. Jamilya Chisholm, "Fade to White," *Village Voice*, January 22, 2002, http://www.villagevoice.com/2002/01/22/fade-to-white/; K. Lewis et al., "Need for Interventions to Prevent Skin Bleaching," 789–91.

CONCLUSION: SEDIMENTED MEANINGS AND COMPOUNDED POLITICS

1. John Battersby, "Apartheid Museum a Testament to Triumph over Adversity," *Sunday Independent*, October 28, 2001; Paul Olivier, "White Parties Back Apartheid Museum," *Citizen*, November 29, 2001; Rachel L. Swarns, "South African Museum Recreates Apartheid," *New York Times*, December 10, 2001; Sean O'Toole, "The Structure of Memory: Johannesburg's Apartheid Museum," *Artthrob* 55, March 2002, www.arthrob.co.za/02mar/reviews/apartheid.html; Deborah Graham, "Apartheid Museum Voted No. 1," *Citizen*, October 3, 2005.

2. Charlotte Bauer, "Speaking for Itself, and for All of Us," *Sunday Times*, December 2, 2001; Anne Simmons, "Shame on Show at Apartheid Museum," *Cape Times*, December 7, 2001; Robyn Sassen, "Apartheid: Now in Museum Form," on the blog "Just Another Day in Africa," at *PopMatters*, April 30, 2002, https://www.popmatters.com/sassen020501-2496174194.html (accessed January 18, 2018).

3. Colin Mitchell, "Scarred for Life by Skin Cream," *Drum*, May 29, 1997, 8–9; David Beresford and Martin Bright, "Buying a Dream, but Sold a Lie," *Weekly Mail and Guardian*, September 3, 1999; "Banned, but Still Available," *Sunday Times*, December 12, 1999. Also see, M. McCloy, "A Lighter Shade of Dark," *Mail and Guardian*, January 31–February 6, 1997; N. Pillay, "Women Left Scarred by Illegal Skin Lighteners," *Sunday Argus*, April 27, 1997, cited in Khan, "Fanta Face, Coca-Cola Body," 15.

4. On the impact of neo-liberal policies on pharmaceuticals in Africa, see Peterson, *Speculative Markets*.

5. "The Perils of Paleness," *Mail and Guardian*, January 21–February 6, 1997, 28; Corinna Schuler, "Africans Look for Beauty in Western Mirror," *Christian Science*

Monitor, December 23, 1999; Sam Mathe, "Curse of the Cosmetic Creams," Drum, February 10, 2000, 92–93; "Skin Lighteners 'Harmful,'" City Vision Western Cape, October 26, 2001.

6. Interviews with Hilary Carman by Lynn M. Thomas, Johannesburg, August 15, 2004, and May 20, 2009; interview with Jameela Aboobaker by Lynn M. Thomas, Durban, July 19, 2007.

7. Email correspondence with Ncoza Dlova, November 8, 2017. For the violent targeting of African refugees with dark skin tones in North Africa, see Dionne Searcey and Jaime Yaya Barry, "Sub-Saharan African Migrants Face Old Enemy in Libya: Bigotry," New York Times, September 12, 2017, https://www.nytimes.com/2017/09/12 /world/africa/migrants-africa-libya.html (accessed February 1, 2018).

8. Mandela's endorsement appeared in a Pure Perfect ad in the Sunday Times, August 3, 2008. Suthentira Govender, "Khanyi Mbau Joins the Lite Brigade," Sunday Times, January 10, 2016, https://www.timeslive.co.za/sunday-times/news/2016–01–10 -khanyi-mbau-joins-the-lite-brigade/ (accessed January 2, 2017); Jacobs et al., "Fifty Shades of African Lightness." On the isiZulu saying, see Thwala, "Bleaching to Become Beautiful?," 122.

9. Tiffany O'Callaghan, "What Could Have Made Sammy Sosa's Skin Lighter?," Time, November 10, 2009, http://healthland.time.com/2009/11/10/what-could-have -made-sammy-sosas-skin-lighter/ (accessed January 2, 2018); "Beyoncé Knowles: L'Oreal Accused of 'Whitening' Singer in Cosmetics Ad," Guardian, August 8, 2008, https://www.theguardian.com/media/2008/aug/08/advertising.usa (accessed January 2, 2018); Sally Evans, "Terry Pics Not 'Whitened,'" Times (Johannesburg), August 18, 2008, 3; Mica Paris, "Why DO So Many of My Fellow Black Stars Want Whiter Skin," Daily Mail, October 23, 2015, http://www.dailymail.co.uk/tvshowbiz/article -3286969/As-Beyonce-steps-palest-shade-MICA-PARIS-asks-black-stars-want-whiter -skin.html (accessed January 2, 2018).

10. Yaba Blay, "Dencia Wants to Set the Record Straight on Whitenicious [Interview]," Ebony, February 3, 2014; Yaba Blay, "Lil' Kim's Lighter, Whiter Skin Is a Sad Indictment of Racism," Daily Beast, April 25, 2016, https://www.thedailybeast.com/lil -kims-lighter-whiter-skin-is-a-sad-indictment-of-racism (accessed January 2, 2018).

11. Theo Nyhara, "'Relax! I Don't Hate Being Black!,'" Drum, November 17, 2011, cover and 10–13.

12. Davids, van Wyk, and Khumalo, "Intravenous Glutathione"; Aneri Pattani, "A New Skin Lightening Procedure Is Short on Evidence," New York Times, August 28, 2017, https://www.nytimes.com/2017/08/28/health/skin-lightening-glutathione -bleaching.html?_r=0 (accessed January 1, 2018). For an interpretation of the rapid spread of glutathione, see Tate, Black Beauty, 107–11.

13. Pumza Fihlani, "Africa: Where Black Is Not Really Beautiful," BBC News, January 1, 2013, http://www.bbc.com/news/world-africa-20444798 (accessed January 18, 2018).

14. Barnes, Cultural Conundrums, 113; Brown-Glaude, "Fact of Blackness?," 37; Tate, Black Beauty, 126; Tate, Skin Bleaching in Black Atlantic Zones.

15. Govender, "Khanyi Mbau."

16. Cooper, *Africa since 1940*, 152–53; Hyslop, "Shopping during a Revolution."

17. Bertelsen, "Ads and Amnesia"; Posel, "Races to Consume"; James, *Money from Nothing*; Posel and van Wyck, *Conspicuous Consumption in Africa*.

18. Nyhara, "'Relax! I Don't Hate Being Black!'"; "Skin Bleaching Scandal in South Africa," *Unreported World*, January 17, 2018, https://www.youtube.com/watch?v=bWHCwXZpH6E&feature=youtu.be (accessed February 1, 2018).

19. Fihlani, "Africa: Where Black Is Not Really Beautiful." For a discussion of Mshoza and "third space skins," see Tate, *Black Beauty*, 33–36.

20. "Lupita Nyong'o Speech on Black Beauty Essence Black Women," *Ebony*, February 24, 2014, https://www.youtube.com/watch?v=ZPCkfARH2eE; Nardine Saad, "How Lupita Nyong'o Got over Believing 'Dark Skin Is Unacceptable,'" *Los Angeles Times*, November 3, 2014, http://www.latimes.com/entertainment/gossip/la-et-mg-lupita-nyongo-glamour-dark-skin-challenges-beauty-20141103-story.html; Heather Saul, "Lupita Nyong'o on Skin Lightening: My Self-Worth Was Compromised by Adverts," *Independent*, August 27, 2016, http://www.independent.co.uk/news/people/lupita-nyong-o-skin-lightening-adverts-compromised-by-self-worth-a7212761.html (all accessed January 12, 2018).

21. On the power of transnational movement to reframe self-perceptions of beauty, see Jarrín, *Biopolitics of Beauty*, 190–96.

22. *Yellow Fever*, written and directed by Ng'endo Mukii, https://vimeo.com/59241525 (accessed January 18, 2018).

23. Beautywell Project, http://www.thebeautywell.org/; Sheila Mulrooney Eldred, "A Minnesota Health Advocate's Crusade Brings Harmful Skin Lightening Out of the Dark," STAT, January 16, 2018, https://www.statnews.com/2018/01/16/skin-lightening-amira-adawe/ (both accessed January 17, 2018); Nancy Rosenbaum, "'You Have Dark Skin and You Are Beautiful': The Long Fight against Skin Bleaching," NPR *Public Radio*, February 25, 2018, https://www.npr.org/2018/02/25/588632658/you-have-dark-skin-and-you-are-beautiful-the-long-fight-against-skin-bleaching (accessed February 25, 2018).

24. Julie Creswell, "Young and in Love . . . with Lipstick and Eyeliner," *New York Times*, November 22, 2017, https://www.nytimes.com/2017/11/22/business/millennials-cosmetics-boom.html (accessed January 12, 2018).

25. Global Industry Analysts, Inc. , "Obsession with Lighter Skin Tones in Asia, the Middle East and Africa Drives Opportunities in the Global Skin Lighteners Market," June 2017, http://www.strategyr.com/MarketResearch/Skin_Lighteners_Market_Trends.asp (accessed March 4, 2018). Also see Glenn, "Consuming Lightness," 166–87.

26. Rebecca Ruiz, "Nivea's Controversial Skin-Lightening Ad Puts Spotlight on the History of White Supremacy," *Mashable*, October 20, 2017, http://mashable.com/2017/10/20/nivea-skin-lightening-cream-ad/#szhu5SOhRaqz (accessed January 9, 2018); Khan, "Fanta Face, Coca-Cola Body," 15. On the international marketing of "Fair & Lovely," see Glenn, "Consuming Lightness."

27. Nchimbi, "Women's Beauty in the History of Tanzania," chaps. 2, 5.

28. Dlova et al., "Women's Perceptions"; Dlova et al., "Skin Lightening Practices."

29. Davids et al., "Phenomena of Skin Lightening."

30. For analysis of skin lightening in a West African country, Ghana, that was not a settler colony but was nonetheless shaped by white supremacist ideology, see Blay, "Ahoofe Kasa!"; Pierre, *Predicament of Blackness*.

31. Dr. Ope Ofodile, "Artificial Depigmentation for Cosmetic Purposes: Prevalence, Consequences and Ethical Concerns," dermatology grand rounds, University of Washington, April 30, 2014. Thanks very much to Dr. Jay Vary for inviting me to this session. Also see Imadojemu and Fiester, "Skin Bleaching."

32. U.S. FDA, "Skin Bleaching Drug Products for Over-the-Counter Human Use; Proposed Rule," *Federal Register* (August 29, 2006): 51152. The proposal would have left Tri-Luma as the only FDA-approved prescription formulation as no other such products had undergone the long and costly drug review process. "Impact of Proposed FDA Restrictions on Hydroquinone," *Dermatologist*, September 4, 2008, https://www.the-dermatologist.com/article/6562 (accessed November 27, 2017).

33. Palm and Toombs, "Letter to the Editor"; Levitt, "Safety of Hydroquinone"; U.S. FDA, "Skin Bleaching Drug Products," Docket FDA-1978-N-0023 at https://www.regulations.gov/docket? D=FDA-1978-N-0023: "Nomination Profile, Hydroquinone, Supporting Information for Toxicological Evaluation by the National Toxicology Program," May 21, 2009; Dr. Michael Swann, University of Missouri-Columbia, November 16, 2006; Dr. Jennifer Cafardi, University of Alabama, November 17, 2006. Some health professionals did voice qualified support for the FDA proposal. U.S. FDA, "Skin Bleaching Drug Products," Docket FDA-1978-N-0023 at https://www.regulations.gov/docket? D=FDA-1978-N-0023: Ms. Babette deWall, November 16, 2006; Daniel Kaas, Assistant Commissioner, Health and Mental Hygiene, New York City, December 21, 2006.

34. U.S. FDA, "Skin Bleaching Drug Products," Docket FDA-1978-N-0023 at https://www.regulations.gov/docket? D=FDA-1978-N-0023: Mrs. Joyce Clark, December 21, 2006; Mrs. Jennifer Szluk, December 21, 2006.

35. U.S. FDA, "Hydroquinone Studies under the National Toxicology Program (NTP)," last modified November 27, 2016, https://www.fda.gov/AboutFDA/CentersOffices/OfficeofMedicalProductsandTobacco/CDER/ucm203112.htm.

36. "CTFA Statement on Hydroquinone," last modified May 15, 2007, https://www.personalcarecouncil.org/newsroom/20070501.

37. "Impact of Proposed FDA Restrictions on Hydroquinone."

38. Jennifer Barrett, "New Secrets for Youthful Skin," *Newsweek*, April 23, 2006, http://www.newsweek.com/new-secrets-youthful-skin-107801 (accessed January 9, 2018); Sally Wadyka, "Skin Deep: Trouble Spots Got You Down? Lighten Up," *New York Times*, July 21, 2005, http://query.nytimes.com/gst/fullpage.html? res=9502E5DC 163FF932A15754C0A9639C8B63 (accessed January 9, 2018). Also see Glenn, "Consuming Lightness," 182–83.

39. Mire, "Scientification of Skin Whitening"; Mire, "'Skin Trade.'" Also see Perry, "Buying White Beauty."

40. Mire, "Scientification of Skin Whitening." Also see Maibach and Elsner, *Cosmeceuticals*.

41. Draelos, "Skin Lightening Preparations"; Glenn, "Consuming Lightness"; Jablonski, *Living Color*, 176–77; Global Industry Analysts, "Obsession with Lighter Skin

Tones." The botanicals are generally regarded as safe but can produce some of hydroquinone's milder side effects, including dermatitis and redness. The more effective of these agents have chemical structures similar to hydroquinone.

42. Mire, "Scientification of Skin Whitening."

43. Harada et al., "Monitoring of Mercury Pollution"; Harada et al., "Wide Use of Skin-Lightening Soap." For more on mercury's resurgence and concealment, see L. Thomas, "Beauty."

44. World Health Organization, "Mercury in Skin Lightening Products."

45. Carson, *Silent Spring*. On toxicity and ill health in Africa, see Livingston, *Improvising Medicine*; Gupta and Hecht, "Toxicity, Waste, Detritus."

46. Dlova, Hendricks, and Martincigh, "Skin-Lightening Creams"; Maneli et al., "Combinations of Potent Topical Steroids."

47. Perry, "Buying White Beauty," 591. Also see Hamann et al., "Spectrometric Analysis of Mercury Content." On products with very high levels of hydroquinone, see Yaba Blay, "Beauty and the Bleach: This Issue Is More Than Skin Deep," *Ebony*, June 20, 2016, http://www.ebony.com/news-views/skin-bleaching#axzz53u1EgaKm (accessed January 11, 2018); "Dying to Be White," UCT *News*, September 10, 2014, https://www.news.uct.ac.za/article/-2014–09–10-dying-to-be-white (accessed January 19, 2018).

48. Luke Feltham, "Panyaza Lesufi Visits School to Probe #StopRacismAtPretoriaGirlsHigh Concerns," *Mail and Guardian*, August 26, 2016; Ra'eesa Pather, "Hair, White Assimilation, and the Girls Who Are Rejecting It," *Mail and Guardian*, August 30, 2016; Hlonipha Mokoena, "From Slavery to Colonialism and School Rules: A History of Myths about Black Hair," *Mail and Guardian*, September 1, 2016; Mark Hunter, "Market Forces Propel Schools' Racism," *The Con*, September 6, 2016. On "white tone" and the politics of schooling in South Africa, see Hunter, *Race for Education*.

Bibliography

ARCHIVES, SPECIAL COLLECTIONS, AND PERSONAL PAPERS

Kenya

Kenyan National Archives, Nairobi
  Popular Magazine Collection

South Africa

Killie Campbell Library, Durban
  Makhanya Papers
National Archive Repository, Pretoria (SAB)

CSO	2
GES	1562, 1727, 1732, 1781, 1788
HEN	617, 618, 620, 4516
LTD	249, 250
NTS	1681, 1877, 7725
RHN	86, 177, 906, 907

National Library of South Africa, Special Collections, Cape Town
  INIL   14165, 14210
Personal Papers of Hilary Carman, Johannesburg (Carman papers)
Personal Papers of Irwin Manoim, Big Media, TimesMedia House, Johannesburg
    (Manoim papers)
Supreme Court of South Africa, Bloemfontein
  *Hollywood Curl (PTY) Limited (First Appellant) and the International Hollywood
    Curl Hairdressers Suppliers and Training Centre (Second Appellant) and Twins
    Products (PTY) Limited (Respondent).* Appeal Case No. 14561 of 1985, vol. 1.
  *Hollywood Curl (PTY) Limited and The International Hollywood Curl Hairdressers
    Suppliers and Training Centre v. Twins Products (PTY) Limited, Judgment
    Supreme Court of South Africa (Appellate Division).* Case No. 281 of 1987, vol. 3.
University of Cape Town, African Studies Library
  Thesis and Manuscript Collection
University of Cape Town, Manuscripts and Archives, Cape Town (UCTMA)
  BC880   Monica and Godfrey Wilson Papers
University of the Western Cape, Robben Island Mayibuye Archives, Cape Town
  MCH280   Black Consciousness
  MCH283   National Medical and Dental Association
University of Witwatersrand, Historical Papers Archive, the Library, Johannesburg (WHP)
  A2675   Karis-Gerhart Collection
  AD843   Correspondence on the Black Press

AD1912   South African Institute of Race Relations Collection (SAIRR)
AD2781   J. D. Mweli Skota Correspondence
AG3199   Legal Resources Centre Collection (LRC)
Western Cape Provincial Archives and Records Service, Cape Town (WCPA)
3/CT 4/1/5/1247
3/CT 4/1/5/1256

Tanzania
University of Dar es Salaam, East Africana Collection
Thesis Collection

United States
Duke University, Rare Book, Manuscript, and Special Collections Library, Durham,
North Carolina (Duke Collection)
J. Walter Thompson Collection (JWT)
Box 2, Young Papers
Box 5, Sidney Berstein
Reel no. 53, Marketing Research Reports
Reel no. 225, Marketing Research Reports
Reel no. 233, Marketing Research Reports
Reel no. 712, Marketing Research Reports
Food and Drug Administration (FDA), U.S. Department of Health and Human Services
"Skin Bleaching Drug Products," Docket FDA-1978-N-0023, https://www.regulations
.gov/docket?D=FDA-1978-N-0023
National Archives and Records Administration, College Park, Maryland (NARA)
RG 88, Records of the Federal Drug Administration (FDA)
RG 122, Records of the Federal Trade Commission (FTC)
Northwestern University, Melville J. Herskovits Library of Africana Studies
Popular Magazine Collection
Schomburg Center for Research in Black Culture, Manuscripts, Archives and Rare
Books Division, New York
Apex News Microfilm
U.S. Library of Congress, Washington, DC
Zonk! and *Drum* Magazines
Yale University, Beinecke Rare Book and Manuscript Library, New Haven,
Connecticut
Zonk! Magazine

FILMS
A Blues for Tiro. Directed by Steve Kwena Mokwena. South Africa: X Productions,
2007.
Cinderella of the Cape Flats. Directed by Jane Kennedy. Johannesburg: Film Resource
Unit, 2004.
Fantacoca. Directed by Agnes Ndibi. In *Africa, Africas.* New York: Distributed by
Women Make Movies, 2001.

Frantz Fanon: Black Skin, White Masks. Directed by Isaac Julien. San Francisco: California Newsreel, 1996.

Yellow Fever. Directed and written by Ng'endo Mukii (2013). https://vimeo.com /59241525 (accessed January 18, 2018).

FORMAL INTERVIEWS

Aboobaker, Jameela. Interviewed by Lynn M. Thomas. Durban, July 19, 2007.

Allan, Tony. Interviewed by Sarah Espi-Sanchis and Lynn M. Thomas. Constantia, Western Cape, July 25, 2008.

Bibi. Interviewed by Patricia Njuki, Stella Bosire, and Lynn M. Thomas. Antonio's Café, Nairobi, June 17, 2009.

Budlender, Geoff. Phone interviewed by Lynn M. Thomas. Cape Town, July 25, 2008.

Carman, Hilary. Interviewed by Lynn M. Thomas. Johannesburg, August 15, 2004, and May 20, 2009.

Dike, Fatima. Interviewed by Moss Lulama and Lynn M. Thomas. Cape Town, July 7, 2009.

Gwantai, Mary. Interviewed by Lynn M. Thomas. Meru School, Meru, June 8, 2009.

Hutt, Peter. Phone interviewed by Lynn M. Thomas. Seattle, WA, November 2, 2017.

Khubeka, Abigail. Interviewed by Lynn M. Thomas. Soweto, May 21, 2009.

Krok, Solomon. Interviewed by Lynn M. Thomas. Johannesburg. August 8 and 12, 2008.

Kungu, Alfred. Interviewed by Lynn M. Thomas. Private Office, Nairobi Hospital, June 16, 2004.

Malgas, Cynthia. Interviewed by Lynn M. Thomas. Cape Town, July 21, 2008.

Maseko, Eunice. Interviewed by Lynn M. Thomas. Johannesburg, August 4, 2008.

Molefe, Joyce, and Notumato Tyeku (pseudonyms). Interviewed by Moss Lalama and Lynn M. Thomas. Langa, July 10, 2008.

Mosweu, Lorato (pseudonym). Interviewed by T. Mpho and Lynn M. Thomas. Thembisa, May 18, 2009.

Nyamu, Agnes. Interviewed by Patricia Njuki and Lynn M. Thomas. Langata, Nairobi, May 28 and June 1, 2009.

Owili, Malaki. Interviewed by Lynn M. Thomas. Private office, Aga Khan Hospital, Nairobi, June 16, 2004.

Rolfe, Phillip. Interviewed by Sarah Espi-Sanchis and Lynn M. Thomas. Mt. Edgecome, KwaZulu-Natal, July 29, 2008.

Roux, François and factory employees. Interviewed by Sarah Espi-Sanchis and Lynn M. Thomas. Middleburg, July 14, 2008.

Schap, Gerald. Interviewed by Sarah Espi-Sanchis and Lynn M. Thomas. Cape Town, July 22, 2008.

Sydo, Dia. Interviewed by Sarah Espi-Sanchis and Lynn M. Thomas. Athlone, Cape Town, July 22, 2008.

Vaphi, Don, Leticia Vaphi, and Primrose Coki. Interviewed by Lulama Moss and Lynn M. Thomas. Langa, Cape Town, July 20, 2008.

Vorster, Joe. Interviewed by Sarah Espi-Sanchis and Lynn M. Thomas. Mossel Bay, Western Cape, July 23, 2008.

NEWSPAPERS AND PERIODICALS

Ghana
Gold Coast Independent. 1935.

India
Times of India. 1973.

Japan
Hokkaido Shinbun. 2003.
Tokyo Cosmetic Industry Association Bulletin. 1957.

Kenya
Daily Nation (Nairobi). 1972, 1996, 1999, 2001.
Drum (East and Central African Edition). 1962.
True Love (Kenya). 1996.
Weekly Review. 1975, 1980.

Nigeria
Lagos Standard. 1909.
Lagos Weekly Record. 1921.

South Africa
Advertising & Selling. 1929, 1951, 1953.
Africa. 1955.
African Market. 1947–48, 1955, 1960.
A.P.O. 1922.
Artthrob. 2002.
Azania News. 1982.
Bantu World. 1932–55.
Bona. 1956–59, 1963–65, 1967–68, 1971, 1973.
Bona (Xhosa Edition). 1958–59.
Business Day. 1990.
Cape Argus. 1930, 1946, 1972, 1990.
Cape Standard. 1936, 1938, 1940, 1943.
Cape Times. 1913, 1926, 1945.
Child Welfare (official publication of the South African National Council for Child
 Welfare). 1927.
Citizen. 2005.
City Press. 1988.
City Vision Western Cape. 2001.
The Con. 2016.
Daily Dispatch. 1989.
Daily Mail. 2015.
Die Burger. 1975.
Die Huisgenoot. 1944, 1946, 1948.
Drum. 1952–53, 1957–59, 1961, 1965, 1990, 2011.
Drum (East African Edition). 1959.

Eastern Province Herald. 1987.

Finance Week. 1989.

Financial Mail. 1987.

Golden City Post. 1956–71.

Graham's Town Journal. 1842.

Hi Note. 1954–55.

Ilanga lase Natal.

Imvo Zabantsundu.

Landstem.

Learn and Teach. 1982.

Mail and Guardian. 1997, 2016.

Natal Witness, and Agricultural and Commercial Advertiser. 1988.

Outspan. 1950.

Pretoria News. 1990.

Rand Daily Mail. 1902–3, 1905, 1909–10, 1937–38, 1961, 1982.

Selling Age—South African Sales Promotion and Packaging. 1956, 1959.

South African Advertising and Selling. 1945.

South African Business Efficiency. 1934, 1935.

South African Government Gazette. 1930.

South African Lady's Pictorial. 1925, 1930.

South African Lady's Pictorial and Home Journal. 1930.

South African Pharmaceutical Journal. 1934, 1935.

South African Pictorial. 1917, 1919, 1920–21.

South African Pictorial: Stage and Cinema. 1920, 1922–23.

South African Retail Chemist. 1953, 1955, 1958.

South African Spectator. 1901.

Sowetan. 1987–90.

The Spur. 1926.

Standard and Diggers' News. 1899.

Star. 1961, 1980, 1982, 1997.

Sun. 1911, 1933–36, 1938, 1948–50, 1953, 1968, 1970–71.

Sunday Independent. 2001.

Sunday Times. 1958, 1977, 1982, 1999, 2001, 2008, 2016.

Sunday Tribune. 1982, 1990.

Times. 2008.

uct *News.* 2014.

Umlindi we Nyanga. 1938.

Umteteli wa Bantu. 1925, 1931, 1933.

Upbeat. 1981.

Urn. 1893.

Veld & Flora. 1996.

Weekly Mail. 1990.

Weekly Mail and Guardian. 1999.

Zonk! 1949–52, 1954, 1956–57, 1959–60, 1962–64.

United Kingdom

BBC. 2013.

British Medical Journal. 1893.

Guardian. 2018.

Independent. 2016.

Times (London). 1785, 1788, 1800, 1806, 1894, 1939, 1978.

United States

American Druggist and Pharmaceutical Record. 1906, 1917–19, 1921.

Apex News. 1936, 1939–40.

Atlanta Daily World. 1941, 1964, 1970.

Baltimore Afro-American. 1924, 1928–29, 1932–33, 1949, 1960.

Bay State Banner. 1972.

Bistoury: A Quarterly Medical Journal, Devoted to the Exposition of Charlatanism in Medicine. 1871, 1876.

Boston Cultivator. 1849.

Chicago Defender. 1935, 1943, 1947–49, 1958, 1960, 1970.

Chicago Tribune. 2007.

Christian Observer. 1895.

Christian Science Monitor. 1999.

Citizen. 1982, 1987.

Drug and Cosmetic Industry. 1932, 1935, 1937, 1939, 1940, 1943, 1945, 1962.

Druggists' Circular and Chemical Gazette. 1891–94.

Ebony. 1959, 1968, 1978, 2014.

Esquire. 1968.

Harper's Bazaar. 1900.

Herald Times. 1987.

Hygeia. 1926–27.

Jet. 1952, 1970, 1973.

Ladies' Home Journal. 1893.

Lancet Medical News. 1861.

Los Angeles Times. 1992, 2014.

McClure, the Magazine of Romance. 1927.

Medical Record. 1884, 1905, 1915.

Negro World. 1925.

New Remedies. 1874, 1880.

New York Age. 1933.

New York Amsterdam News. 1929, 1932, 1949, 1962, 1966.

New York Times. 1918, 1927, 1939, 1962, 1992–93, 2001, 2005, 2016–18.

Philadelphia Tribune. 1960, 1976.

Pittsburgh Courier. 1926, 1955.

Press, Advertising, and Radio Review. 1956, 1965.

Printers' Ink Monthly. 1929.

Salos. 1987.

Scientific American. 1861, 1875, 1895.

STAT. 2018.

Time. 2011.

Tri-State Defender (Memphis, TN). 1959.

Village Voice. 2002.

Vogue. 1941.

Washington Post. 1905, 1913, 1924, 1929, 1932, 1936, 1960, 1967, 1970, 1972, 1975.

Worker's Herald. 1926–28.

Youth's Companion. 1888.

Zimbabwe

Herald. 1987.

OTHER SOURCES

Adamson, Joy. *The Peoples of Kenya.* New York: Harcourt, Brace & World, 1967.

Adhikari, Mohamed. *Not White Enough, Not Black Enough: Racial Identity in the South African Coloured Community.* Athens: Ohio University Press, 2005.

Adhikari, Mohamed. "Predicaments of Marginality: Cultural Creativity and Political Adaptation in Southern Africa's Coloured Communities." In *Burdened by Race: Coloured Identities in Southern Africa,* edited by Mohamed Adhikari, viii–xxxii. Cape Town: University of Cape Town Press, 2009.

Adler, Karen S. "'Always Leading Our Men in Service and Sacrifice': Amy Jacques Garvey, Feminist Black Nationalist." *Gender & Society* 6, no. 3 (1992): 346–75.

"Advertisements as Affecting Black People." *SASO Newsletter* (November/December 1975): 11–12.

Ahmed, Sara. "Animated Borders: Skin, Colour and Tanning." In *Vital Signs: Feminist Reconfigurations of the Bio/logical Body,* edited by Margrit Shildrick and Janet Price, 45–65. Edinburgh: Edinburgh University Press, 1998.

Ahmed, Sara, and Jackie Stacey. *Thinking through the Skin.* New York: Routledge, 2001.

Akeyeampong, Emmanuel. *Drink, Power and Cultural Change: A Social History of Alcohol in Ghana, c. 1800 to Recent Times.* Portsmouth, NH: James Currey, 1996.

Albrecht, Sybelle. "Introducing Dr. Rina Venter." *Nursing RSA* 4, no. 11 (November/December 1989): 16–17.

Alegi, Peter. "Rewriting Patriarchal Scripts: Women, Labor, and Popular Culture in South African Clothing Industry Beauty Contests, 1970s–2005." *Journal of Social History* (Fall 2008): 31–56.

Alexander, Amanda, and Andile Mngxitama. "Interview with Deborah Matshoba." In *Biko Lives! Contesting the Legacies of Steve Biko,* edited by Andile Mngxitama, Amanda Alexander, and Nigel C. Gibson, 275–83. New York: Palgrave Macmillan, 2008.

Allman, Jean, editor. *Fashioning Africa: Power and the Politics of Dress.* Bloomington: Indiana University Press, 2004.

Ally, Shireen. *From Servants to Workers: South African Domestic Workers and the Democratic State.* Ithaca, NY: Cornell University Press, 2009.

Ally, Shireen. "'Ooh, eh eh ... Just One Small Cap Is Enough!' Servants, Detergents, and Their Prosthetic Significance." *African Studies* 72, no. 3 (2013): 321–52.

Ally, Shireen. "Oppositional Intellectualism as Reflection, Not Rejection, of Power: Wits Sociology, 1975–1989." *Transformation* 59 (2005): 66–97.

Anderson, Carol. *Eyes Off the Prize: The United Nations and the African American Struggle for Human Rights, 1944–1955*. Cambridge: Cambridge University Press, 2003.

Appadurai, Arjun, editor. *The Social Life of Things: Commodities in Cultural Perspective*. Cambridge: Cambridge University Press, 1986.

Armstrong, James C., and Nigel A. Worden. "The Slaves, 1652–1834." In *The Shaping of South African Society, 1652–1840*, edited by Richard Elphick and Hermann Giliomee, 109–83. Second edition. Middleton, CT: Wesleyan University Press, 1988.

Arndt, Kenneth A., and Thomas B. Fitzpatrick. "Topical Use of Hydroquinone as a Depigmenting Agent." *Journal of American Medical Association* 194, no. 9 (November 29, 1965): 117–19.

Ashforth, Adam. "Weighing Manhood in Soweto." *CODESRIA Bulletin* 3/4 (1999): 51–58.

Baldwin, Davarian. *Chicago's New Negroes: Modernity, the Great Migration, and Black Urban Life*. Chapel Hill: University of North Carolina Press, 2007.

Baldwin, Davarian. "From the Washtub to the World: Madam C. J. Walker and the 'Re-creation' of Race Womanhood, 1900–1935." In *The Modern Girl Around the World: Consumption, Modernity, and Globalization*, edited by the Modern Girl Around the World Research Group, 55–76. Durham: Duke University Press, 2008.

Ballantine, Christopher. "Gender, Migrancy, and South African Popular Music in the Late 1940s and the 1950s." *Ethnomusicology* 44, no. 3 (Autumn 2000): 376–407.

Ballantine, Christopher. *Marabi Nights: Early South African Jazz and Vaudeville*. Johannesburg: Ravan, 1993.

Balter, Michael. "Early Start for Human Art? Ochre May Revise Timeline." *Science* 323 (January 30, 2009): 569.

Bambara, Toni Cade, editor. *The Black Woman: An Anthology*. New York: Mentor, 1970.

Bank, Andrew. "The 'Intimate Politics' of Fieldwork: Monica Hunter and Her African Assistants, Pondoland and the Eastern Cape, 1931–1932." In *Inside African Anthropology: Monica Wilson and Her Interpreters*, edited by Andrew Bank and Leslie J. Bank, 67–94. Cambridge: Cambridge University Press, 2013.

Bank, Andrew. "Liberals and Their Enemies: Racial Ideology at the Cape of Good Hope, 1820 to 1850." Ph.D. diss., Cambridge University, 1995.

Bank, Leslie J. "Witchcraft and the Academy: Livingstone Mqotsi, Monica Wilson, and the Middledrift Healers, 1945–1957." In *Inside African Anthropology: Monica Wilson and Her Interpreters*, edited by Andrew Bank and Leslie J. Bank, 224–53. Cambridge: Cambridge University Press, 2013.

Banks, Ingrid. *Hair Matters: Beauty, Power, and Black Women's Consciousness*. New York: New York University Press, 2000.

Banner, Lois. *American Beauty*. New York: Knopf, 1983.

Bantu Press (Pty.) Ltd. *The Approach to Bantu Press Advertising*. Johannesburg: Bantu Press, 1948.

Bantu Press (Pty.) Ltd. *Black Gold! A New Market*. Johannesburg: Bantu Press, 1945.

Barnard, Rita. "Contesting Beauty." In *Senses of Culture: South African Culture Studies*, edited by Sarah Nuttall and Cheryl-Ann Michael, 344–62. Oxford: Oxford University Press, 2000.

Barnes, Natasha. *Cultural Conundrums: Gender, Race, Nation, and the Making of Caribbean Cultural Politics*. Ann Arbor: University of Michigan Press, 2006.

Barr, R. D., P. H. Rees, P. E. Cordy, A. Kungu, B. A. Woodger, and H. M. Cameron. "Nephrotic Syndrome in Adult Africans in Nairobi." *British Medical Journal* (April 15, 1972): 131–34.

Barr, R. D., B. A. Woodger, F. R. C. Path, and P. H. Rees. "Levels of Mercury in Urine Correlated with the Use of Skin Lightening Creams." *American Journal of Clinical Pathology* 59, no. 1 (January 1973): 36–40.

Barthes, Roland. "Rhetoric of the Image." In *Semiotics: An Introductory Anthology*, edited by Robert E. Innis, 190–205. Bloomington: Indiana University Press, 1985.

Bayart, Jean-François. "Africa in the World: A History of Extraversion." *African Affairs* 99 (2000): 217–67.

Beavon, Keith. *Johannesburg: The Making and Shaping of the City*. Pretoria: UNISA Press, 2004.

Becker, S. W., and Malcolm C. Spencer. "Evaluation of Monobenzone." *Journal of American Medical Association* 180, no. 4 (April 28, 1962): 93–98.

Bennett, James. "Mercolized Wax." *Cosmetics and Skin*. Accessed January 23, 2012. http://cosmeticsandskin.com/aba/mercolized-wax.php.

Benthien, Claudia. *Skin: On the Cultural Border between Self and the World*. Translated by Thomas Dunlap. New York: Columbia University Press, 2002.

Bentley-Phillips, B., and Margaret A. H. Bayles. "Butylated Hydroxytoluene as a Skin Lightener." *Archives of Dermatology* 109 (February 1974): 216–17.

Bentley-Phillips, B., and Margaret A. H. Bayles. "Correspondence: Acquired Hypomelanosis: Hyperpigmentation Following Reactions to Hydroquinones." *British Journal of Dermatology* 90, no. 232 (1974): 232–33.

Bentley-Phillips, B., and Margaret A. H. Bayles. "Cutaneous Reactions to Topical Application of Hydroquinone." *South African Medical Journal* 49 (August 9, 1975): 1391–95.

Berg, Maxine. *Luxury and Pleasure in Eighteenth-Century Britain*. Oxford: Oxford University Press, 2005.

Berger, Iris. "An African American 'Mother of the Nation': Madie Hall Xuma in South Africa, 1940–1963." *Journal of Southern African Studies* 27, no. 3 (2001): 547–66.

Berger, Iris. *Threads of Solidarity: Women in South African Industry*. Bloomington: Indiana University Press, 1992.

Berglund, Axel-Ivar. *Zulu Thought-Patterns and Symbolism*. Cape Town: David Philip, 1976.

Bergner, Gwen. "Who Is That Masked Woman? Or, the Role of Gender in Fanon's *Black Skin, White Masks*." *PMLA* 110, no. 1 (1995): 75–88.

Berlant, Lauren. *Cruel Optimism*. Durham: Duke University Press, 2011.

Berry, Sarah. *Screen Style: Fashion and Femininity in 1930s Hollywood*. Minneapolis: University of Minnesota Press, 2000.

Bertelsen, Eve. "Ads and Amnesia: Black Advertising in the New South Africa." In *Negotiating the Past: The Making of Memory in South Africa*, edited by Sarah Nuttall and Carli Coetzee, 221–41. Oxford: Oxford University Press, 1998.

Bickford-Smith, Vivian. "Black Ethnicities, Communities, and Political Expression in Late Victorian Cape Town." *Journal of African History* 36, no. 3 (1995): 443–65.

Bickford-Smith, Vivian. *Ethnic Pride and Racial Prejudice in Victorian Cape Town*. Cambridge: Cambridge University Press, 1995.

Bickford-Smith, Vivian, E. van Heyningen, and Nigel Worden. *Cape Town in the Twentieth Century: An Illustrated History*. Claremont, South Africa: David Philip, 1999.

Biko, Steve. "The Definition of Black Consciousness." In *Steve Biko—I Write What I Like*, edited by Aelred Stubbs C.R., 48–53. San Francisco: Harper and Row, 1978.

Biko, Steve. "Some African Cultural Concepts." In *Steve Biko—I Write What I Like*, edited by Aelred Stubbs C.R., 40–47. San Francisco: Harper and Row, 1978.

Biko, Steve. "What Is Black Consciousness?" In *Steve Biko—I Write What I Like*, edited by Aelred Stubbs C.R., 99–119. San Francisco: Harper and Row, 1978.

Biko, Steve. "White Racism and Black Consciousness." In *Steve Biko—I Write What I Like*, edited by Aelred Stubbs C.R., 61–72. San Francisco: Harper and Row, 1978.

Bird, William Wilberforce, and H. T. Colebrooke. *State of the Cape of Good Hope, in 1822*. London: John Murray, 1823.

Blanco-Dávila, Feliciano. "Beauty and the Body: The Origins of Cosmetics." *Plastic and Reconstructive Surgery* 105, no. 3 (2000): 1196–204.

Blay, Yaba. "Ahoofe Kasa! Skin Bleaching and the Function of Beauty among Ghanaian Women." *JENdA: A Journal of Culture and African Women Studies* 14 (2009): 51–85.

Blay, Yaba. "Skin Bleaching and Global White Supremacy: By Way of Introduction." *Journal of Pan African Studies* 4, no. 4 (2011): 4–46.

Blay, Yaba, editor. Special Issue of *JENdA: A Journal of Culture and African Women Studies* 14 (2009).

Blay, Yaba. "Yellow Fever: Skin Bleaching and the Politics of Skin Color in Ghana." Ph.D. diss., Temple University, 2007.

Blay, Yaba, and Christopher A. D. Charles, editors. Special Issue of *Journal of Pan African Studies* 4, no. 4 (2011).

Bloch, Graeme. "Room at the Top?—The Development of South Africa's Manufacturing Industry, 1939–1969." *Social Dynamics* 7, no. 2 (1981): 47–57.

Bonner, P. L. "'Desirable or Undesirable Basotho Women?' Liquor, Prostitution and the Migration of Basotho Women to the Rand, 1920–1945." In *Women and Gender in Southern Africa to 1945*, edited by Cherryl Walker, 221–50. Cape Town: David Philip, 1990.

Bonner, P. L. "The Transvaal Native Congress, 1917–1929: The Radicalisation of the Black Petty Bourgeoisie on the Rand." In *Industrialisation and Social Change in South Africa: African Class Formation, Culture, and Consciousness, 1870–1930*, edited by Shula Marks and Richard Rathbone, 270–313. New York: Longman, 1982.

Boone, Sylvia Ardyn. *Radiance from the Waters: Ideals of Feminine Beauty in Mende Art*. New Haven, CT: Yale University Press, 1986.

Bozzoli, Belinda. "The Origins, Development and Ideology of Local Manufacturing in South Africa." *Journal of Southern African Studies* 1, no. 2 (1975): 194–214.

Bozzoli, Belinda. *Theatres of Struggle and the End of Apartheid.* Johannesburg: Wits University Press, 2004.

Bozzoli, Belinda, with Mmantho Nkotsoe. *Women of Phokeng: Consciousness, Life Strategy, and Migrancy in South Africa, 1900–1983.* Portsmouth, NH: Heinemann, 1991.

Bradford, Helen. "Framing African Women: Visionaries in Southern Africa and Their Photographic Afterlife, 1850–2004." *Kronos* 30 (2004): 70–93.

Brandel-Syrier, Mia. *"Coming Through": The Search for a New Cultural Identity.* Johannesburg: McGraw-Hill, 1978.

Brandel-Syrier, Mia. *Reeftown Elite: A Study of Social Mobility in a Modern African Community on the Reef.* London: Routledge and K. Paul, 1971.

Breckenridge, Keith. *Biometric State: The Global Politics of Identification and Surveillance in South Africa, 1850 to the Present.* Cambridge: Cambridge University Press, 2014.

Breckenridge, Keith, and Gabrielle Hecht. "Confronting African Histories of Technology: A Conversation with Keith Breckenridge and Gabrielle Hecht." *Radical History Review* 127 (January 2017): 87–102.

Brooks, George. "The Signares of Saint Louis and Gorée: Women Entrepreneurs in Eighteenth-Century Senegal." In *Women in Africa: Studies in Social and Economic Change,* edited by Nancy J. Hafkin and Edna G. Bay, 19–44. Stanford, CA: Stanford University Press, 1976.

Broster, Joan A. *The Tembu: Their Beadwork, Songs, and Dances.* New York: Purnell, 1976.

Brown, J. Tom. *Secwana Dictionary: Secwana-English and English-Secwana.* South Africa London Missionary Society, 1925.

Brown, James. "Say It Loud: I'm Black and I'm Proud." *Say It Loud: I'm Black and I'm Proud.* Los Angeles: Vox, 1968.

Brown, Kathleen. *Foul Bodies: Cleanliness in Early America.* New Haven, CT: Yale University Press, 2009.

Brown, Marie Grace. *Khartoum at Night: Fashion and Body Politics in Imperial Sudan.* Stanford, CA: Stanford University Press, 2017.

Brown-Glaude, Winnifred. "Don't Hate Me 'Cause I'm Pretty: Race, Gender and the Bleached Body in Jamaica." *Social and Economic Studies* 62, no. 1 (2013): 53–78.

Brown-Glaude, Winnifred. "The Fact of Blackness? The Bleached Body in Contemporary Jamaica." *small axe* 24 (October 2007): 34–51.

Bruch, Mary K., and Elaine Larson. "An Early Historical Perspective on the FDA's Regulation of OTC Drugs." *Infection Control and Hospital Epidemiology* 10, no. 11 (1989): 527–28.

Buckley, Liam. "Portrait Photography in a Postcolonial Age: How Beauty Tells the Truth." In *Portraiture and Photography in Africa,* edited by John Peffer and Elisabeth L. Cameron, 287–312. Bloomington: Indiana University Press, 2013.

Buggenhagen, Beth. "A Snapshot of Happiness: Photo Albums, Respectability and Economic Uncertainty in Dakar." *Africa* 84, no. 1 (2014): 78–100.

Bunche, Ralph J., and Robert R. Edgar. *An African-American in South Africa: The Travel Notes of Ralph J. Bunche, 28 September 1937–1 January 1938.* Athens: Ohio University Press, 1992.

Bunting, Brian. *Who Runs Our Newspapers? The Story behind the Non-White Press.* Cape Town: New Age, 1959.

Burgess, Thomas. "Cinema, Bell Bottoms, and Miniskirts: Struggles over Youth and Citizenship in Revolutionary Zanzibar." *International Journal of African Historical Studies* 35, no. 2–3 (2002): 287–313.

Burke, Timothy. "'Fork Up and Smile': Marketing, Colonial Knowledge and the Female Subject in Zimbabwe." *Gender and History* 8, no. 3 (1996): 118–34.

Burke, Timothy. *Lifebuoy Men, Lux Women: Commodification, Consumption, and Cleanliness in Modern Zimbabwe.* Durham: Duke University Press, 1996.

Burns, Catherine. "Louisa Mvemve: A Woman's Advice to the Public on the Cure of Various Diseases." *Kronos* 23 (1996): 108–34.

Burns, Catherine. "Reproductive Labors: The Politics of Women's Health in South Africa, 1900 to 1960." Ph.D. diss., Northwestern University, 1995.

Burns, Catherine. "A Useable Past: The Search for 'History in Chords.'" In *History Making and Present-Day Politics: The Meaning of Collective Memory in South Africa,* edited by Hans Erik Stolten, 351–62. Stockholm: Nordiska Afrikainstitutet, 2007.

Buszek, Maria Elena. *Pin-Up Grrrls: Feminism, Sexuality, Popular Culture.* Durham: Duke University Press, 2006.

Califf, Robert M., Jonathan McCall, and Daniel B. Mark. "Cosmetics, Regulations, and the Public Health: Understanding the Safety of Medical and Other Products." *JAMA Internal Medicine* 177, no. 8 (August 2017): 1080–82.

Callaci, Emily. *Street Archives and City Life: Popular Intellectuals in Postcolonial Tanzania.* Durham: Duke University Press, 2017.

Callaway, Henry. *Nursery Tales, Traditions, and Histories of the Zulus, in Their Own Words, with a Translation into English, Volume I.* Westport, CT: Negro Universities, 1970. (Originally published in 1868).

Camp, Stephanie M. H. "Black Is Beautiful: An American History." *Journal of Southern History* 81, no. 3 (2015): 675–90.

Campbell, Alec, Larry Robbins, and Michael Taylor, editors. *Tsodilo Hills: Copper Bracelet of the Kalahari.* East Lansing: Michigan State University Press, 2010.

Campbell, James. "The Americanization of South Africa." In *"Here, There and Everywhere": The Foreign Politics of American Popular Culture,* edited by R. Wagnleitner and E. May, 34–63. Hanover, NH: University of New England Press, 2000.

Campbell, James. *Songs of Zion: The African Methodist Episcopal Church in the United States and South Africa.* Chapel Hill: University of North Carolina Press, 1995.

Campbell, James. "T. D. Mweli Skota and the Making and Unmaking of a Black Elite." Unpublished paper presented to the University of the Witwatersrand History Workshop, February 9–14, 1987.

Campt, Tina. *Image Matters: Archive, Photography, and the African Diaspora in Europe.* Durham: Duke University Press, 2012.

Canizares, O., F. U. Jaramillo, and F. K. Vegas. "Leukomelanoderma Subsequent to the Application of Monobenzyl Ether of Hydroquinone: A Vitiligoid Reaction Observed in Columbia and Venezuela." *AMA Archives of Dermatology* 77 (1958): 220–23.

Carman, H. A. "Memorandum on the Use of Skin Lightening Creams in South Africa with Specific Reference to Hydroquinone-Containing Preparations." *Integument: Newsletter of the Dermatological Society of South Africa* (1987): 8–11.

Carpenter, Daniel P. *Reputation and Power: Organizational Image and Pharmaceutical Regulation at the FDA*. Princeton, NJ: Princeton University Press, 2010.

Carson, Rachel. *Silent Spring*. New York: Houghton Mifflin, 1962.

Cell, John W. *The Highest Stage of White Supremacy: The Origins of Segregation in South Africa and the American South*. Cambridge: Cambridge University Press, 1982.

Charles, Christopher A. D. "Liberating Skin Bleachers: From Mental Pathology to Complex Personhood." *JENdA: A Journal of Culture and African Women Studies* 14 (2009): 86–100.

Cheng, Anne Anlin. *Second Skin: Josephine Baker and the Modern Surface*. New York: Oxford University Press, 2011.

Chilson, Francis. *Modern Cosmetics: The Formulation and Production of Cosmetics, Together with a Discussion of Modern Production and Packaging Methods and Equipment*. New York: Drug and Cosmetic Industry, 1934.

Clark, G. Robert. "The Federal Food Drug, and Cosmetic Act and the Cosmetic Chemist." In *Cosmetics: Science and Technology*, edited by Edward Sagarin, 1277–316. New York: Interscience, 1957.

Clarke, Christa. *The Activist Collector: An African American Woman in Pre-Apartheid South Africa*. Newark, NJ: Newark Museum and Lucia/Marquand, forthcoming.

Clowes, Lindsay. "'Are You Going to Be MISS (or MR) Africa?' Contesting Masculinity in *Drum* Magazine, 1951–1953." *Gender and History* 13, no. 1 (2001): 1–20.

Clowes, Lindsay. "'A Modernised Man? Changing Constructions of Masculinity in *Drum* Magazine, 1951–1984." Ph.D. diss., University of Cape Town, 2002.

Cock, Jacklyn. "Domestic Service and Education for Domesticity: The Incorporation of Xhosa Women into Colonial Society." In *Women and Gender in Southern Africa to 1945*, edited by Cherryl Walker, 76–96. Cape Town: David Philip, 1990.

Cohen, Colleen Ballerino, Richard R. Wilk, and Beverly Stoeltje. "Introduction: Beauty Queens on the Global Stage." In *Beauty Queens on the Global Stage: Gender, Contests, and Power*, edited by Colleen Ballerino Cohen, Richard R. Wilk, and Beverly Stoeltje, 1–11. New York: Routledge, 1996.

Cohen, Lizabeth. *A Consumers' Republic: The Politics of Mass Consumption in Postwar America*. New York: Knopf, 2003.

Cole, Jennifer. *Sex and Salvation: Imagining the Future in Madagascar*. Chicago: University of Chicago Press, 2010.

Coleman, Deirdre. "Janet Schaw and the Complexions of Empire." *Eighteenth-Century Studies* 36, no. 2 (2003): 169–93.

Colenso, John W. *Zulu-English Dictionary*. Fourth edition. Natal: Vause, Slatter, 1905. (Originally published in 1861.)

Colson, Elizabeth, and Thayer Scudder. *For Prayer and Profit: The Ritual, Economic, and Social Importance of Beer in Gwembe District, Zambia, 1950–1982*. Stanford, CA: Stanford University Press, 1988.

Comaroff, Jean. *Body of Power, Spirit of Resistance: The Culture and History of a South African People*. Chicago: University of Chicago Press, 1985.

Comaroff, Jean. "The Empire's Old Clothes: Fashioning the Colonial Subject." In *Cross-Cultural Consumption: Global Markets, Local Realities*, edited by David Howes, 19–38. New York: Routledge, 1996.

Comaroff, Jean. "Medicine, Colonialism, and the Black Body." In *Ethnography and the Historical Imagination*, edited by John L. Comaroff and Jean Comaroff, 215–34. Boulder, CO: Westview, 1992.

Comaroff, Jean, and John L. Comaroff. *Ethnography and the Historical Imagination*. Boulder, CO: Westview, 1992.

Comaroff, Jean, and John L. Comaroff. "Occult Economies and the Violence of Abstraction: Notes from the South African Postcolony." *American Ethnologist* 26, no. 2 (May 1999): 279–303.

Comaroff, Jean, and John L. Comaroff. *Of Revelation and Revolution: The Dialectics of Modernity on a South African Frontier*. Vol. 2. Chicago: University of Chicago Press, 1991.

Conor, Liz. *The Spectacular Modern Woman: Feminine Visibility in the 1920s*. Bloomington: Indiana University Press, 2004.

Cook, Ernest Fullerton, Charles H. LaWall, and Joseph P. Remington. *Remington's Practice of Pharmacy*. Eighth edition. Philadelphia: J. B. Lippincott, 1936.

Cooper, Frederick. *Africa since 1940: The Past of the Present*. Cambridge: Cambridge University Press, 2002.

Copeland, Senator Royal S. "Protection for the Public." *Scientific American* (November 1938): 257–58.

Coplan, David. "The African Musician and the Development of the Johannesburg Entertainment Industry, 1900–1960." *Journal of Southern African Studies* 5, no. 2 (April 1979): 135–64.

Coplan, David. *In Township Tonight! South Africa's Black City Music and Theatre*. Chicago: University of Chicago Press, 1985.

Coplan, David. "South Africa Radio in a Saucepan." In *Radio in Africa: Publics, Cultures, Communities*, edited by Liz Gunner, Dina Ligaga, and Dumisani Moyo, 134–48. Johannesburg: Wits University Press, 2011.

Coplan, David. "You Have Left Me Wandering About: Basotho Women and the Culture of Mobility." In *"Wicked" Women and the Reconfiguration of Gender in Africa*, edited by Dorothy Hodgson and Sheryl McCurdy, 188–211. Portsmouth, NH: Heinemann, 2001.

Cornwell, Lee. "Letter to the Editor: Skin Lighteners and Professional Ethics." *South African Pharmaceutical Journal* 45, no. 6 (June 1978): 216.

Corsi, Jerome R. *The Obama Nation: Leftist Politics and the Cult of Personality*. New York: Threshold Books, 2008.

Couzens, Tim. "'Moralizing Leisure Time': The Transatlantic Connection and Black Johannesburg (1918–1936)." In *Industrialisation and Social Change in South Africa: African Class Formation, Culture, and Consciousness, 1870–1930*, edited by Shula Marks and Richard Rathbone, 314–37. New York: Longman, 1982.

Couzens, Tim. *The New African: A Study of the Life and Work of H. I. E. Dhlomo.* Johannesburg: Ravan, 1985.

Couzens, Tim. "A Short History of 'World' (and Other Black SA Newspapers)." *Inspan Journal* 1, no. 1 (1978): 69–92.

Craig, Maxine. *Ain't I a Beauty Queen? Black Women, Beauty, and the Politics of Race.* Oxford: Oxford University Press, 2002.

Craig, Maxine. "The Decline and Fall of the Conk; Or, How to Read a Process." *Fashion Theory* 1, no. 4 (1997): 399–420.

Cramp, Arthur J. *Nostrums and Quackery: Articles on the Nostrum Evil, Quackery and Allied Matters Affecting the Public Health; Reprinted, with or without Modifications, from the Journal of the American Medical Association.* Chicago: Press of the American Medical Association, 1911–36.

Cramp, Arthur J. *Nostrums and Quackery and Pseudo-Medicine.* Vol. 3. Chicago: American Medical Association, 1936.

Crankshaw, Owen. "Class, Race and Residence in Black Johannesburg, 1923–1970." *Journal of Historical Sociology* 18, no. 4 (2005): 353–93.

Crenshaw, Kimberlé W. "Mapping the Margins: Intersectionality, Identity Politics, and Violence against Women of Color." *Stanford Law Review* 43, no. 6 (1991): 1241–99.

Crush, Jonathan, and Charles Ambler, editors. *Liquor and Labor in Southern Africa.* Athens: Ohio University Press, 1992.

"CTFA Statement on Hydroquinone." May 15, 2007. Accessed November 27, 2017. https://www.personalcarecouncil.org/newsroom/20070501.

Curran, R. E. "British Food and Drug Law—A History." *Food Drug Cosmetic Law Journal* 6, no. 4 (April 1951): 247–68.

Davids, Lester M., Jennifer C. van Wyk, and Nonhlanhla P. Khumalo. "Intravenous Glutathione for Skin Lightening: Inadequate Safety Data." *South African Medical Journal* 106, no. 8 (2016): 782–86.

Davids, Lester M., Jennifer C. van Wyk, Nonhlanhla P. Khumalo, and Nina G. Jablonski. "The Phenomena of Skin Lightening: Is It Right to Be Light?" *South African Journal of Science* 112, no. 11/12 (2016): 1–5.

Davis, Angela Y. "Afro Images: Politics, Fashion, and Nostalgia." *Critical Inquiry* 21 (Autumn 1994): 37–45.

Daymond, M. J., Dorothy Driver, Sheila Meintjes, Leloba Molema, Chiedza Musengezi, Margie Orford, and Nobantu Rasebotsa, editors. *Women Writing Africa: The Southern Region.* New York: Feminist Press at the City University of New York, 2003.

De la Pena, Carolyn Thomas. "'Bleaching the Ethiopian': Desegregating Race and Technology through Early X-Ray Experiments." *Technology and Culture* 47 (January 2006): 27–55.

De Lange, M. "Some Traditional Cosmetic Practices of the Xhosa." *Annual Cape Provincial Museum* 3 (1963): 85–95.

Decary, Raymond. *Mœurs et coutumes des Malgaches.* Paris: Payot, 1951.

Decker, Alicia C. *In Idi Amin's Shadow, Gender, and Militarism in Uganda.* Athens: Ohio University Press, 2014.

Deford, Frank. *There She Is: The Life and Times of Miss America.* New York: Viking, 1971.

Denton, Cleveland R., Aaron B. Lerner, and Thomas B. Fitzpatrick. "Inhibition of Melanin Formation by Chemical Agents." *Journal of Investigative Dermatology* 18, no. 2 (1952): 119–35.

Deppe, R. K. "A Comparative Study of Motives Observed in Selected Pictorial Advertisements Directed at the Bantu." Research Report No. 39, Bureau of Market Research, University of South Africa. Pretoria, 1974.

Deppe, R. K. "A Study of the Attitudes of Urban Blacks to Advertising." Research Report No. 38, Bureau of Market Research, University of South Africa. Pretoria, 1975.

Dhlomo, R. R. R. *An African Tragedy*. Lovedale, South Africa: Lovedale Institution, 1928.

Dhlomo, R. R. R. "An Experiment in Colour." *African Observer* 3, no. 4 (August 1935): 67–80. Republished in *H. I. E. Dhlomo Collected Works*, edited by Nick Visser and Tim Couzens. Johannesburg: Ravan, 1985.

Diamandopoulos, A., L. Kolonas, and M. Grapsa-Kotrotsou. "Use of Lead Cosmetics in Bronze-Age Greece." *Lancet* 344 (1994): 754–55.

A Dictionary of South African English on Historical Principles. Oxford: Oxford University Press, 1996.

Digby-Junger, Richard. "The *Guardian, Crisis, Messenger*, and *Negro World*: The Early-20th-Century Black Radical Press." *Howard Journal of Communications* 9, no. 3 (1998): 263–82.

Dlamini, Jacob. *Native Nostalgia*. Sunnyside, South Africa: Jacana Media, 2009.

Dlova, Ncoza C., Saja H. Hamed, Joyce Tsoka-Gwegweni, and Anneke Grobler. "Skin Lightening Practices: An Epidemiological Study of South African Women of African and Indian Ancestries." *British Journal of Dermatology* 173, no. 52 (July 2015): 2–9.

Dlova, Ncoza C., Saja H. Hamed, Joyce Tsoka-Gwegweni, Anneke Grobler, and Richard Hift. "Women's Perceptions of the Benefits and Risks of Skin-Lightening Creams in Two South African Communities." *Journal of Cosmetic Dermatology* 13 (2014): 236–44.

Dlova, Ncoza C., Nicole E. Hendricks, and Bice S. Martincigh. "Skin-Lightening Creams Used in South Africa." *International Journal of Dermatology* 51, Suppl. 1 (2012): 51–53.

Dlova, Ncoza C., Funanani T. Nevondo, Elizabeth M. Mwangi, Beverley Summers, Joyce Tsoka-Gwegweni, Bice S. Martincigh, and Dulcie A. Mulholland. "Chemical Analysis and *in vitro* UV-Protection Characteristics of Clays Traditionally Used for Sun Protection in South Africa." *Photodermatology, Photoimmunology and Photomedicine* 29 (2013): 164–69.

Dogliotti, M., I. Caro, R. G. Hartdegen, and D. A. Whiting. "Leucomelanoderma in Blacks: A Recent Epidemic." *South African Medical Journal* 48 (August 3, 1974): 1555–58.

Dogliotti, M., and M. Leibowitz. "Granulomatous Ochronosis—a Cosmetic-Induced Skin Disorder in Blacks." *South African Medical Journal* 56, no. 19 (1979): 757–60.

Doke, C. M., and B. W. Vilakazi. *Zulu-English Dictionary*. Johannesburg: Witwatersrand University Press, 1948.

Dooling, Wayne. "Poverty and Respectability in Early Twentieth-Century Cape Town." *Journal of African History* 59, no. 3 (2018): 411–35.

Dorman, Jacob S. "Skin Bleach and Civilization: The Racial Formation of Blackness in 1920s Harlem." *Journal of Pan African Studies* 4, no. 4 (2011): 47–80.

Dorsey, Clete S. "Dermatitic and Pigmentary Reactions to Monobenzyl Ether of Hydroquinone." *AMA Archives of Dermatology* 81, no. 2 (1960): 123–26.

Downing, John Godwin. "Cosmetics—Past and Present." *Journal of the American Medical Association* 102, no. 25 (1934): 2088–91.

Draelos, Zoe Diana. "Skin Lightening Preparations and the Hydroquinone Controversy." *Dermatologic Therapy* 20 (2007): 308–13.

Drew, Allison. *Discordant Comrades: Identities and Loyalties on the South African Left.* Burlington, VT: Ashgate, 2000.

Driver, Dorothy. "*Drum* Magazine (1951–9) and the Spatial Configurations of Gender." In *Text, Theory, Space: Land, Literature and History in South Africa and Australia,* edited by Kate Darian-Smith, Liz Gunner, and Sarah Nuttall, 231–42. London: Routledge, 1996.

"Drug and Cosmetic Provisions of the Federal Food, Drug, and Cosmetic Act and General Regulations for Its Enforcement." In *Cosmetics Science and Technology,* edited by Edward Sagarin, 1265–76. New York: Interscience, 1957.

Dubow, Saul. *Scientific Racism in Modern South Africa.* Cambridge: Cambridge University Press, 1995.

Dyer, Richard. *White: Essays on Race and Culture.* New York: Routledge, 1997.

Eales, Kathy. "Patriarchs, Passes, and Privilege: Johannesburg's African Middle Classes and the Question of Night Passes for African Women, 1920–1932." In *Holding Their Ground: Class, Locality, and Culture in Nineteenth- and Twentieth-Century South Africa,* edited by P. Bonner, I. Hofmeyr, D. James, and T. Lodge, 105–39. Johannesburg: Ravan, 1989.

Earle, Roxanne. "Can the Nubian Change His Skin, or the Leopard His Spots?" *African Wildlife* 30, no. 6 (1976): 8.

Ebrahim-Vally, Rehana. "Beauty and Race in the South African Context." Unpublished paper presented at "The Burden of Race?" conference at University of Witwatersrand, Johannesburg, July 2001.

Edmonds, Alexander. "The Biological Subject of Aesthetic Medicine." *Feminist Theory* 14, no. 1 (2013): 65–82.

Eiselen, W. W. M. (Delivered in his absence by Mr. Turton, Chief Commissioner for Bantu Affairs in Natal). "The Elasticity of the Bantu Consumer Market." In *Second Advertising Convention in South Africa, Sponsored by the Society of Advertisers Ltd., Durban, 21st–24th September, 1959.* Johannesburg: Statistic Holdings (Pty.) Ltd., 1959.

El Hamel, Chouki. *Black Morocco: A History of Slavery, Race, and Islam.* Cambridge: Cambridge University Press, 2013.

Elphick, Richard, and Hermann Giliomee, editors. *The Shaping of South African Society, 1652–1840.* Second edition. Middleton, CT: Wesleyan University Press, 1988.

Elphick, Richard, and Robert Shell. "Intergroup Relations: Khoikhoi, Settlers, Slaves and Free Blacks, 1652–1795." In *The Shaping of South African Society, 1652–1840,* edited by Richard Elphick and Hermann Giliomee, 184–239. Second edition. Middleton, CT: Wesleyan University Press, 1988.

Erasmus, Zimitri, editor. *Coloured by History, Shaped by Place: New Perspectives on Coloured Identities in Cape Town.* Colorado Springs, CO: International Academic, 2001.

Erasmus, Zimitri. "Hair Politics." In *Senses of Culture: South African Culture Studies,* edited by Sarah Nuttall and Cheryl-Ann Michael, 380–92. Oxford: Oxford University Press, 2000.

Erasmus, Zimitri. *Race Otherwise: Forging a New Humanism in South Africa.* Johannesburg: Wits University Press, 2017.

Erickson, Peter. "'God for Harry, England, and Saint George': British National Identity and the Emergence of White Self-Fashioning." In *Early Modern Visual Culture: Representation, Race, Empire in Renaissance England,* edited by Peter Erickson and Clark Hulse, 315–45. Philadelphia: University of Pennsylvania Press, 2000.

Erlank, Natasha. "Gender and Masculinity in South African Nationalist Discourse, 1912–1950." *Feminist Studies* 29, no. 3 (2003): 653–71.

Erlmann, Veit. *African Stars: Studies in Black South African Performance.* Chicago: University of Chicago Press, 1991.

Erlmann, Veit. *Music, Modernity, and the Global Imagination: South Africa and the West.* New York: Oxford University Press, 1999.

European Communities. "Twenty-Fourth Commission Directive 2000/6/EC of 29 February 2000 Adapting to Technical Progress Annexes II, III, VI and VII to Council Directive 75/768/EEC on the Approximation of the Laws of the Member States Relating to Cosmetic Products." *Official Journal of the European Communities* (March 1, 2000): 42–44.

Fair, Laura. *Pastimes and Politics: Culture, Community, and Identity in Post-Abolition Urban Zanzibar, 1890–1945.* Athens: Ohio University Press, 2000.

Fanon, Frantz. *Black Skin, White Masks.* Translated by Richard Philcox. New York: Grove Press, 2008. (Originally published in French in 1952.)

Feinstein, C. H. *An Economic History of South Africa: Conquest, Discrimination, and Development.* New York: Cambridge University Press, 2005.

Feldman, David, J. Wesley Pike, and John S. Adams. *Vitamin D.* New York: Academic, 2011.

Feldstein, Ruth. *How It Feels to Be Free: Black Women Entertainers and the Civil Rights Movement.* New York: Oxford University Press, 2013.

Felski, Rita. "'Because It Is Beautiful': New Feminist Perspectives on Beauty." *Feminist Theory* 7, no. 2 (2006): 273–82.

Fenner, Byron. *Fenner's Twentieth Century Formulary and International Dispensatory: A Complete Formulary and Hand-Book.* Westfield, NY: B. Fenner, 1904.

Ferguson, James. *Expectations of Modernity: Myths and Meanings of Urban Life on the Zambian Copperbelt.* Berkeley: University of California Press, 1999.

Ferme, Mariane C. *The Underneath of Things: Violence, History, and the Everyday in Sierra Leone.* Berkeley: University of California Press, 2001.

Fernandes, Des. "Hydroquinone—A Harmful Agent." *South African Medical Journal* (September 20, 1990): 829.

Festa, Lynn. "Cosmetic Differences: The Changing Faces of England and France." *Studies in Eighteenth Century Culture* 34 (2005): 25–54.

Feyder, Sophie. "Portraits of Resilience: Writing a Socio-Cultural History of a Black South African Location with the Ngilima Photographic Collection, Benoni, 1950s–1960s." Ph.D. diss., Leiden University, 2016.

Feyder, Sophie. "A Space of One's Own: Studio Photography and the Making of Black Urban Femininities in the 1950s East Rand." *Safundi: The Journal of South African and American Studies* 15, nos. 2–3 (2014): 227–54.

Fieldhouse, David K. "Unilever in South Africa." *South African Journal of Economic History: Economic Interpretations of 19th Century Imperialism* 11, no. 2 (1996): 144–93.

Findlay, George. *Miscegenation: A Study of the Biological Sources of Inheritance of the South African European Population.* Pretoria: Pretoria News and Printing Works, 1936.

Findlay, G. H. "Ochronosis Following Skin Bleaching with Hydroquinone." *American Academy of Dermatology Journal* 6, no. 6 (June 1982): 1092–93.

Findlay, G. H., and H. A. De Beer. "Chronic Hydroquinone Poisoning of the Skin from Skin-Lightening Cosmetics: A South African Epidemic of Ochronosis of the Face in Dark-Skinned Individuals." *South African Medical Journal* 57, no. 6 (1980): 187–90.

Findlay, G. H., J. G. L. Morrison, and I. W. Simson. "Exogenous Ochronosis and Pigmented Colloid Milium from Hydroquinone Bleaching Creams." *British Journal of Dermatology* 93 (1975): 613–22.

Fleming, Tyler, and Toyin Falola. "Africa's Media Empire: Drum's Expansion to Nigeria." *History in Africa* 32 (2005): 133–64.

Flint, Karen. "Competition, Race, and Professionalization: African Healers and White Medical Practitioners in Natal, South Africa in the Early Twentieth Century." *Social History of Medicine* 14 (2001): 199–221.

Flint, Karen. *Healing Traditions: African Medicine, Cultural Exchange, and Competition in South Africa, 1820–1948.* Athens: Ohio University Press, 2008.

Ford, Tanisha C. *Liberated Threads: Black Women, Style, and the Global Politics of Soul.* Chapel Hill: University of North Carolina Press, 2015.

Forman, L. "A Note on the Depigmentation Properties of Monobenzylether of Hydroquinone." *British Journal of Dermatology* 65, no. 11 (November 1953): 406–9.

Frazier, E. Franklin. *Black Bourgeoisie.* Glencoe, IL: Free Press, 1957.

Frederikse, Julie, Keyan Tomaselli, Joe Muller, and Muff Anderson. *Culture and the Media: How We Are Made to See.* Durban: Contemporary Cultural Studies Unit, 1985.

Fredrickson, George. *Black Liberation: A Comparative History of Black Ideologies in the United States and South Africa.* Oxford: Oxford University Press, 1995.

Fredrickson, George. *Racism: A Short History.* Princeton, NJ: Princeton University Press, 2002.

Fredrickson, George. *White Supremacy: A Comparative Study in American and South African History.* New York: Oxford University Press, 1981.

Friedel, Evelyne A. "Regulation of Cosmetics in the Common Market." *Food Drug Cosmetic Law Journal* 46, no. 3 (1991): 429–40.

Friedman, Jonathan. "The Political Economy of Elegance: An African Cult of Beauty." In *Consumption and Identity,* edited by Jonathan Friedman, 167–87. Chur, Switzerland: Harwood Academic, 1994.

Gaines, Jane. "*The Scar of Shame*: Skin Color and Caste in Black Silent Melodrama." In *Representing Blackness: Issues in Film and Video*, edited by Valerie Smith, 61–81. New Brunswick, NJ: Rutgers University Press, 1997.

Gaines, Kevin. *Uplifting the Race: Black Leadership, Politics, and Culture in the Twentieth Century*. Chapel Hill: University of North Carolina Press, 1996.

Gaitskell, Deborah, Judy Kimble, Moira Maconachie, and Elaine Unterhalter. "Class, Race and Gender: Domestic Workers in South Africa." *Review of African Political Economy* 10, no. 27/28 (1983): 86–108.

Garvey, Amy Jacques. "I Am a Negro—and Beautiful." In *Modern Black Nationalism: From Marcus Garvey to Louis Farrakhan*, edited by William Van Deburg. New York: New York University Press, 1997. (Originally published in *Negro World*, July 20, 1926.)

Garvey, Marcus. "The 'Colored' or Negro Press." In *Philosophy and Opinions of Marcus Garvey or Africa for the Africans*, compiled by Amy Jacques Garvey. Dover, MA: Majority, 1986. (Originally published c. 1919–23.)

Gastrow, Shelagh. "Elizabeth Hendrina Venter." In *Who's Who in South African Politics*, third revised edition, 351–52. London: Hans Zell, 1990.

Gatewood, Willard. *Aristocrats of Color: The Black Elite, 1880–1920*. Bloomington: Indiana University Press, 1990.

George, Timothy. *Minamata: Pollution and the Struggle for Democracy in Postwar Japan*. Cambridge, MA: Harvard University Press, 2002.

Gerhart, Gail. *Black Power in South Africa*. Berkeley: University of California Press, 1978.

Gettens, Rutherford J., Hermann Kühn, and W. T. Chase. "Lead White." In *Artists' Pigments: A Handbook of Their History and Characteristics*, vol. 2, edited by Ashok Roy. Washington, DC: National Gallery of Art, 1986.

Gibbons, Ann. "How Africans Evolved a Palette of Skin Tones." *Science* 358, no. 6360 (October 13, 2017): 157–58.

Gill, Tiffany M. *Beauty Shop Politics: African American Women's Activism in the Beauty Industry*. Urbana: University of Illinois Press, 2010.

Ginsburg, Rebecca. *At Home with Apartheid: The Hidden Landscapes of Domestic Service in Johannesburg*. Charlottesville: University of Virginia Press, 2011.

Glaser, Clive. *Bo-Tsotsi: The Youth Gangs of Soweto, 1935–1976*. Portsmouth, NH: Heinemann, 2000.

Glassman, Jonathon. *War of Words, War of Stones: Racial Thought and Violence in Colonial Zanzibar*. Bloomington: Indiana University Press, 2011.

Glenn, Evelyn Nakano. "Consuming Lightness: Segmented Markets and Global Capital in the Skin-Whitening Trade." In *Shades of Difference: Why Skin Color Matters*, edited by Evelyn Nakano Glenn, 166–89. Stanford, CA: Stanford University Press, 2008.

Glenn, Evelyn Nakano, editor. *Shades of Difference: Why Skin Color Matters*. Stanford, CA: Stanford University Press, 2008.

"Global Perspectives on Colorism." Special Issue of *Washington University Global Studies Law Review* 14, no. 4 (2015).

Goeckerman, William H. "A Peculiar Discoloration of the Skin." *Journal of the American Medical Association* 84, no. 7 (1925): 606–7.

Goldin, Ian. *Making Race: The Politics and Economics of Coloured Identity in South Africa*. New York: Longman, 1987.

Goodhew, David. *Respectability and Resistance: A History of Sophiatown*. Westport, CT: Praeger, 2004.

Goodhew, David. "Working-Class Respectability: The Example of the Western Areas of Johannesburg, 1930–55." *Journal of African History* 41, no. 2 (2000): 241–66.

Gordon, Lady Duff. *Letters from the Cape*. Edited by John Purves. London: Humphrey Milford, 1921.

Gqola, Pumla Dineo. "Contradictory Locations: Blackwomen and the Discourse of the Black Consciousness Movement (BCM) in South Africa." *Meridians: Feminism, Race, Transnationalism* 2, no. 1 (2001): 130–52.

Green, Adam. *Selling the Race: Culture, Community, and Black Chicago, 1940–1955*. Chicago: University of Chicago Press, 2007.

Greenberg, Leon A., and David Lester. *Handbook of Cosmetic Materials: Their Properties, Uses, Toxic and Dermatologic Actions*. New York: Interscience, 1954.

Groenewald, Gerald. "Slaves and Free Blacks in VOC Cape Town, 1652–1795." *History Compass* 8, no. 9 (2010): 964–83.

Guelke, Leonard. "Freehold Farmers and Frontier Settlers, 1657–1780." In *The Shaping of South African Society, 1652–1840*, second edition, edited by Richard Elphick and Hermann Giliomee, 66–108. Middletown, CT: Wesleyan University Press, 1988.

Gunn, Fenja. *The Artificial Face: A History of Cosmetics*. New York: Hippocrene, 1973.

Gupta, Pamila, and Gabrielle Hecht, editors. "Toxicity, Waste, Detritus in the Global South: Africa and Beyond." Special Issue of *Somatosphere* (2017–18). Accessed July 4, 2018. http://somatosphere.net/toxicity.

Guthrie, L. M. "Successes and Failures in Bantu Marketing—the Lessons to Be Learned." In *The Urban Bantu Market: Understanding Its Complexities and Developing Its Potential—Proceedings of a 2-Day Seminar Held in February 1969, Durban, Natal*, National Development and Management Foundation, 63–74. Johannesburg: National Development and Management Foundation of South Africa, 1969.

Guyer, Jane, and Samuel Belinga. "Wealth in People as Wealth in Knowledge: Accumulation and Composition in Equatorial Africa." *Journal of African History* 36, no. 1 (1995): 91.

Gwilliam, Tassie. "Cosmetic Poetics: Coloring Faces in the Eighteenth Century." In *Body and Text in the Eighteenth Century*, edited by Veronica Kelly and Dorothea Von Mücke, 144–59. Stanford, CA: Stanford University Press, 1994.

Hadfield, Leslie A. *Liberation and Development: Black Consciousness Community Programs in South Africa*. East Lansing: Michigan State University Press, 2016.

Hall, Bruce. *A History of Race in Muslim West Africa, 1600–1960*. Cambridge: Cambridge University Press, 2014.

Hall, Kim. *Things of Darkness: Economies of Race and Gender in Early Modern England*. Ithaca, NY: Cornell University Press, 1995.

Hall, R. E., editor. *The Melanin Millennium: Skin Color as 21st Century International Discourse*. Dordrecht: Springer, 2013.

Hall, Ronald. *An Empirical Analysis of the Impact of Skin Color on African-American Education, Income, and Occupation*. New York: Mellen, 2005.

Hall, Simon. "Farming Communities of the Second Millennium: Internal Frontiers, Identity, Continuity and Change." In *Cambridge History of South Africa, Volume I, From Early Times to 1885,* edited by Carolyn Hamilton, Bernard K. Mbenga, and Robert Ross, 112–67. Cambridge: Cambridge University Press, 2010.

Hall, Stuart. "What Is This 'Black' in Black Popular Culture?" In *Black Popular Culture,* edited by Gina Dent, 21–36. New York: New Press, 1998.

Hamann, Carsten R., Waranya Boonchai, Liping Wen, Emi Nishijima Sakanashi, Chia-Yu Chu, Kylin Hamann, Curtis P. Hamann, Kumar Sinniah, and Dathan Hamann. "Spectrometric Analysis of Mercury Content in 549 Skin-Lightening Products: Is Mercury Toxicity a Hidden Global Health Hazard?" *Journal of American Academy of Dermatology* 70, no. 2 (2014): 281–86.

Hamm, Charles. "'The Constant Companion of Man': Separate Development, Radio Bantu and Music." *Popular Music* 10, no. 2 (May 1991): 147–73.

Hamsi (Marie Kathleen Jeffreys), with an introduction by Meg Samuelson. "Though I Am Black, I Am Comely." In *Women Writing Africa: The Southern Region,* edited by M. J. Daymond, Dorothy Driver, Sheila Meintjes, Leloba Molema, Chiedza Musengezi, Margie Orford, and Nobantu Rasebotsa, 229–31. New York: Feminist Press at the City University of New York, 2003.

Hanretta, Sean. "Women, Marginality and the Zulu State: Women's Institutions and Power in the Early Nineteenth Century." *Journal of African History* 39, no. 3 (1998): 389–415.

Hansen, Devon. "Shades of Change: Suntanning and the Twentieth-Century American Dream." Ph.D. diss., Boston University, 2007.

Hansen, Karen Tranberg. *Distant Companions: Servants and Employers in Zambia, 1900–1985.* Ithaca, NY: Cornell University Press, 1989.

Hansen, Karen Tranberg. *Salaula: The World of Secondhand Clothing and Zambia.* Chicago: University of Chicago Press, 2000.

Hansen, Karen Tranberg, and D. Soyini Madison, editors. *African Dress: Fashion, Agency, Performance.* London: Bloomsbury Academic, 2013.

Harada, Masazumi, Shigeharu Nakachi, Taketo Cheu, Hirotaka Hamada, Yuko Ono, Toshihide Tsuda, Kohichi Yanagida, Takako Kizaki, and Hideki Ohno. "Monitoring of Mercury Pollution in Tanzania: Relation between Head Hair Mercury and Health." *Science of the Total Environment* 227 (1999): 249–56.

Harada, Masazumi, Shigeharu Nakachi, Koa Tasaka, Sakae Sakashita, Kazue Muta, Kohichi Yanagida, Rikuo Doi, Takako Kizaki, and Hideki Ohno. "Wide Use of Skin-Lightening Soap May Cause Mercury Poisoning in Kenya." *Science of the Total Environment* 269 (2001): 183–87.

Hardon, Anita, and Emilia Sanabria. "Fluid Drugs: Revisiting the Anthropology of Pharmaceuticals." *Annual Review of Anthropology* 46 (2017): 117–32.

Hardwick, N., L. W. van Gelder, C. A. van der Merwe, and M. P. van der Merwe. "Exogenous Ochronosis: An Epidemiological Study." *British Journal of Dermatology* 120 (1989): 229–38.

Harries, Patrick. "Photography and the Rise of Anthropology: Henri-Alexandre Junod and the Thonga of Mozambique and South Africa." *Encounters with Photography.* Accessed November 10, 2001. http://www.museums.org.za/sam/conf/enc/harries.htm.

Harris, Angela P. "Introduction: Economies of Color." In *Shades of Difference: Why Skin Color Matters*, edited by Evelyn Nakano Glenn, 1–5. Stanford, CA: Stanford University Press, 2008.

Harris, John E. "Did Michael Jackson Have Vitiligo?" January 19, 2016. Accessed March 12, 2017. http://www.umassmed.edu/vitiligo/blog/blog-posts1/2016/01/did -michael-jackson-have-vitiligo/.

Hart, Gillian. "Denaturalizing Dispossession: Critical Ethnography in the Age of Resurgent Imperialism." *Antipode* 38, no. 5 (2006): 977–1004.

Hassim, Shireen. *Women's Organizations and Democracy in South Africa: Contesting Authority*. Madison: University of Wisconsin Press, 2006.

Hayes, Patricia. "Introduction: Visual Genders." *Gender and History* 17, no. 3 (2006): 519–37.

Hayes, Patricia, and Andrew Bank, guest editors. *Kronos*. Special Issue: Visual History 27 (2001).

Hayman, Graham, and Ruth Tomaselli. "Ideology and Technology in the Growth of South African Broadcasting, 1924–1997." In *Currents of Power: State Broadcasting in South Africa*, edited by Ruth Tomaselli, Keyan Tomaselli, and Johan Muller, 23–83. Bellville, South Africa: Anthropos, 1989.

Hecht, Gabrielle. *Being Nuclear: Africans in the Global Uranium Trade*. Cambridge, MA: MIT Press, 2012.

Hellmann, Ellen. "Native Life in a Johannesburg Slum Yard." *Africa* 8, no. 1 (1935): 34–62.

Hellmann, Ellen. *Rooiyard: A Sociological Survey of an Urban Native Slum Yard*. Cape Town: Oxford University Press, Rhodes-Livingstone Papers No. 13, 1948.

Hendrickson, Hildi, editor. *Clothing and Difference: Embodied Identities in Colonial and Post-Colonial Africa*. Durham: Duke University Press, 1996.

Henshilwood, Christopher S., Francesco d'Errico, Karen L. van Nieker, Yvan Coquinot, Zenobia Jacobs, Stein-Erik Lauritzen, Michel Menu, and Renata Garcia-Moreno. "A 100,000-Year-Old Ochre-Processing Workshop at Blombos Cave, South Africa." *Science* 334 (October 14, 2011): 219–22.

Henshilwood, Christopher S., Francesco d'Errico, and Ian Watts. "Engraved Ochres from the Middle Stone Ages Levels at Blombos Cave, South Africa." *Journal of Human Evolution* 57 (2009): 27–47.

Herring, Cedric, Verna M. Keith, and Hayward Horton, editors. *Skin Deep: How Race and Complexion Matter in the Color Blind Era*. Urbana-Champaign: University of Illinois Press, 2004.

Herskovits, Melville J. "Some Physical Characteristics of the American Negro Population." *Social Forces* 6, no. 1 (1927).

Herzig, Rebecca. *Plucked: A History of Hair Removal*. New York: New York University Press, 2015.

Higginbotham, Evelyn. *Righteous Discontent: The Women's Movement in the Black Baptist Church, 1880–1920*. Cambridge, MA: Harvard University Press, 1993.

Hill, Walter, and Barbara Burger. "Aristocrats of Color: Photographic Images of Life at Black Colleges in the 1930s." *Journal of Blacks in Higher Education* 22 (1998): 116–20.

Hobbs, Allyson. *A Chosen Exile: A History of Racial Passing in American Life*. Cambridge, MA: Harvard University Press, 2014.

Hochschild, Jennifer L., and Vesla Weaver. "The Skin Color Paradox and the American Racial Order." *Social Forces* 86, no. 2 (2007): 643–70.

Hofmeyr, Isabel. "AHR Conversation: On Transnational History." *American Historical Review* (December 2006): 1440–64.

Hofmeyr, Isabel. *The Portable Bunyan: A Transnational History of "The Pilgrim's Progress."* Princeton, NJ: Princeton University Press, 2004.

Holt, Thomas C. "Marking: Race, Race-making, and the Writing of History." *American Historical Review* 100, no. 1 (February 1995): 1–20.

hooks, bell. *Ain't I a Woman: Black Women and Feminism*. Boston: South End Press, 1981.

hooks, bell. *Black Looks: Race and Representation*. Boston: South End Press, 1992.

Hope, Donna P. "Fashion Ova Style: Contemporary Notions of Skin Bleaching in Jamaican Dancehall Culture." *JENdA: A Journal of Culture and African Women Studies* 14 (2009): 101–26.

Horrell, Muriel, compiler. *A Survey of Race Relations in South Africa, 1958–9*. Johannesburg: South African Institute of Race Relations, 1960.

Horrell, Muriel, compiler. *A Survey of Race Relations in South Africa, 1967*. Johannesburg: South African Institute of Race Relations, 1968.

Horwitz, Ralph. *Expand or Explode: Apartheid's Threat to South African Industry*. Cape Town: Business Bookman, 1957.

Houghton, D. Hobart. *The South African Economy*. Cape Town: Oxford University Press, 1964.

Hull, Richard. *American Enterprise in South Africa: Historical Dimensions of Engagement and Disengagement*. New York: New York University Press, 1990.

Hunt, Nancy Rose. "The Affective, the Intellectual, and African Gender History." *Journal of African History* 55 (2014): 331–45.

Hunt, Nancy Rose. *A Colonial Lexicon of Birth Ritual, Medicalization, and Mobility in the Congo*. Durham: Duke University Press, 1999.

Hunter, Margaret L. *Race, Gender, and the Politics of Skin Tone*. New York: Routledge, 2005.

Hunter, Mark. "The Bond of Education: Gender, the Value of Children, and the Making of Umlazi Township in 1960s South Africa." *Journal of African History* 55, no. 3 (2014): 467–90.

Hunter, Mark. *Love in the Time of AIDS: Inequality, Gender, and Rights in South Africa*. Bloomington: Indiana University Press, 2010.

Hunter, Mark. *Race for Education: Gender, White Tone, and Schooling in South Africa*. Cambridge: Cambridge University Press, 2019.

Hunter, Monica. *Reaction to Conquest: Effects of Contact with Europeans on the Pondo of South Africa*. New York: Oxford University Press, 1936.

Hurst, Rachel Alpha Johnstone. *Surface Imaginations: Cosmetic Surgery, Photography, and Skin*. Montreal: McGill-Queen's University Press, 2015.

Hutchings, Anne, with Alan Haxton Scott, Gillian Lewis, and Anthony Cunningham. *Zulu Medicinal Plants: An Inventory*. Pietermaritzburg: University of Natal Press, 1996.

Hutt, Peter Barton. "A History of Government Regulation of Adulteration and Misbranding of Cosmetics." In *Cosmetic Regulation in a Competitive Environment*, edited by Norman F. Estrin and James M. Akerson, 1–41. New York: Marcel Dekker, 2000.

Hutt, Peter Barton. "Legal Distinction in the United States between a Cosmetic and a Drug." In *Cosmeceuticals and Active Cosmetics*, third edition, edited by Raja K. Sivamari, Jared Jagdeo, Peter Elsner, and Howard I. Maibach, 429–42. Boca Raton, FL: CRC Press, 2016.

Hyslop, Jon. "Shopping during a Revolution: Entrepreneurs, Retailers and 'White' Identity in the Democratic Transition." *Historia* 50 (2005): 173–90.

Iliffe, John. *The Emergence of African Capitalism*. London: Macmillan, 1983.

Iliffe, John. *Honour in African History*. New York: Cambridge University Press, 2004.

Illouz, Eva. *Cold Intimacies: The Making of Emotional Capitalism*. Cambridge: Polity Press, 2007.

Illouz, Eva, editor. *Emotions as Commodities: Capitalism, Consumption and Authenticity*. New York: Routledge, 2018.

Illouz, Eva, and Yaara Benger. "Emotions and Consumption." In *The Wiley Blackwell Encyclopedia of Consumption and Consumer Studies*, edited by Daniel Thomas Cook and J. Michael Ryan, 1–6. New York: John Wiley and Sons, 2015.

Imadojemu, Sotonye, and Autumn Fiester. "Skin Bleaching as a Dermatologic Intervention: Complicity or Service?" *JAMA Dermatology* 149, no. 8 (August 2013): 901–2.

"Impact of Proposed FDA Restrictions on Hydroquinone." *The Dermatologist*, September 4, 2008. Accessed November 27, 2017. https://www.the-dermatologist.com/article/6562.

Ingold, Tim. "Toward an Ecology of Materials." *Annual Review of Anthropology* 41 (2012): 427–42.

Isaacs, Nathaniel. *Travels and Adventures in Eastern Africa: Descriptive of the Zoolus, Their Manners, Customs with a Sketch of Natal*. Edited and revised by Louis Herrman and Percival R. Kirby. Cape Town: C. Struik, 1970.

Ito, M. "Monobenzylether-Hydroquinone Leucomelanderma." *Tahuku Journal of Experimental Medicine* 65, 5 Supp. (1957): 64–75.

Ivaska, Andrew. *Cultured States: Youth, Gender and Modern Style in 1960s Dar es Salaam*. Durham: Duke University Press, 2011.

Iyengar, Sujata. *Shades of Difference: Mythologies of Skin Color in Early Modern England*. Philadelphia: University of Pennsylvania Press, 2005.

Jablonski, Nina G. "The Evolution of Human Skin and Skin Color." *Annual Review of Anthropology* 33 (2004): 585–623.

Jablonski, Nina G. *Living Color: The Biological and Social Meaning of Skin Color*. Berkeley: University of California Press, 2012.

Jablonski, Nina G. *Skin: A Natural History*. Berkeley: University of California Press, 2006.

Jacobs, Meagan, Susan Levine, Kate Abney, and Lester Davids. "Fifty Shades of African Lightness: A Bio-psychosocial Review of the Global Phenomenon of Skin Lightening Practices." *Journal of Public Health in Africa* 7, no. 552 (2016): 67–70.

Jacobson-Widding, Anita. *Red-White-Black as a Mode of Thought: A Study of Triadic Classification by Colours in the Ritual Symbolism and Cognitive Thought of the Peoples of the Lower Congo*. Uppsala: Amqvist and Wiksell, 1979.

Jaji, Tsitsi Ella. *Africa in Stereo: Modernism, Music, and Pan-African Solidarity*. New York: Oxford University Press, 2014.

James, Deborah. *Money from Nothing: Indebtedness and Aspiration in South Africa*. Stanford, CA: Stanford University Press, 2014.

Japanese Ministry of Environment web page. Accessed January 24, 2018. http://www.env.go.jp/chemi/tmms/tobira/riyo.html.

Jarrín, Alvaro. *The Biopolitics of Beauty: Cosmetic Citizenship and Affective Capital in Brazil*. Durham: Duke University Press, 2017.

Jesitus, John. "Distant Decisions: U.S. Lags behind EU, Others in Regulating Hydroquinone." *Dermatology Times* (July 2007): 67.

Jha, Meeta Rani. *The Global Beauty Industry: Colorism, Racism, and the National Body*. New York: Routledge, 2016.

Johnson, Paul. "'Talking the Talk and Walking the Walk': The Spring Queen Festival and the Eroding Family Cult in the Western Cape Garment Industry." Unpublished paper presented to the Oral History Project Seminar, Centre for African Studies, Rondebosch, University of Cape Town, October 7, 1993.

Jones, Geoffrey. *Beauty Imagined: A History of the Global Beauty Industry*. Oxford: Oxford University Press, 2010.

Jones, Geoffrey. "Blonde and Blue-Eyed? Globalizing Beauty, c.1945–c.1980." *Economic History Review* 61, no. 1 (2008): 125–54.

Jordan, Winthrop D. *White over Black: American Attitudes toward the Negro, 1550–1812*. New York: W. W. Norton, 1968.

Kambili, Cyprian. "Ethics of African Tradition: Prescription of a Dress Code in Malawi 1965–73." *Society of Malawi Journal* 55, no. 2 (2002): 80–99.

Kaplan, D. E. "The Politics of Industrial Protection in South Africa, 1910–1939." *Journal of Southern African Studies* 3, no. 1 (1976): 70–91.

Karim-Cooper, Farah. *Cosmetics in Shakespearean and Renaissance Drama*. Edinburgh: Edinburgh University Press, 2006.

Kay, Gwen. *Dying to Be Beautiful: The Fight for Safe Cosmetics*. Columbus: Ohio State University Press, 2005.

Kay, Stephen. *Travels and Researches in Caffraria*. New York: Harper, 1834.

Keegan, Timothy. *Colonial South Africa and the Origins of the Racial Order*. Charlottesville: University of Virginia Press, 1996.

Kelly, Edward W. "Pigmented Skin Lesions: Treatment with Monobenzyl-ether of Hydroquinone." *Journal of Michigan State Medical Society* 55, no. 3 (1956): 303–4, 314.

Kelly, Olson. "Cosmetics in Roman Antiquity: Substance, Remedy, Poison." *Classical World* 102, no. 3 (2009): 291–310.

Kemp, Amanda. "'Up from Slavery' and Other Narratives: Black South African Performances of the American Negro." Ph.D. diss., Northwestern University, 1997.

Kemp, Amanda, and Robert Vinson. "'Poking Holes in the Sky': Professor James Thaele, American Negroes, and Modernity in 1920s Segregationist South Africa." *African Studies Review* 44, no. 1 (2000): 141–59.

Kenya. National Assembly Debates, 1968, 1971.

Kerr, Audrey Elisa. *The Paper Bag Principle: Class, Colorism, and Rumor and the Case of Black Washington, D.C.* Knoxville: University of Tennessee Press, 2006.

Khan, Farieda. "Beauty, Myths and Trees." *Agenda* 12, no. 29 (January 1996): 37–42.

Khan, Farieda. "Black Beauty, White Mask." *Veld and Flora* (March 1996): 15.

Khan, Farieda. "Fanta Face, Coca-Cola Body: The Use of Chemical Skin Lightening Preparations in South Africa, Past and Present." Unpublished manuscript, c. 1998.

Kibukamusoke, J. W., D. R. Davies, and M. S. R. Hutt. "Medical Memoranda: Membranous Nephropathy Due to Skin-Lightening Cream." *British Medical Journal* (June 22, 1974): 646–47.

Kirby, Percival R., editor. *Andrew Smith and Natal: Documents Relating to the Early History of That Province.* Cape Town: Van Riebeeck Society, 1955.

Klein, Allen. *How to Suntan for Health and Fun.* Emaus, PA: Rodale, 1938.

Koller, Theodor. *Cosmetics: A Handbook of the Manufacture, Employment, and Testing of All Cosmetic Materials and Cosmetic Specialties.* Translated by Charles Salter. London: Scott, Greenwood & Son, 1920. (Originally published in 1902.)

Korhonen, Anu. "Washing the Ethiopian White: Conceptualising Black Skin in Renaissance England." In *Black Africans in Renaissance Europe*, edited by T. F. Earle and K. J. P Lowe, 94–112. New York: Cambridge University Press, 2005.

Kracauer, Siegfried. *The Mass Ornament: Weimar Essays.* Edited and translated by Thomas Levin. Cambridge, MA: Harvard University Press, 1995.

Kratz, Corinne A. *Affecting Performance: Meaning, Movement, and Experience in Okiek Women's Initiation.* Washington, DC: Smithsonian Institution, 1994.

Krige, Eileen Jensen. *The Social System of the Zulus.* Pietermaritzburg: Shuter & Shooter, 1936.

Krige, Eileen Jensen, and J. D. Krige. *The Realm of a Rain-Queen: A Study of the Pattern of Lovedu Society.* New York: Oxford University Press, 1943.

Kuper, Leo. *An African Bourgeoisie: Race, Class, and Politics in South Africa.* New Haven, CT: Yale University Press, 1965.

Laden, Sonja. "'Making the Paper Speak Well,' or, the Pace of Change in Consumer Magazines for Black South Africans." *Poetics Today* 22, no. 2 (Summer 2001): 515–48.

Laden, Sonja. "Who's Afraid of a Black Bourgeoisie? Consumer Magazines for Black South Africans as an Apparatus of Change." *Journal of Consumer Culture* 3 (2003): 191–216.

Lafrance, Marc. "Skin Studies: Past, Present and Future." *Body and Society* 24, no. 1–2 (2018): 3–32.

Lamb, Ruth deForest. *American Chamber of Horrors: The Truth about Food and Drugs*. New York: Farrar and Rinehart, 1936.

Landau, Paul Stuart. *Popular Politics in the History of South Africa, 1400–1948*. Cambridge: Cambridge University Press, 2010.

Landau, Paul Stuart. *The Realm of the Word: Language, Gender, and Christianity in a Southern African Kingdom*. Portsmouth, NH: Heinemann, 1995.

Landau, Paul Stuart, and Deborah Kaspin, editors. *Images and Empires: Visuality in Colonial and Postcolonial Africa*. Berkeley: University of California Press, 2002.

Langschmidt, W. "Some Characteristics of the Urban Bantu Market." In *The Urban Bantu Market: Understanding Its Complexities and Developing Its Potential— Proceedings of a 2-Day Seminar Held in February 1969, Durban, Natal*, edited by the National Development and Management Foundation. Johannesburg: National Development and Management Foundation of South Africa, 1969.

Larkin, Brian. *Signal and Noise: Media, Infrastructure, and Urban Culture in Nigeria*. Durham: Duke University Press, 2008.

Larsen, Nella. *Passing*. New York: Knopf, 1929.

Lasker, Lawrence. "A Whiter Shade of Black." *Esquire* (July 1968): 62–65.

Lee, Christopher J. *Unreasonable Histories: Nativism, Multiracial Lives, and the Genealogical Imagination in British Africa*. Durham: Duke University Press, 2014.

Lekgoathi, Sekibakiba Peter. "Bantustan Identity, Censorship and Subversion on Northern Sotho Radio under Apartheid, 1960s–80s." In *Radio in Africa: Publics, Cultures, Communities*, edited by Liz Gunner, Dina Ligaga, and Dumisani Moyo, 117–33. Johannesburg: Wits University Press, 2011.

Levin, Cheryl Y., and Howard Maibach. "Exogenous Ochronosis: An Update on Clinical Features, Causative Agents and Treatment Options." *American Journal of Clinical Dermatology* 2, no. 4 (2001): 213–17.

Levine, Lawrence. *Black Culture and Black Consciousness: Afro-American Folk Thought from Slavery to Freedom*. New York: Oxford University Press, 1977.

Levitt, Jacob. "The Safety of Hydroquinone: A Dermatologist's Response to the 2006 Federal Register." *Journal of the American Academy of Dermatology* 57, no. 5 (November 2007): 854–72.

Lewis, Desiree. "Women and Gender in South Africa." In *South Africa: The Challenge of Change*, edited by Vincent Maphai. Harare, Zimbabwe: SAPES, 1994.

Lewis, Desiree, and Mary Hames. "Gender, Sexuality and Commodity Culture." *Agenda* 25, no. 4 (2011): 2–7.

Lewis, Kelly M., Karie Gaska, Navit Robkin, Amber Martin, Emily Andrews, and Justin Williams. "The Need for Interventions to Prevent Skin Bleaching: A Look at Tanzania." *Journal of Black Studies* 43, no. 7 (2012): 787–805.

Lewis, Kelly M., Solette Harris, Christina Camp, Willbrord Kalala, Will Jones, Kecia L. Ellick, Justin Huff, and Sinead Young. "The Historical and Cultural Influences of Skin Bleaching in Tanzania." In *The Melanin Millennium: Skin Color as 21st Century International Discourse*, edited by R. E. Hall, 19–38. Dordrecht: Springer, 2013.

Lindsay, Lisa A. *Atlantic Bonds: A Nineteenth-Century Odyssey from America to Africa*. Chapel Hill: University of North Carolina Press, 2017.

Lindsley, Syd Saramalia. "Girl Pictures: The Politics of Sexuality and Female Display in the Twentieth-Century United States." Ph.D. diss., University of Washington, 2011.

Livingston, Julie. *Improvising Medicine: An African Oncology Ward in an Emerging Cancer Epidemic*. Durham: Duke University Press, 2012.

Livingstone, David. *Missionary Travels and Researches in South Africa*. New York: Harper and Brothers, 1858.

Lockhart, R. J. J., and L. J. A. Loewenthal. "Occupational Leukoderma." *South African Medical Journal* 23, no. 43 (October 22, 1949): 867–68.

Lorincz, Allan L. "Studies on the Inhibition of Melanin Formation." *Journal of Investigative Dermatology* 15, no. 6 (December 1950): 425–32.

Loubser, M. "Market Potentials of Consumer Goods and Services for Non-White Population Groups in the Main Urban Areas of the Republic of South Africa in 1975." *Bureau of Market Research, University of South Africa, Research Report No. 57*. Pretoria, 1977.

Louw, P. Eric. *The Rise, Fall, and Legacy of Apartheid*. Westport, CT: Praeger, 2004.

Magaziner, Daniel. *The Art of Life in South Africa*. Athens: Ohio University Press, 2016.

Magaziner, Daniel. *The Law and the Prophets*. Athens: Ohio University Press, 2010.

Magaziner, Daniel. "Pieces of a (Wo)man: Feminism, Gender and Adulthood in Black Consciousness, 1968–1977." *Journal of Southern African Studies* 37, no. 1 (2011): 45–61.

Mager, Anne Kelk. *Beer, Sociability, and Masculinity in South Africa*. Bloomington: Indiana University Press, 2010.

Magubane, Zine. *Bringing the Empire Home: Race, Class, and Gender in Britain and Colonial South Africa*. Chicago: University of Chicago Press, 2004.

Maibach, Howard I., and Peter Elsner, editors. *Cosmeceuticals: Drugs vs. Cosmetics*. New York: Marcel Dekker, 2000.

Makeba, Miriam, with James Hall. *Makeba: My Story*. New York: New American Library, 1987.

Malangu, N., and G. A. Ogunbanjo. "Predicators of Topical Steroid Misuse among Patrons of Pharmacies in Pretoria." *South African Family Practice* 48, no. 1 (2006): 14a–e.

Malcolm X. "After the Bombing—February 14, 1965." In *Malcolm X Speaks: Selected Speeches and Statements*, edited by George Breitman, 157–77. New York: Pathfinder, 1992. (Originally published in 1965.)

"Malcolm X Speech in Los Angeles (May 5, 1962)." *World History Archive and Compendium*. Accessed January 23, 2018. https://worldhistoryarchive.wordpress.com /2017/02/03/malcolm-x-speech-in-los-angeles-may-5-1962/.

Mamdani, Mahmood. *Imperialism and Fascism in Uganda*. Trenton, NJ: Africa World Press, 1984.

Maneli, M. H., L. Wiesner, C. Tinguely, L. M. Davids, Z. Spengane, P. Smith, J. C. van Wyk, A. Jardine, and N. P. Khumalo. "Combinations of Potent Topical Steroids,

Mercury and Hydroquinone Are Common in Internationally Manufactured Skin-Lightening: A Spectroscopic Study." *Clinical and Experimental Dermatology* 41 (2016): 196–201.

Mangena, M. J. Oshadi. "The Black Consciousness Philosophy and the Woman's Question in South Africa: 1970–1980." In *Biko Lives! Contesting the Legacies of Steve Biko*, edited by Andile Mngxitama, Amanda Alexander, and Nigel C. Gibson, 253–66. New York: Palgrave Macmillan, 2008.

Manoim, Irwin S. "The Black Press 1945–1963: The Growth of the Black Mass Media and Their Role as Ideological Disseminators." M.A. thesis, University of Witwatersrand, 1983.

Mapumulo, M., and B. M. Legwate. "Problems of Retailing to the Bantu Market: 1. Bantu Urban Areas." In *The Urban Bantu Market: Understanding Its Complexities and Developing Its Potential—Proceedings of a 2-Day Seminar Held in February 1969, Durban, Natal*, edited by the National Development and Management Foundation, 33–35. Johannesburg: National Development and Management Foundation of South Africa, 1969.

Marais, G. "Structural Changes in Manufacturing Industry 1916 to 1975." *South African Journal of Economics* 49, no. 1 (1981): 16–27.

Marchand, Roland. *Advertising the American Dream: Making Way for Modernity, 1920–1940.* Berkeley: University of California Press, 1985.

"The Marcus Garvey and Universal Negro Improvement Association Papers Project." UCLA African Studies Center. Accessed August 24, 2018. http://www.international.ucla.edu/africa/mgpp/.

Marks, Shula. *Divided Sisterhood: Race, Class, and Gender in the South African Nursing Profession.* New York: St. Martin's, 1994.

Marks, Shula, editor. *Not Either an Experimental Doll: The Separate Worlds of Three South Africa Women.* Bloomington: Indiana University Press, 1987.

Marks, Shula. "Patriotism, Patriarchy and Purity: Natal and the Politics of Zulu Ethnic Consciousness." In *The Creation of Tribalism in Southern Africa*, edited by Leroy Vail. Berkeley: University of California Press, 1991.

Martin, Morag. "Doctoring Beauty: The Medical Control of Women's Toilettes in France, 1750–1820." *Medical History* 49, no. 3 (2005): 351–68.

Martin, Morag. *Selling Beauty: Cosmetics, Commerce, and French Society, 1750–1830.* Baltimore, MD: Johns Hopkins University Press, 2009.

Marzulli, F. N., and Daniel W. C. Brown. "Potential Systemic Hazards of Topically Applied Mercurials." *Journal of the Society of Cosmetic Chemists* 23, no. 13 (1972): 875–86.

"MASA Bulletin: MASA's Agenda for 1989." *South African Medical Journal* 75 (January 21, 1989): 46.

Mashinini, Emma. *Strikes Have Followed Me All My Life: A South African Autobiography.* London: Women's Press, 1989.

Matthews, James. *Black Voices Shout! An Anthology of Poetry.* Cape Town: BLAC, 1974.

Matthews, James, and Gladys Thomas. *Cry Rage!* Johannesburg: Spro-Cas, 1972.

Matumo, Z. I., compiler. *Setswana English Setswana Dictionary*. Gaborone: Macmillan and Botswana Book Centre, 1993.

Mayer, Philip, with contributions by Iona Mayer. *Townsmen or Tribesmen: Conservatism and the Process of Urbanization in a South African City*. Cape Town: Oxford University Press, 1961.

Mazrui, Ali. "A Discourse on Mixed Reactions to—Miniskirts." *Sauti ya Mabibi* 1, no. 8 (1969): 2–5, 8, 17, 21.

Mbembe, Achille. "African Modes of Self-Writing." *Public Culture* 14, no. 1 (2002): 245–46.

McClintock, Anne. *Imperial Leather: Race, Gender and Sexuality in the Colonial Contest*. New York: Routledge, 1995.

McCoskey, Denise Eileen. "Naming the Fault in Question: Theorizing Racism among the Greeks and Romans." *International Journal of the Classical Tradition* 13, no. 2 (2006): 243–67.

Mda, Zakes. *The Heart of Redness*. New York: Picador, 2000.

Mertens, Alice, and Joan A. Broster. *African Elegance*. New York: Purnell, 1973.

Mesthrie, Rajend, et al., editors. "Language Contact 1: Maintenance, Shift and Death." In *Introducing Sociolinguistics*, 242–70. Edinburgh: Edinburgh University Press, 2009.

Meyerowitz, Joanne. "Women, Cheesecake, and Borderline Material: Responses to Girlie Pictures in the Mid-Twentieth-Century U.S." *Journal of Women's History* 8, no. 3 (Fall 1996): 9–35.

Miller, Daniel. *Capitalism: An Ethnographic Approach*. New York: Berg, 1997.

Mini, B. M., editor. *The Greater Dictionary of Isi Xhosa*. Vol. 2, *K–P*. Alice, South Africa: University of Fort Hare, 2003.

Mintz, Sidney. *Sweetness and Power: The Place of Sugar in Modern History*. New York: Penguin, 1985.

Mire, Amina. "The Scientification of Skin Whitening and the Entrepreneurial University-Linked Corporate Scientific Officer." *Canadian Journal of Science, Mathematics and Technology Education* 12, no. 3 (2012): 272–91.

Mire, Amina. "Skin-bleaching: Poison, Beauty, Power and the Politics of the Colour Line." *New Feminist Research* 28, no. 3/4 (2000): 13–38.

Mire, Amina. "'Skin Trade': Genealogy of Anti-ageing 'Whiteness Therapy' in Colonial Medicine." *Medicine Studies* 4 (2014): 119–29.

Mishra, Neha. "India and Colorism: The Finer Nuances." *Washington University Global Studies Law Review* 14, no. 4 (2015): 725–50.

Mitchell, Sally. *The New Girl: Girls' Culture in England, 1880–1915*. New York: Columbia University Press, 1995.

Mkele, Nimrod. "Advertising to the Bantu." In *Second Advertising Convention in South Africa, Sponsored by the Society of Advertisers Ltd., Durban, 21st–24th September, 1959*, 116–35. Johannesburg: Statistic Holdings (Pty.) Ltd., 1959.

Mngxitama, Andile, Amanda Alexander, and Nigel C. Gibson. "Biko Lives." In *Biko Lives! Contesting the Legacies of Steve Biko*, edited by Andile Mngxitama, Amanda Alexander, and Nigel C. Gibson, 13–15. New York: Palgrave Macmillan, 2008.

Modern Girl Around the World Research Group (Alys Eve Weinbaum, Lynn M. Thomas, Priti Ramamurthy, Uta G. Poiger, Madeleine Y. Dong, and Tani E. Barlow), editors. *The Modern Girl Around the World: Consumption, Modernity, and Globalization.* Durham: Duke University Press, 2008.

Modern Girl Around the World Research Group (Alys Eve Weinbaum, Lynn M. Thomas, Priti Ramamurthy, Uta G. Poiger, Madeleine Yue Dong, and Tani E. Barlow), editors. "The Modern Girl Around the World: Cosmetics Advertising and the Politics of Race and Style." In *The Modern Girl Around the World: Consumption, Modernity, and Globalization,* edited by the Modern Girl Around the World Research Group, 25–54. Durham: Duke University Press, 2008.

Modern Girl Around the World Research Group (Alys Eve Weinbaum, Lynn M. Thomas, Priti Ramamurthy, Uta G. Poiger, Madeleine Yue Dong, and Tani E. Barlow). "The Modern Girl around the World: A Research Agenda and Preliminary Findings." *Gender and History* 17, no. 2 (August 2005): 280.

Modern Girl Around the World Research Group (Alys Eve Weinbaum, Lynn M. Thomas, Priti Ramamurthy, Uta G. Poiger, Madeleine Yue Dong, and Tani E. Barlow). "The Modern Girl as Heuristic Device: Collaboration, Connective Comparison, Multidirectional Citation." In *The Modern Girl Around the World: Consumption, Modernity, and Globalization,* edited by the Modern Girl Around the World Research Group, 1–24. Durham: Duke University Press, 2008.

Moffat, Robert. *Missionary Labours and Scenes in Southern Africa.* New York: Johnson Reprint, 1967. (Originally published in 1842.)

Mofokeng, Santu. "The Black Photo Album." In *Anthology of African and Indian Ocean Photography,* edited by Pascal Martin Saint Léon, N'Goné Fall, and Frédérique Chapuis, 68–75. Paris: Revue Noire, 1998.

Mofokeng, Santu. "Trajectory of a Street-Photographer: South Africa 1973–1998." In *Democracy's Images: Photography and Visual Art after Apartheid,* 42–45. Umeå, Sweden: Bildmuseet, 1998.

Mofokeng, Santu, with an essay by James T. Campbell. *The Black Photo Album/Look at Me, 1890–1950.* Gottingen: Steidl, 2012.

Mokoena, Hlonipha. *Magema Fuze: The Making of a Kholwa Intellectual.* Pietermaritzburg: University of KwaZulu-Natal Press, 2011.

Monk, Jr., Ellis P. "The Cost of Color: Skin Color, Discrimination, and Health among African-Americans." *American Journal of Sociology* 121, no. 2 (2015): 396–444.

Moolman, B. A., and M. Loubser. "Market Potentials of Consumer Goods and Services for Non-White Population Groups in the Five Main Metropolitan Areas of the Republic of South Africa in 1970." Bureau of Market Research, University of South Africa, Research Report No. 34. Pretoria: 1977.

Morel, Marion (Marion Welsh). "It's Gotta Be Cash for a Cookie." Original in *Drum* (1959), with an introduction by Dorothy Driver. In *Women Writing Africa: The Southern Region,* edited by M. J. Daymond et al., 252–54. New York: Feminist Press, 2003.

Morgan, Robin, editor. *Sisterhood Is Powerful: An Anthology of Writings from the Women's Liberation Movement.* New York: Random House, 1970.

Morobe, Murphy. "Towards a People's Democracy: The UDF View." *Review of African Political Economy* 40 (December 1987): 81–87.

Morrison, Toni. *The Bluest Eye*. New York: Vintage Books, 2007. (Original edition published by Holt, Rinehart and Winston, 1970.)

Motsemme, Nthabiseng. "Distinguishing Beauty, Creating Distinctions: The Politics and Poetics of Dress among Young Black Women." *Agenda* 57 (2003): 12–18.

Motsuenyane, M. "Black Consciousness and the Economic Position of the Black Man in South Africa." In *Black Renaissance: Papers from the Black Renaissance Convention*, edited by Thoahlane Thoahlane, 47–52. Johannesburg: Ravan, 1975.

Mphahlele, Ezekiel. *Down Second Avenue*. London: Faber and Faber, 1959.

Mqotsi, Livingstone, and Nimrod Mkele. "A Separatist Church: Ibandla lika-Krestu." *African Studies* 5, no. 2 (1946): 106–42.

Mufson, Steve. *Fighting Years: Black Resistance and the Struggle for a New South Africa*. Boston: Beacon Press, 1990.

Muholland, Dulcie A., Elizabeth M. Mwangi, Ncoza C. Dlova, Nick Plant, Neil R. Crouch, and Phillip H. Coombes. "Non-toxic Melanin Production Inhibitors from *Garcinia livingstonei* (Clusiaceae)." *Journal of Ethnopharmacology* 149 (2013): 570–75.

Murillo, Bianca. *Market Encounters: Consumer Cultures in Twentieth-Century Ghana*. Athens: Ohio University Press, 2017.

Murphy, Michelle. *Sick Building Syndrome and the Problem of Uncertainty: Environmental Politics, Technoscience, and Women Workers*. Durham: Duke University Press, 2006.

Mustafa, Hudita Nura. "Portraits of Modernity: Fashioning Selves in Dakarois Popular Photography." In *Images and Empires: Visuality in Colonial and Postcolonial Africa*, edited by Paul S. Landau and Deborah D. Kaspin, 172–92. Berkeley: University of California, 2002.

Musuva. *Peeping through the Reeds: A Story about Living in Apartheid South Africa*. Milton Keynes: AuthorHouse, 2010.

Mutongi, Kenda. "'Dear Dolly's' Advice: Representations of Youth, Courtship, and Sexualities in Africa, 1960–1980." *International Journal of African Historical Studies* 33, no. 1 (2000): 1–23.

Nash, Linda. "From Safety to Risk: The Cold War Contexts of American Environmental Policy." *Journal of Policy History* 29, no. 1 (2017): 1–33.

Nchimbi, Rehema Jonathan. "Women's Beauty in the History of Tanzania." Ph.D. diss., University of Cape Town, 2005.

Nealon, D. F. *Report of Studies on Nadinola Bleaching Cream*. Paris, TN: National Toilet, 1946.

Negri, Antonio. "Value and Affect." *boundary 2* 26, no. 2 (1999): 77–88.

Nelson, Alondra. *The Social Life of DNA: Race, Reparations, and Reconciliation after the Genome*. Boston: Beacon Press, 2016.

Ngubane, Harriet. *Body and Mind in Zulu Medicine: An Ethnography of Health and Disease in Nyuswa-Zulu Thought and Practice*. London: Academic, 1977.

Nguyen, Mimi Thi. "The Biopower of Beauty: Humanitarian Imperialisms and Global Feminisms in an Age of Terror." *Signs* 36, no. 2 (2011): 359–83.

Nixon, Robert. *Homelands, Harlem and Hollywood: South African Culture and the World Beyond.* New York: Routledge, 1994.

Noble, Vanessa. *A School of Struggle: Durban's Medical School and the Education of Black Doctors.* Scottsville: University of KwaZulu-Natal Press, 2013.

Nordlund, James J. "Hydroquinone: Its Value and Safety." *Future Drugs* (2007): 283–87.

Norval, A. J. *A Quarter of a Century of Industrial Progress in South Africa.* Cape Town: Juta, 1962.

Norwood, Kimberly Jade. *Color Matters: Skin Tone Bias and the Myth of a Post-Racial America.* New York: Routledge, 2014.

Ntantala, Phyllis. *A Life's Mosaic: The Autobiography of Phyllis Ntantala.* Berkeley: University of California Press, 1993.

Nussbaum, Felicity A. "Women and Race: 'A Difference of Complexion.'" In *Women and Literature in Britain, 1700–1800,* edited by Vivien Jones, 69–88. Cambridge: Cambridge University Press, 2000.

Nuttall, Sarah, editor. *Beautiful/Ugly: African and Diaspora Aesthetics.* Durham: Duke University Press, 2006.

Nuttall, Sarah. "Surface, Depth and the Autobiographical Act: Texts and Images." *Life Writing* 11, no. 2 (2014): 161–75.

Nuttall, Sarah, and Cheryl-Ann Michael, editors. *Senses of Culture: South African Culture Studies.* Oxford: Oxford University Press, 2000.

Obama, Barack. *Dreams from My Father: A Story of Race and Inheritance.* New York: Three Rivers Press, 1995.

Ochoa, Marcia. *Queen for a Day: "Transformistas," Beauty Queens, and the Performance of Femininity in Venezuela.* Durham: Duke University Press, 2014.

Odhiambo, Tom. "Inventing Africa in the Twentieth Century: Cultural Imagination, Politics and Transnationalism in *Drum* Magazine." *African Studies* 65, no. 2 (2006): 157–74.

O'Donoghue, Marianne N., Yelva L. Lynfield, and Vincent Derbes. "Letter to Editor: Orchronosis Due to Hydroquinone." *Journal of the American Academy of Dermatology* 8 (January 1983): 123.

Ofodile, Ope. "Artificial Depigmentation for Cosmetic Purposes: Prevalence, Consequences and Ethical Concerns." Unpublished presentation, Dermatology Grand Rounds, University of Washington. April 30, 2014.

Oliver, Edward A., Louis Schwartz, and Leon H. Warren. "Occupational Leukoderma." *Archives of Dermatology and Syphilology* 42, no. 6 (December 1940): 993–1014.

Oliver, Edward A., Louis Schwartz, and Leon H. Warren. "Occupational Leukoderma: Preliminary Report." *Journal of the American Medical Association* 113, no. 10 (September 2, 1939).

Olumide, Mercy. *The Vanishing Black African Woman: A Compendium of the Global Skin Lightening Practice.* Vols. 1 and 2. Cameroon: Langaa RPCIG, 2016.

Omi, Michael, and Howard Winant. *Racial Formation in the United States.* Third edition. New York: Routledge, 2015. (Originally published in 1986.)

Osseo-Asare, Abena Dove. *Bitter Roots: The Search for Healing Plants in Africa.* Chicago: University of Chicago Press, 2014.

Oumeish, Oumeish Youssef. "The Cultural and Philosophical Concepts of Cosmetics in Beauty and Art through the Medical History of Mankind." *CID Clinics in Dermatology* 19, no. 4 (2001): 375–86.

Ozier, C. W. "Skin Lighteners and Bleach Creams." In *Cosmetics: Science and Technology*, edited by Edward Sagarin, 213–21. New York: Interscience, 1957.

Palm, Melanie D., and Ella L. Toombs. "Letter to the Editor: Hydroquinone and the FDA—the Debate?" *Journal of Drugs in Dermatology* 6, no. 2 (2007): 122.

Palmer, G. F. D. "Some Aspects of the Development of Secondary Industry in South Africa since the Depression of 1929–1932." *South African Journal of Economics* 22, no. 1 (1954): 148–59.

Parle, Julie. "'A Drug, Like a Scalpel, in an Unskilled Hand Is a Dangerous Weapon...': South African Struggles over Pharmaceutical Regulatory Authority, 1930s–1960s." Unpublished paper presented at WISER, University of Witwatersrand, March 2016.

Parrish, Charles H. "Color Names and Color Notions." *Journal of Negro Education* 15 (1946): 13–20.

Patkar, Kunda B. "Herbal Cosmetics in Ancient India." *Indian Journal of Plastic Surgery* 41 (2008): 134–37.

Peck, S. M., and Harry Sobotka. "Effect of Monobenzyl Hydroquinone on Oxidase Systems in Vivo and in Vitro." *Journal of Investigative Dermatology* 4, no. 4 (August 1941): 325–29.

Peiss, Kathy. *Hope in a Jar: The Making of America's Beauty Culture*. New York: Metropolitan, 1998.

Perry, Imani. "Buying White Beauty." *Cardozo Journal of Law and Gender* 12 (Spring 2006): 579–609.

Peterson, Bhekizizwe. "The Bantu World and the World of the Book: Reading, Writing, and 'Enlightenment.'" In *Africa's Hidden Histories: Everyday Literacy and Making the Self*, edited by Karin Barber, 236–57. Bloomington: Indiana University Press, 2006.

Peterson, Bhekizizwe. *Monarchs, Missionaries and African Intellectuals*. Trenton, NJ: Africa World, 2000.

Peterson, Kristin. *Speculative Markets: Drug Circuits and Derivative Life in Nigeria*. Durham: Duke University Press, 2014.

Phillips, James I., Charles Isaacson, and Hilary Carman. "Ochronosis in Black South Africans Who Used Skin Lighteners." *American Journal of Dermatology* 8, no. 1 (1986): 14–21.

Phillips, Ray E. *The Bantu in the City: A Study of Cultural Adjustment on the Witwatersrand*. Lovedale, South Africa: Lovedale Press, 1938.

Pierre, Jemima. "'I Like Your Colour!' Skin Bleaching and Geographies of Race in Urban Ghana." *Feminist Review* 90 (2008): 9–29.

Pierre, Jemima. *The Predicament of Blackness: Postcolonial Ghana and the Politics of Race*. Chicago: University of Chicago Press, 2013.

Pinney, Christopher, and Nicolas Peterson, editors. *Photography's Other Histories*. Durham: Duke University Press, 2003.

Pinnock, Patricia Schonstein. *Xhosa: A Cultural Grammar for Beginners*. Cape Town: African Sun, 1994.

Pivin, Jean Loup. "The Icon and the Totem." In *Anthology of African and Indian Ocean Photography*, edited by Pascal Martin Saint Léon, N'Goné Fall, and Frédérique Chapuis. Paris: Revue Noire, 1998.

Pointer, Sally. *The Artifice of Beauty: A History and Practical Guide to Perfumes and Cosmetics*. Gloucestershire, UK: Sutton Limited, 2005.

Pollack, Julius H. "Hyperpigmentation Improved by Treatment with Monobenzyl Ether of Hydroquinone." *Archives of Dermatology and Syphilology* 61, no. 5 (May 1950): 873–75.

Poole, Deborah. *Vision, Race, and Modernity: A Visual Economy of the Andean Image World*. Princeton, NJ: Princeton University Press, 1997.

Popenoe, Rebecca. *Feeding Desire: Fatness, Beauty, and Sexuality among a Saharan People*. New York: Routledge, 2004.

Posel, Deborah. "Race as Common Sense: Racial Classification in Twentieth-Century South Africa." *African Studies Review* 44, no. 2 (2001): 87–113.

Posel, Deborah. "Races to Consume: Revisiting South Africa's History of Race, Consumption and the Struggle for Freedom." *Ethnic and Racial Studies* 33, no. 2 (2010): 151–75.

Posel, Deborah. "What's in a Name? Racial Categorisations under Apartheid and Their Afterlife." *Transformation* 47 (2001): 50–74.

Posel, Deborah, and Ilana van Wyk, editors. *Conspicuous Consumption in Africa*. Johannesburg: Wits University Press, forthcoming.

Powell, Eve Troutt. *A Different Shade of Colonialism: Egypt, Great Britain, and the Mastery of the Sudan*. Berkeley: University of California Press, 2003.

Pray, W. Steven. *A History of Nonprescription Product Regulation*. New York: Pharmaceutical Products Press, 2003.

Presbury, David. "Hydroquinones: A National Disgrace!" *Diseases of the Skin* 2, no. 2 (1988): 1.

Presholdt, Jeremy. *Domesticating the World: African Consumerism and the Genealogies of Globalization*. Berkeley: University of California Press, 2008.

Ramamurthy, Priti. "Feminist Commodity Chain Analysis: A Framework to Conceptualize Value and Interpret Perplexity." In *Gendered Commodity Chains: Seeing Women's Work and Households in Global Production*, edited by Wilma Dunaway, 38–52. Stanford, CA: Stanford University Press, 2014.

Ramphele, Mamphela. *Across Boundaries: The Journey of a South African Woman Leader*. New York: Feminist Press, 1995.

Ramphele, Mamphela. *A Bed Called Home: Life in the Migrant Labour Hostels of Cape Town*. Athens: Ohio University Press, 1993.

Ramphele, Mamphela. "The Dynamics of Gender within Black Consciousness Organisations: A Personal View." In *Bounds of Possibility: The Legacy of Steve Biko and Black Consciousness*, edited by Barney Pityana, Mamphela Ramphele, Malusi Mpumlwana, and Lindy Wilson, 214–27. Atlantic Highlands, NJ: Zed Books, 1991.

Ramphele, Mamphela, and Emile Boonzaier. "The Position of African Women: Race and Gender in South Africa." In *South African Keywords: The Uses of Abuses of*

Political Concepts, edited by Emile Boonzaier and John Sharp, 153–66. Cape Town: David Philip, 1988.

Ranuga, Thomas. "Frantz Fanon and Black Consciousness in Azania (South Africa)." *Phylon* 47, no. 3 (1986): 182–91.

Ratele, Kopano. "Men and Masculinities: Psychology and Politics." In *The Gender of Psychology,* edited by Tamara Shefer, Floretta Boonzaier, and Peace Kiguwa, 165–81. Cape Town: University of Cape Town Press, 2006.

Rauwerda, Antje M. "Whitewashing *Drum* Magazine (1951–1959): Advertising Race and Gender." *Continuum: Journal of Media and Cultural Studies* 21, no. 3 (September 2007): 393–404.

Raven-Hart, R., translator. *Cape Good Hope, 1652–1702: The First Fifty Years of Dutch Colonisation as Seen by Callers, Volumes I and II.* Cape Town: A. A. Balkema, 1971.

Ray, Carina E. *Crossing the Color Line: Race, Sex, and the Contested Politics of Colonialism in Ghana.* Athens: Ohio University Press, 2015.

Ribane, Nakedi. *Beauty: A Black Perspective.* Durban: University of KwaZulu-Natal Press, 2006.

Richards, Audrey I. *Chisungu: A Girls' Initiation Ceremony among the Bemba of Northern Rhodesia.* New York: Routledge, 1956.

Riehl, Anne. "'Let Nature Paint Your Beauty's Glory': Beauty and Cosmetics." In *The Face of Queenship: Early Modern Representations of Elizabeth I,* 37–63. New York: Palgrave Macmillan, 2010.

Robbins, Lawrence H. "*Sebilo*: 19th Century Hairdos and Ancient Specularite Mining in Southern Africa." *International Journal of African Historical Studies* 49, no. 1 (2016): 103–31.

Robbins, Lawrence H., Michael L. Murphy, Alec C. Campbell, and George A. Brook. "Intensive Mining of Specular Hematite in the Kalahari ca. A.D. 800–1000." *Current Anthropology* 39, no. 1 (1998): 144–50.

Robertson, Jennifer. "Japan's First Cyborg? Miss Nippon, Eugenics and Wartime Technologies of Beauty, Body and Blood." *Body and Society* 7, no. 1 (2001): 1–34.

Robinson, Henry Peach. *The Studio: And What to Do in It.* New York: Arno, 1973.

Rodgers, H. J. *Twenty-Three Years under a Sky-Light, or Life and Experiences of a Photographer.* New York: Arno, 1973.

Rodney, Walter. *How Europe Underdeveloped Africa.* London: Bogle L'Ouverture, 1972.

Rooks, Noliwe M. *Hair Raising: Beauty, Culture, and African American Women.* New Brunswick, NJ: Rutgers University Press, 1996.

Rosenbaum, Nancy. "'You Have Dark Skin and You Are Beautiful': The Long Fight against Skin Bleaching." *NPR Public Radio,* February 25, 2018. Accessed February 25, 2018. https://www.npr.org/2018/02/25/588632658/you-have-dark-skin-and -you-are-beautiful-the-long-fight-against-skin-bleaching.

Ross, C. M. "Skin Disease in the Venda." *South African Medical Journal* (April 16, 1966): 302–8.

Ross, Robert. *Clothing: A Global History; or the Imperialists' New Clothes.* Cambridge: Polity Press, 2008.

Ross, Robert. *A Concise History of South Africa.* Second edition. Cambridge: Cambridge University Press, 2008.

Ross, Robert. "The Politics of African Household Budget Studies in South Africa." *History in Africa* 43 (2016): 205–28.

Ross, Robert. *Status and Respectability in the Cape Colony, 1750–1870: A Tragedy of Manners.* Cambridge: Cambridge University Press, 1999.

Ross, Robert. "Sumptuary Laws in Europe, the Netherlands, and the Dutch Colonies." In *Contingent Lives: Social Identity and Material Culture in the* VOC *World*, edited by Nigel Worden, 382–91. Rondebosch: University of Cape Town Press, 2007.

Ross, Robert. *Things Change: The Transformation in South African Material Culture, 1800–2000.* Manuscript in preparation.

Roth, Lorna. "Looking at Shirley, the Ultimate Norm: Colour Balance, Image Technologies, and Cognitive Equity." *Canadian Journal of Communication* 34 (2009): 111–36.

Roux, Edward. *Time Longer Than Rope: A History of the Black Man's Struggle for Freedom in South Africa.* Madison: University of Wisconsin Press, 1964.

Ruiz, Rebecca. "Nivea's Controversial Skin-Lightening Ad Puts Spotlight on the History of White Supremacy." *Mashable,* October 20, 2017. Accessed January 9, 2018. http://mashable.com/2017/10/20/nivea-skin-lightening-cream-ad /#szhu5SOhRaqz.

Russell, Kathy, Midge Wilson, and Ronald E. Hall. *The Color Complex: The Politics of Skin Color among African Americans.* New York: Harcourt Brace Jovanovich, 1992.

Russell, Patricia Denise. "Styling Blackness: African American Hair Styling Practices in Late Twentieth Century America and the Phenomenology of Race." Ph.D. diss., University of Chicago, 2002.

Ryan, Mike. *A History of Organised Pharmacy in South Africa, 1885–1950.* Cape Town: Society for the History of Pharmacy in South Africa, 1986.

Sachs, Wulf. *Black Hamlet.* Baltimore, MD: Johns Hopkins University Press, 1996. (Originally published in 1937.)

Saffer, D., H. Tayob, and P. L. A. Bill. "Correspondence: Continued Marketing of Skin-Lightening Preparations Containing Mercury." *South African Medical Journal* 50, no. 39 (1976): 1499.

Samuelson, Meg. Introduction to Hamsi (Marie Kathleen Jeffrey), "Though I Am Black, I Am Comely." In *Women Writing Africa: The Southern Region,* edited by M. J. Daymond, Dorothy Driver, Sheila Meintjes, Leloba Molema, Chiedza Musengezi, Margie Orford, and Nobantu Rasebotsa, 229. New York: Feminist Press at the City University of New York, 2003.

Samuelson, Meg. "The Urban Palimpsest: Re-presenting Sophiatown." *Journal of Postcolonial Writing* 44, no. 1 (2008): 73–75.

Sanders, Mark. *Complicities: The Intellectual and Apartheid.* Durham: Duke University Press, 2002.

Saraswati, L. Ayu. *Seeing Beauty, Sensing Race in Transnational Indonesia.* Honolulu: University of Hawai'i Press, 2013.

Sassen, Robyn. "Apartheid: Now in Museum Form." On the blog "Just Another Day in Africa" at *PopMatters*, April 30, 2002. Accessed January 18, 2018. https://www.popmatters.com/sassen020501-2496174194.html.

Schama, Simon. *The Embarrassment of Riches: An Interpretation of Dutch Culture in the Golden Age*. Berkeley: University of California Press, 1988.

Schapera, Isaac. *Married Life in an African Tribe*. London: Faber and Faber, 1940.

Schmidt, Benjamin. "Collecting Global Icons: The Case of the Exotic Parasol." In *Collecting across Cultures: Material Exchanges in the Early Modern Atlantic World*, edited by Daniela Bleichmar and Peter C. Mancall, 31–57. Philadelphia: University of Pennsylvania Press, 2011.

Schmidt, Elizabeth. "Race, Sex, and Domestic Labor: The Question of African Female Servants in Southern Rhodesia, 1900–1939." In *African Encounters with Domesticity*, edited by Karen Tranberg Hansen, 221–41. New Brunswick, NJ: Rutgers University Press, 1992.

Schoeman, Karel. *The Face of the Country: A South African Family Album, 1860–1910*. Cape Town: Human and Rosseau, 1996.

Schulz, E. J. "Skin Disorders in Black South Africans: A Survey of 5,000 Patients Seen at Ga-Rankuwa Hospital, Pretoria." *South African Medical Journal* 62 (November 27, 1982): 864–67.

Schulz, E. J., and M. A. Sher. "Rescinding of Legislation to Ban Hydroquinone-Containing Bleaching Creams." *South African Medical Journal* 77 (April 7, 1990): 372.

Schulz, E. J., Beverley Summers, and R. S. Summers. "Correspondence: Inappropriate Treatment of Cosmetic Ochronosis with Hydroquinone." *South African Medical Journal* 73 (January 9, 1988): 59–60.

Schuyler, George S. *Black No More*. New York: Macaulay, 1931.

Schuyler, George. "Madam C. J. Walker." *Messenger* 6 (August 1924): 251–66.

Schwartz, Louise. "Occupational Pigmentary Changes in the Skin." *Archives of Dermatology and Syphilology* 56 (1947): 592–600.

Scully, Pamela. *Liberating the Family? Gender and British Slave Emancipation in the Rural Western Cape, South Africa, 1823–1853*. Portsmouth, NH: Heinemann, 1997.

Segrave, Kerry. *Suntanning in 20th Century America*. Jefferson, NC: McFarland, 2005.

Shadle, Brett L. *The Souls of White Folk: White Settlers in Kenya, 1900s–1920s*. Manchester: Manchester University Press, 2015.

Shevde, Natasha. "All's Fair in Love and Cream: A Cultural Case Study of Fair & Lovely in India." *Advertising and Society Review* 9, no. 2 (2008).

Simmons, Anne. "Shame on Show at Apartheid Museum." *Cape Times*, December 7, 2001.

Simons, H. J., and R. E. Simons. *Class and Colour in South Africa, 1850–1950*. Harmondsworth, UK: Penguin, 1969.

"Skin Bleaching Scandal in South Africa." *Unreported World*, January 17, 2018. Accessed February 1, 2018. https://www.youtube.com/watch?v=bWHCwXZpH6E&feature=youtu.be.

Smith, Woodruff. *Consumption and the Making of Respectability, 1600–1800*. New York: Routledge, 2002.

Soga, John Henderson. *The Ama-Xosa: Life and Customs*. Lovedale, South Africa: Lovedale Press, 1932.

Sopher, David E. "Indigenous Uses of Turmeric (*Curcuma domestica*) in Asia and Oceania." *Anthropos* 59, no. 1/2 (1964): 93–127.

South Africa. Act No. 23 of 1923. Customs and Excise Duties Amendment. *Statutes of the Union of South Africa 1925*. Cape Town: Government Printer, 1923.

South Africa. Act No. 36 of 1925. Customs Tariff and Excise Duties Amendment. *Statutes of the Union of South Africa 1925*. Cape Town: Government Printer, 1925.

South Africa. Act No. 13 of 1928. Medical, Dental and Pharmacy. *Statutes of the Union of South Africa 1928*. Cape Town: Government Printer, 1928.

South Africa. Act No. 5 of 1937. Medical, Dental and Pharmacy Amendment. *Statutes of the Union of South Africa 1937*. Cape Town: Government Printer, 1937.

South Africa. *Government Gazette*. 1972, 1974–75, 1980, 1983, 1987–88, and 1990.

South Africa. *Report of the Commission of Inquiry into the Press, Second Report*. Pretoria: Government Printer, 1964.

South Africa. *Sixth Census of the Population of South Africa, Enumerated 5th May, 1936, Volume I, Population—Sex and Geographical Distribution of the Population*. Pretoria: Government Printer, 1938.

South Africa, Board of Trade and Industries. *Report No. 282: Investigation into Manufacturing Industries in the Union of South Africa (First Interim Report)*. Cape Town: Cape Times, 1945.

South Africa, Bureau of Census and Statistics. *Population Census, 1960, Sample Tabulation, No. 3, Major Occupational Groups: Whites, Coloureds and Asiatics*. Pretoria: Government Printer, 1962.

South Africa, Bureau of Census and Statistics. *Population Census, 1960, Sample Tabulation, No. 5, Industry Divisions, Age Groups, and Major Occupational Groups: Bantu*. Pretoria: Government Printer, 1963.

South Africa, Office of Census Statistics. *Official Year Book of the Union and of Basutoland, Bechuanaland Protectorate, and Swaziland*. Pretoria: Government Printer, 1937.

South African Federated Chamber of Industries. *National Directory of Manufacturers 1931*. Second edition. Cape Town: South African Federated Chamber of Industries, n.d.

Soyinka, Wole. *Art, Dialogue and Outrage: Essays on Literature and Culture*. New York: Pantheon Books, 1993.

Spelman, Elizabeth V. "Gender and Race: The Ampersand Problem in Feminist Thought." In *The Inessential Woman: Problems of Exclusion in Feminist Thought*, 114–32. Boston: Beacon Press, 1988.

Spencer, Malcolm C. "Hydroquinone Bleaching." *Archives of Dermatology* 84 (July–December 1961): 131–34.

Spencer, Malcolm C. "Topical Use of Hydroquinone for Depigmentation." *Journal of the American Medical Association* 194 (1965): 962–64.

Springer, Kimberly. "Black Feminists Respond to Black Power Masculinism." In *The Black Power Movement: Rethinking the Civil Rights-Black Power Era*, edited by Peniel E. Joseph, 105–18. New York: Routledge, 2006.

Springer, Kimberly. *Living for the Revolution: Black Feminist Organizations, 1968–1980*. Durham: Duke University Press, 2005.

Steenekamp, J. J. A. *Changes in the Income and Expenditure Patterns of Multiple Urban Non-White Households*. Bureau of Market Research, University of South Africa, Research Report No. 36. Pretoria, 1973.

Steenekamp, J. J. A. "Inkomste- en bestedingspatrone van stedelike meervoudige nie-Blanke in die Republiek van Suid-Afrika: 'n vergelykende studie." Ph.D. diss., University of South Africa, 1975.

Steenkamp, W. F. J. "Bantu Wages in South Africa." *South African Journal of Economics* 30, no. 2 (1962): 93–118.

Stein, Sarah Abreveya. *Plumes: Ostrich Feathers, Jews, and a Lost World of Global Commerce*. New Haven, CT: Yale University Press, 2008.

Steinmetz, George. *The Devil's Handwriting: Precoloniality and the German Colonial State in Qingdao, Samoa, and Southwest Africa*. Chicago: University of Chicago Press, 2007.

Stevenson, Michael, and Michael Graham-Stewart. *Surviving the Lens: Photographic Studies of South and East African People, 1870–1920*. Vlaeberg, South Africa: Femwood Press in association with M. Stevenson and M. Graham-Stewart, 2001.

Stolar, Robert. "Induced Alterations of Vitiliginous Skin." *Annals of the New York Academy of Sciences* 100 (February 1963): 58–75.

Stone, Judith. *When She Was White: The True Story of a Family Divided by Race*. New York: Miramax Books, 2007.

Storey, William Kelleher. *Guns, Race, and Power in Colonial South Africa*. Cambridge: Cambridge University Press, 2008.

Strutt, Daphne. *Fashion in South Africa, 1652–1900: An Illustrated History of Styles and Materials for Men, Women and Children, with Notes on Footwear, Hairdressing, Accessories and Jewellery*. Cape Town: Balkema, 1975.

Stuart, James, and D. McK. Malcolm, editors. *The Diary of Henry Francis Fynn*. Pietermaritzburg: Shuter and Shooter, 1950.

Stuurman, Siep. "François Bernier and the Invention of Racial Classification." *History Workshop Journal* 50 (2000): 1–21.

Sutton, Denise H. *Globalizing Ideal Beauty: Women, Advertising, and the Power of Marketing*. New York: Palgrave Macmillan, 2009.

Swiderski, Richard. *Quicksilver: A History of the Use, Lore and Effects of Mercury*. London: McFarland, 2008.

Switzer, Les. "*Bantu World* and the Origins of a Captive African Commercial Press." In *South Africa's Alternative Press: Voices of Protest and Resistance, 1880s–1960s*, edited by L. Switzer, 189–212. Cambridge: Cambridge University Press, 1997.

Switzer, Les. "*Bantu World* and the Origins of a Captive African Commercial Press in South Africa." *Journal of Southern African Studies* 14, no. 1 (1988): 351–70.

Switzer, Les, and Donna Switzer. *The Black Press in South Africa and Lesotho: A Descriptive Bibliographic Guide to African, Coloured and Indian Newspapers, Newsletters and Magazines 1836–1976.* Boston: G. K. Hall, 1979.

Taraborrelli, J. Randy. *Michael Jackson: The Magic, the Madness, the Whole Story, 1958–2009.* New York: Birch Lane Press, 2009.

Tate, Shirley Anne. *Black Beauty: Aesthetics, Stylization, Politics.* Burlington, VT: Ashgate, 2009.

Tate, Shirley Anne. *Skin Bleaching in Black Atlantic Zones: Shade Shifters.* London: Palgrave Macmillan, 2016.

Taylor, Janelle S. "Surfacing the Body Interior." *Annual Review of Anthropology* 34 (2005): 741–56.

Taylor, Jean Gelman. "Painted Ladies of the VOC." In *Contingent Lives: Social Identity and Material Culture in the VOC World,* edited by Nigel Worden, 512–37. Rondebosch: University of Cape Town Press, 2007.

Taylor, Jean Gelman. *The Social World of Batavia: European and Eurasian in Dutch Asia.* Madison: University of Wisconsin Press, 1983.

Taylor, Jeremy. *Ag Pleez Deddy! Songs and Recollections.* Pretoria: Jeremy Taylor, 1992.

Thomas, Bridget M. "Constraints and Contradictions: Whiteness and Femininity in Ancient Greece." In *Women's Dress in the Ancient Greek World,* edited by Lloyd Llewellyn-Jones. London: Duckworth and the Classical Press of Wales, 2002.

Thomas, Lynn M. "Beauty." *Somatosphere,* January 15, 2018. Accessed January 15, 2018. http://somatosphere.net/2018/01/beauty.html.

Thomas, Lynn M. "Gendered Reproduction: Placing Schoolgirl Pregnancies in African History." In *Africa after Gender?,* edited by Stephan Miescher, Catherine Cole, and Takyiwaa Manuh, 48–62. Bloomington: Indiana University Press, 2006.

Thomas, Lynn M. "Love, Sex, and the Modern Girl in 1930s Southern Africa." In *Love in Africa,* edited by Jennifer Cole and Lynn M. Thomas, 31–57. Chicago: University of Chicago Press, 2009.

Thomas, Lynn M. *Politics of the Womb: Women, Reproduction, and the State in Kenya.* Berkeley: University of California Press, 2003.

Thomas, Lynn M. "Skin Lighteners in South Africa: Transnational Entanglements and Technologies of the Self." In *Shades of Difference: Why Skin Color Matters,* edited by Evelyn Nakano Glenn, 188–210. Stanford, CA: Stanford University Press, 2008.

Thomas, Lynn M., and Jennifer Cole. "Introduction: Thinking through Love in Africa." In *Love in Africa,* edited by Jennifer Cole and Lynn M. Thomas, 1–30. Chicago: University of Chicago Press, 2009.

Thompson, J. Walter, Company (South Africa) Limited. *African Market Division: A Statistical Overview of the African Market in South Africa, 1973 Issue.*

Thompson, J. Walter, Company (South Africa) Limited. *African Market Division: A Statistical Overview of the African Market in South Africa, 1974 Issue.*

Thompson, J. Walter, Company (South Africa) Limited. *Markets to the North: A Continuing Survey of Merchandising and Advertising Opportunities in the Union of South Africa's Principal Export Territories.* Cape Town: Cape Times Ltd., 1954.

Thompson, Krista P. *Developing Blackness: Studio Photographs of "Over the Hill" Nassau in the Independence Era.* Nassau: National Art Gallery of the Bahamas, 2008.

Thompson, Krista P. *Shine: The Visual Economy of Light in African Diasporic Aesthetic Practice.* Durham: Duke University Press, 2015.

Thwala, Zinhle. "Bleaching to Become Beautiful? The Use of Skin Lighteners and the Effects on IsiZulu-Speaking African Women in Madadeni Township in Newcastle, KwaZulu-Natal, 1950s to 2000s." M.A. thesis, University of KwaZulu-Natal, Pietermaritzburg, 2017.

Tiley, A. "Problems of Retailing to the Bantu Market, Part 2: Central Business Areas." In *The Urban Bantu Market: Understanding Its Complexities and Developing Its Potential—Proceedings of a 2-Day Seminar Held in February 1969, Durban, Natal,* edited by the National Development and Management Foundation of South Africa. Johannesburg: National Development and Management Foundation of South Africa, 1969.

Tobias, Phillip V. "The Biology of the Southern African Negro." In *The Bantu-Speaking Peoples of Southern Africa,* second edition, edited by W. D. Hammond-Tooke, 3–45. London: Routledge & Kegan Paul, 1974.

Tomaselli, Kenyan, and Ruth Tomaselli. "Between Policy and Practice in the SABC, 1970–1981." In *Currents of Power: State Broadcasting in South Africa,* edited by Ruth Tomaselli, Keyan Tomaselli, and Johan Muller, 84–152. Bellville, South Africa: Anthropos, 1989.

Tousignant, Noémi. *Edges of Exposure: Toxicology and the Problem of Capacity in Postcolonial Senegal.* Durham: Duke University Press, 2018.

Tsing, Anna Lowenhaupt. *Friction: An Ethnography of Global Connection.* Princeton, NJ: Princeton University Press, 2005.

United Kingdom. *The Cosmetic Products Regulations 1978.* Statutory instrument no. 1354. London: HMSO, 1978.

Unterhalter, Beryl. "Changing Attitudes to 'Passing for White' in an Urban Coloured Community." *Social Dynamics* 1, no. 1 (1975): 53–62.

U.S. Congress. *Congressional Record.* 1971.

U.S. Department of Commerce. *Advertising in the Union of South Africa.* Washington, DC: United States Government Printing Office, 1936.

U.S. Environmental Protection Agency. "Citronella (Oil of Citronella) (021901) Fact Sheet." November 1999.

U.S. *Federal Register.* 1972–74, 1978, 1982, and 2006.

U.S. Food and Drug Administration (FDA), Department of Health and Human Services. "Hydroquinone Studies under the National Toxicology Program (NTP)." Last updated November 27, 2015. Accessed November 27, 2017. https://www.fda.gov/AboutFDA/CentersOffices/OfficeofMedicalProductsandTobacco/CDER/ucm203112.htm.

Vail, Gilbert. *A History of Cosmetics in America.* New York: Toilet Goods Association, 1947.

van der Geest, Sjaak, Susan Reynolds Whyte, and Anita Hardon. "The Anthropology of Pharmaceuticals: A Biographical Approach." *Annual Review of Anthropology* 25 (1996): 153–78.

Van der Reis, A. P. *Motivational Factors in Bantu Buying Behaviour.* Bureau of Market Research, University of South Africa, Research Report No. 15. Pretoria, 1966.

Van der Reis, A. P. *Some Aspects of the Acceptability of Particular Photographic Models to the Bantu.* Bureau of Market Research, University of South Africa, Research Report No. 29. Pretoria, 1972.

Van der Vliet, Virginia. "Growing Up in Traditional Society." In *The Bantu-Speaking Peoples of Southern Africa,* edited by W. D. Hammond-Tooke. Boston: Routledge & Kegan Paul, 1974.

Van Kessel, Ineke. *"Beyond Our Wildest Dreams": The United Democratic Front and the Transformation of South Africa.* Charlottesville: University Press of Virginia, 2000.

Van Niekerk, Robert. "The Evolution of Health and Welfare Policies in South Africa: Inherited Institutions, Fiscal Restraint, and the Deracialization of Social Policy in the Post-Apartheid Era." *Journal of African American History* 88, no. 4 (2003): 361–76.

Van Onselen, Charles. "The Witches of Suburbia: Domestic Service on the Witwatersrand, 1890–1914." In *Studies in the Social and Economic History of the Witwatersrand, 1886–1914,* vol. 2, *New Nineveh,* 1–73. London: Longman, 1982.

Veriava, Ahmed, and Prishani Naidoo. "Remembering Biko from Here and Now." In *Biko Lives! Contesting the Legacies of Steve Biko,* edited by Andile Mngxitama, Amanda Alexander, and Nigel C. Gibson, 233–52. New York: Palgrave Macmillan, 2008.

Vilakazi, Absolom. *Zulu Transformations: A Study of the Dynamics of Social Change.* Pietermaritzburg: University of Natal Press, 1962.

Vinikas, Vincent. *Soft Soap, Hard Sell: American Hygiene in an Age of Advertisement.* Ames: Iowa State University Press, 1992.

Vinson, Robert Trent. *The Americans Are Coming! Dreams of African American Liberation in Segregationist South Africa.* Athens: Ohio University Press, 2012.

Visser, Nick, and Tim Couzens, editors. *H. I. E. Dhlomo Collected Works.* Johannesburg: Ravan, 1985.

von Eschen, Penny. *Race against Empire: Black Americans and Anticolonialism, 1837–1957.* Ithaca, NY: Cornell University Press, 1997.

Vukani Makhosikazi Collective (Jane Barrett, Aneene Dawber, Barbara Klugman, Ingrid Obery, Jennifer Shindler, and Joanne Yawitch). *South African Women on the Move.* London: Catholic Institute for International Relations, 1985.

Wagatsuma, Hiroshi. "The Social Perception of Skin Color in Japan." *Daedalus* 96, no. 2 (1967): 407–43.

Walker, Alice. "If the Present Looks Like the Past, What Does the Future Look Like?" In *In Search of Our Mothers' Gardens,* 290–312. New York: Harcourt Brace Jovanovich, 1983.

Walker, Brett. *Toxic Archipelago: A History of Industrial Disease in Japan.* Seattle: University of Washington Press, 2010.

Walker, Susannah. *Style and Status: Selling Beauty to African American Women, 1920–1975.* Lexington: University of Kentucky Press, 2007.

Wallace, Florence Elizabeth. "Color in Homer and in Ancient Art." *Smith College Classical Studies* 9 (December 1927): 1–83.

Walters, Ronald G. "The Negro Press and the Image of Success: 1920–1939." *Midcontinent American Studies Journal* 11, no. 2 (1970): 36–55.

Ward, Stephen. "The Third World Women's Alliance: Black Feminist Radicalism and Black Power Politics." In *The Black Power Movement: Rethinking the Civil Rights-Black Power Era*, edited by Peniel E. Joseph, 119–44. New York: Routledge, 2006.

Watson, Graham. *Passing for White: A Study of Racial Assimilation in a South African School*. New York: Tavistock, 1970.

Watts, Ian. "The Pigments from Pinnacle Point Cave 13B, Western Cape, South Africa." *Journal of Human Evolution* 59 (2010): 392–411.

Webb, Colin De B., and John B. Wright, editors and translators. *The James Stuart Archive of Recorded Oral Evidence Relating to the History of the Zulu and Neighbouring Peoples*. Vols. 1–4. Pietermaritzburg: University of Natal Press, 1976.

Weinbaum, Alys Eve. "Racial Masquerade: Consumption and Contestation of American Modernity." In *The Modern Girl Around the World: Consumption, Modernity, and Globalization*, edited by the Modern Girl Around the World Research Group (Alys Eve Weinbaum, Lynn M. Thomas, Priti Ramamurthy, Uta G. Poiger, Madeleine Y. Dong, and Tani E. Barlow), 120–46. Durham: Duke University Press, 2008.

Weiss, Brad. "Dressing at Death: Clothing, Time, and Memory in Buhaya, Tanzania." In *Clothing and Difference: Embodied Identities in Colonial and Post-Colonial Africa*, edited by Hildi Hendrickson, 133–54. Durham: Duke University Press, 1996.

Weiss, Brad. *Sacred Trees, Bitter Harvests: Globalizing Coffee in Northwest Tanzania*. Portsmouth, NH: Heinemann, 2003.

Weiss, Brad. *Street Dreams and Hip Hop Barbershops: Global Fantasy in Urban Tanzania*. Bloomington: Indiana University Press, 2009.

Weiss, M., E. del Fabbro, and R. Kolisang. "Cosmetic Ochronosis Caused by Bleaching Creams Containing 2% Hydroquinone." *South African Medical Journal* 77 (April 7, 1990): 373.

Wells, Julia C. "Eva's Men: Gender and Power in the Establishment of the Cape of Good Hope, 1652–74." *Journal of African History* 39, no. 3 (1998): 417–37.

Wells, Julia M. "Sun Hats, Sundowners, and Tropical Hygiene: Managing Settler Bodies and Minds in British East and South-Central Africa, 1890–1939." *African Historical Review* 48, no. 2 (2016): 68–91.

Wendl, Tobias. "Entangled Traditions: Photography and the History of Media in Southern Ghana." RES: *Anthropology and Aesthetics* 39 (2001): 78–101.

Werble, Wallace. "The Federal Trade Commission and the Cosmetic Chemist." In *Cosmetics: Science and Technology*, edited by Edward Sagarin, 1317–35. New York: Interscience, 1957.

Werner, Michael, and Bénédicte Zimmermann. "Beyond Comparison: *Histoire Croisée* and the Challenge of Reflexivity." *History and Theory* 45 (February 2006): 30–50.

West, Cornel. "A Genealogy of Modern Racism." In *Race Critical Theories*, edited by Philomena Essed and David Theo Goldberg, 90–112. New York: Blackwell, 2002.

"What Is Wrong with Black Consciousness? (Some Common Questions and Answers)." *Solidarity: Official Organ of the Black Consciousness Movement of Azania* 13 (December 1986): 23–24.

Wheeler, Roxann. *The Complexion of Race: Categories of Difference in Eighteenth-Century British Culture.* Philadelphia: University of Pennsylvania Press, 2000.

Whisson, Michael G., and William Weil. *Domestic Servants: A Microcosm of "The Race Problem."* Johannesburg: South African Institute of Race Relations, 1971.

White, Amos, and Luella White. *Dawn in Bantuland: An African Experiment.* Boston: Christopher House, 1953.

White, Luise. "Precarious Conditions: A Note on Counter-Insurgency in Africa after 1945." *Gender and History* 16, no. 3 (2004): 603–25.

White, Luise. "Sex, Soap, and Colonial Studies." *Journal of British Studies* 38, no. 4 (October 1999): 478–86.

White, Shane, and Graham J. White. *Stylin': African American Expressive Culture from Its Beginnings to the Zoot Suit.* Ithaca, NY: Cornell University Press, 1998.

White, Walter. "Has Science Conquered the Color Line?" *Look* 13, no. 18 (August 30, 1949): 94–95.

White, Walter. *A Man Called White.* New York: Arno Press, 1969. (Originally published in 1948.)

Wicomb, Zoe. *Playing in the Light.* New York: New Press, 2006.

Willan, Brian. *Sol Plaatje: South African Nationalist, 1876–1932.* London: Heinemann, 1984.

Williams, Carla. "The Erotic Image Is Naked and Dark." In *Picturing Us: African American Identity in Photography,* edited by Deborah Willis, 128–34. New York: New Press, 1994.

Williams, Hywel. "Skin Lightening Creams Containing Hydroquinone." *British Medical Journal* 305 (October 17, 1992): 903–4.

Williams, Megan E. "'Meet the Real Lena Horne': Representations of Lena Horne in *Ebony* Magazine, 1945–1949." *Journal of American Studies* 43, no. 1 (2009): 117–30.

Williams, Rhonda Y. "Black Women, Urban Politics, and Engendering Black Power." In *The Black Power Movement: Rethinking the Civil Rights-Black Power Era,* edited by Peniel E. Joseph, 79–104. New York: Routledge, 2006.

Williamson, Judith. "Woman Is an Island: Femininity and Colonization." In *Studies in Entertainment: Critical Approaches to Mass Culture,* edited by Tania Modleski, 99–118. Bloomington: Indiana University Press, 1986.

Willis, Deborah. *Posing Beauty: African American Images from the 1890s to the Present.* New York: W. W. Norton, 2009.

Willis, Justin. *Potent Brews: Social History of Alcohol in East Africa 1850–1999.* Athens: Ohio University Press, 2002.

Wilner, Ortha L. "Roman Beauty Culture." *Classical Journal* 27, no. 1 (1931): 26–38.

Wilson, Monica, and Archie Mafeje. *Langa: A Study of Social Groups in an African Township.* Oxford: Oxford University Press, 1963.

Winston, Brian. "A Whole Technology of Dyeing: A Note on Ideology and the Apparatus of the Chromatic Moving Image." *Daedalus* 114, no. 4 (1985): 105–23.

Wipper, Audrey. "African Women, Fashion, and Scapegoating." *Canadian Journal of African Studies* 6, no. 2 (1972): 329–49.

Wolcott, Victoria. *Remaking Respectability: African American Women in Interwar Detroit.* Chapel Hill: University of North Carolina Press, 2001.

Woloshyn, Tania Anne. "Soaking Up the Sun's Rays." *Wellcome History* 53 (Summer 2014): 6–7.

Woodcock, Janet. "Modernizing the Other Side of the Counter: FDA Oversight of Nonprescription Drugs." *Health Affairs Blog,* June 9, 2016. Accessed November 3, 2017. http://www.healthaffairs.org/do/10.1377/hblog20160609.055243/full/.

Woodson, Dorothy C. *Drum: An Index to "Africa's Leading Magazine," 1951–1965.* Madison: African Studies Program, University of Wisconsin-Madison, 1988.

Woodward, James P. "Consumer Culture, Market Empire, and the Global South." *Journal of World History* 23 (2012): 375–98.

Worden, Nigel, Elizabeth Van Heyningen, and Vivian Bickford-Smith, editors. *Cape Town: The Making of a City.* Kenilworth, South Africa: David Philip, 1998.

World Health Organization. "Mercury in Skin Lightening Products." 2011. Accessed January 10, 2018. http://www.who.int/ipcs/assessment/public_health/mercury _flyer.pdf.

Wright, Arthur. *Color Me White: The Autobiography of a Black Dancer Who Turned White.* Smithtown, NY: Exposition Press, 1980.

Wright, Charlotte Crogman. *Beneath the Southern Cross: The Story of an American Bishop's Wife in South Africa.* New York: Exposition, 1955.

Xaba, Thokozani T. "Witchcraft, Sorcery or Medical Practice? The Demand, Supply and Regulation of Indigenous Medicines in Durban, South Africa (1884–2002)." Ph.D. diss., University of California, Berkeley, 2004.

Yang, Chi-ming. *Performing China: Virtue, Commerce, and Orientalism in Eighteenth-Century England, 1660–1760.* Baltimore, MD: Johns Hopkins University Press, 2011.

Zelizer, Viviana. *The Purchase of Intimacy.* Princeton, NJ: Princeton University Press, 2005.

Index

Italicized page numbers indicate illustrations.

women (continued)
185; as spokesmodels, 66, 70, *99*, *113*, 114, 129, 164, *165*, 177. *See also* modern girls
Women in the National Association for the Advancement of Colored People, 217
Women of Phokeng (Bozzoli), 88
The World, 121, *178*. *See also Bantu World*
World Health Organization, 233–34
World War II, 19, 80, 100
The Wretched of the Earth (Fanon), 174, 192

X, Malcolm, 173–74, 199
Xhosa. *See* isiXhosa
Xitsonga, 49

Yellow Fever, 227–*28*
yellow ochre, 59
"Ysabel" Lemon Cold Cream, 78

Zambia, 223
Zanzibar, 167
Zimbabwe, 11–12, 194, 218
Zonk!, 10, 109–14, *112*, 119, 124; beauty contests and, 128, *130*, 132, 134, *135*; films and, 136, *137*, 138, *139*; photography techniques in, 140, 141, *142*, *143*; and skin lighteners, 84, 98, *99*, 121, *130*, *137*
Zulu. *See* isiZulu
Zuma, Jacob, 199